THE PSYCHODYNAMICS OF FAMILY LIFE

THE

Psychodynamics

OF

Family Life

DIAGNOSIS AND TREATMENT
OF FAMILY RELATIONSHIPS

BY NATHAN W. ACKERMAN, M.D.

PUBLISHERS Basic Books, Inc. NEW YORK

72 73 74   12 11 10 9 8 7 6 5 4 3 2 1

To my wife, Gwendolyn,
my daughters, Jeanne and Deborah,
my other kinfolk, and
The Family of Man

FOREWORD

W HEN ARTHUR ROSENTHAL asked me to write a foreword to this
new paperback edition of the late Nat Ackerman's classic book, I accepted immediately and without reservation.

Why had I reacted so fast? Out of the past came painful memories. I re-
called how this book, when I first confronted it in 1958, had provoked in me
sharply hostile reactions. My own ideas of the family and family therapy seemed
to me to have gone beyond those of Ackerman, and to have been more revolutionary. As our differences emerged in public and were followed by years of
competitive sparring, they raised barriers to professional and personal openness.
Was I now really welcoming a public chance to expose old wounds?

But the later years brought about a change in our relations. The publication
of *Family Process* threw us together as colleagues. A friendship of growing
closeness and trust began and deepened, terminated too soon by his sudden
death. This mutual respect and affection led us to reconsider our differences and
contentions. I could now feel gratitude for his fierce passion to promote family
well-being. I came to know and admire his willingness to set aside all other
priorities to handle a family crisis at first hand. In our similar roles as adminis-
trators, we came to share hopes, anxieties, problems, plans, and commitments. We
exchanged ideas about techniques and theories of family therapy and about the
training of professional persons, and were moving together into the expanding
field of family relations with the community. Best of all, we no longer seemed to

need a platform to express our differences; we had learned the advantages and delights of directness with each other.

I reread this book, then, in a new frame of mind. And I felt ready to appraise it afresh.

This was and remains a daring book. It challenges one of the most fundamental orientations of our culture, our preoccupation with the self. It frees us from cultural cliches of individualism and redirects our attention to the basic social processes that either strengthen human well-being or destroy our capacities to cope. It brings us directly in touch with the social matrix of the family through which our natures and relations are shaped. It sets forth with compassion the necessary social conditions that must prevail in everyday life and in treatment if we are to ameliorate personal and family problems.

Ackerman, perhaps more than anyone else in the family field, had the necessary qualifications for building a bridge from the theories prevailing when he published this work to the current and forthcoming "social psychology and social psychopathology of family life" which was his acknowledged aim. Into encounters with professionals he carried credentials of training, practice, and an established reputation as a psychoanalyst. For the sake of helping disturbed people he could risk unconventional family points of view and still hold his psychoanalytically-oriented readers. When he wrote about patients and their relatives, one knew he was talking about real families; now I, too, could see the compassion with which he had struggled to help them.

This book—and Ackerman's life—carried the day for the family. He came to be honored near and far by those whose ideas he was rejecting. With his exquisite sensitivity, he seemed always to convey the impression of moving ahead by inches when he was leaping ahead by furlongs. It is all here in this book— the deference to Freud and the words of psychoanalysis, the concerns over problems given their psychiatric names (schizophrenia, psychosomatics, neuroses, and psychotherapy), the table of psychiatric disorders in children boldly printed into the middle of the gentle poetic language for his radical ideas. To know where we have been in the family field, read his work; it epitomizes the early history.

Seen afresh, after a decade and a half, his book would not be worth reprinting if it had not been so far ahead of its time, if it were not now so up-to-date. Ackerman could not have anticipated in detail the common social concerns of the 1970s, but none of today's problems is foreign to his comprehension nor to his presentation of underlying forces which disturb persons, families, and society as a whole. He prepares us for the deeper significances of the women's liberation movement, the drug culture, peer supremacy in adolescents and their alienation from adult society, the transience of many marriages, the situations of minority and poverty groups, the penalties for being old and our ruthlessness in destroying one another and our environment. He was setting a course toward solving our social problems, toward establishing humane social programs, toward socially-oriented diagnosis and treatment, toward family research, toward training others how to help families and other social units, and toward ultimate prevention of our human disorders. Since our social crises are immense; our progress in coping with them, slow; and our understanding of their sources, rudimentary, his guidance for us remains highly relevant.

One should not seek in this book a primer for family therapy. Succeeding publications by many authors, including Dr. Ackerman, present the work of the therapist in concrete detail not possible here. Look here for something far more important—a point of view. Through this book we can learn to stand where Ackerman stood and look out with his eyes at age-old and new problems that he saw, perceive them more clearly, and move together with him nearer to mastery over them.

John Bell

October 1972

PREFACE

THIS BOOK is the outgrowth of an idea, a point of view, concerning mental illness and health. It presents a way of understanding health through the emotional "give and take" of family relationships. It outlines a conceptual approach to emotional disturbance in the individual through analysis of the psychological content of his family experience.

The concepts in this book have been germinating for a long time. They have developed gradually during twenty-five years of psychiatric practice. An early publication, "The Family as a Social and Emotional Unit," appeared in the *Bulletin of the Kansas Mental Hygiene Society* in 1937; since that time, other papers have been published in a wide range of periodicals. Now, in this volume, I am attempting to present a unitary conception of the mental health problems of family life—a tentative view, to be sure, but a sufficient foundation, I hope, for further fruitful study of a complex area.

This effort results from the recognition of a long series of problems arising in psychiatric practice that have persistently defied solution. As a clinician seeking to help distressed and disoriented people live better, I was plagued by perplexity and doubt. Did I really know what I was doing? Did I have the requisite knowledge, the wisdom, to help my patients dissolve away their fright and confusion and find a path back to health? It seems to me that I could not answer with a firm *yes*, that something basic was missing in my understanding of the very disturbances I was trying to cure. Health, after all, is an expression of the entire life process; it encompasses the entirety of the human organism's vital relations with his environment. In the diagnosis and treatment of disturbed persons, did clinicians give full respect to this principle? The answer was hardly clear, but the question led me to this attempt to view the disturbances of the individual—child or adult—in the larger frame of his on-going experience of emotional integration into his family group.

This approach attempts to correlate the dynamic psychological processes of individual behavior with family behavior in order to be able to place individual clinical diagnosis and therapy within the broader frame of family diagnosis and therapy. It has been necessary, therefore, to explore a series of interrelated themes: the interdependence of individual and family stability at every stage of growth from infancy to old age; the role of family in the emotional development of the child; the family as stabilizer of the mental health of the adult; the family as conveyor belt for anxiety and conflict and as a carrier of the contagion of mental illness; the interplay of conflict between family and community, conflict in family relationships, and conflict within individual family members; and breakdown in adaptation and illness as symptoms of the group pathology of the family.

With this wider orientation comes a host of troublesome questions: What is the nature of the discordance and discontinuity in the relations of individual and society that predisposes to breakdown and illness? What is similar in the dynamic relatedness of child and adult to the surrounding family and community environment? What is different? In the diagnosis and therapy of the adult patient, do we examine his family and extended group environment with the same care and precision we apply to his inner mental life? If not, why not? What is the specific deficiency of present-day standards of psychiatric classification? Why is it that efforts at improving psychiatric diagnosis tend to reach an impasse?

And there are other plaguing difficulties: When an emotionally sick person responds well to psychotherapy and unravels his inner knots, how does he then maintain his emotional health? It is one thing to be cured; it is quite another to stay healthy. One cannot do it all alone. To keep one's health, one must continuously share it with other healthy persons. One must find a group climate in which one can continue to grow and actualize one's potentials in healthy human relationships. But the groups from which an emotionally sick person comes are themselves warped. How does the successfully treated patient, his personality, so to speak, decontaminated, create new groups that have healthy aims and values? Where does he turn to find a healthy mate, one who will complement his needs and strivings as marital partner, parent, worker, and member of the community? To stay well, he needs the help of others. He must, in effect, build for himself a new image of self, new values, and a new culture. What help does he require? From whom? What forces in society can he call upon for this kind of help?

Often, when family diagnosis and therapy are mentioned, many who work in the field show a certain mistrust and reluctance and, to some extent, create an obstacle to the development of this approach. The mistrust is rooted in the fear of violating the traditional psychotherapeutic role. What is the propriety of a therapist's dealing openly with intimate matters when more than one member of the family is involved? Can confidential material be so handled? Under what conditions must an individual's privacy be completely safeguarded? Under what conditions may his personal secrets be exposed to family scrutiny for legitimate therapeutic purposes? With great frequency I have found that these intimate matters, these so-called secrets, turn out not to be real secrets at all. Far more often they are common family knowledge, surrounded by a tacit conspiracy of silence. What is involved here is not so much a true secret but rather a barrier to emotional communication, a barrier to the free sharing of certain experiences. Some forms of privacy are needed and healthy. Others are pathogenic. When a therapist supports a sick need for privacy, he affirms guilt and fear; he reinforces the patient's isolation. Therapists are often overanxious about the preservation of privacy, sometimes more anxious than the patients and their families. A patient must develop faith in his therapist, and the therapist must not betray that faith. But, in the long view, this hinges on the therapist's understanding and skill. Faith and trust do not derive from the encouragement of sick kinds of privacy and isolation. Nor do faith and trust derive from taking sides with one individual against other members of his family. If the patient is helped to face his true problem, excessive privacy and the preservation of guilt-ridden secrets become less important and increased closeness and communication with family members more important. Surely the trust of a patient is not won in a day, but, as the patient's security increases, he will welcome the dissolution of barriers to greater intimacy and sharing with his family members.

Some therapists ask whether family treatment does not incur the risk of involving them over their depth with multiple family members in a way that complicates both transference and countertransference. They feel confident of controlling their relations with one patient but are less sure of their therapeutic control in contacts with multiple family members. The apprehension of loss of control increases the therapist's anxiety. Again and again, therapists claim that the maintenance of a one-to-one private relation with the patient (and the exclusion of other family members) simplifies their task; it forestalls complications. Is this not an illusion? One may well ask: for whom does this forestall complications, the patient and his family or the therapist? Whatever complications exist are inherent in the patient's life situation. The task of therapy cannot be simplified by the magic device of avoiding contact with other family members. Life is not simple, nor are the problems of family relationships simple. When a therapist refuses to see other family members, he has not thereby reduced the complexity of his position. He is a silent presence in the patient's family life anyway. Even though the therapist rejects face-to-face contact with other family members, he is a live image to them. He is a psychic force in the day-by-day emotional interchange among family members. In this sense, the therapist can no more avoid relatedness to the family group than can the patient cut off relations with his family while undergoing therapy. The real question is not the artificial control of the simplicity or complexity of the therapeutic situation, but rather the need to explore the dynamic implications of different methods. Does one deal with these family members *in absentia*, through a medium, or does one deal with them directly? The position of the therapist cannot be an easy or simple one with any approach. It is conceivable that a therapist who deals exclusively with one patient faces one set of complications, whereas a therapist who deals with multiple family members faces another. In other words, the complications may be differently structured in the two approaches. There is the further question of which set of complications a particular therapist prefers to deal with. Why? And how?

For these questions I have tried to find answers. Some will be of particular interest to psychiatrists and psychoanalysts, some to clinical psychologists, social workers, and social scientists. But there are other professional men and women who are profoundly concerned with the problem of mental health: educators, the clergy, community leaders, etc. I hope that they too will find something of value here. I have tried to express these concepts in straightforward, unprofessional language, avoiding technical jargon as far as possible, for today concern with these problems goes far beyond the professional worker in the field. The lay reader may also find some of these ideas useful and practical.

Unfortunately, in contemporary society the tasks of psychotherapy, prevention of mental illness, promotion of positive mental health, and education in general seem to be profoundly divorced. Should they be? The basic purpose of this book is to bring a clear light to the challenging problem of the interdependence of individual, family, and society. It is an attempt to build an integrated, dynamic conception of the mental health problems of family living, relating the family outward to society and inward to the individual member. In such an undertaking all of us must ultimately be concerned.

Nathan W. Ackerman

New York
July 1958

ACKNOWLEDGMENTS

WITHIN THE PAST DECADE, there has been a remarkable spurt of interest in developing a direct approach to the mental health of the family as a whole. Outstanding contributions have been made by a special group of workers: Erich Lindemann, Gerald Caplan, John Spiegel, Don Jackson, David Mendell, Seymour Fisher, Adelaide Johnson, Stanley Szurek, Bela Mittelman, Martin Grotjahn, and, among the social scientists, Marjorie Behrens, Florence Kluckhohn, Gregory Bateson, Otto Pollack, Reuben Hill, Ernest Burgess, Talcott Parsons, Robert Bales, and others. The work of these investigators has been a stimulus to my own.

To the fifty families who provided my clinical material I owe a very special kind of debt. Close studies of these families contributed to the development of a theoretical frame for the understanding of the relations of family process and mental health. A fraction of this family material also appears here as illustrative case studies.

Innumerable people and countless sources in the literature have exerted influence on the theoretical orientation, but special mention is due Marjorie Behrens, M. Robert Gomberg, Iago Galston, Martin Grotjahn, and Otto Klineberg. The late Dr. Gomberg, former director of the Jewish Family Service of New York City, gave me not only his critical evaluation of the theoretical framework but his sustained support and personal encouragement as well. I am deeply saddened by the knowledge that he will not see the finished book to which he

contributed so much: his untimely death occurred on April 25, 1958, very shortly
after he had delivered a lecture on "Stabilizing the Family for Health and Social
Effectiveness" at the New York Academy of Medicine.

Dr. Galdston, Executive Secretary of the Committee on Medical Information at the New York Academy of Medicine, gave me much encouragement and
penetrating criticisms of certain aspects of this work.

Marjorie Behrens served as my assistant. She contributed unstintingly of
her talent, influenced the conceptualization of basic problems and, in particular,
the development of methods and procedures for family study. Deserving of special mention is her contribution to the home visit as an aid to family diagnosis
and therapy. I am exceedingly grateful for her help.

The manuscript in its first version was thoughtfully reviewed and criticized
by a number of friends and colleagues including Max Lerner, Erich Fromm,
Martin Grotjahn, Otto Klineberg, and Edward Hornick. I also wish to express
my thanks to Dr. George Daniels, Director of the Columbia Psychoanalytic
Clinic, and to Dr. Lawrence Kolb, Professor of Psychiatry and Director of the
Department of Psychiatry, Columbia University, for their approval of the manuscript.

I am especially grateful to Arthur Rosenthal of Basic Books, Inc., for his un-
limited help and understanding in the editing of this book.

Finally, thanks are due to a series of professional publications whose editors
have graciously allowed me to adapt earlier articles for the purposes of this book:

The International Journal of Group Psychotherapy, for "Group Psychotherapy with a Mixed Group of Adolescents";

Zeitschrift für diagnostische Psychologie und Persönlichkeitsforschung,
Band V, Heft 3/4, Sonderheft Gruppenpsychotherapie, published by Hans
Huber, Bern, Switzerland, 1957, for "Five Issues in Group Psychotherapy";

The International Journal of Social Psychiatry, for "The Principles of
Shared Responsibility for Child Rearing";

The American Journal of Psychoanalysis, for "A Changing Conception of
Personality" and "Goals in Therapy—A Symposium";

American Journal of Psychiatry, for "Toward an Integrative Therapy of
the Family";

The American Journal of Orthopsychiatry, for "Group Dynamics: I: Social
Role and Total Personality," "Disturbances of Mothering and Criteria for Treatment," and "A Study of Family Diagnosis" (the last with Marjorie L. Behrens);

Social Casework, for "Mental Hygiene and Social Work Today and Tomorrow," "The Diagnosis of Neurotic Marital Interaction," and "The Home Visit
as an Aid in Family Diagnosis and Therapy" (the last with Marjorie L.
Behrens);

Journal of Jewish Communal Service, for "Mental Health and the Family in the Current World Crisis";

Psychiatry, for "Interpersonal Disturbances in the Family: Unsolved Problems in Psychotherapy";

Psychosomatic Medicine, for "Personality in Arterial Hypertension" and Personality Factors in Neurodermite";

Columbia University Press, for "The Adaptive Problems of the Adolescent Personality," in *The Family in a Democratic Society,* edited by Community Service Society, 1949;

Grune & Stratton, Inc., for "Interlocking Pathology in Family Relationships," in *Changing Concepts of Psychoanalytic Medicine,* edited by Sandor Rado and G. E. Daniels, 1956;

The Williams & Wilkins Company, for "Character Structure in Hypertensive Persons," in *Life Stress and Bodily Disease,* edited by Harold G. Wolff *et al.,* 1950.

CONTENTS

PART 3

Therapeutic Aspects

PART 4

Wider Perspectives

THE PSYCHODYNAMICS OF FAMILY LIFE

MENTAL HEALTH, SOCIAL CHANGE, AND FAMILY

THE SOCIO-CULTURAL revolution that characterizes our time has spurred mistrust and fear among nations, altered the face of family life, and unsettled established patterns of individual, family, and community. No piece of earth, no person, no community is immune. Human beings and human relations have been plunged into a state of turbulence while the machine surges far ahead of man's wisdom concerning himself. The shrinking of space and the cramped intimacy of people living in clashing cultures call for new understanding, a new vision of the relations of man to man and man to society. Somehow we must implement the human striving for health, security, and enrichment of the spirit in a single world community, find the way to live together, and establish a family of mankind. As Toynbee[1] says, we must learn the "difficult art of dwelling together in unity, like brothers." The present-day issues of mental health no longer concern only the sick individual. They involve the entire structure of the community and are deeply affected by the contemporary world crisis.

In an environment that is continually changing, unstable, unpredictable, we sense danger but the danger is ill-defined. Although a basic criterion of mental health is accurate perception of external reality, such perception is difficult indeed in our rapidly changing social scene. No one knows what is happening or what to expect. We are inadequately informed and hardly know what is real and what is imaginary. This makes it difficult at best to chart an effective course of action, and we are in danger of falling prey to panic and confusion, irrational suspicion, prejudice, war, and genocide.

In the disordered relations of person and environment, the first line of defense is to find a realistic solution for conflict, a solution that preserves and enhances personal development. The second line of defense is to contain the conflict within the person while seeking an effective solution. The third line of defense is irrational "acting out." The final defense is progressive emotional retreat leading ultimately to disintegration of personality. We see in current tensions between person and environment a shift to the third line of defense: "acting out." This spells danger.

In the contemporary social crisis there is little reason for complacency on anyone's part. Especially the physician, psychiatrist, social worker, educator, and religious leader—all those committed to healing and protecting the distressed and disabled—must work together to safeguard the essential values of the family of man. At the same time we must be continually vigilant against the cultivation of machine-like efficiency, against the development of trained technicians who operate with precision but are numb to the sufferings of people. Those who cease to feel cease to learn; the numb become dumb. We must not allow ourselves to be seduced by the sick values of the machine age, the very values that we seek to cure.

How are we more specifically to determine the magnitude of the challenge of mental health? It is traditional to quote statistics about the numbers of mentally afflicted and to count in dollars and cents the cost of mental illness to the community. To do so is to reflect the Western habit of measuring the importance of all things human by a process of counting—counting people and dollars. The statistics—and they are appalling—are easily available.[2] But can we measure the value of human life in dollars? Is it not totally misleading to approach the well-being of the human community through a process of bookkeeping? Statistics can give us only part of the story.

There are three distinct though interrelated facets of the problem of mental health: the study and treatment of mental illness, a program of prevention, and a program of promotion of positive mental health. It is not a simple problem. The human devastation of mental illness and its immeasurable damage to the welfare of the community poses a critical challenge. But this is only the negative aspect. The immense exertion required to neutralize the destructiveness of mental illness cannot be separated from the necessity for a community-wide plan aimed at prevention and also at promotion of positive mental health.

Because in recent years public interest in the urgency of this problem has grown considerably, allotments of public money for psychiatric research and the training of personnel in the mental health field are increasing constantly.

In ever greater numbers psychiatrists are tending to leave the mental hospitals and move into the open community to meet the increasing demands for their services in psychotherapy, child and family guidance, and marital counseling, and to cope with the wider ramifications of mental illness, delinquency, and social maladjustment in the community at large.

It is by no means the psychotic fraction of our population which has spurred this migration of psychiatrists from hospitals into the open community. It is rather the people who are "normal" or "near normal" who place this large claim on the special help of psychiatrists. The popularization of ideas having to do with mental health, the conspicuousness of parlor talk concerning psychiatry, and even the many jokes about psychiatrists are no accident. They are in themselves manifestations of a larger trend in our culture pattern, which makes mental health an earnest concern for everyone. In our changing society, the striving for mental health is no luxury; it is a "must"!

In this changing climate, the very definition of mental health has changed. We must now be able to define mental health in a positive way, not merely as absence of mental illness, not solely in terms of individual personality or such ambiguities as "maturity, harmony, and happiness." Freud himself offers a pithy definition of mental health as *lieben und arbeiten* (to love and to work), but has anyone anywhere ever worked or loved alone? Karl Menninger[3] states that "mental health is the adjustment of human beings to the world and to each other with a maximum of effectiveness and happiness." And Erich Fromm[4] says that "from the standpoint of function in society one can call a person normal or healthy if he is able to fulfill his social roles—if he is able to participate in the reproduction of society. From the standpoint of the individual we look upon health or normalcy as the optimum of growth and happiness of the individual." The expert committee on mental health of the World Health Organization suggested that mental health is the "capacity to establish harmonious interpersonal relations." [5]

Marie Jahoda[6] offers five criteria for the consideration of mental health: (1) the absence of mental illness, (2) the normality of behavior, (3) the adjustment to environment, (4) the internal unity of personality, (5) the correct perception of reality. These criteria, however, refer to partial processes on different planes of experience. Several pertain to mechanisms that maintain the internal harmony of the personality; others allude to the individual's relations with environment.

Jahoda further suggests three main elements: (1) active adjustment or attempts at mastery of environment as distinct both from the ability to adjust and from indiscriminate adjustment through passive acceptance of environmental conditions; (2) unity of personality, the maintenance of stable, internal integration, which remains intact notwithstanding the flexibility of behavior which derives from active adjustment; (3) the ability to perceive the world and self correctly.

Generally speaking, the distinction between healthy and sick, normal and abnormal, has been examined from two standpoints: (1) normal as statistically average and sick as statistically unusual; (2) normal as an approximation of a dynamic model of ideally healthy personality functioning and sick as a conspicuous deviation from this theoretical model. At some points these criteria overlap; at others they have no relation whatever; and at still others they contradict one another.

For example, a certain type of behavior may be sufficiently common in a given community to be accepted or at least tolerated as "normal"; nevertheless, a careful psychiatric examination by current standards may reveal conspicuous distortions in the internal mechanisms of personality. Insofar as such behavior deviates sharply from the dynamic model of an ideally healthy person, it is judged to be a psychopathological illness. Conversely, an individual whose behavior is socially atypical and veers from the common norms of a community may, upon careful psychiatric appraisal, reveal no significant defects of personality and may therefore be diagnosed as a mentally healthy person. Usually, however, disturbances in the inner mental life of the individual are mirrored in disturbances of social relations. The concepts of "normal" behavior which prevail in a given community influence greatly people's reactions to nonconforming types of conduct. Such social judgments translated into everyday behavior of persons toward one another may heighten the tendencies toward illness in an individual or may affect the processes of recovery.

Less and less do we blame everything that goes wrong on the one person who suffers from mental illness. We are beginning to broaden our view and examine mental illness as an expression of the significant relations of the individual with his social group as well as the balance of internal psychic processes. In this sense mental illness can be examined at three levels: (1) what goes on psychically within one person; (2) what happens between this person and his human environment; (3) what is distorted in the social processes of the environment itself. In other words, mental illness here is understood as a sick process that takes place partly inside the person and partly outside; a person may be thought of as being more or less sick or more or less healthy. The individual's emotional involvement in one set of human relations or another mobilizes predominantly either the sick or the healthy tendencies. The manner in which these tendencies come into play in personal relationships largely determines how other persons will react to the individual. It is the emotional content of these social experiences that qualifies the individual's capacity to deal with his personal conflicts and defend himself against excessive amounts of anxiety.

It cannot be forgotten that at any point in time the individual is the repository of a group experience. His identity is at once both individual and social. He is a mirror image, a microcosm of his family group. At a given moment in life, he epitomizes a whole hierarchy of family configurations, each of which corresponds to his individual personality at a particular stage of growth. A meaningful conception of mental health can be achieved only as we relate the functioning of the individual to the human relations patterns of his primary group. The historical focus on the individual has brought a wealth of knowledge of internal mental processes, but it has also imposed a blindness as to the urgency of evaluating illness as family process as well. Criteria for emotional illness and health cannot be restricted to the individual; they must encompass the individual within the group and the group as well. The ills of individual, family, and society are a continuum.

Among the normal, individual differences are tremendous; among the sick, too, there are individual differences. But among the sick the significance of these differences grows dim as compared with the conspicuous qualities of rigidity, stereotypy, and repetitiveness that are so characteristic of psycho-pathological states. The striking difference between healthy and sick persons is the plasticity of adaptive behavior in the healthy as compared with the rigid, constricted, automatized sameness of sick patterns of behavior. Among the latter the adaptive value of social interaction is gradually lost; there is a tendency to constriction and sameness. Among the healthy there is a tremendous range and diversity of behavior.

If, therefore, we rule out of our definition of mental health rigidity and constriction, which are so often characteristic of illness, if we rule out the "average" and the "usual," which may be found on closer analysis to be psychiatrically sick, and if we keep in mind the fact that islands of illness and islands of health may coexist in varying proportion in the same person, we must begin our thinking in terms of a process of balance and adaptation. Mental health is not a static quality in the private possession of anyone. It is not self-sustaining. It can be maintained only by continuous exertion and with the emotional togetherness and support of others. Ideally, it is the result of balanced and creative personal functioning that fulfills the best of man in social relations. It is the outcome of a capacity for optimal fulfillment of the individual's potential for group living. It means successful and satisfying performance. It alludes in a general sense to such attributes as maturity, stability, realism, altruism, a sense of social responsibility, effective integration in work and in human relations. It implies confidence and courage in facing new experience. It implies a value system in which the individual's welfare is joined to that of others; in other words, it implies a concern for the common good. As has been indicated, mental health is a quality of living, a process. It is achieved by a continuing struggle for better personal adaptation. It cannot be maintained in isolation, for satisfying emotional union with others is necessary for its preservation. It is concerned not only with inner harmony but also with optimal relatedness of person, family, and society. It implies the capacity to grow, to learn, to live fully, to love, and to share with others the adventure of life.

And yet with our new and broader definition of mental health, we are still sadly lacking in ways and means of achieving our goals. Again and again we see mental illness and health examined only at their first level—what goes on psychically within one person. What happens between this person and his environment and what is distorted in the social processes of that environment are sometimes ignored by clinicians and other mental health workers. In fact, however, "the mind is inside, it is outside, it is everywhere all the time." As Angyal[7] puts it, "We have a number of sciences related to the person but we do not have a science of the person. Human physiology, psychology and sociology deal with artificially separated single aspects of the human organism. It is paradoxical but unfortunately true that psychiatry is an application of a basic science which does not yet exist." In a similar vein, Jurgen Reusch[8] expresses his opinion:

> Today we conceive of the individual as a living organism whose social relations are combined into a complex organization, whose inner world of experience is closely related to his social operations, and whose soma materially makes possible his various activities—such a view necessitates a more unitary approach to man—one which will enable us to represent physical, psychological and social events within one system of denotation. If such an undertaking were to be successful, it would provide for an entirely new perspective of the intricate relations of mind, body and socioeconomic events and would furnish a framework which would consider simultaneously the individual and his surrounding, both in health and disease.

In a very real sense, Freud, with his uniquely brilliant penetration of the mechanisms of the individual psyche, left clinicians and mental health workers with a peculiar heritage: Health is "love and work," but human beings do not love and work alone. The child is shaped by the influence of environment, by parental care, love, and discipline, but the adult too is profoundly affected by his family and the surrounding community patterns. Yet Freud, in his theoretical constructions, chose to give prior emphasis to heredity, constitution, and the predetermined biological unfolding of instinctual patterns. He made his bow to the social man, but his investigation of social-psychopathological processes was negligible. Freudian theory presents a curious paradox.

Freud illuminated the relations of parent and child, but the light which he shed on mother and child and father and child also cast some shadows. The father is depicted as the towering authority who protects or menaces, gives strength or castrates. The mother is depicted as the great giver or depriver, wielding the limitless power of giving or withholding love and approval. Then, too, there is the eternal triangle of mother, father, and child. Some aspects of family life were sharply spotlighted while others were left in the dark. And it is one thing to state the emotional needs of a child and another to make over parents and family to meet those needs.

From these considerations arises my conviction that the single, most encompassing reason for our conspicuous failure thus far to prevent mental illness derives from our failure to cope with the mental health problems of family life. We have somehow kept ourselves so busy, so preoccupied with studying and treating the suffering of individuals, that we have, in effect, blinded ourselves to the significance of the concurrent struggles of the family for mental health and to the way in which the ongoing content of family experience affects the emotional struggles of its adult members. I do not mean to imply that the treatment of the individual patient, the alleviation of the very real sufferings of a single human being, is unimportant or unnecessary. To the contrary. But I do question the effectiveness of any such treatment that does not take into consideration the sum total of this individual, which must of necessity include his environment and his interactions with it.

A basic problem arises first in the area of diagnosis, for without adequate diagnosis there can hardly be adequate therapy. The prevailing diagnostic systems are essentially descriptive rather than dynamic, developmental, and etiological. The special criteria emphasized in these systems vary; they may be symptoms, configurations of conflict, or total personality profiles. But in such diagnostic frameworks, the individual is conceptually atomized and cut off from the close group into which his personality functions are integrated. Diagnostic categories depend mainly on symptom clusters; they reflect little of total personality organization and of the preferred modes of social adaptation. The central concern is with the mechanisms of symptom formation, those deviant, irrational, ego-alien (nonassimilable) units of behavior which in varying degree are walled off from the residual healthy parts of the personality. But it is now known that the same symptom may have effects that are benign in one person and malignant in another. It is also recognized that a given symptom may have different effects for the same person at different times in his life and in different family or other group circumstances.

The issue, therefore, is not so much the form of the symptom but rather the way in which the individual's integrative capacity deals with the central conflict and the manner in which his family relationships affect this outcome. Because of the subtleties of such processes, in a situation in which two people have the same pathological symptoms it is possible to succeed in promoting mental health in one case and fail in the other. The final outcome in adaptation rests not merely on the nature of the individual's conflicts and symptoms but on his total resources for dealing with them; that is, on the integrative potential of his personality and the psychological character of the family group of which he is a part.

These principles in turn may be related to another clinical observation. In the psychiatric field we have sometimes been prone to make inaccurate, sometimes inappropriate appraisals of the behavior of certain persons because of a one-sided, excessive emphasis on the pathological trends. We overlook other trends reflecting residual health, both in the primary patient and in his family environment. This consideration is of practical importance in that, in the last analysis, the rehabilitation of emotionally distressed or disabled persons rests on our ability to make maximal use of what is residually healthy in such individuals and their families. It is an easy matter to confirm the validity of this principle if we examine carefully the emotional functioning of a person in the several significant areas of life adaptation—sexual, social, occupational, etc. When we do this, we inevitably find that the person acts more sick in some places in life and less sick in others, that the degree of disablement that comes from the illness varies with the life task that is undertaken and the quality of relations with other persons with whom the task is shared.

So also misleading diagnoses are sometimes made when the clinician depends too heavily on a single office interview and does not get adequate data on the patient's total life performance. Or the psychiatrist may diagnose on the basis of a single significant personal relationship (e.g., the marital) without checking life performance in other personal relationships. All these tendencies to diagnose and therefore treat in terms of only a part of the whole person are responsible for the limited success of much therapy.

Furthermore, the tendency to isolate conceptually the individual from his family renders prediction of the course of illness virtually impossible. The proper unit of prediction cannot be the person alone but must be the person-family environment as an integrated unit. The dynamic balance of individual and group influences the precipitation of illness, the course of illness, the possibility of recovery, and the risk of relapse. Yet the great importance of day-by-day family experience is all but ignored in much current practice.

It is the failure to assess the environment or to achieve effective control of it that often limits the results of psychiatric treatment. If one family member enters individual therapy, any change in the patient's attitudes and behavior alters the reciprocal behavior of other family members and, in turn, the change in their behavior affects the experience of the primary patient. Often a patient may be initially accessible but soon bogs down and blocks further progress because he is emotionally locked in a warped role in his family group. Yet all too often there is no effort to modify these pathogenic patterns of family-role relations. Such processes are profoundly affected by the fact that the chain of family relations serves as a kind of conveyor belt, a carrier for pathogenic intensities of emotional disturbance. Over a span of time the critical focus of conflict and anxiety may move from one family member to another or gravitate first to one family pair and then to another. Conflict in a family relationship may be partly internalized, or internal conflict may be partly externalized. The patterns of interpersonal conflict within the family affect the vicissitudes of control of internalized conflict. Individual diagnosis and therapy cannot alone deal with these difficulties or promote the kind of mental health that today's turbulent society demands.

If we are to approach these problems anew, dissatisfied with existing systems and techniques, we must, it seems to me, acknowledge the fact that mental health cannot be understood within the limited confines of individual experience. The concentrated study of individual personality is significant and fruitful in its own right, but it is not enough A broader approach to mental health must embrace the dynamics of the family group as well. And it must extend even farther to the complex weave of the interrelations of individual, family, and wider community.

Therefore, my central purpose is to evolve a conceptual frame within which it is possible to define the relations between the emotional functioning of the individual and the psychosocial functioning of the family group. My immediate goals are three: First, I hope to develop a theoretical framework for the evaluation of the psychosocial functioning of family groups. Second, I hope to find means for the systematic correlation of the emotional functioning and mental health of the individual with the emotional functioning and mental health of the family group. Third, I hope to develop a method for the observation and differential description of families according to their mental health and, correspondingly, a method for systematic comparison of contrasting types of families. To simplify the statement of these goals, I use the brief term "family diagnosis." Such an undertaking requires new hypotheses, new methods of research and validation, and different ways of applying basic psychodynamic principles to the empirical tasks of bettering the mental health of the community.

The potential values of the cultivation of a system of family diagnosis are numerous. There is the opportunity to re-examine prevailing theories regarding the development of personality disorders in children; to study the role of family in the mental health of adult persons; to illuminate the processes of integration of personality into familial and extrafamilial roles; to explore the problems and consequences of adaptation to multiple roles with conflicting requirements; and to consider the part these events play in the precipitation of and subsequent rehabilitation after mental illness. In addition, there is the opportunity to correct recognized deficiencies in methods of psychiatric diagnosis, psychotherapeutic practice, and prediction of behavior and the chance to fashion new tools in the tasks of prevention. Last but not least, there is the challenge to discern the role of family patterns and values in the mental health of the individual, family, and wider community.

Surely the tremendous accretion of new knowledge in the fields of psychiatry, social science, and interpersonal communication opens the way to something better. The development of family diagnosis and family therapy offers this promise.

Part 1

THEORETICAL ASPECTS

CHAPTER 1

THE PSYCHODYNAMICS OF
THE FAMILY

NONE OF US lives his life alone. Those who try are foredoomed; they disintegrate as human beings. Some aspects of life experience are, to be sure, more individual than social, others more social than individual; but life is nonetheless a shared and a sharing experience. In the early years this sharing occurs almost exclusively with members of our family. The family is the basic unit of growth and experience, fulfillment or failure. It is also the basic unit of illness and health.

The family is a designation for an institution as old as the human species itself. The family is a paradoxical and elusive entity. It assumes many guises. It is the same everywhere; yet it is not the same anywhere. Throughout time it has remained the same; yet it has never remained the same. The steady transformation of family through time is the product of an unceasing process of evolution; the form of family molds itself to the conditions of life which dominate at a given time and place. On the contemporary scene, the family is changing its pattern at a remarkably rapid rate; it is accommodating in a striking way to the social crisis which is the mark of our period in history. There is nothing fixed or immutable about family, except that it is always with us. It is small wonder, therefore, that we accept its role in our lives so naturally, so unthinkingly. In one sense, we have had thousands of years in which to grow accustomed to it, and yet, in another, each generation in turn must learn again how to live with it.

What is the irreducible minimum of family? Is it the mating of male and female to produce and care for progeny, or is it a fundamental expression of the social nature of man, his need to be part of a group? Or are these really the same?

Some students of family, notably Westermark and his followers, express the conviction that there has been a uniform development of family from the anthropoid ancestors of man to civilization in a predominantly monogamous form within which the father filled a significant place. Other students, Briffault and his disciples, assert the opposite view that the organization of family had mainly a maternal basis and that the role of the father was transient, relatively peripheral, and unimportant. In time, however, the father assumed a permanent place in the family group. In the words of Otto Klineberg,[1] "society imposes upon the man the duty of caring for his children as a sort of payment for the rights he has in his wife."

Some forms of family have been patterned distinctly as an economic unit and tied relatively little to its biological matrix. Family has not always signified father, mother, and children. It has sometimes represented a complicated household functioning as a unit and composed of all those living under one roof or submitting to the authority of one supreme head—a group of persons unified for the purpose of effective social regulation.

Thus family bonds are made up of a fusion of factors: biological, psychological, social, and economic. Biologically, the family serves to perpetuate the species. It is the basic unit of society that provides for the union of male and female to produce offspring and to assure their nurture and training. The relations of male and female and sexual mores play a lesser role than the care of the young. The historical background of family is complicated. Marriage and family have been divided. Sex and marriage have been divided. The evolutionary shift from hunting to agriculture as a way of life brought with it a shift from the matriarchal to the patriarchal family and the development of property value. The industrial revolution brought with it profound changes in the family pattern. What nuclear energy and the space age will bring no one can predict.

But the family's biological functions can be fulfilled only in an appropriate organization of social forces. Psychologically, the members of the family are bound by mutual interdependence for the satisfaction of their respective affectional needs. Economically, they are bound by mutual interdependency for the provision of their material needs.

The pattern of family organization is in no sense static or sacred. Despite popular superstition, marriage is not made in heaven; the family is not a God-ordained, perfect system. Neither is the family the pillar of society. Rather society molds the function of family to its greatest usefulness.

Thus the family is in every sense the product of evolution. It is a flexible unit that adapts delicately to influences acting upon it both from without and within. In its external relations it must adapt to prevalent customs and mores and must make wide and workable connections with racial, religious, social, and economic forces. But internally the family must also come to terms with the basic biological bonds of man and woman and of mother and child.

This issue is not at all whether the family is biological or social. It can hardly be "either-or." There is a fundamental continuity between individual, family, and society. But the biosocial organization of behavior at each of these levels is distinct.

The family is sometimes characterized as an organism. The connotations of the term "organism" instantaneously suggest the biological core of family. It attaches to family the qualities of living process and functional unity. It suggests that the family possesses a natural life history of its own—a period of germination, a birth, a growth and development, a capacity to adapt to change and crisis, a slow decline, and, finally, dissolution of the old family into the new.

Throughout the entire process the psychological unity of the family is continuously molded by both external conditions and by its internal organization. Just as in the growth of the individual there are critical turning points, so in the life of the family there are critical periods when the bond of the family itself may be strengthened or weakened. The family of one generation is born, lives and dies, and, like the individual, it achieves a kind of immortality in its offspring. Within one generation the configuration of the family undergoes significant shifts at each phase of transition. It is one kind of structure in the period of childbearing, another when the children reach pubescence and the parents enter their prime, and still another when children mature, marry, go their several ways, and the parents turn senescent.

Moreover, every man has not one family but several. He has the family of his childhood, the family of marriage and parenthood, and the "sunset family" —the family of grandparenthood. In each of these periods of family living, the individual must integrate his emotional dispositions into the appropriate family roles.

Although there is a striking analogy between the organismic properties of the individual and the vital phenomena of family life, which is expressed in interdependence of the parts and specialization of functions, this analogy can be carried only part way. The individual organism is characterized by its physical unity. The members of a family do not adhere in the same way as the organs of the body, although they do adhere in space under the same roof or within the same community.

Adaptive shifts in family pattern are determined both by its internal organization and its external position in the community. It is commonly recognized that the weave of family relations may be affected in a wide variety of ways by either a friendly, supportive social environment or a hostile and dangerous one. A social environment which imposes danger may cause a family to go asunder; the unity of the family may crumble as it is invaded by external force. Or, by contrast, a family may react with a defensive strengthening of its solidarity. A friendly external environment that provides opportunity for self-expression and reward in the wider community may loosen the bonds of family and invite increased social mobility for its members. Or, if the family is so organized internally, it may respond with greater closeness and increased satisfaction for individual members within the fold. And we know that with a change of family pattern in response to social change the bonds of love and loyalty may be fortified or weakened; the sharing of experience, division of labor, and the apportionment of authority between male and female parent may undergo marked change.

From within, the family must adjust to a wide range of vicissitudes that affect the relations of each family member to every other. Under favorable conditions, the emotions of love and loyalty prevail and family harmony is maintained. Under conditions of excessive tension and conflict, mutual antagonism and hatred are aroused and the integrity of the family is threatened.

The family may be likened to a semipermeable membrane, a porous covering sac, which allows a selective interchange between the enclosed members and the outside world. "Reality" seeps through the pores of the sac selectively to affect the enclosed members in a way predetermined by the quality of the sac. The influence exerted by the family members on the outside world is also affected by the quality of the sac. Adverse conditions within the sac or in the surrounding environment may destroy it, in which case the enclosed members lose their protective envelope. Menacing external conditions may cause the pores of the sac to shrink, thereby contracting the sac and holding the members more tightly within it. A family sac thus constricted and isolated from the environment cannot carry out its functions normally or long survive. Favorable external conditions expand the sac and promote a more fluid interaction with the external world. Excess tension within the sac arising from a state of imbalance among the enclosed members may warp the sac. Unless balance is restored, the accumulated internal pressure will eventually burst it.

Basically, the family does two things: It insures physical survival and builds the essential humanness of man. The satisfaction of basic biological needs is essential to survival, but the mere sating of these needs by no means guarantees the unfolding of the qualities of humanness. It is the family experience of togetherness that is the matrix for development of this humanness. This togetherness is epitomized in the union of mother and child and is further reflected in the bond of identity of individual and family, of family and wider community.

Concretely, the social purposes served by the modern family are:

1. the provision of food, shelter, and other material necessities to sustain life and provide protection from external danger, a function best fulfilled under conditions of social unity and cooperation;
2. the provision of social togetherness which is the matrix for the affectional bond of family relationships;
3. the opportunity to evolve a personal identity, tied to family identity, this bond of identity providing the psychic integrity and strength for meeting new experience;
4. the patterning of sexual roles, which prepares the way for sexual maturation and fulfillment;
5. the training toward integration into social roles and acceptance of social responsibility;
6. the cultivation of learning and the support for individual creativity and initiative.

Clearly the configuration of family determines the forms of behavior that are required in the roles of husband and wife, father, mother, and child. Mothering and fathering, and the role of the child, acquire specific meaning only within a defined family structure. Thus the family molds the kinds of persons it needs in order to carry out its functions, and in the process each member reconciles his past conditioning with present role expectations. Clearly this process is a continuing one, for the psychological identity of a family changes over a period of time. And within the framework of this process, each member at times conforms and, at other times and within limits, actively alters these role expectations.

The currents of feeling that move between family members are myriad in kind and of all degrees of intensity. Each of these emotional currents may, under altered conditions, provoke its antagonist. The emotional tone that governs the relationship between any two members of a family has a development peculiarly its own, but this development is continuously influenced by the emotional climate that characterizes the entire family. It is the changing manifold of emotional currents and cross-currents that defines the unique interpersonal atmosphere of the family. It is against the background of this family atmosphere, constantly in flux, that a child's personality and social reactions are developed.

The family may be fairly regarded as a kind of exchange unit; the values exchanged are love and material goods. Within the family sphere there is a flow of these values in all directions. Generally, however, the parents are the prime givers. To use a simple formula, the emotional attitudes and actions of any one member of the family are expressed in what he needs, how he seeks to get it, what he is willing to give in return, what he does if he does not get it, and how he responds to the needs of others. The whole process of distribution of satisfactions in the family is governed by the parents. It rests largely with them whether the expectations of each member from every other are destined to have reasonable fulfillment. At its best, this process is a smooth-running one, and a general atmosphere of mutual love and devotion prevails. If, however, the family atmosphere is full of sudden turns and shifts, deep feelings of frustration may result, inevitably accompanied by resentment and hostility. The interchange of feeling between family members revolves centrally about this oscillation between love and hate.

In the usual course of events in family life, it is the fate of all to experience some measure of disappointment; in consequence of this, there is stirred some anger and fear. An excess of disillusionment, pain, and hatred may prove a serious detriment to healthy development. However, the experiencing of some measure of disappointment, the development of tolerance to frustration, and the acceptance of less than complete fulfillment are essential to emotional growth. Without these there would be an insufficient spur to new experience and new achievement.

It is apparent that children experience both love and hate toward their parents. The reasonably satisfied, happy child succeeds effectively in subordinating his hate, mainly loves, and identifies with his parents, molding himself in their image. The thwarted, unhappy child experiences excessive hate and may identify with his parents on a basis of hate and fear rather than love, defiantly renounce identity with them, or develop a pathologically severe conscience out of fear of parental retaliation.

The effective control of this balance between love and hate is largely determined by the attitudes of the parents, though these are in turn influenced by the attitudes and behavior of the children. The characters of the parents have already been deeply etched as a result of their own early family conditionings. They may carry over from this original experience the same attitudes that their parents showed them; or, if they have felt badly treated by their own parents, they may now display a set of attitudes exactly the opposite of those they themselves experienced in childhood.

The manner in which parents characteristically show their love for one another and for their children is of utmost significance in determining the emotional climate of the family. Conflict evokes hostile tension, which when unabated threatens family disorganization. When the parents love one another, the child loves both parents; when the parents hate one another, the child is compelled to side with one against the other. This induces fear since he must then be prepared to lose the love of the parent he rejects in favor of the other one. The emotional climate of the family is a steadily evolving one. It is not one of unending sameness. The shift in the quality of family interaction is often subtle.

At birth, the infant has a certain hereditary potential, but in the larger sense he has no self, no mind, no personality of his own. His individuality is patterned stage by stage out of the primary oneness of mother and infant. Out of this original oneness emerges difference. The perception of difference may be a spur to learning provided the self-esteem of the individual is sustained by the bond of identification. A healthy separation of the child's individual self is contingent on the maintenance of a healthy emotional togetherness of child and mother. If the togetherness is impaired, the process of separation is distorted. If the separation experience is impaired, the sense of togetherness is injured.

The relations of individual identity and family identity are characterized by the delicate interplay of processes of merging and differentiation. As the individual matures, marries, and creates a new family, his identity becomes fused in these new relationships, is modified and further differentiated. Thus identity is a constantly evolving process. Individual identity requires support from family identity, and family identity in turn requires support from the wider community.

The family's task is to socialize the child and foster the development of his identity. There are two central processes involved in this development: first, the movement from a position of infantile comfort and dependence toward adult self-direction and its attendant satisfactions; second, the movement from a place of infantile, aggrandized, omnipotent importance to a position of lesser importance, that is, from dependence to independence and from the center of the family to the periphery. Both processes are psychological functions of the family as a unit. In the interests of the emotional health of the child it is essential that these processes be imperceptibly gradual.

In the case of the marital relationship the situation differs, of course. Each partner comes to the union with a personal identity already formed. Though formed, it is nevertheless incomplete. Male and female are drawn to each other through a process of empathic attraction. Each yearns to complete the self through union with the other. The psychic identity of the marital couple derives from this union. But the emotion of love is more than sex. It is a total emotional response and requires an echo.

It is the interaction, merging, and redifferentiation of the individualities of the partners of this marital pair that molds the identity of the new family. Just as a child's personality internalizes something of each parent and also evolves something new, so too the identity of a new family incorporates something of the self-image of each marital partner and the image of their respective families-of-origin and also develops something unique and new.

From the joined identity of the marital pair each partner seeks further development as an individual, as well as the fulfillment of family goals. If the identity of the marital relationship is impaired, the process of further differentiation of each individual partner will likewise be impaired. The psychological identity of the marital pair shapes the child, but the child also shapes the parental pair to his needs. It is the interaction of family members in reciprocal role relations that provides the stimulus to appropriate receptivity to new experience and the cultivation of individual initiative. The psychological identity of the marital pair, as well as the evolving identity of each individual partner, becomes the core of the expanding identity of the new family.

Under optimal conditions it is possible to achieve a level of positive emotional health beyond that which characterized the families-of-origin. The younger generations of parents may raise healthier children than the older one, even while over-reacting against their parents' "mistakes."

Maternal and paternal behavior cannot be linked in a simple, one-to-one causal relationship with the individual personalities of the parents. Rather mothering and fathering represent interdependent, reciprocal role adaptations molded by the total psychological configuration of the family group, over and above the determinants that derive from the individual backgrounds of the two parents. Thus, the behavior of father, mother, or child cannot be evaluated in a social vacuum or in the exclusive context of parent-child interaction but must rather be regarded as a functional expression of the total interpersonal experience that characterizes the life of the family.

The interrelations of the identity of the marital or parental couple and the individual identity of each partner are delicately balanced. It is something like losing oneself in the larger family identity only to find oneself again, this time, hopefully, in an improved version. Out of this marital and parental fusion in a healthy family comes a richer, stronger individual identity. The differentiation of the separate self is as important as is the basic family togetherness. The quality of difference in family relations need not be felt as a threat, any more than sex difference is a threat. Instead it should be welcomed as proof of the complementation of the self, the opportunity for new learning and greater fulfillment.

The emotional disturbances of most people converge on the experiences of day-to-day family living. The emotional "give and take" of these relationships is the dead center of all forces that "make or break" mental health. The family group executes the crucial task of socializing the child, and shapes the development of his personality, thus determining in great part his mental fate. Those processes by means of which the child absorbs or rejects, wholly or in part, his family atmosphere determine his character. For the adult person, the day-by-day experiences of family living play a central part in stabilizing and enhancing mental health, advancing personal satisfaction, promoting success in social integration, and stimulating new growth of personality. The family provides the specific kinds of learning experience that enable a person to fit himself into a variety of life situations. The home is the arena in which a person acquires practice and increasing dexterity in filling a wide range of social roles.

Family relationships regulate the flow of emotion, facilitating some paths of emotional release and inhibiting others. The family configuration controls the quality and quantity of emotional expression, as well as its direction. The family supports some individual strivings while subordinating others. Likewise, it patterns the form and range of opportunities for security, pleasure, and self-realization. It structures the sense of responsibility the individual must feel for the welfare of others. It provides models for success and failure in personal and social performance.

It gives form to the subjective images of danger, which are a part of all social striving, and influences the accuracy or confusion of these perceptions of danger. Whether an individual reacts to a sense of threat with "fight or flight" is in turn affected by the conviction of support and loyalty in family ties or feelings of alienation and betrayal. Family interaction may intensify or lessen anxiety; it patterns the human setting in which conflicts are expressed and contributes to success or failure in the solution of these conflicts. In the struggle, the choice of particular defenses against anxiety is also selectively influenced by the family pattern.

Finally, family interaction molds the range of impact between phantasy and reality and thus influences the growth of perception of reality. The individual seeks out those qualities of family experience that are congenial to his personal strivings. He interacts selectively with those features of family life that are favorable to the pursuit of personal aims, pleasure goals, and the relief of conflict and guilt.

The stability of the family and that of its members hinges on a delicate pattern of emotional balance and interchange. The behavior of each member is affected by every other. A shift in the emotional interaction of one pair of persons in a given family alters the interaction processes of other family pairs. In a triangular relationship, one member may bind or disrupt the psychic unity of the other two. Emotional illness may integrate or disintegrate a family relationship. The emotional illness of one member may complement that of another or may have effects that are antagonistic. Some forms of illness may be shared by two or more members of a family. A crisis in the life of the family may exert pervasive and far-reaching effects on the mental health of the family and its individual members.

The interrelations of individual and family behavior need to be scrutinized in these dimensions: (1) the group dynamics of the family; (2) the dynamic processes of emotional integration of the individual into his family role; (3) the internal organization of individual personality and its historical development.

The phenomena of family role constitute the bridge between the internal processes of personality and the group pattern of the family. The family roles of husband and wife, father and mother, parent and child, child and sibling, are intrinsically interdependent and reciprocal. Each family member is required to integrate himself into multiple roles and also into extrafamilial roles. We must be concerned here with several questions: the relative success or failure of adaptation into the required family roles, how each role affects every other, how one family pair influences another, and the degree to which adaptation in one role reinforces or impedes adaptation in another.

Three empirically documented principles are immediately relevant to such an effort:

1. Abnormal behavior in adult persons has significant roots in the experience of childhood integration into a particular family but continues to be molded by current family experience.
2. The diagnostic evaluation and therapy of emotional disturbance in a child, viewed as an individual apart from his family environment, is impossible. The proper unit for study and treatment is the child seen as part of the family, the family as part of the child.
3. Personality disorders and disturbances in social adaptation of adult persons may be better understood if examined not in isolation but rather as a dynamic changing pattern, influenced continuously by the reciprocal effects of family interaction. Deviant behavior is thus seen not merely as a projection of a fixed intrapersonality distortion but also as a functional expression of emotional interplay in significant personal relationships. The way in which the person perceives the image of others influences his image of self, and vice versa. This is a two-way process, continuously molding feeling, attitude, and action.

The family is a primary group. It is intermediate between the individual and wider society. In the study of behavior, we have been prone either to examine the individual as an intact, isolated entity or to examine the effects on behavior of the individual's position in the wider social structure. The investigation of the psychodynamics of the family as a unit and the processes of individual integration into the family group, previously neglected, opens up a new avenue of research. The relations of individual personality and the group-dynamic processes of family living constitute an essential link in the chain of causation of states of mental illness and health.

Arthur Miller,[2] the playwright, asks this question:

How may a man make of the outside world a home? How and in what ways must he struggle, what must he strive to change and overcome within himself and outside himself if he is to find the safety, the surroundings of love, the ease of soul, the sense of identity and honor, which all men have connected in their memories with the idea of family?

CHAPTER 2

FREUD AND THE PSYCHOANALYTIC
VIEW OF FAMILY

THE CONCEPTS of Freud are endlessly rich in their reflections on the nature of human experience. Yet hidden in these reflections lies the profound riddle of the interrelations of individual development and family "belongingness" as they evolve in time. The riddle is persistently echoed in a measure of indecision about how far personality is individual, how far it is familial or social, how far it unfolds autonomously from within, how far it is influenced from without, and how far it moves inward and backward rather than outward and forward. It is the riddle of the relations between the inner and outer face of personality, the secrets of which are not yet fully revealed. They are still somewhat obscured in the reciprocal processes of integration and individuation in family life.

We would surely fail to give Freud the measure of respect and honor that is his due if we did not come to grips with the limitations of his conceptual picture of man that now are revealed by the newer knowledge of personality dynamics and group behavior. It is this more recently accumulated knowledge, enriched by the cross-fertilization of psychoanalysis, social science, and communication theory that enables us now to re-examine the role of family in mental health.

The value of Freud's theory of personality rests not so much on the literal correctness of this or that facet of the system, but rather in the tremendous inspiration it provided for exploration and testing of an endless range of provocative ideas about human behavior. Freud's own concepts left the field wide open for modification and further development of a theory of personality. However, the rigid and excessively literal interpretation of his conceptual system by some of his adherents has created difficulty. One may well raise the question as to whether these vocal and staunch supporters of the "master" or the so-called "revisionists" are the more truly loyal. I count myself among the revisionists. I believe Freud's ideas must be put to the test.

The more literal and dogmatic interpretation of the Freudian theoretical system falls somewhere short of providing a unified framework for tracing the path of transition from the family of childhood to the family of adulthood. It discloses with remarkable brilliance how man perceives and falsifies his image of family, but it does not elucidate with equal clarity how man assimilates and uses the more correctly perceived experiences, the "realities" of family life. The Freudian image of love as a positive, healthy force in family relations is incomplete. So, too, is the view of the impact between old and new experience. Therefore, the psychodynamics of learning, the forward-moving, creative phase of development remains only vaguely outlined.

The Freudian theory* focuses attention on the role of family in the shaping of personality and mental health of the child, but it gives priority to inborn instincts. It dramatizes the biological core of man, while diminishing the role of society. It dwells heavily on the permanent patterning of personality in the first years of life, while reducing the importance of later levels of social participation. It raises to a dizzy height the primacy of irrational unconscious processes, while underrating man's powers of reason. It points to parents and family as the epitome of all social influence on behavior, yet it paradoxically plays down the social factor in the causation of states of illness and health. The salient emphasis is on the projection of irrational, anxiety-ridden phantasy; the interpersonal reality of the contemporary group environment is largely bypassed.

Freud's writings reflect an inexhaustible fertility of imagination about man's inner mind, but show also some persistent ambiguity in interpreting the role of the environment. The concept of superego leads directly to parents and family, but there is a tendency to bypass or postpone systematic appraisal of the relations of individual and group. Freud's perspective implied an ambivalent attitude toward society, one might say to life itself. It appeared as if Freud were for the individual and against culture. He expressed a deep pessimism toward civilization; he perceived the individual and culture as being set against one another. Culture and personal freedom were incompatible. Man pays a penalty, he believed, for whatever benefits he derives from civilization; with inimitable irony,

---

* In drawing these generalizations regarding Freud's own theory, full consideration should be given to the import of later modifications of psychoanalytic theory.

he expressed his wonder as to whether civilization was worth the price. Freud's pessimism toward life and social relations was active, not passive. He seemingly attached a personal value judgment to the realities of human existence, the realities of family and wider society. In his view, reality was intrinsically a source of danger and pain, but unavoidable. At best, one resigned oneself to the disillusioning sadness of it. In the light of present day knowledge, one might again ask: How far did he understand love, creativity and emotional health as a positive force in human relations?

Freud conceived the family as the instrument for disciplining the child's biologically fixed instinctual urges and enforcing repression of their spontaneous release. He described the child as a polymorphous, perverse little animal. The child epitomizes animal pleasure. The parent personifies reality and the restraints of society. The child is a pleasure-bent anarchist. The parent is anti-pleasure. In this aspect of family relations, parent and child are imaged as virtual enemies to one another. It is as if the basic life values of parent and child are at war. At best they might live together in an uneasy truce, each exacting sacrifice of the other. From one angle at least, this attitude lends to the ethos of family relations something of a puritanical tinge, a self-sacrificial, duty-bound conception of the role of the parent, and a view of the pleasure drives of the child as being subhuman and anti-social. If the child indulges his pleasure cravings, does this inevitably impose a sacrifice on the parent? Does it inflict pain? If the parent asserts his guiding and controlling position, does this necessarily deprive the child of pleasure? Is it really so that what gratifies the child hurts the parent and vice versa? I do not believe so. What is good, satisfying, and healthy for the one ought fundamentally to be the same for the other.

There is something obscured in Freud's conceptual picture, certainly obscured, if not actually missing. It is, I repeat, love as a positive force in family relations, a mutually enhancing experience, which provides the impetus to social learning. It is the joining of man and wife, and parent and child, in the fulfillment of love within the realities of family living which spurs learning. The ideological content of Freudian psychoanalysis highlights the trends toward fixation and regression; it emphasizes the inertia of emotional development. But it does not disclose the secrets of forward movement of personality, the capacity to learn, the element of creativity in man's development. Freud, creative giant that he was, confessed his sense of failure and futility in attempting to find an explanation for creativity. By his own admission, he did not understand the creative urge of the artist.

Freud saw with dramatic clarity man's failure to learn and grow creatively. He provided penetrating answers to the questions: How is it that man perceives his family experience in a faulty way? How is it that he becomes emotionally blind and repeats over and over the same human errors? How is it that he re-enacts in adulthood the irrationalities of his family of childhood and becomes impervious to new experience? But how is it at the other pole that he learns and grows? What is healthy development?

Freud conceptually opposed parent and child somewhat in the same way that he opposed reality and pleasure and culture and personal freedom. He saw vividly the oppositional but not the joining aspect of these relations. This he understood less well. It is surely not inevitable that parent and child, reality and pleasure, culture and personal freedom, are inalterably opposed. Nor is it that old and new experience are incompatible. Under conditions of emotional health each may be the true complement of the other. Was this perhaps Freud's blind spot? Is it not in fact the merging of these contrasting and complementary forces that is essential to learning and creativity?

Unsupported by present-day knowledge of the role of culture in molding family constellation and parental functioning, Freud tended in his time to design stereotyped conceptions of the family roles of father, mother, and child. He made the man the dominant figure of the family group, subordinated the woman and perceived her largely as an inferior edition of the man. According to Ian Suttie,[1] Freud had "a grudge against mothers and a mind blindness for love; . . . he concentrated on father and sex to the exclusion of mother and love."

While elaborating the theory of the oedipus complex, he tended to isolate parent-child relations from the totality of family experience. The vector of his thinking seemed to move mainly from inside the human organism to outside. He could not then clearly visualize a two-directional process in which the influence on behavior exerted from outside inward was as significant as its opposite. His conceptual approach tended to divorce the internal processes of mind from the social environment.

It is perhaps this feature of Freud's theoretical structure which fostered a trend toward a divorce of the inside of the mind from the outside, emphasizing the individual while neglecting the group. Throughout the development of psychoanalytic thought, we see evidence of this bias, a tendency to schism between biological and social, conscious and unconscious experience, pleasure and pain, reality and phantasy. The chemistry of learning, however, compounds these elements. Freud was intensely absorbed in the search for the purity of internal mental mechanisms. Social force was implicitly treated as a contamination. He favored the individual man, the biological man. He went further: He interpreted culture as the projection of man's instincts onto the social scene.

This historically determined, one-sided emphasis on the individual, and on the inside of the mind, complicated the task of conceptualizing the interrelations of individual development and family process. In this respect psychoanalytic theory is incomplete; it is deficient in its illumination of the dynamics of the family group as an integrated psychic whole. It does not give us a positive healthy image of family relations. It does not elucidate learning and creative development.

It is a strange paradox that, despite the psychoanalytic axiom that the mental fate of the individual rests on his family experience, there have been thus far so few studies of the family group as a unit. Parts of the family phenomena have been brilliantly illuminated; yet even these parts have been lighted up only in certain directions. And the elusive mystery of still other parts persists. In particular, the relations of the adult's emotional stability to his family position are poorly understood. This is due partly to the long conceptual leap from the family of childhood to the family of adulthood without adequate study (until now) of the intermediate stage of adolescent adaptation to family group. Flügel's book, The Psycho-analytic Study of the Family,[2] does not unfortunately deal with the dynamics of the family as a unit. It offers mainly interesting conjectures as to the possible role of Freudian mechanisms in family relations—the unconscious, guilt, ambivalence, incest, castration, etc. It dramatizes the irrational, the conflictual aspects, but fails to depict these within the frame of the realities of family function.

Child-parent relations are the core of the psychoanalytic view of human development. It is these very relationships that, as transference phenomena, occupy the center of the stage in psychoanalytic therapy. Yet in psychoanalysis direct observations of family interaction have not been carried out until very recently, and only now is their importance beginning to be recognized. The attitude of classical Freudians has been, in effect, that the patient's phantasies and dreams are the royal road to the unconscious, that it is relatively unessential to know the realities of the social environment. In its most extreme form, this attitude leads to the idea that if a psychoanalyst interests himself in the social realities that surround his patient, he will "spoil his ear for the unconscious." (Psychoanalysts functioning in child and family social agencies have met this particular extreme of prejudice in a striking form.) Analysts in training were sometimes told by their instructors that if they interested themselves in the environmental factors of family life, they would become contaminated as analysts; they would injure their talents for perceiving unconscious processes. I myself have been accused by colleagues of being uninterested in the unconscious. On the contrary, I believe that an accurate understanding of the unconscious is possible only when one interprets unconscious dynamics in the context of the conscious organization of experience, the total integrative patterns of personality, and the prevailing interpersonal realities.

The usual approach of psychoanalysts to the phenomena of family life has been indirect rather than direct. It is still common practice for analysts to refuse to interview other family members on the premise that this would interfere with the conduct of the patient's analysis. This means that the analyst is solely dependent for information concerning family experience on the emotionally biased views of his individual patient. Traditionally, the analyst detects the distorted perceptions of the patient in the processes of transference, but his evaluation of disparity between real and unreal is unaided by objective knowledge of family interaction. Thus, the reality-testing powers of the analyst are handicapped. The traditional custom of the psychoanalyst, to avoid interviewing other family members lest this complicate his relations with his patient, needs to be re-examined for its dynamic implications.

Several relevant considerations must be carefully weighed: Is it correct to regard the day-by-day emotional interactions of a patient with his family as complications in the task of analytic therapy, or are they of the essence? Insofar as these processes are regarded as complications, they surely cannot be excluded from the private relation of analyst with his patient. They are carried with the patient into his analytic experience and asserted most rigorously. They are not magically erased by the analyst's determined isolation of himself from the patient's family. Complications of a sort they may be, but they are clearly of the essence as well.

The analyst who rigidly disregards other family members courts trouble. He may throw the continuity of the course of therapy into jeopardy. If he treats a wife and refuses to interview her husband, he should not be surprised if his bill remains unpaid. If he appears to strengthen the aggression of one partner against the other, he will sometimes be accused of being a home-breaker, causing divorce, or inducing a breakdown in the untreated partner. There is no safety in ritual avoidance of other family members. In the relations of individual and family there is a mutuality of misperception that parallels the patient's transference misperceptions of the analyst. If the analyst interviews his patient together with other family members, he achieves a tremendous gain in his reality-testing capacity. Contact with family need not complicate the therapy of the primary patient. The issue is rather how contact is made and how appropriately it is used.

In classical technique the analyst has available to him the patient's image of self, his image of his family members, his image of the analyst; the analyst has available his image of self and his image of the patient. But he has no dependable, accurate image of the patient's family members or of their image of the patient. Were he to observe the two-way emotional interchange of patient and family, he would then be in a position to match his perception of the patient and his family relationships not only against the patient's perceptions, but also against the family members' perception of the patient.

Psychoanalysis is believed to be the only specific therapy for neuroses. And it is generally agreed that the main determinants of neuroses are social, that is, essentially familial in origin. In the psychoanalytic therapy of neuroses, there have been notable successes and also dramatic failures. It is of some value to focus special attention on the failures insofar as they may shed light on relevant processes in the patient's contemporary family life.

It is assumed that psychoanalytic therapy corrects the patient's twisted perceptions of the family of his childhood and that, as these are modified toward reality, the patient will catch up with an accurate picture of the family relationships of his adult life. In classical analytic process, the role of present realities is temporarily subordinated. This is the matrix for the unfolding of transference neurosis. For a period, the unreality of transference achieves not merely a position of prominence but one of dominance. Ultimately and by successive stages, the irrational content of transference is worked through and matched against the realities of the analytic relationship. The qualities of the analyst's person are not revealed until the later stages. Thus, the check with reality is delayed. This theoretical framework implies that the realities of present family relationships will wait until the patient catches up with himself and achieves a realistic definition of his contemporary family problems. This theory provides the rationale for the principle of postponement of crucial life decisions during analysis.

But decision-making is of the essence of life. It means action. Action is the core of aliveness. Without decision, there is no action, no movement; there can be no life. Is there not a magic delusion involved in the idea that time and life can be stopped in their tracks while the patient prepares himself emotionally to deal realistically with his contemporary problems. Ideally perhaps, classical psychoanalytic technique works best in a group environment that is stable, fixed, definable, and predictable. But where do we find this environment in our present-day community? We don't; we find the opposite. What happens in analytic therapy when the group environment and the relations of individual and group are unstable, discontinuous, difficult to define and predict? Since the structure of society and family is undergoing revolutionary change and is profoundly different today from what it was at the turn of the nineteenth century, perhaps it is in order to rethink the role of transference in psychotherapy.

Years ago, Robert Fleiss pointed out that under conditions of radical social change and imminent external danger like those in Nazi Germany it was virtually impossible to do psychoanalytic therapy. Perhaps in the turbulence of present-day society we are approaching a similar condition. The agitation in the human relations patterns of our day is echoed in the character disorders that are now so universally the psychoanalyst's problem. Intrinsic to the dynamics of character disorder are the contagion and sharing of the experience of pathogenic conflict. Character disorders do not exist alone; they function in pairs and three-somes. For every person suffering from a character disorder there are one or more partners who share the pathology. In such persons, the defenses that come into prominence are projection, substitution of aggression for anxiety, magic thinking, isolation, and "acting out." The implementation of such defenses, especially "acting out," calls for the complicity of a partner. Character disorders are a social as well as an individual phenomenon. Mutual and complementary "acting out" is frequent in contemporary family patterns.

The analyst's ability to help a patient move toward recovery through a correct interpretation of transference and resistance and his ability to define the clash of real and unreal may fail if neither patient nor analyst possesses an accurate picture of the relevant interpersonal realities. In the analytic situation, the analyst is presumed to embody these realities within his own person. The patient is expected to get well gradually as he perceives, stage by stage, the contradictions between his transference image of the analyst and what the analyst really represents. But the analyst personifies not only the reality of his own person; he must epitomize the realities of the patient's current interpersonal environment as well. It is obligatory, therefore, that the analyst have an accurate picture of the patient's family life and other significant group involvements. Otherwise, the analytic therapy will flounder. The challenge is not only to interpret the inappropriate transference expectations but also to enable the patient to accept, understand, and use something that is new and different, *i.e.*, to learn from experience.

We know that the neuroses of the various family members reinforce one another through family contagion. The traditional procedure of referring neurotically involved members of the patient's family to other analysts for therapy is a relatively feeble device for improving the emotional health of family relationships, for empirical experience reveals that the technique of individual analytic treatment for each neurotic family member by separate analysts often fails to ameliorate the pathological interactions of the family.

Still another unsolved problem in psychoanalytic therapy is that which derives from certain forms of resistance to change in the patient, this resistance being continually fortified by his emotional position in his family. Sometimes the individual, emotionally speaking, is the virtual prisoner of an unhealthy family role. Occasionally, it may appear that he is locked in an unhealthy extrafamilial role, for example, in a submissive relationship with a tyrannical employer. If so, he is also generally bound to a similarly unhealthy family role. It is the family pattern that imprisons him to the job role. Subjectively the patient may feel protected in this role and yet be harmed by it. Although the security in the role is illusory, the patient clings to it because it symbolizes parental protection. In order to change he must gamble; he must trade something he already knows for a way of life he does not yet know. The patient holds tenaciously to what seems familiar and safe, and the analyst is unable to wrench him loose.

When we view this problem in the context of current family relationships it becomes clear that, at least in some instances, it is not possible to achieve the cure of one person without simultaneously altering his family system. The emotional inertia of the individual partly expresses the inertia of the family group within which he functions. We recognize this principle very well in the case of child patients where, to affect cure, we undertake to treat family as well as child. But we are less prone to give recognition to analogous processes in the group life of the adult patient.

It is easy to recognize in this picture a familiar phenomenon, to which the psychoanalyst gives the name "secondary emotional gain." This term implies a kind of compromise formation in which a patient consoles himself for the suffering and impediment of his neurosis with situational advantages. He exploits his neurotic disability for purposes of winning attention, protection, or special favors, avoiding responsibility, or wreaking vengeance on parent figures. The patient attempts in this way to ease the stress and pain of his present position in the group. In effect, he demands a special bribe from those about him as compensation for his submission to a social role in life in which he feels cheated of a full reward. This bribe is supposed to assuage his anger. The phenomenon of secondary gain is thus linked to a patient's neurotic willingness to be tied to a failing role; while his family supports and compensates him in this role, it does not permit him to escape from it.

This problem poses a special difficulty in psychoanalytic therapy. The obstacles in the way of separating the patient from a neurotically sick, failing family role and the associated secondary emotional gain often prove formidable. The psychoanalyst's position is weak if he cannot lessen the family's support of these patterns of secondary gain, as well as treat the individual patient. In the historical development of psychoanalytic theory, the processes of secondary gain have been conceived as relatively peripheral and not significantly tied to the fate of central conflicts. Because the phenomena of secondary gain are a vital link between individual and group, perhaps secondary gain should be reassessed as to its significance for ego integration and social role adaptation.

The lesson to be drawn is clear: The autonomy of the individual is relative, not absolute. The characteristics of an individual are predictable only within a concrete situation. The individual is personally responsible for his conduct only within certain limits. It is a sheer impossibility, at times, for an individual to buck his group all by himself. To accept change or be motivated toward it, he requires the group to change along with him. This makes it necessary to consider the family as a subject for therapy, as well as the individual member. Surely, there are individuals with an irrepressible urge to change and grow regardless of the inertia of the surrounding group, but these are the exceptional persons. Most people change only as the group changes with them.

Still another unsolved problem in analytic therapy is the influence that the changed behavior in the patient produces on those family members who share his everyday life. As the patient changes, he affects the behavior of other members of this family; similarly, as they change, the nature of their change further affects the patient. The process is circular. It is incumbent upon the analyst, therefore, to know accurately the patient's contemporary family environment.

These considerations are of direct relevance to clinical judgments as to which cases are treatable and which are untreatable. Some cases are deemed to be untreatable precisely because the individual is appraised in isolation from his involvement in the family group. The resistance to the acceptance of therapy or the fixity of the neurotic patterns of motivation are not adequately examined within the frame of the patient's family role involvement and the pathology of the family group itself. If these questions are examined more thoroughly, it is likely that the judgments of patients as being hopeful or hopeless for psychoanalytic therapy will be reached differently.

There is the related question of how best to prepare certain patients for psychoanalytic therapy. In many instances, the emotional preparation for the initiation of psychotherapy proves to be inadequate because the efforts are directed exclusively to a single individual in isolation. In actuality, something often needs to be done to modify the emotional climate of the entire family group. At the very least, certain warped family relationships in which the patient's conflicts are locked need to be altered before such a patient can be properly receptive to the influence of psychoanalytic therapy.

The same problems reveal themselves another way in the field of psychoanalysis of children. Child psychoanalysts by tradition work mainly or exclusively with their individual child patient. The inappropriate attitudes of the mother toward these patients are judged to be the product of the mother's personal neurosis. The child analyst undertakes therapy of the child patient, and when necessary the mother is referred for therapy of her neurosis to another analyst. More rarely, the same child analyst may choose also to treat the mother. In the main, however, child analysts have no contact with the family as a group. They make no direct observations of the disturbed patterns of interaction that characterize the family as a unit. In other words, child analysts have little direct information concerning the realities of family life. A short time ago, I asked such an analyst if she treated the mothers of her child patients. Her reply was: "Oh, heavens, no!"

In general, the practice of the classical method of child analysis has lessened, but the practice of child psychotherapy, combining treatment of child and parent and oriented pointedly to the realities of family, has increased by leaps and bounds. It is thus of great interest to ask why less and less child analysis and more and more child psychotherapy. I believe the single most important reason is not, as many have said, the alleged inconveniences of child analytic practice but rather that the classical technique fails often to produce a cure. To whatever extent child analysis cuts itself away from the realities of group interaction in family life, it is doomed to die. Any form of child therapy, if it is to be successful, must surely avoid isolation from a parallel program for dealing with the mental health problems of the family group. Looking to the future of child analysis, systematic study of family process must surely grow in importance.

I have become increasingly skeptical of traditional clichés and stereotyped formulations regarding the psychodynamic relations of child and family. Such conceptions as oedipus conflict, seduction, inconsistent discipline, overprotection, overindulgence, and narcissistic exploitation of the child can in no way be adequately understood unless the interaction processes of the family, as well as the personalities of each member, are subjected to systematic study. It has become crystal clear, for example, that such a trend as parental seduction of the child is an empty phrase unless it is explored fully in terms of the sexual maladjustment between the parents with the associated patterns of conflict and emotional alienation. "Rejection" has become a hackneyed term. It is often used to cover a real ignorance of the history of the child's sense of betrayal by the parent. Where there is rejection, it needs to be qualified in terms of its intensity, its form of expression, and its relative specificity for the given child; in terms of the role of the rejecting motive in the economy of the mother's personality and the role of the rejecting behavior in the total psychosocial economy of the family life. (See Chapter 11, Disturbances of Parental Pairs.)

At present it is extremely difficult to implement the conceptual structure of child analysis in an integrated theory of child development and adaptation. Freud's formulation of the psychosexual stages of the child's development, valuable as it is in its own right, fails to provide a satisfactory scheme. A serious difficulty emerges from the tendency of this theory to dissociate the biological and social components of behavior. When the psychoanalyst characterizes a person according to his psychosexual make-up as oral, anal, or genital, his term generally carries a dual connotation: (1) a specific level of instinctual organization, (2) an implied level of ego maturation or total personality organization related to the dominant patterns of instinctual drive. This twofold meaning is ambiguous and confusing. The reference to a presumed level of personality integration is vague and ill-defined, and the dynamic relations of biological drive to personality organization and to the dominant modes of social adaptation are not clearly communicated. To say this is by no means to discount the value of the psychosexual concept but merely to point to some of its present-day limitations.

The validity of current theories regarding the emotional relations of child and family rests to a large extent on empirical wisdom deriving largely from psychotherapeutic experience. Such formulations depend mainly on the acuity and skill of the individual clinician. Truly amazing sometimes is the astuteness of the psychiatric clinician in drawing cogent, useful, and, within limits, reliable dynamic interpretations. But the fact remains that such conclusions are usually fragmentary and selective. Beyond the sphere of a few central correlations, the interpretations of the emotional interaction of child and family become progressively vague and eventually reach the point of mere conjecture. In the end, such a situation becomes critical and makes it impossible to judge which dynamic interpretations are right and which are wrong.

In relation to the child patient, the main emphasis in such formulations has been on the correlation of specific types of child reaction with specific parental attitudes: rejection, inconsistency of discipline, overindulgence, overprotection; and the relation of specific body behavior in the child (oral, anal, genital, etc.) to specific anxieties in the parent. Some correlations are made to the child's reactions to rivals for the exclusive possession of the mother's love and to his reactions to the punishing authority of the parent. Finally, conflict in the child is related to conflict between child and parent or between the parents.

Unfortunately these partial patterns of interaction are not viewed in the appropriate psychosocial context. Parental behavior is usually inadequately defined and, accordingly, analysis of the child's alleged pattern of response is rendered suspect. The determinants of parental role functioning are multiple. They derive partly from individual personality but are otherwise influenced by the parent's interaction with the child, the other parent, the family group, and the community. In addition, parental behavior, in accordance with these multiple influences, may undergo significant shifts at different stages of the development of the child and family.

In a lecture here in 1954, Anna Freud [3] emphasized the inevitable role of frustration and conflict in the emotional development of the child. She pointed out that the child must always experience some "delay and rationing" in the satisfaction of his needs; this is the background for the continuing struggle between pleasure and pain. Of historical importance was her pointed assertion that in the search for the causes of neurotic development in the child, the early emphasis on the father as the authority figure and as the source of the castration threat gave way to increasing recognition of the importance of the mother as the parent who disciplines through the power of deprivation. There was a strong backward push in time from a first emphasis on oedipal conflict as the core of neurosis to a more recent and sharper emphasis on pre-oedipal conflict, from the father who denies sexual pleasure to the child to the mother who denies the child oral satisfaction. Whatever the level of conflict, it is the ego that mediates the struggle between pleasure and renunciation. According to Anna Freud the ego takes its cue from the environment.

But here curiously enough she stops. Although she states that there are some mothers who are continuously rejecting, some intermittently rejecting, some who reject the child for accidental reasons, and some whose very devotion is interpreted by the child as rejection, she goes no further in interrelating the emerging ego functions of the child with the social patterns of the family as a whole.

She makes the point, however, that the child reacts with anxiety both to the parent who is punitive and to the parent who is permissive. In other words, a child requires parental control to feel protected; without it, he feels abandoned and insecure. Obviously then optimal child-rearing involves a modicum of satisfaction of basic needs, some inevitable frustrations, and an appropriate quality of social control exercised through the authority of the parent.

But under what conditions does control mean protection to the child and under what conditions does it become a threat? This is the very heart of the matter, and it hinges on the connotations of Anna Freud's statement that the child's ego takes its cue from the environment. It is generally recognized that control is experienced by the child as protection if the child's basic needs are understood and reasonably satisfied. Problems of discipline can be understood only as they are joined to the basic experience of security in family relations. If this is not the case, the child perceives control as a hostile assault and, by stages, becomes impervious to parental discipline. The central issue is how and by what processes the growing child internalizes the significant psychic content of his family environment. What is the dynamic correlation of ego, superego, and the social interaction patterns of the family?

In psychoanalytically oriented formulations, certain selected patterns of interaction are suggested between the child's unconscious needs and particular elements of parental behavior, or between the overt actions of the child and the unconscious wishes of the parent. Such correlations are clearly partial in nature; they hypothesize a relation between a piece of the child and a piece of the parent. This piece of the child—usually a set of conflicted unconscious needs—is not defined in its proper relation to the whole child, nor is the whole child seen in accurate perspective with regard to the whole parent, or to the full breadth of the relationship between the parents, or to the psychosocial configuration of the family as a whole. It is self-evident that an accurate definition of the interrelation of child and family requires that a part of the child's emotional life be viewed in relation to the total personality of the child and his total pattern of adaptation to the family environment.

In a quizzical though facetious mood, a South American analyst once raised this question: "Is psychoanalytic theory regressing? It seems always to go backward. First, it was the oedipus conflict and castration fear; then came the theory of aggression, anal sadism, and the death instinct; now we revert to oral insecurity, oral deprivation. Which is right?" Clearly, no one of these ideas provides a full answer. They are each of them partial theories. They are either all of them right or all of them wrong, depending upon how we put them together into a unified view of the human being.

Psychoanalytic concepts have ushered in a revolution in personality theory. But these concepts evolved piecemeal. It is time to integrate them and design a broader frame of reference within which it is possible more effectively to conceptualize and treat a person's disturbance within the matrix of his position in his primary group—the family.

CHAPTER 3

FREUD AND CHANGING CONCEPTIONS OF PERSONALITY— A PERSONAL SYNTHESIS

THE PSYCHOANALYTIC VIEW of man's nature had a revolutionary impact on the evolution of personality theory. It constituted a major breakthrough in the development of a science of psychodynamics. Its contribution was dramatic, its influence on medicine and the social sciences profound. By comparison, other approaches to personality, academic psychology, and social psychology seemed feeble.

But once again the dichotomy of biological man and social man introduced an element of ambiguity into Freudian theory. Because Freud put off until later the issues of adaptation to time, place, and social conditions, we are even now trying to find our way out of the conceptual complications of his one-sided, biological orientation to personality. The ways in which the attempt is being made are many. Yet most of us would agree that the categorization of analysts either as "instinctual theorists" or as "culturalists" is at the present time rather arbitrary. The urge to divide analysts into two broad, opposing classes is understandable, but the result makes little sense. Certainly there are analytic schools that carry the flag for major differences in theory, but it is also true that the members of any one school often hold varying opinions on a number of theoretical questions. Each analyst weighs the evidence in his own way and orients himself to the issues of personality theory accordingly. As long as such theoretical differences persist we can be sure that we do not have the right answer.

This chapter, subtitled "A Personal Synthesis," is an attempt to make clear my own position.

Are the basic determinants of behavior, the primary factors in personality, biological or social? Here rests the essential ambivalence in the psychoanalytic approach to personality, the dilemma with which psychoanalysts have plagued themselves for many years. Waelder[1] posed the question in these terms:

> Is it man who creates his environment, or the environment which shapes the individual? The individual creates things but the outside world—reality—determines the survival value of his creations. . . . Perhaps the environment in large measure controls which of the inborn drives of the child, or his ego drives are encouraged or discouraged.

In the light of present-day knowledge, it seems that the question is an irrelevant one because biological and social forces are complementary and indivisible. In the history of science the posing of an impossible question has at times resulted in a fruitless waste of time. Hindsight now makes the issue appear all too simple. The real truth seems to be that psychoanalysts have plagued themselves with a needless and wrong kind of question. The posing of the dilemma in these terms, as I see it, both oversimplifies and distorts the real issue.

When it is asserted that man creates things whereas reality determines the survival value of his creations, what is really implied is that it is man in the generic and plural sense—man emotionally interrelated with other men, man related to his personal and social history—who creates things, not the individual man in isolation. The source of creativity, then, is rather man's effort to find meaning in the world of men, not individual man by himself. Again, when Waelder says that the environment controls which of the inborn drives of the child or his ego drives are encouraged or discouraged, we must recognize that the ego by definition absorbs the realities of social process.

The cornerstone of Freud's theory of personality rests on a group of core concepts: [2] the organization of instinctual drives; the primacy of unconscious mental processes; the polarity of the pleasure and reality principles, the concept of trauma; the role of conflict, anxiety, and defense; the genetic structuring of personality; the topography of the psychic apparatus; the tendency to restoration of equilibrium among conflicting psychic forces; finally, the principle of inertia and economy in the adaptation of the human organism to the conditions of life.

These are potent dynamic principles. They incite no end of controversy. Freud himself was an intrepid explorer, searching out the empirical evidence for his hypotheses and proceeding to test the validity of each in turn. Where proof was insufficient he adopted a tentative attitude, leaving to the future the affirmation or the negation of the given hypothesis. It should be borne in mind, however, that Freud studied mental functions in piecemeal fashion. He investigated partial aspects of personality. There is some doubt as to how far he himself viewed his concepts as a holistic or integrated theory of human behavior.*

My personal synthesis of personality theory makes use of Freudian dynamics for understanding the internal mental processes but emphasizes the adaptational view of personality, man in society.† It endeavors to neutralize Freud's tendency to divorce the individual from the group, to dissociate the inside of the mind from the outside. The central problem which demands solution is the integration of knowledge of the internal stabilizing mechanisms of personality with knowledge of the processes of adaptation through time to changing conditions of life, both internal and external. In day-by-day dealing with clinical problems, I find it necessary to modify some facets of the Freudian theoretical structure.

The orientation to personality theory here offered is not static; it is a tentative, groping, progressively evolving one. The main impetus toward an explicit statement of orientation comes from a personal sense of bafflement and defeat, a persistent conviction of frustration in coping with certain problems in clinical psychiatry and psychotherapy. In particular, a thoughtful confrontation of certain issues in the psychiatry of children exposes sharply some of the deficiencies of our present-day formulations in the psychiatry of adults. If we apply the framework of a child's interaction with family as a theoretical model to the problem of the adaptation of the adult to society, it seems possible to construct a more useful integration of dynamic concepts for the further development of personality theory, for the Freudian system in its classical representations seems not to provide a satisfactory answer.

My views have been molded by a certain range of experience in the practice of psychoanalytic psychiatry, in the application of psychodynamic formulations to social problems, and by the assimilation of the contributions of a broad group of workers in the psychiatric, psychoanalytic, and related fields of behavioral science. In addition to Freud, other teachers representing a variety of orientations to psychoanalytic thought have been influential. In this group were both "instinctualists" and "culturalists." Against this background, the importance of joining the dynamics of individual and group behavior became apparent. For further progress, it seemed to me essential to encompass within a single theoretical frame the integrative patterns of personality and the dynamics of interper-

---

* "Psychoanalysis has never claimed to give a perfect theory of human psychic life but has only demanded that its discoveries be used for the completion and correction of knowledge we have gained elsewhere." [3]

† My approach to personality theory reflects considerable agreement with Gardner Murphy's biosocial theory.[4]

sonal relations, to interpret unconscious mental processes and the related conflicts within the broader context of the individual's conscious experience and integration into group relationships.

I have been deeply influenced by the literature of the social sciences and by experiences of collaboration with social scientists in interdisciplinary research. I have felt the impact of ideas deriving from topological and gestalt theory, communications research, animal psychology, and neurophysiology. Through these various influences I have been impelled to favor a holistic-dynamic approach to the theory of behavior rather than the atomistic-mechanical approach.[5]

Among psychoanalysts I am of course not alone in seeking to reconcile the polarities of the biological core of man and his assimilation into social life. There are others whose work represents a trend toward revision of classical Freudian theory and with which I am in sympathy. My own point of view is similar though not identical to theirs.

For example, Thomas French[6] says:

In the early years of psychoanalytic investigation, Freud concentrated his interest on the repressed and unconscious parts of the personality. He resolutely postponed study of the higher mental functions until he had thoroughly explored the unconscious. . . . Our use of Freud's structural concepts has not really corrected his one-sided interpretation.

It was the recognition of this that impelled French to initiate his extensive research on the integrative mechanisms of personality.

Kardiner,[7] who together with Linton developed the hypothesis of "basic personality," says:

The libido theory was designed as a special theory of neurosis, not as a theory of adaptation. The arrival of ego psychology is testimony to this. Instead of trying to derive social evolution from ontogenesis, we try the opposite—to derive ontogenesis from social evolution.

It is not repression that causes culture, but the reverse.

Society is not an organism and cannot be described in terms of ontogenetic process.

Freud [gave recognition] to the environment but did not include it in his frame of reference.

The libido theory is incomplete, an over-simplification. (It) made a closed system or rather a self-sealing system, which meant pedanticism and limitation of research.

The libido theory is inadequate as a conceptual tool for investigation.

Erikson,[8] in *Childhood and Society*, writes:

> The drives man is born with are not instincts, nor are his mother's complementary drives instinctive in nature. Neither carry in themselves the patterns of completion, of self-preservation, of interaction with any segment of nature; tradition and conscience must organize them. . . .
>
> Man's [inborn instincts] are drive fragments to be assembled, given meaning and organized during a prolonged childhood by methods of child training and schooling which vary from culture to culture and are determined by tradition. . . . [Man] learns to exist in time and space as he learns to be an organism in the time-space of his culture.
>
> It was clear to him [Freud] and it becomes clearer to us—who deal with new areas of the mind (ego), with different kinds of patients (children, psychotics), with new applications of psychoanalysis (society)—that we must search for the proper place of the libido theory in the totality of human life. . . .
>
> We must become sensitive to the danger of forcing living persons into the role of marionettes of a mythical Eros—to the gain of neither therapy nor theory.

Masserman,[9] in his effort to integrate the theories of psychoanalysis and biodynamics, offers a broad adaptational base for the theory of personality. He sets forth his biodynamic principles as follows:

I. All organisms are actuated by their physiological needs.

II. Every organism reacts, not to some absolute reality, but to its own interpretations of its milieu in terms of its individual needs, special capacities and unique experiences.

III. Whenever the goal directed activities of an organism are partially or totally frustrated by external obstacles, the organism either changes its techniques in further attempts to reach the same goal or deviates its behavior toward a partial or complete substitution of goals (*i.e.*, neurotic).

IV. When two or more urgent motivations of an organism are in sufficiently serious conflict for the adaptive patterns attendant to each to be simultaneously called forth and when these are mutually exclusive to a point of paralyzing impasse, then the organism experiences mounting tension and apprehension reaching various levels of anxiety, while its behavior, somatic and muscular, become progressively more disorganized, regressive and bizarrely symbolic (*i.e.*, psychotic).

Ian Suttie,[10] on the other hand, interprets the Freudian conceptual system in this way:

1. It ignores the mother for the father.
2. It denies tenderness—filial or parental.
3. It interprets socialization merely as overcoming of sex jealousy by coercion and fear.
4. It regards hate as a spontaneous, ineradicable appetite and all motive as egoistic.
5. It regards all cultural interests as substitute gratification and all else as materialistic and ultilitarian interest.

As I see it, the Freudian illumination of the depth processes of personality now needs to be reassessed and, wherever valid, such insights need to be reformulated within a broader theoretical framework that gives recognition to the essential continuity of individual, family, and society.

Freud's theoretical system did away with the dichotomy of mind and body. It joined man's mind to his biological structure. It stressed organismic process, the vicissitudes of drives, and the role of unconscious mental mechanisms. In the light of accumulated evidence to date, however, some of the limitations of this classical system are brought to light. Freud's concepts dealt mainly with partial psychic processes, those forces within personality which produce the pathological formations to which we give the name "symptoms." In considerable part the total patterns of personality organization and the relations of these to the dominant modes of social adaptation were neglected. To some extent manifestations of unconscious experience were divorced from the conscious organization of experience and the striving for successful adaptation to the social environment here and now.

Freud's theory gives a one-sided emphasis to the erogenous zones and fails to lend itself to an integrated evaluation of the functions of personality. It gives insufficient consideration to the nonsexual drives, particularly to tender love as a primary emotion. It overlooks the role of group membership in actual behavior and the principle of self-image. It isolates inner and outer reality, separates the inside of the mind from the outside. But as Munroe[11] says in her book, *Schools of Psychoanalytic Thought,*

> In Freud's Vienna, it was easier perhaps to dichotomize instinctual drives and society.
>
> In his observation of the universal character of man's inner development, Freud saw no alternative to almost total rejection of theories that pretended to explain behavior by a scientific investigation of the social conditions under which it occurred.

Many of Freud's disciples have speculated about the meaning of Freud's own ambivalent attitude toward his libido theory. Why in the vagaries of mood did he tend at times to dismiss his theory as mythology and yet at other times demand that it be taken literally and with the utmost seriousness? Freud's views were influenced by the biological orientation and mechanistic philosophy of his time. They reflect the then current views of cause and effect relationships and were conceptually influenced by the laws of thermodynamics. These laws were presumed to apply to closed-energy systems. But man is not a closed-energy system. Outside influences and materials are absorbed, transformed, and discharged by the living organism. There is continuous contact and communication with the environment. The closed-circle hypothesis of life process is not tenable.

For its theoretical relevance, I quote Max Planck[12] on the thermodynamic laws:

The energy of the world remains constant. . . . The entropy of the world tends toward the maximum. [Entropy signifies the transformation of energy from usable to non-usable forms.]

Planck qualifies this principle as follows:

The energy and the entropy of the world have no meaning because such quantities can have no accurate definition. . . . The energy of any system of bodies changes according to the measure of effects produced by external bodies. It remains constant only if the system be isolated.

Freud conceptualized the adult individual as a relatively isolated psychic system. He underrated the importance of interchange of energy and information with external agents.

Planck continues:

Since, strictly speaking, every system is acted on by external agents, —for complete isolation cannot be realized in nature—the energy of a finite system may be approximately, but never absolutely constant.

The more widely extended a system, we assume, the more approximately will the energy remain constant (if action at a distance be excluded). A small error will be committed in assuming the energy of our solar system to be constant. A smaller one if the system of all known fixed stars be included.

By this same token, the smaller and more circumscribed the system, the less will the energy remain a constant; the narrower the system, the greater the effect of external agents. The behavior system of the individual organism is a narrow one. Therefore, the energy of this system cannot be constant; the effect of external agents must be great indeed.

Freud's interpretation of libido implies the presence in man of a fixed quantity of energy. This seems doubtful. Human personality is more properly interpreted as an open behavior system. Vital phenomena and the problems of adaptation must be viewed in a broad biosocial frame. In the last analysis, what is biological is also social, and what is social is also biological.

From the social sciences, particularly anthropology, comes the relativity theory and the cross-cultural approach to personality. Here behavior is viewed as being shaped by the individual's integration into a social system and requires us to design hypotheses for the dynamic relations of personality and social role adaptation. As Ralph Girard[13] puts it, the human being has "roots in his biological make-up and fruits in his human interrelations." The interplay of genetic and other physiological processes with environment begins with conception and continues incessantly until death.

From such animal psychologists as Herbert Birch[14] come data that behavior that has seemed to be inborn, fixed, and instinctual is dependent for its specificity on particular kinds of social interaction between one part of the organism and another, as well as between organism and environment. This is additional evidence, if any be needed, that heredity and environment cannot be defined apart from one another.

From neurophysiology we derive the principle that the same physiological phenomena that involve energy exchange may parallel the exchange of information and vice versa. The communication of information from one part of the organism to another may be dynamically analogized to communication between one person and another. In other words, communication between parts of the self, between mind and body, runs parallel to the relations between the self and other selves.

Also, from neurophysiology comes the principle that fundamentally whatever is organic is functional and whatever is functional is organic. "An idea or a series of ideas in the abstract cannot fire a neurone";[15] that is, an idea is some kind of biochemical process that involves energy transformation in the brain. Recently Heath *et al.*[16] demonstrated recordable alterations in electrical potentials from the septal and hippocampal regions deep in the brain in patients responding to conflicting situations in their social milieu. All this new knowledge should, I believe, be utilized to the utmost as we work toward an ultimate theory of personality.

In psychoanalytic personality theory I find particularly unclear these areas: (1) the relations of phantasy and reality; (2) ego development and social interaction; (3) the emergence of self-identity from the original symbiotic union of infant and parent, and the entrenchment and expansion of such personal identity through interpersonal identification; (4) the relations of personal identity to body image; (5) the struggle to stabilize identity in the face of anxiety and conflict, to derive support for this identity from group integration; (6) the need to modify identity in accordance with the vicissitudes of maturation and social adaptation.

Of special significance is the whole area of the psychodynamics of learning, the impact between old and new perceptions, the resolution of discrepancies between real and unreal, and the achievement of new levels of mastery of experience.

The "either-or" approach (i.e., either the biological processes or social forces are the main determinants of personality) is simply not tenable in the light of present-day evidence. It is a polemic which raises a false and irrelevant question, one for which there can be no scientific answer. To dichotomize the biological and the social components of the life process distorts the content of the problem. It invites prejudice and the taking of one side or the other by means of religious conversion rather than scientific formulation of the issues of behavior. It obscures some aspects of the relations of mind and body; it tends to perpetuate some misleading distinctions between organic and functional; it confuses the relations of past and present determinants of behavior; it tends one-sidedly to overemphasize individuality, to dissociate the individual organism from environment, to confuse the issue of individual and social identity. It is sometimes forgotten that what we call individuality absorbs social process in the primary union of infant and mother, child and family.

Therefore, I feel strongly that we must do away with "either-or." Personality is the product of the interaction and merging of the individual organism and its environment; it is also the product of the progressive differentiation of the organism from environment. It is the integrative instrument for the processes of adaptation. Personality, therefore, beginning with birth, is biopsychosocial. So is family; so is society; but at each of these levels the biosocial integration has different properties.

I do not regard personality, family, social structure, and culture patterns as closed systems, or as separate and independent entities, but rather as interrelated and interacting parts of a unified whole, which change and shift over time. Individual and group are reciprocal and interdependent. Each influences the other selectively in the process of change. The intactness of individual personality is relative rather than absolute. Man is an open system; there is continual interchange of energy between the organism and its outer environment. The functions of personality are dually oriented to internal processes and the social environment. Each direction of orientation influences the other.

In a basic sense, then, individuality is relevant mainly to the physical separateness of the single organism; beyond that, behavior and mind are organized by processes of growth and socialization, social communication with parts of the self, one's own body, and social interaction with others. Therefore, intrapsychic and interpersonal processes can only be defined each in relation to the other.

The homeostatic function has as its purpose not the goal of static equilibrium, but rather a fluid, flexible adaptation to changing life conditions. Personality stays the same and yet cannot ever stay the same; this is the paradox of the homeostatic principle. (See Chapter 5, Homeostasis of Behavior.) Stability within the self and stability of interaction with environment are temporarily conditioned, interdependent phenomena. Stability of the internal mechanisms of the personality depends therefore in part on the continuity and predictability of the social environment. Under stress, stability within the self may be maintained transitionally by a radical shift in the balance of interaction with environment, or stability of interaction with environment may be maintained by a radical shift of the balance of forces within the organism. Over a span of time stability within and stability without are mutually contingent.

The factors of heredity and environment can only be defined each in relation to the other. "No heredity without environment; no environment without heredity." Heredity sets limits to the developmental potential of personality, but social experience gives it concrete form. At birth the infant is not a *tabula rasa*. There are significant hereditary and congenital differences between one infant and the next. Infants vary in physical type, intellectual potential, temperament, metabolic pattern, affectivity, motor activity, and nervous response. Nonetheless, the influence of environment is immeasurably great in molding the ultimate expression of potentials, whether they are intellectual capacity, digestive functioning, or whatever.

Of all the species in the animal world, man is the least shackled to a fixed pattern of instinctually determined behavior. He is least automatized. He is comparatively free to respond flexibly and expansively to his environment. The dependence of the human infant on the mother's care and love is a long one; deprived of this protective union the infant cannot survive. But the plasticity and tremendous range of potential development of the individual comes on the condition of prolonged dependence of infant on mother.

I regard the child's adaptation to his environment and the progressive differentiation of his personality as a biosocial process. The channels of expression and control of physiological needs are organized by the social interaction of child and parent. The socialization of the child reflects the personality of the parent and the typical interpersonal relationships of the family group. The child-mother interaction can only be evaluated in the frame of the psychosocial structure of the larger unit, the family. Cultural influences are transmitted to the child through the parents acting as culture carriers. The family is the psychic agency of society, the cradle of personality.

Thus, I regard the progressive stages of personality organization of the child as advancing levels of biosocial integration with, and differentiation from, the environment. The basic drives of the child are to be evaluated within the frame of changing integrations of personality and changing integrations of the individual into family relationships. At each stage of maturation, drive, defense, perception of self, perception of persons in the environment, conflict, and anxiety are partial phases of integral units of adaptation. The urges for food, love, preservation of self, and sexual expression are structured by the continuous interplay of image of self and image of interpersonal experience with the significant others in the family. Behavior is goal-directed. The direction of striving is determined by personal identity and value orientation. Pleasurable experience is sought, pain avoided. Pleasure may come with need satisfaction or new learning, the adventuresome exploration and expanding mastery of the outer world.

Anxiety mounting to critical intensity may induce a lag or distortion of perception of the prevailing realities. It may induce disorganization of the adaptive patterns and the phenomena of regression and fixation. I do not conceive aggression and destructiveness as the expression of a death instinct but rather as a derailment of healthy adaptation, a defense, a means of controlling environment, of counteracting frustration and anxiety, and of asserting the identity of the self in interpersonal situations. Unconscious mental phenomena achieve communicable meaning only in the time-space continuum of conscious perception, the striving for mastery, and the social development of personality.

The orifices of the body, the skin, the activity of internal organs and muscle systems may be conceived not only as zones of experience of pleasure and avoidance of pain but also as somatic agencies for the interchange of energy between the inner and outer environment and, also, as subverbal means of interpersonal communication. The language of the body conveys messages to other significant persons regarding the dominant affective mood, states of need, pleasure, or apprehension of danger. At each stage of maturation, it is the balance of the primary emotions, pleasure in love relations, rage, and fear, that governs interpersonal adaptation and so determines healthy forward development of the individual or withdrawal, arrest, and regression.

The human being is a social animal. He seeks out his own kind. From birth on, the primary urge is toward the maintenance of interpersonal contact and communication. The inevitable experiences of disappointment and frustration stir conflict. This is expressed in a continuous struggle between the need for closeness with others and the disposition to turn back into the self. The exploration of the self in a state of aloneness influences further orientation to relations with others. This conflict of orientation to self and others is differently organized at each stage of maturation.

The capacity for tender union with others, for empathic communication and identification is present early. Tender emotion is an expression of the basic social nature of man, rather than a secondarily desexualized drive. With healthy maturation, tenderness and sex become merged. The capacity for tender closeness is enhanced by satisfaction of basic needs and is crippled and marred by deprivations of a traumatizing nature.

In coping with the stress of life, the individual may correctly define a problem and discover a realistic solution. His failure to do so leads to a series of further reactions: the effort to contain the harmful effects of frustration and conflict until a solution can be found; or the tendency to discharge tension through irrational actions; or the tendency to become disorganized, i.e., to "break down."

Orientation to the issues of personality theory is in no sense an academic matter. It has immediate practical relevance to all levels of practice in the mental health field and to every aspect of research in the sciences of behavior. I have presented here a point of view, a personal synthesis of prevailing ideas, concerning the structure and function of personality. It is nothing final, only a tentative conception that provides a basis for further exploration of relevant questions.

CHAPTER 4

SOCIAL ROLE AND PERSONALITY

JUST AS PERSONALITY cannot be conceived in a social vacuum, so also social process cannot be conceived in a personality vacuum. Social process abstracted from the behavior of people has no meaning. In order to elucidate social process both inside and outside the family group, the individual's adaptive relations to significant small groups and to wider society must be defined. Social action is the extension of mind into organized patterns of human relations, whether in the family or in a wider group.

It is not possible to distinguish the individual mind from the group mind any more than it is possible conceptually to isolate the individual from the group or understand the group apart from the individuals of which it is composed. The mind of the individual already contains a deposit of social events recorded out of the past. It meets each new social situation with both the perceptions of the new experience and the deposits of the old. The action which ensues is a function of the psychic interplay of perceptions conditioned by past experience and the new situation.

In the interaction between individual and group three levels of phenomena are involved: the structure of the environment, interpersonal relations, and the internal organization of personality. These phenomena are often interpreted as distinct processes. They are in fact, however, facets of a larger unit, the life process itself. They encompass the expressions of personality within a defined environment. They function together as interconnected parts of a feed-back system. In circular fashion events which take place at any one of these levels overlap with and interpenetrate events at the others.

The functions of personality are, as we have seen, oriented in two directions: toward the internal processes of the organism and toward the social environment. At the same time, there is continuous interplay between the relations of the person with self and relations with other persons. When one thinks of a person's psychic relations with his environment, it is difficult to say where the person ends and the environment begins, to sharply demarcate what is inside the person and what is outside. In this sense, the borders of the person cannot be sharply delimited; person and environment merge in the intermediate zone.

As a bridge between the processes of intrapsychic life and those of social participation, it is useful to employ the concept of social role. Within the frame of this concept, it is possible to express the extensions of psychic processes into social events. Sociology, social psychology, and anthropology approach the problems of role through the use of special concepts and techniques. They apply the term in two distinct ways, meaning either the "role" of the person in a specific, transient, social position or the characteristic "role" of the individual in society as determined by his social class status. Working in the psychodynamic frame of reference, I shall use the term to represent an adaptational unit of personality in action. "Social role" is here conceived as synonymous with the operations of the "social self" or social identity of the person in the context of a defined life situation.

In the jargon of everyday life, a distinction is often drawn between the inner and outer self. To contrast the "social self," or outer self, with the "private self," or inner self, is to emphasize those functions of personality that are externally oriented. The private self may be conceived as the inner social relation of "I and me." It is a kind of concentration of the relations of "I and me," an inward orientation which temporarily subordinates the impact of other persons. The relations of "I and me" are presumed to be more constant; the relations of "I and they" less constant. The outer or social self changes with social conditions; the inner self (individual identity) presumably stays much the same. Under some conditions the inner self is realized or even enhanced in the expressions of the outer self. Or the inner self may be submerged or denied in the social, conforming representations of personality.

Sometimes the outer self is seen as a social front, a façade behind which is concealed the true self. When the environment goes counter to the need of the inner self, the outer self provides protective coloring, a kind of mask needed for safe adaptation. Or there may be a conflict between the requirements of two overlapping social selves, which imposes an extra strain on the inner self. The inner self represents the private core of the being. It is the older aspect of the self. It is individual and yet social, too, since it contains the residue of family experience of childhood. The inner self yields least to immediate social exigencies. It is the essence of individuality.

Under some social conditions the inner and outer selves achieve a smooth blend, as, for example, in the case of a social worker whose personal needs and professional role are in close harmony. Under other conditions the inner and outer selves may clash at times so critically as to shake the personality to its very roots. This occurs if the role requirements of the present life situation create an experience of danger, toward which the older self is vulnerable and against which it cannot mobilize sufficient defense. For example, a young woman's dream of being an actress is crushed by parental prohibition; she is forced to become an office secretary and reacts with acute depression.

One may suppose that in a given individual certain sets of social roles abet and strengthen one another, while others are antithetical. For example, the roles of businessman, Rotarian, and captain of a bowling team may be congenial, whereas the roles of soldier, family man, and independent entrepreneur may be antithetical. The harmony or conflict of requirements of several concurrent roles determine the degree of strain which is imposed upon the personality.

I should like to elaborate further the dynamic interrelations of social role adaptation and personality for two reasons: (1) to discern useful socio-psychological criteria for a dynamic concept of social role, whether inside or outside the family; (2) to discuss the relations between social role and personality and to illustrate them in the common psychopathological conditions.

Let us start once again with the assumption that social role is that aspect of personality that is integrated in social action. The behavioral forms expressed in this role are determined by a series of factors: the propensities of personality, the processes of group participation and identification, and other temporal-situational phenomena. The concept of social role implies the capacity of the personality to modify its form in varying degree, in accordance with the adaptational requirements of the individual's position in society. The individual's orientation in this phase of social participation presupposes a set of goals and values commensurate with his position in the given group. What is involved here is a particular quality of perception of reality (interpreted in the context of interpersonal relationships), the implementation within the context of the given role of specific techniques of emotional control, specific defenses against anxiety, and the effort to find solutions to personal conflict and achieve gratification of personal needs.

It is recognized that a given personality type may be capable of fulfilling a range of social roles; *i.e.*, a particular person may be related functionally to a number of social positions and yet remain essentially himself. With his particular personality configuration he adapts one way on his job, somewhat differently in his church or social club, and still another way within his family. Yet he is the same person in each of these group situations. A contrasting personality type would over time fit himself into these roles in a different way.

In some forms of sociological investigation there has been a tendency to disregard the personality factor as unimportant. The rationale is something to the effect that, because the same social role may be filled by different kinds of persons, the study of social events can ignore differences in personality. The feasibility of this approach depends upon the problem under investigation. It is permissible to disregard the personality variable only in the study of those forms of social participation in which individual differences matter relatively little, as, for example, in the payment of taxes. In the study of social behavior strongly dependent on individual differences—for example, the rearing of children—the neglect of the personality factor will lead to serious error.

From the psychodynamic point of view, the omission of the factor of differences of personality is inadmissible. As soon as one introduces the factor of time and explores differences of social behavior from one point in time to another, the personality variable can no longer be ignored. Over the span of time the pattern of integration of personality into social role and its consequences vary with the characteristics of the personality enacting the role. The quality of social integration is influenced by the factor of individual motivation, which must be examined at both conscious and unconscious levels. In the final analysis different persons execute the same role in different ways if one observes the process of change through time.

There are numerous variations in the relations between social role adaptation and individual personality that tend to strengthen the point that distinct personality types do not execute the same role in the same way and with the same end results, for example: the effects of anxiety on social role behavior; the possible range and variability of social roles that can be assumed by a given individual; the clarity, stability of the role, and its central or peripheral significance in relation to the individual's inner emotional life. More will be said of this later.

It may be useful to illustrate by diagram the manner in which individual personality adapts its specific tendencies to suit several distinct social roles, each appropriate to participation in or identification with a distinct group.

Role A corresponds to personality component A. The integration of personality into the role in Group A involves the investment of a large segment of the individual or private self; it encompasses within the role the individual's personal needs and conflicts. The defenses implemented are highly personal.

Role B corresponds to personality component B. The integration of personality into the role in Group B involves the investment of a lesser segment of the individual self; to some varying extent the individual's personal needs and conflicts are involved, but less centrally than in Role A. The defenses implemented are personal but less so.

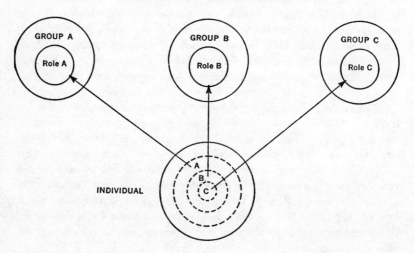

SOCIO-ECONOMIC STRUCTURE
Social Institutions
CLOSE GROUPS
INTO WHICH INDIVIDUAL IS
INTEGRATED IN FACE-TO-FACE RELATIONSHIPS

Role C corresponds to personality component C. The integration of the personality into the role in Group C involves a minimal segment of the individual self. The commitment of self to the social role is superficial. The needs and conflicts of the individual self are removed from this role. The defenses implemented are impersonal and imitative of the group pattern.

If instead of talking in terms of abstract roles A, B, and C, we take the case of Mr. Ellis as an example, we have a man of forty-nine who behaves in somewhat different ways in each of three groups within which he has special roles. He is a successful business executive, he is a leading figure in several community philanthropic organizations, and he has a part within his family group. The relevant personality traits are his overevaluation of his intelligence, which is expressed as manipulative shrewdness, his need to enhance self-esteem by social prestige, his competitiveness, and his underlying anxieties about his masculinity and his feelings of aloneness.

In his business role Mr. Ellis insinuates himself as a person born to executive leadership, with a special talent for exactitude and an omniscent capacity for predicting changes in business conditions. He projects the picture of himself as indispensable protector of other men's capital investments and on this basis sets a high price on his executive services. Under this pattern of self-aggrandizement, he conceals a basic need to live comfortably off the resources of others.

In his philanthropic activities, Mr. Ellis seeks to win recognition as an outstanding leader and strives for top positions on community boards, etc. In these organizations, he endeavors to sell his unique talent and indispensability in order to win the place of highest prestige.

Within his family group, the mask falls away. It is his wife who maintains their active social life and who wins friends and arranges dinner parties. He clings tenaciously to her, requiring her to function as the front for his relations with the wider community. Sexually impotent, he gives up in his attempt to fulfill his role as sexual partner. Moreover, he leaves the responsibilities of parenthood entirely to her. As businessman and outstanding figure in the community he succeeds; in his role of husband he deeply fails.

In the configuration of each distinct role the emotional participation of the person in a unit of action reflects a unique pattern of integration. This is represented in a distinct combination of components of behavior which go to make up the social role: the perception of interpersonal relations, the compliance with or protest against group pressure, the assertion or subordination of the individual self, the effort to solve personal conflicts, and the selection of particular defenses against anxiety. In those adaptational forms of personality that are fitted to a range of roles, each role evokes a somewhat different arrangement of conflict and induces different quantities of anxiety. The anxiety influences the success or failure of adaptation, and in turn the quality of adaptation influences the intensity of anxiety. The vicissitudes of anxiety therefore affect the outcome of the role.

The individual may find it easier to search out a solution to conflict in one role, more difficult in others; the weaknesses or defects of the personality may produce exaggerated consequences in one role and in another they may be minimized or even counteracted. The particular configurations of defense employed will be significantly different in the separate roles. Each role calls forth a mobilization of different reality skills and defenses. The success or failure of adaptation is partly contingent upon the measure of support the individual derives from his group relations. Other persons may buttress for this individual a favored self-image and a necessary defense against anxiety.

Society and family are, we know, the nutritional medium in which the identity of a person gradually emerges. The identity of the group structures the content of personal identity. As the individual matures, he achieves an identity which is at once both individual and social, and the two aspects are not clearly separable.

The individual component of personal identity is represented in the older, early acquired traits. This is the more durable and the less modifiable aspect of personality. It represents the organized behavior tendencies of the individual, those specific, relatively stable integrations of behavior which have been patterned by the early interaction of biological disposition and family relations. This is the core of the personality, the more personal, private, relatively fixed aspect of self.

In a strict sense the genetic process of individuation is never complete. Individuation moves forward on the basis of processes of togetherness with family, that is, identification of child and parent. A child never completely separates its psyche from parental influence, and in an analogous sense the adult's identity is always being influenced through the accretion of new layers of interpersonal influence.

In the processes of maturation, the achievement of individuality and independence is a matter of degree; only a state of relative biosocial independence is ever attained, whether in the context of the child's need of mother or the adult's need of society.

The social identity of a person epitomizes the continued interdependence of individual and society. The social component of a person's identity is represented in the later acquired, more peripheral aspects of personality. This is the less durable, more modifiable layer of character. It is less personal, less private, less fixed. It is this relatively more external layer of personality which permits the greater degree of penetration and modification by current social pressures. It is, therefore, more malleable and more tentative, influenced by time and the processes of group belongingness.

In a given time and social situation, certain components of personality are mobilized in action, while other components are temporarily subordinated. With a change in time and group situation, a shift of emotional integration occurs with a corresponding shift of integration into another social role; that is, other components of the self are moved into a dominant position in preparation for a particular type of social participation.

This is the essence of the process of social adaptation. In this process, the individual may react to social pressure with compliance, protest, or withdrawal. There is also a fourth possibility: If the social pressures are overwhelming and exceed the individual's resources for plastic adaptation, the organism may respond by disintegrating its old form and structuring a new one which shows distinct properties of its own. This is what seems to happen in the psychotic forms of integration, in some forms of war neurosis, and in psychosomatic disorders.

In the Freudian formulation of personality, one-sided emphasis is placed on the state of opposition between individual and society. Just as often, however, the two sets of forces may act in the same direction and reinforce one another. Under certain conditions, the forces of society and the individual are antithetical; under altered conditions, these same forces may mutually complement one another.

The relations between individual and society may in one sense be analogized to those between child and mother. The emotional tendencies of child and mother may at times be mutually complementary, at other times mutually opposed. The child incorporates selected parts of the mother which may strengthen or weaken his own evolving self. At later stages of maturation similar principles pertain to the relations between the individual and other persons and society as a whole.

Personality and society cannot be considered apart. Human adaptation is shaped both by the organization of the internal forces of personality and the external forces of society. Just as the biologist recognizes that the broader unit of study for the life process is not the single organism but rather the colony, so in an analogous sense personality must be scrutinized in the context of the processes of group life and the individual's part in the group. Psychoanalysts and sociologists both recognize the need for a broader conceptual frame within which to define and measure the operations of personality. Psychoanalysts require a theory of social organization; sociologists require a theory of personality. In fact, as we have seen, a scientific theory of personality is hardly possible except in the context of a broader theory of social organization. Just as the dominant patterns of social organization influence both the form and content of individual behavior, so social process likewise plays a considerable role in the determination of states of mental illness and health. The effect of society on personality, therefore, is not merely a surface one; it influences deeper processes as well. Exactly here lies the importance of the social organization of the family unit as an intermediary between the individual and society.

Viewing the phenomenon from the opposite side, the person seeks out selectively a social environment that is congenial to the expression of specific individual needs. To some limited extent, the individual has the power to change or shape his environment or to set up priorities for interaction with some elements of the surrounding situation while rejecting contact with others. He may choose those forms of interaction that are favorable to the desired direction of self-expression. In a sense he can choose his own social roles.

Concretely, this involves the interrelation between selected elements of the environment and the pursuit of particular ego aims, pleasure goals, relief of guilt, reinforcement of favorable defenses, and solutions of inner conflict. In another direction, the individual may seek out an environment favorable to the need for an irrational "acting out" of unconscious urges; he may seek opportunities for the projection of elements of his inner conflict onto the social scene.

It is common knowledge that certain individuals are capable of integrating their personalities into a particular form only as they derive support from the environment for such integration. In this sense, certain forms of personality balance are parasitic. The intactness and stability of the self in such instances depend on the support of the environment. A young mother, seventeen years old, manages the care of her household and baby very well so long as her own mother remains with her. When her mother leaves, she falls apart emotionally, gets panicky and disorganized. Her adaptation to the roles of mother and housekeeper disintegrates.

At times the forms of adaptation appear in the guise of automatic obedience to the forces of the environment. This is clinically important insofar as the adaptational success or failure of certain persons rests with such parasitic dependence on environmental protection. We see it exemplified not only in certain symbiotic two-person relationships, but also in the intense clinging quality with which an individual may attach to certain groups. For example, a young married woman still extremely dependent on her mother feels herself empty and without worth. A large part of her time is devoted to exquisite attention to her appearance, her clothes, and her manners. Her mother is a detached, shallow, emotionally hollow person, who for many years had adjudged herself the best-dressed woman in their community. Thus the relationships with her mother and with her community reinforce this young woman's unhealthy adaptation.

There is, in contrast, the type of person who relates to his environment and maintains role adaptation through a pattern of sustained opposition. This is an instance of an inverted form of dependence on the social environment. A young man working in his father's business preserves emotional balance by means of persistent fighting with his father. When his father dies and he can no longer defy and quarrel with him, he becomes confused and slips into flagrant delinquencies. Behavior of this sort is thus exemplified in terms either of automatized obedience or of habitual defiance. In situations involving severe or persistent conflict between person and environment, the environment may prove to be the stronger force, and in consequence there may be any degree of damage to the intactness of individual personality and failure in adapting to required social roles.

In the process of adaptation, the social role of the individual may serve either a positive or a negative psychological function. In mature, well-integrated personalities, a social role can reflect the strength of the individual expressed positively in participant group action. Here there is no conflict between the individual and the social components of self. They are mutually reinforcing. In weaker persons, handicapped by specific emotional disabilities and generalized immaturity, the individual and social aspects of self may come sharply into conflict. The effort of integrating a particular social role may exact an excessive price in terms of anxiety and conflict within the individual self; or conflict within the individual may damage or prevent the effective execution of a given social role. Such discord between individual and social aspects of self are common in a variety of psychopathological types.

In group participation, the identity of the individual is either strengthened or weakened. In a positive sense, an individual may assert his strength through group participation; on the other hand, the weaker the person's sense of individual identity the greater the need for support from the group. The deeper the anxiety about self the more intense is the dependence on group belongingness. In this context, social role signifies a compensatory, defensive, and negative function.

For years the etiology of psychoneurotic behavior has been the subject of controversial discussion, some investigators stressing the role of conflict in buried past experience, and others, conflict in current experience. If the issue is reformulated, this controversy may no longer be meaningful. It has been kept alive by inadequate understanding of the dynamic interplay of person and environment. To ask whether past or current experience is the causation of neurosis is to pose a wrong kind of question.

The phenomenological conception of social role sheds light on this problem. It offers a dynamic link between society and the individual; it provides a theoretical frame for the relations between the older, genetically entrenched aspects of personality and the more modifiable, more recently acquired aspects. This hypothesis provides the possibility of reconciling the past and present components of neurosis.

All components of causation of present neurotic behavior must by definition be part of the present dynamics of the situation. Such factors must be current as functioning elements of the personality or as elements of the environmental situation or both. That part of the past that is relevant to present causation is the "live past," not the "dead past"; that is, that part of past experience, perception, need, and conflict that has been incorporated into the motivational patterns of the evolving self and continues now as a live part of the current personality structure. As such it influences the potentialities of adaptive behavior and the possible range of adaptation to varied social roles. Current factors in the environment influence the social levels of personality integration and may in some circumstances penetrate down through the social layers to affect the inner and older aspects of personality as well.

The relations between social role and personality are readily observable in clinical practice. In psychoanalytic practice, one often has occasion to appraise the emotional capacity of an adult for fulfilling in various groups the roles of child, boy or girl, man or woman. For example, a female patient, married, with two children, is capable of fulfilling the role of wife but unable to assume the role of mother, or vice versa; a married male patient assumes the role of boy but is unable to meet the requirements of the role of man; other patients may be adequate or outstanding in their professional role but utterly incompetent in their family roles, or the exact opposite; or one sees successful execution of a role as political leader and incompetence in the marital role.

Certain individuals are able to achieve close relations with one or two people but are unable to play an effective role in groups; they simply do not make contact with groups of people. In contrast, many social leaders in this culture who are outstanding in their success in manipulating groups have a shockingly defective capacity for close, personal relations with individuals. One discerns here selective emotional processes that make possible successful adaptation in one role and failure in another.

It should be very clear that even in the case of an emotionally handicapped person it is possible for the consequences of the handicap to be intensified in one role and minimized in another. It is known, for example, that some psychopathic personalities and neurotics achieve a more successful adaptation in military life than in civilian life.

Still another approach to the question of the relations between personality and role is through the examination of the usual pattern of social functioning of particular personality types, both normal and psychopathological. In the "normal" person one assumes the capacity for flexible integration into a variety of social roles even when their requirements in some measure conflict. In our culture, some forms of social integration of personality are more stable and constant than others.

The hysterical personality is characterized by a flair for the dramatic, a romantic leaning, exhibitionism, heavy reliance on wish-fulfilling phantasy, and suggestibility. The hysteric is noted for his capacity for dissociating the separate components of a multiple identity. Hysterical personalities display an all-or-none tendency in their adaptive processes. When they are obedient to external reality, they tend to deny or suppress the inner reality—the needs inherent in their phantasy life. When dominated by their phantasy life they tend to ignore or blunt external reality. They seem unable to harmonize the two levels of reality, inner and outer. Such shifts of internal psychic balance are implicated in the tasks of integrating personality into different social roles. Thus, the hysteric's tendency to dissociation is reflected in a favoring of one or another type of social identity, depending upon the stimuli that derive from the group environment. Hitler has been described as hysterical and paranoid. World history was fatefully influenced by an extraordinary complementarity between the prewar social environment of Germany, the emotional state of the masses, and Hitler's mental condition. The German group psychological situation was receptive to the pathological exhibitionism of Hitler. The hysterical and paranoid role of the leader was not only accepted but strongly fortified by the mood of the masses.

In the obsessional personality, we see something different. Here the structure of personality is such that the strongest characteristic is obedience to social compulsion and renunciation of personal sexual and aggressive urges. The obsessional is more rigid; the shift of role from one group to another occurs within a more limited range. There is usually no major move away from the prevailing orientation to self, which is represented in a profound tendency toward ritual submission to social command and denial of basic drives. Accordingly, there are only minor shifts of role, the form of which is influenced by the characteristic mechanism of symbolic substitution. The goal of seeking security through obedience to social compulsion and renunciation of basic drives persists. On the other hand, it is also true that the obsessional person buys off his conscience with ritual negation of self; and, after that, he compensates with the assertion of cruelty. In any case, he is characterized by loss of spontaneity and a much reduced emotional plasticity. This is the chief reason for the obsessional's distress in meeting the requirements of varied social situations. The rigid, superficial, conforming aspects of the obsessional person impart a quality of insincerity to his role behavior.

The schizophrenic by contrast contemptuously casts off ordinary conventions. Often this is the most appealing feature of the schizophrenic. With respect to fluidity of social behavior and diversity of social roles the schizophrenic comes closer to the hysteric than to the obsessional. Rapid shifts of role influenced by group stimuli are often seen. At one pole there is an identification of the self-image with the deep bodily surgings, unintegrated with the influence of social contacts. And in contrasting group situations there is an identification of the self-image with the presumed constraints and hostile, menacing aspects of the surrounding environment, activating the urge to deny the body altogether. In either case the schizophrenic experiences great difficulty in effectuating a consistent social behavior.

The schizophrenic is characteristically apprehensive of loss or destruction of self. If he identifies himself with his bodily drives, he tends to renounce social participation for fear of his own destructive powers or fear of being injured through the exposure of his body to retaliatory attack. This renunciation is one kind of destruction of self. On the other hand, if the schizophrenic denies his body and identifies himself with the restrictive, hostile elements of his environment, he again renounces social participation because of his intense hostile feeling toward other persons, whom he blames for the required sacrifices of the vital pleasures of his body. This is again a kind of destruction of self. The schizophrenic's preoccupation with the threat of destruction evoked by closeness to other persons induces withdrawal and resistance to social participation.

We often see schizophrenics who automatically assume the mannerisms of the persons by whom they are surrounded—a phase of their uncontrolled obedience to social pressure. Or they may show a bizarre pattern of opposition to those same influences. In any case, in some schizophrenic individuals one does see remarkable shifts in adaptive behavior, with lightning transitions in role stimulated by the patient's awareness of the hostile or sympathetic climate of the personal environment.

Looking at the dynamics of role adaptation in still another way, I have been impressed with the close association between the emergence of psychosomatic disorders and the adaptive breakdown of a characteristic role pattern—or more accurately, with the psychosomatic disintegration associated with unresolved conflict between the requirements of antithetical social roles. In the hypertensive person, there is neither the ability to effectuate a role of dependence on and submission to the environment nor the ability successfully to master the environment with hostile aggressive power. The two roles are incongruous and cannot be reconciled. I have myself been tempted to characterize the hypertensive personality as an individual who is a would-be psychopath, a person who in phantasy is motivated by the desire to live like a psychopath but does not dare. The fright of retaliation is overwhelming. But neither is the hypertensive individual able to accept the dependent and submissive role.

The patient who breaks down with peptic ulcer can neither assume a role of passive oral dependence on his environment nor achieve the opposed role of superior omnipotent strength and self-sufficiency.

The person who breaks down with an acute skin disorder is invested in a certain role relationship in which he suffers a deep injury to his pride. He can neither accept the implications of this blow to his vanity nor can he restore the pre-injured, successful social self. Instead one sees him fuming with indignation and bursting with fury. He gets red in the face and blows hot and cold.

The skin, in a somatic sense, is the partition between person and environment. In one sense, changes in skin are surface phenomena, relatively peripheral experiences. Yet through the skin and the surface membranes of the orifices of the body are mediated all the vital processes of exchange between organism and environment. In this sense, changes in skin function may have critical importance for the deepest biological functions of the organism. An apt analogy for this theme is the pheomenon of huge skin burns; if large areas of skin are injured, the entire vital processes of the organism are in jeopardy, and the very life of the individual is at stake. In an analogous sense, one wonders if an environmental threat to the efficacious performance of certain social roles does not endanger the integrity of the entire personality.

The effect of anxiety on the dynamics of social role may show itself in two opposite ways: it may induce increasing instability and a tendency to rapid change of roles; or it may induce increasing rigidity. In either case adaptive efficiency is impaired. The quantity of anxiety generated is influenced by the degree of harmony or conflict between the individual, older aspects of identity and the newer aspects of social identity. The personality performance in a given social role will be affected by the relative harmony or conflict between the social expression of self and the inner image of self, influenced both by conscious and unconscious factors and also by the corresponding intensity of anxiety. There is the related question of the degree of psychic distance between the individual self and the social self; in terms of emotional content, the social role may be relatively peripheral or relatively close to the individual self. Such relations will determine the degree to which an individual's identification with a given group is genuine or false, spontaneous or forced, healthy or anxiety-ridden.

The issues of assimilation of personality to role requirements need to be weighed in the light of a special trend in our culture; namely, the unusual degree of strain and anxiety that accompanies the effort of social adaptation. The relations of person and society in our time are characterized by a confusion of norms, a lack of clarity as to what society expects of the individual in the fulfillment of social roles. With this is associated a widespread tendency toward loneliness. Hostile, competitive feelings are overstimulated, and the need for defenses against and escape from these emotions is very great. One of the outstanding characteristics in our society is the individual's emotional isolation and lack of security in group living. The need for group belongingness is profound, but the thwarting of this need is extensive. This seems to be one of the manifestations in our society of the competitive patterns of group organization and exaggerated intergroup tensions, but it is also partly an expression of a particular kind of evolution of individual personality in our cultural group from childhood up.

Still another aspect of the relations of individual personality to social role pertains to the dominant emotion which is implicated in the individual's identification with the group. Such identification, as Fritz Redl has pointed out, may be mediated through the dominant emotion of love or through fear and hate. It is an unfortunate fact that all too frequently in our society an individual is integrated into a group through emotional needs relating to fear and hate rather than love. The patterns of prejudice against minorities, the fear, mistrust, and belligerence toward other nations, mirror this characteristic trend.

If we approach human behavior according to Kurt Lewin's field concepts (*i.e.*, society is the total space in which personality manifestations are to be appraised), a hierarchical scheme of the relevant phenomenological levels may be represented as follows:

HIERARCHICAL SCHEME FOR REPRESENTATION OF ROLE OR SOCIAL SELF

SOCIO-ECONOMIC STRUCTURE

SOCIAL INSTITUTIONS

CLOSE FACE-TO-FACE GROUPS WITHIN WHICH INDIVIDUAL IS INTEGRATED

SOCIAL ROLE, SOCIAL SELF, OR SOCIAL IDENTITY

Strivings, Values, and Expectations
   (Security, pleasure, self-fulfillment)
Self-Image ⟷ Image of Other Persons
Self-Assertion ⟷ Self-Subordination
   (Mastery or Compliance)
Satisfaction or Frustration
Conflict, Anxiety, Defense

INDIVIDUAL SELF

Inner Self-Image
Drives, conflict, anxiety, defense
Conscious ⟷ Unconscious Determinants
Constitutional Factors

This diagram depicts the manner in which the phenomena of social role are influenced from without by group organization and from within by the factors deriving from individual personality (older aspects). We see the continuity of personality with the environment, the phenomena of social role or social self as intermediate between the fixed intrapsychic patterns of personality and the dynamics of group integration. The particular configuration of a given role derives its cue from the goals and values that orient the individual's part in the group. Goals have to do with security, pleasure, and self-fulfillment. Values represent a function of the individual's relations to society; they provide meanings that direct the path of social action. Values are oriented both toward self and toward one's relations to other persons. They involve a particular attitude toward personal strivings, influenced by the perceptual response to culture-conditioned patterns of interpersonal relations.

It is clear then that multiple factors, deriving partly from the group organization and partly from the individual structure of personality, determine the configuration of social role. The more pertinent of these are itemized in the diagram: the goals and value orientation, the interplay of self-image and image of other persons, the pattern of compliance with or protest against social pressures, the assertion or subordination of the individual self, the projection of inner need and conflict into the role, and the selection of specific defenses against anxiety.

THE HOMEOSTASIS OF BEHAVIOR

THE THEME "homeostasis" is very much in fashion today. It is a favorite topic of discussion in both medicine and the behavioral sciences. Its sudden prominence can hardly come as a surprise, for the current key word in professional groups dealing with human problems is "integration." The battleground of theory has shifted from a concern with the way in which particular parts of the mind work to the way in which these parts work together. The debate has moved over to the what, how, and why of integration. The revolution in technology and in communications and the resulting contraction of the human world have brought sharply into focus the problems of the individual's position in society. The tighter network of human relations, no longer permitting isolation, creates new problems of adaptation. It poses new questions concerning the emotional and social integration of the individual into the group.

At one pole there is the link of psychoanalysis with social sciences in the exploration of questions of personality and role adaptation; at the other pole the link of psychoanalysis and physiology in the investigation of psychosomatic illness. In the over-all picture there is a dramatic spread of interest in the role of social and cultural factors in mental illness and health. In the pursuit of such questions an understanding of the principle of homeostasis is a *sine qua non*.

The term "homeostasis" refers to the vital principle that preserves the intactness and continuity of the human organism, the capacity for maintaining effective, coordinated functioning under constantly changing conditions of life. It has to do with the relations of the organism both to its inner and outer environment. But the transposition of the concept of homeostasis as expounded by Walter Cannon and Claude Bernard[1] to the sphere of balanced functioning of the mind and the dynamic equilibrium of the individual with his social environment is a recent development.

Is such transposition appropriate? Is it timely? And if so, are the principles of human behavior and our readiness to integrate individual and group dynamics sufficiently advanced to make feasible an operational concept of homeostasis of personality? My answer is affirmative.

For the contemporary scientist, mind and body are one. If the term "homeostasis" is to carry meaning, it must apply to the totality of life process; it must strictly avoid the false dichotomization of mind and body. The functions of mind mediate between the intact, live, physical being and his environment. Mind unfolds between biological and social levels of experience. In a basic sense, biology, psychology, and sociology are artificially separated single aspects of the science of behavior. A unified theory must join these systems of thought. Because this is so, it becomes important to seek out the expressions of the homeostatic principle at all three levels: body, mind, and society.

Cannon[2] says,

> It seems not impossible that the means employed by more highly involved animals for preserving uniform and stable their economy (i.e., for preserving homeostasis) may present some general principles for the establishment, regulation and control of steady states that would be suggestive of other organizations, even social and industrial, which suffer from distressing perturbations.

Here we see Cannon himself offering the speculation that the homeostatic principle operates at the mental and group organization levels as well as in the body. He extends his understanding of the homeostatic function in the body to the sphere of the mind and to the organization of society. In this sense, the physiological concept of homeostasis is elaborated by analogy to refer to the integrative, balancing function of the mind and to the dynamic equlibrium between the individual and his surrounding group.

Let us consider more carefully what this may mean at the mental and social levels. This is imperative because of the extensive confusion that currently marks professional deliberations of this question. The term "homeostasis" means literally "staying the same." It implies the adaptive capacity to stabilize the self in the face of the continuously shifting demands of life. The individual is subjected to unremitting pressure from stimuli arising from both within and without. These pressures offer a potential threat to the integrity and continuity of the live organism. They bring about a continuing alteration of the balance of forces within the organism. Homeostasis thus signifies the capacity to resist and modify such incursion in order to maintain that level of balance and integration that is necessary for the preservation of life activity and for further development.

Exactly here is the profound paradox at the very heart of the homeostatic concept. We have said that homeostasis, literally translated, means "staying the same," that is, the capacity to restore steady states following upsets of balance. But no living organism ever stays the same. Cannon understood this very well. He embraced in his interpretation of homeostasis the ability to adapt to change. For example, in his description of rage he included the outflow of adrenalin, increased blood sugar, and increased capacity for appropriate action in the face of danger. It is a basic condition of life process that the organism must not only adjust but must simultaneously change, grow, and shift its functions according to its stage of maturation and environmental position; otherwise it dies. There is, therefore, a fundamental incompatability between "staying the same" and remaining alive. In the deepest biological sense, to "stay the same" is a certain warrant of death. A correct appreciation of the nature of this paradox is of crucial importance.

How then shall we interpret the connotation of "staying the same?" In one sense, the organism must stay the same, and yet, in another, it must maintain a state of perpetual readiness for change and growth. This is what is meant by the maintenance of dynamic equilibrium in the internal life of the organism and in its fluid interchange with the surrounding environment. On this point, Cannon cogently remarks, "Through self-regulation . . . we preserve stability in the highly unstable of which we are composed."

Let us take a further step in unraveling this riddle. It is perhaps closer to the truth to conceive that the exact purpose of homeostasis is to protect, not stability in any static sense, but rather a creative but controlled "instability"* of the organism in consonance with the necessary conditions for maturation and for expanding relations with the outer world? In other words, in the interpretation of this concept I am shifting the emphasis to the exact opposite of the connotation of "staying the same." I am suggesting that "homeostasis," or the principle of dynamic equilibrium, signifies the capacity for creative, fluid adaptability to change, which at the same time assures that measure of coordinated control that prevents the organism from being overwhelmed by a barrage of stimuli in excess of the organism's capacity to accommodate (the final effect of which would, of course, be disorganization). The principle thus rein-

* "Instability" is here used to emphasize readiness for change.

terpreted is conceived as creative, controlled "instability"; it regulates response to experience not in order to maintain sameness, but rather to preserve a resilient capacity for change while preventing change from becoming too rapid —so rapid as to disintegrate resources for adaptation and growth.

In this interpretation, what is emphasized is the positive, dynamic aspect rather than the static negative aspect, a life principle represented in the ideal as an optimal degree of fluid, productive "instability," which provides for the organism the highest measure of plasticity of adaptation and growth while coordinating vital activities.

The essence of life is change, growth, learning, adaptation to new conditions, and creative evolution of new levels of interchange between person and environment. In this context, life process cannot be secure and stable in any absolute sense; it is intrinsically fluid, changing, and unstable. Without this "instability" there can be no growth, no adaptation, no learning, no creativity. But this is a controlled "instability," controlled so as to offset a too rapid and destructive change. In this scheme, we envisage the homeostatic principle as a kind of shock barrier, both for body and mind, which enables expansion of the organism while protecting its integrity.

One phase of the function of stabilization serves a conservative purpose; it makes possible the continuity of "sameness" in time. Yet the exact conditions of the past can never be maintained. The second phase of the function of stabilization is the accommodation to new conditions of life. As these conditions change, so does the organism change and undergo further evolution. If either of these capacities is critically impaired, the continuity of life is inconceivable. Homeostasis is the instrumentality of vital process, the mechanism of growth, not stultification.

Let us call to mind the way in which the body reacts to any sudden, disruptive, mutilative assault. There is a physiological shock barrier. When a person is mutilated in an automobile accident, the injured area for a short time freezes, becomes anesthetic and numb to pain. The body mobilizes its emergency defense. Then comes acute pain, and the body summons a further series of protective devices for controlling the danger.

In a striking analogous way, when the mind is subjected to a shocking invasion, there is an instantaneous mobilization of emergency psychic defense so as to minimize the excess of trauma. Sometimes this emergency defense extends to the point of total magic denial, a kind of numbing of the mind. Shortly thereafter other defenses are activated so as to reduce the impact of the shock and provide a longer period of time for its gradual assimilation.

It is a misconception to consider as "homeostatic" the strivings toward a state of static equilibrium that we observe clinically in certain patients. This is not homeostasis; this is psychopathology. The striving for static equilibrium can lead only to a weakening of the vital resources of the person and ultimately to a kind of psychic dying, if not actual physical death.

I can exemplify this point in several ways. In formulating his theory of a death instinct, Freud[4] alluded to a drive toward restoration of a state of quiescence, a static equilibrium in which the tensions of energy release all but cease. Freud likened this tendency to a yearning for something akin to a state of nirvana or the blissful state of rest and contentment of the embryo in the mother's womb.

By far the vast majority of psychoanalysts reject Freud's theory of the death instinct. A simpler and more convincing explanation is readily available for the striving to reduce tension, to reach a state of quiescence, for the phenomena of "repetition compulsion," and for self-destructive behavior. The striving for a static equilibrium can be understood as a secondary process, a defensive avoidance of shock and frustration, or as an escape from psychic pain; that is, such behavior can be looked upon as an aspect of failure, defeat, or derailment of the life drive, rather than as a primary death instinct. In any case, the motivational constellations that Freud identified with his death instinct point dramatically to the connection between a striving for static equilibrium and retreat from life. The homeostatic process actuates and protects life. It does not foster fear and withdrawal from life.

Let us consider, for example, the clinical condition in infants called marasmus, in which there is a slow but persistent ebbing of life. In this condition there is a paralysis of vital activity, a stultification of the processes of equilibrium within the organism and in the zone between organism and environment. It represents a failure of homeostasis. There is also the clinical condition in children that Leo Kanner[5] originally described as autism. The specific features of this condition are a tendency to progressive isolation, retreat into fantasy, and increasing rigidity; there is also an insistence on sameness and routinization of all aspects of life experience. The autistic child resists every aspect of change in the environment. This condition is conceived by many to be either the equivalent or a forerunner of schizophrenia. Here the need for a static sameness, the frozen defense against change, endangers the integrity of the organism.

Still other illustrations may be drawn from the field of psychosomatic illness. A forty-year-old woman recurrently developed ulcer pain exactly at the time that certain rigid defenses intended to maintain a static equilibrium between her image of self and other persons broke down. These defenses involved a rigid denial of the image of herself as a child, hungry, helpless, exposed, and vulnerable, and the over-assertion of a compensatory image of self, omnipotent, self-sufficient, able to provide her own food. When these defenses failed, she was foiled in her escape into her alienated, emotionally detached, all-powerful state of being. As soon as this occurred, she was gripped with pain, her stomach tightened up rigidly, and she was unable to eat. With the cramping of the stomach and her inability to eat, her mind became filled with thoughts of death. Here we have an instance of a rigid striving for a static equilibrium that is incompatible with the maintenance of life.

A twenty-eight-year-old man with elevated blood pressure was fearful of his aggressive employer. He feared the employer's criticism and the possible loss of his job. He imagined that his boss would assault him physically in a fit of irritability. He was in dread of such humiliation and injury. He held the secret phantasy of avenging himself by spitting on his boss. He entertained other consoling phantasies of erupting with a burst of rage and destroying his employer. But he feared that without a job he would starve. He could not effectively repress this conflict. It boiled over into his consciousness and dominated his waking life. Outwardly, he was compliant. His face was wiped clean of all expression of feeling; he wore a bland, composed mask. But all the time he was "burning up inside." He could neither resign himself to his position of dependence and submission nor effectuate his secret defense of asserting magic, omnipotent power. He became acutely anxious and depressed; he suppressed his rage, and his blood pressure rose. In the context of these several clinical examples, the defensive need for a static equilibrium leads to a form of emotional disorganization and dying.

Conflict in the zone of relations between person and environment feeds back into the mind to affect the regulatory control of internal conflict and the choice of defense against internal conflict. Homeostatic control of external relations with the environment is characterized by a far greater range of plasticity of adaptation than is homeostatic control of internal events. The effective coordination and stabilization of the internal life of the organism is more fixed, while the homeostatic balance of external relations to environment is more variable. This difference is due to the advanced development of the cortex in man, which provides the power of introspection and the capacity to predict future problems of adaptation, to examine the range of possible responses to experience, and therefore to exercise through the powers of reason some measure of discrimination and choice as to the preferred mode of social adaptation. It is man's expanded control of his external environment that in one sense creates new problems of adaptation to his internal physiological environment, e.g., the "diseases of civilization," but it also makes possible within limits adaptive modification of his control of physiological need.

Let us consider the most subtle form of homeostatic control in the body, namely, temperature control. This is a most delicate mechanism; a beautiful example of a near perfect homeostatic operation. This is a form of physiological regulation, the product of long evolutionary processes that developed in accommodation to the specific climate of this earth. Its perfect functioning requires assistance from the outside. Human beings protect the homeostatic temperature control of the body with clothes; they heat their places of habitation or resort to mechanical cooling of the home and even of mattresses.

It is true that an abruptly changing climate can play havoc with the reflex temperature control of the body. It is also true, I believe, that individuals undergoing prolonged exposure to cold are less apt to freeze to death if they have the support of warm, encouraging companions; if they are not alone, their chance of survival is greater. At the other extreme, individuals subjected to intense heat tolerate it better and show less irritability if they have congenial companions.

Now let us consider heat and cold at the psychic level, that is, the need of human beings to maintain a certain optimal psychic temperature. It is no accident that we speak of a human being's need of warmth and closeness or of the craving for the snugness and safety of the hearth. There is nothing so cozy as a fireplace. What is the relation between a person's inner feeling of warmth and the temperature of his personal surroundings? Within specified limits, a person may preserve inside himself a sense of emotional warmth even when he lives among a group of cold, impersonal, hostile people. But he is able to maintain this inner warmth just so long and no longer. Beyond a certain point, his psyche begins to turn frigid. He gradually becomes aloof, suspicious, withdrawn. He freezes his emotions and ceases to trade feelings with those about him.

There is, for example, some hypothetical suspicion that schizophrenia is related to a failure of "psychic temperature" control in the early relations of infant and mother. In persons of schizoid disposition, there is a tendency for the emotional expressions of the mouth to go dead. The play of the mouth as an organ of emotional exchange ceases. The mouth goes numb: it ceases to ask; it ceases to give. With this interruption of trade of emotions via the mouth, the individual enters a state of static relation with his environment. This state is a failure of homeostasis and in every sense becomes a "living death."

The social nature of man, his need of human warmth and closeness make it apparent that at the psychological and social levels homeostasis can be understood only within the continuum of individual, family, and society. "Homeostasis" at the individual level is contingent upon "homeostasis" of family, and, in turn, "homeostasis" of family rests upon "homeostasis" of society. These relations do not move in one direction only; they are, of course, circular and convoluted.

In the broadest sense, nothing ever remains the same. Change is of the essence of life; change at any one level of experience influences change at every other. Homeostasis of personality, therefore, cannot be conceived in isolation; it becomes a meaningful principle only as it is applied to all levels of organization of life process, not only individual, family, and social community, but to those levels that involve the interrelations of human and other species of life and the relations of human beings with physical nature.

If, for the moment, we examine the relations of mother and child, we can say that the potential homeostasis of the child is a function of the symbiotic union of mother and child. Initially, the infant's capacity for homeostasis is limited. His survival hinges on the mother's homeostatic capacity. The mother's powers of stabilization, in consonance with the requirements of growth and change, must cloak the need of both persons functioning as one. Any deficiency or distortion in the mother's homeostatic powers will instantly be revealed in a disturbance of complementarity and interchange between mother and infant. It will result in an impairment of the infant's homeostatic development.

Whether the inappropriate mothering emerges as neglect, overstimulation, or direct, hostile assault, the infant will tend toward a more rigid, constricted, static equilibrium and the homeostatic capacity of the infant will in consequence be injured. Neglect of the infant's needs evokes an excess of stimuli from within the organism. A superabundance of handling of the infant or direct, hostile assault stirs turmoil and tension. The excess of stimulation, whether from without or from within, overwhelms the infant, exceeds his shock barrier, and overrides his capacity to slow the pace of change, in keeping with his limited resources for adaptation.

It is true, of course, that the general direction of development is from a position of biosocial union with mother to a separate existence, from dependence on mother to self-dependence. As the infant matures he moves toward autonomy. But autonomy in human development is a frequently misunderstood concept. Autonomy may be of either a healthy or a pathological kind. Pathological separation is not a true autonomy. A healthy, genuine autonomy emerges only as a satisfying and healthy union is maintained.

Togetherness and separation are the head and tail of the same coin. No togetherness, no true autonomy. If togetherness is distorted, so is the quality of separation. A true development of autonomy is superimposed on a satisfying union. Autonomy does not supplant union; it is added to it. In the understanding of the genesis of homeostasis of personality, it is of the utmost importance to grasp this principle. If the mother-child union is distorted, the development of homeostatic competence in the child fails.

This principle is clearly expressed in the mutuality of health in infant and mother. Angyal[3] has stated that as the infant progresses toward autonomy, it expands at the expense of the environment. In the context of infant-mother relations, are we to interpret this literally? I do not believe that we can.

In a fundamental biological sense, it is not true that the infant expands at the expense of the mother, except under abnormal conditions. There is a powerful body of evidence to show that under normal conditions the welfare of infant and mother are one. What is good for the infant is also good for the mother and vice versa. The mother need make no sacrifice for the child. From the works of Margaret Ribble[4] and Theresa Benedek,[5] we learn that the mother's health, both physical and mental, is actually enhanced through her care of the child. Breast feeding promotes rapid contraction of the uterus after birth, favors a rapid restoration of glandular balance in the mother, etc. Through a good quality of psychological union with the infant, the mother fosters homeostasis and effective development of autonomy in both persons; in so doing, she promotes health both in the infant and in herself.

The mother makes no sacrifice, therefore, for the welfare of her child. The belief that a good mother is self-sacrificial, that the child expands at the mother's expense, is a myth that dies hard. It is a persistent theme in the perceptual elaborations of neurotic patients. It comes back again and again in a variety of guises: A mother may die in childbirth. She must give till it hurts. Unless she is willing to sacrifice she is a "bad" mother. Loving is proved by the mother's pain and loss. The mother's surrender of self is a noble, aggrandizing thing. "We owe our mother a debt we can never repay." Under abnormal conditions, there may be a core of truth to the theme of sacrifice. Under healthful conditions, this cannot be the case.

Neurotic mothers are notorious for their martyred agonies, their self-pitying dramatic displays, their exploitation of the theme of sacrifice. In actuality, however, martyred mothers make no sacrifice. If anything, they do precisely the opposite. They exploit their children. They exact an emotional sacrifice. They press upon the children with their imagined wounds, with constant reminders of all they have done for them. Neurotic children take this maternal display seriously; they are mowed down by guilt and seek penance in propitiatory behavior. They attempt in a futile way to make up to their mothers for the presumed sacrifice. Such patterns of neurotic interaction bind the child to mother, deform the quality of togetherness, and sharply restrict the range of development toward a mature autonomy. The relevance of this trend for the unfolding of a competent homeostasis of personality is self-evident.

Now let us look similarly at the vicissitudes of the relations of male and female. What role does homeostasis play in the sexual pair? Male and female are incomplete without one another. They seek completion through union. We have heard much concerning the shift in the role of the female in contemporary society. The woman has "emancipated" herself through the feminist movement. She is no longer treated as chattel. With the development of contraception, she has ceased to be a breeding machine. She is not any longer enslaved to home and children. She has achieved independence. She has more leisure, exercises greater powers of choice, and enjoys greater sexual freedom.

But we hear also of the "battle of the sexes," the rivalry of male and female for a position of dominance. We hear of "Momism," the overweening aggressiveness of women, and the weak, submissive spinelessness of many men. What has happened to the complementarity, the natural union and completion of male and female in one another? There is a great change, to be sure, but it is not in the position of women in society alone. If the behavior of women is now different, it is in relation to the changed behavior of men. A shift in the one sex entails a shift in the other.

It is true that women enjoy greater freedom. But have they learned what to do with it? Have they really matured? Have they used their increased sexual freedom to come into their own as women? Are they really more feminine? The relations of male and female are in a state of flux. Perhaps the potential for a better quality of sexual complementarity exists in the present fluid instability of male-female relations. But at present the pattern of balance between the sexes too often gets derailed. If women were actually becoming more feminine, then men should be becoming more masculine. What do we actually see? In many parts of society, men seem to be turning less masculine. If so, we can only assume that women are not becoming more feminine but less so.

The issue is not one of orgastic capacity in women. The test of femininity is not merely their ability to experience orgasm. This is much too narrow a view. Some women can be orgastic without being truly feminine; they become conditioned to orgastic response in a setting in which they experience sexual relations as a hectic, violent, competitive battle with the male. Orgasm comes to mean triumph. To judge femininity by the presence or absence of orgastic response is to mechanize the woman, to view her female body only as a sexual machine. This is a twisted, obsessive, and critically inadequate criterion for femininity. The standard of femininity must be one that reflects the total quality of the woman's adaptation to the man and to her child, not just her sexual performance.

Today's women are freer, often more assertive, but they compete like men and in so doing move away from femininity. If they compete, it is better that they compete as women, not as men. Men and women both are oriented to the struggle for competitive dominance. The effect of this, in the long view, is to obscure the essential difference and the essential mutuality of male and female, to alienate the two sexes. Men become less masculine, women less feminine. Both suffer a distortion and loss of psychosexual identity. A further complication results when the disturbed psychosexual identity of a pair of parents confuses the emotional development of their child.

Yet there need be no clash, no sacrifice of the one to the other with resultant damage to the child. Increased freedom for both sexes should mean the realization of a better complementarity and "homeostatic" balance between them. Ideally, there is an interweaving of the balance of equilibratory forces all along the line. "Homeostasis" of mother and child and man and wife are linked to the homeostasis of the entire family group. The balance of relations of mother and child are affected by the balance between mother and father, father and child, child and sibling, etc. Moving a step further, the internal organization of the family is influenced by the family's position in the larger community.

Let us return, however, to the more specific issues of homeostasis of individual personality. In the classical psychoanalytic framework, homeostasis is the integrative process of the personality, the instrument that interrelates and balances the component functions of personality. We think specifically of the intimate interconnections of such ego functions as perception, association, memory, judgment, discrimination, control, and defense. We must surely realize that each is not one or another differentiated function operating in isolation, but all of them act together in a certain harmony. It is the design of all of these partial operations, expressed as a functional unity, that is pertinent to the issue of homeostasis. Ego itself is not an autonomous operation; neither is superego; neither is id. A distortion is introduced as we anthropomorphize these abstract constructs and view them as separate entities. They do not exist as such. The ego itself, to use the phrase of Anna Freud, takes its cue from the processes of social interaction within the family.

Psychoanalysis itself has made much of the distinction between ego and self. The two are not viewed as identical. The self-image is considered to be a complex structure, gradually evolving from progressive stages of identification with parents. This sequence culminates in the establishment of a separate personal identity. The self is a holistic concept. On the other level, the ego represents specific, partial integrative functions, which make possible the entrenchment of a sense of self. The superego in turn is presumed to place discriminatory ethical judgments of right and wrong on conflicts between ego and id. Homeostasis is the process that governs and coordinates the interrelations of these part functions of the personality, no one of which is meaningful without the other.

There arises then the question of the definition of self, the relations of the subjective and objective aspects of self, the "I" and the "me," the relations of individual and social aspects of self. The "I" is the representation of the autonomous self, the active, initiating, mastering aspect of self. It is the part of the self that makes objects of other selves. The "me" is the object of other selves. This then raises the question: Is there one self or many selves?

The self shifts in accordance with the integration of personality into different social roles. One may conceive of multiple social selves mobilized to meet the needs of a variety of social situations but all of them held together by the preservation of a more basic self-image, which we speak of as the individual self. The individual self or inner self is the component of self that is oldest and most stable. It is the primary self-identity established in the early processes of identification with parents, rooted in the first and oldest group experience, the family of childhood. It is what we mean by the term "individuality." It is the least yielding to immediate exigencies of experience, but it continues to be molded by an unending series of new group integrations and identifications. The distinction between individual and social self lies in a series of superimposed layers of social influence that exert their effects on the person in the dimension of time.

The individual layers of self are the oldest; beyond that, through the span of time, the individual integrates into a range of social selves. Each layer of self-identity corresponds to a particular group with which this identity is linked. The principle of homeostasis expresses itself in this time-conditioned, hierarchical series of selves integrated into changing group structures.

Homeostasis means the preservation of a certain center of self, with the addition of new dimensions to the self in a never-ending series of group integrations. It is within this conceptual frame that we must try to understand the interrelations of intrapsychic and interpersonal patterns of organization, and it is self-evident that preservation of self cannot mean isolation. The mechanism of emotional isolation leads ultimately to a disownment of self, depersonalization and loss of self. The preservation of self represents rather an ever-expanding matrix of joined identity with other persons, which at the same time adds strength to the core of the self. Barricading or isolating the self from an expanding process of social identification condemns the individual to feed on himself psychically and guarantees a premature psychic death. It is something akin to a snake devouring his own tail. Thus, intrapsychic equilibrium can in no way be divorced from interpersonal equilibrium. At any point in time, personality is simultaneously oriented to inner and outer experience. Each direction of orientation continuously influences the other. If we define the intrapsychic organization of a person, we are inferentially referring to his probable interpersonal performance and vice versa. In this context, stability and growth of the self must be seen as fundamentally tied to stability and growth of interpersonal relations.

CHAPTER 6

FAMILY IDENTITY, STABILITY, AND BREAKDOWN

HAVING CONSIDERED the empirical and conceptual questions germane to family diagnosis and treatment, we endeavor now to build a theoretical frame within which useful hypotheses for the dynamic interrelations of individual and family behavior may be devised. We seek to establish a method of family diagnosis—a method for identifying the family as a psychological entity in and of itself, a way of assessing its psychosocial configuration and mental health functioning, a basis of classification and differential diagnosis of family types, and finally a means of establishing the specific dynamic interrelations of individual and family behavior. The ultimate goal is the social psychology and social psychopathology of family life.

Systematically, the criteria demanded by such an undertaking are:

1. criteria for the differential classification of family types according to their psychosocial configuration and mental health functioning;
2. criteria for evaluating the emotional integration of individuals into their family roles; also for identifying the emotional mechanisms by which adaptation to one family role supports or conflicts with the requirements of other familial and extrafamilial roles;
3. criteria (within the definition of family types) for evaluating emotional disturbances of family pairs and threesomes;
4. criteria for the disturbances of individual members, which emphasize the dynamic interdependence of the mental health of individual and family;

also for the emotional mechanisms by which the maturing individual separates his image of self from the image of family while maintaining a level of joined identity.

For such purposes it is necessary to gather a considerable body of data derived from several distinct though interrelated phenomenological levels. The relevant behavior components are the relative autonomy of the individual; his emotional integration into family group (*i.e.*, the adaptation of his personality to the required family roles); the fit or lack of fit for the same individual of significant familial or extrafamilial roles; the extent to which the reciprocal role behavior of other family members supports or threatens the stability of the individual; and the psychological identity and value orientation of the family group and its external adaptation to the community.

The data so obtained should illuminate at each successive stage of development the interrelations of individual and family, thus providing both horizontal and longitudinal configurations of the relevant phenomena. In such an undertaking, the dimensions of diagnostic thinking are expanded beyond the limits of the internal economy of personality so as to embrace three interrelated sets of processes: (1) what goes on inside the individual; (2) what goes on between this individual and other significant family members; (3) the psychosocial patterns of the family as a whole.

The goal is to establish the relations of the emotional balance within the individual to the balance of role adaptation in family pairs and threesomes, and the relations of this balance in turn to the emotional balance of the family group itself. In order to embrace these multiple, overlapping, and interpenetrating processes within a unified theoretical framework, it is necessary to find means for identifying the whole, the parts, and the relations of the parts to the whole. In seeking to answer this need, I have tried to develop a basic conceptual scheme, a set of interrelated core concepts within which the relevant relationships can be understood. I have experimented with a series of such schemes, testing each against the specific data of clinical studies of family life. I have attempted to analyze such empirical data, moving from outside inward, from the family group to the individual, and from inside outward, from the individual to the family group. I have also experimented in another way, taking as a starting point the interplay of family members in their respective family roles and moving from there inward to the individual and outward to the family as a whole.

At the present stage I have arrived at a tentative theoretical scheme, which is by no means final but may be the foundation for further development. It consists of a small group of core concepts by which the psychosocial dynamics of family life may be operationally defined. They are guiding concepts that attempt to answer for the dynamics of family functioning: the who and what of family life, the how, and the resulting functional patterns of the family. These concepts are, in brief, the following: (1) psychological identity, which subsumes strivings, expectations, and values; (2) stability of behavior, expressed as (a) the continuity of identity in time; (b) the control of conflict; (c) the capacity to change, learn, and achieve further development; adaptability and complementarity in new role relationships.

In exploratory studies of a series of families of different types, it has seemed useful to apply these dimensions to the task of evaluating the psychosocial processes of family life. The questions, who, what, and how, and the corresponding dimensions of identity and stability can be applied to the examination of both individual and family behavior. This scheme must be considered as a unity. No one dimension can be considered apart from its relations to every other.

Identity

The concept "psychological identity and values" refers to direction and content of striving, while stability refers to organization and expression of behavior in action.

Any human entity—an individual, a pair of related persons, or a group—possesses a unique psychic representation. I speak of this as identity. It is part of the cycle of life that people strive to express and fulfill the potentials of their identity in the context of on-going social relations. A joined pair of persons or a group may be conceived as possessing a unique identity in the same sense that an individual does. Psychological identity is not a static configuration; it evolves and changes through time. It is an amalgam of elements of old and new, of depth and surface experience. It is molded by the individual's interaction with his interpersonal environment; it leaves its imprint on that environment. At any one moment in time psychological identity can be defined only as an abstraction, because human development cannot ever be halted in the path of time and space. Psychological identity refers to a self-concept, expressed in the strivings, goals, expectations, and values of a person or group of persons. It answers the question "Who am I?" or "Who are we?" in the context of a given life situation. It qualifies a particular kind of person or persons, what they stand for, where they are going, their purpose and meaning in life.

The psychological identity of an individual or of a family pair or group is its psychic center of gravity. It is the "I and me" or the "we and us," the unique configuration of psychic self-representation around which all interpersonal experience is woven and by which this same identity is further modified in the passage of time. It orients personal strivings to relations with others. At a given point in time the individual has an image of his personal identity and his family identity, both continuously being influenced by the images which outside persons hold of these same identities. The image of self and image of family are reciprocally interdependent. At each stage of development, personal identity is linked to and differentiated from the identity of parents and family in a special way. This relationship begins with the symbiosis of the child-mother pair; it is molded by processes of primary identification of child and parents; and it undergoes further change as the child gradually differentiates his separate self and expands his identification with other family members. The organization of individual identity at any point in time, therefore, epitomizes a corresponding family identity.

If one conducts the experiment of asking a child, "Who are you? What do you think of yourself?" one rarely gets an answer. It is a question that tends to bewilder and immobilize the child. Depending upon the degree of immaturity and incompleteness of the child's self, he pieces together a reply, but he cannot do it easily. Because he does not experience his personal identity apart from family identity, it is most difficult for him to speak of himself in any clearly separate way. On the other hand, if one observes clinically the same child's nonverbal communications—his attitudes, postures, and actions—both alone and with his family group, one may draw reasonable inferences as to the child's sense of personal identity as related to his family identity.

If one pursues the same experiment with an adult person, the results are varied and often unpredictable. An adult person, generally regarded as an autonomous being, is assumed to know his own identity. Nevertheless, his reply to "Who are you? What is your opinion of yourself?" is often hedged and qualified by his inner image of his interrogator, and the interrogator's presumed image of him. Such an answer inevitably expresses the circular interdependence of image of self with image of others; it echoes the primary interrelatedness of self-identity with family identity.

One may also observe that, in proportion to the depth of personality impairment in the adult, the response to the question will tend to be like that of the child. In emotionally disordered, immature adult persons the self-concept or identity tends to be conflicted, fragmented, and confused. The individual experiences himself in unintegrated parts; he is unable to pull the pieces of himself together into a whole person. This fragmentation in turn reflects a corresponding fragmentation of his image of family identity. The more distorted the personality, the less healthy are the basic layers of joined identity with family and the deeper the failure to differentiate an integrated separate self.

Moving a step further, one may try to conceptualize the psychological identity of a family pair, such as mother and child, or husband and wife, and also the psychological identity of the family group as an integrated unit. In the context of a family relationship or group, psychological identity refers to elements of joined psychic identity—the strivings, values, expectations, actions, fears, and problems of adaptation, mutually shared in or complemented by the role behaviors of members of the family group. In essence this is a segment of shared identity, reflected in layers of joined experience, and enacted in the reciprocal, or complementary family role behaviors of these joined persons.

It is this feature of family living that gives form to the standards and ideals of the family—the lines of authority, sexual differentiation, division of labor, and child-rearing attitudes. The psychological identity of a family pair or group determines the manner in which elements of sameness and difference among the personalities of family members are held in a certain balance. In some families, the interplay of members in their various family roles emphasizes the trends toward sameness over the trends toward difference. In other families, the opposite pattern may prevail. In disordered family groups, differences may be so intensified as to create a formidable barrier, which critically impairs the matrix for joined identity.

Stability

Psychological identity and stability of behavior must be considered together. The evolution of the identity of the individual, family pair, and family group through time achieves a clear definition only as we examine in a parallel procedure the stability of family functions. Stability of behavior is itself the end-product of complex, interdependent processes. The more important of these are: the continuity of identity in time; the control of conflict; the capacity to change, learn, fill new life roles, and achieve further development; and finally, the complementarity of family role relations. These are conceived as interwoven processes by which identity and stability are expressed in action. This manifold of family processes must be approached as a unity. It is hardly possible to evaluate family dynamics in any one of these dimensions except in the context of the others. In the over-all view of individual and family adaptation, it should be possible to define the balance of forces which contributes to successful adaptation and emotional health or the tendency to breakdown and illness.

Stability in its first phase epitomizes the capacity to maintain the sameness or continuity of a person or a group of persons through time. It is the maintenance of the integrity and continuity of identity under the pressure of changing life conditions. It assures the intactness and the wholeness of personal behavior in the face of the dangers of new experience. This is the conservative phase of the functions of stability. Its internal aspect is represented in the regulation of the balance of intrapsychic forces. This balance is maintained through the coordinated functioning of multiple mental processes—perception, memory, association, judgment, and control of emotion, anxiety, and conflict—through the implementation of specific mastery techniques and defenses. Such regulatory mechanisms, operating in harmony, control internal psychic equilibrium and contribute to the stabilization of personal identity in group integration.

Stability in interpersonal relations is a function of the interplay of the orientation to self and to group. The interaction of family members in their respective family roles governs the quality of stability of family relationships. It affects the capacity to cope with family conflict and restore balance following an emotional upset. Such stability may be maintained on the basis of a relatively static or rigid pattern of family role reciprocity or on the basis of a more flexible capacity to accommodate to change and achieve a new and improved level of reciprocity. One aspect of the function of stability fulfills the conservative requirement of protecting sameness and continuity; another aspect must make room for new experience, learning, and further development. The receptivity to new experience, the capacity to learn and grow, is the more open, more adventuresome aspect of life adaptation. It entails risk, but without risk the power to adapt to change and to grow is lost. Effective adaptation requires, therefore, a favorable balance between the need to protect sameness and continuity and the need to accommodate to change. It requires preservation of the old combined with receptivity to the new, a mixture of conservatism and an emotional readiness to "live dangerously." Evaluation of the relations of individual and family requires assessment of both aspects, stability in its conservative, relatively static phase, and stability in its more open, flexible, adventuresome phase, which makes possible adaptation to new experience, learning, and further growth of personality.

The achievement of stability in these aspects is, in turn, influenced by the capacity to cope with conflict. The control of conflict is a special dimension relevant to the relations of individual and family. The failure to find effective solution leads to adaptive breakdown and emotional illness. Within the individual, the core of pathogenic conflict and the associated attempts at control and restitution correspond most closely to the dynamic bases for clinical psychiatric diagnosis. By tracing the fate of the core conflicts within the individual and between family members, one can trace the relations between adaptive breakdown and illness in one individual and pathogenic disturbance in family relationships.

Within the individual, conflict, anxiety, and symptoms defectively controlled represent vulnerability to adaptive breakdown and mental illness. Coexistent with these forces are the potential capacities for finding solutions to such conflict or for establishing a protective equilibrium or compensating for the effects of conflict. Of special importance in this connection is the ability to achieve patterns of family role complementarity. The term "complementarity" refers to specific patterns of family role relations that provide satisfactions, avenues of solution of conflict, support for a needed self-image, and buttressing of crucial forms of defenses against anxiety. Complementarity in family role relations may be further differentiated as being either positive or negative. Positive complementarity exists when the members of family pairs and triads experience mutual fulfillment of need in a way which promotes positive emotional growth of the relationships and of the interacting individuals. Negative complementarity in family relations signifies a buttressing of defenses against pathogenic anxiety but does not significantly foster positive emotional growth. Negative complementarity mainly neutralizes the destructive effects of conflict and anxiety and barricades family relationships and vulnerable family members against trends toward disorganization.

A mutual two-way process of influence is present. The configuration of conflict that prevails in a family pair or group influences the fate of internalized patterns of conflict within individual family members. Family conflict may conceivably provide a path for the solution of individual conflict, or family conflict may push the conflicted individual toward a state of emotional decompensation. But the individual also influences family conflict by projecting elements of his inner emotional life into processes of family interaction. In any case, contemporary patterns of family conflict may potently affect the ultimate outcome of individual conflicts that have been internalized at earlier periods of development.

Conflict in family relations may be benign or malignant. Benign forms may stimulate growth whereas malignant forms may predispose to a breakdown in the emotional balance of family relationships and a breakdown in individual adaptation. This occurs if the family conflict exceeds the potential for complementarity among family members, expressed in terms of their reciprocal role adaptation.

Within this conceptual frame, it is possible to define the pathogenic areas of family conflict, those which push the stabilizing or homeostatic functions toward a state of decompensation and thus intensify trends toward disintegration, regression, breakdown of communication, and emotional alienation. At the opposite pole, it is possible to define the potential in the reciprocity of family role relations for providing paths of solution to conflict, establishing effective compensation or complementarity, and fostering support of new levels of identification. An approximation of these trends enables us to view more clearly the forces that predispose to illness within the broader frame of total functioning and the residual potentials for promoting health.

Because the biosocial organization of behavior is distinct at the levels of individual, family pair, and family group, psychological identity and stability at these several levels carry analogous though not identical meanings. There is an essential continuity between identity and stability in the autonomous individual and identity and stability in the family pair and group. The dynamic interrelations between the identity of the autonomous individual and identity of the family pair or group are influenced by the evolving pattern of family role relations and the stabilization of these relations. These relations are affected by the ability to conserve identity through time, the ability to control conflict, and the ability to adapt to change, learn, and achieve further development.

These concepts are schematically represented in the following diagram:

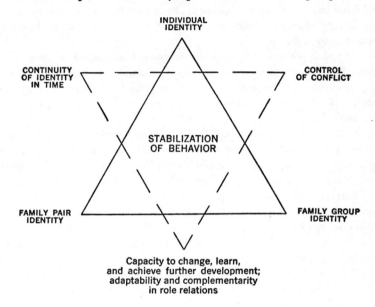

The Chronological Factor

Thus far we have described a conceptual approach to the problem of the dynamic interrelations of individual and family that appraises these relations at a given point in time. If we want to compare the relations of individual and family behavior at the present time with corresponding configurations of past relations, the task may be pragmatically divided into three phases: childhood, adolescence, and adulthood. At each stage of maturation the pattern of relations of individual and family is likely to be distinct. For the child the main problems of adaptation are contained within the family fold—child-mother, child-father, child-sibling. For the adolescent the main problems of adaptation are sexual maturation and differentiation and emotional preparation for the tasks of adult living.

The evolving identity of the adolescent must accommodate to the expanding and changing roles that he must fill within the family and also in the larger community. For the adult the main adaptational problems within the family group lie in the relations of husband-wife, father-mother, parent-child. The requirements of integration into intrafamilial roles must be harmonized with the corresponding requirements of extrafamilial social and occupational roles.

A comparison is drawn traditionally between adaptation in the family of childhood and the family of adulthood. The intermediate phase—adaptation in the family of adolescence—merits special attention because until now it has been somewhat neglected.

The adult person is chronologically mature and has reached the peak of his physical growth. His personality patterns are presumed to be fully differentiated and entrenched; he is regarded as a relatively autonomous person, with greater freedom of choice and control over his environment. This is the adult person in the abstract. In actuality, however, he is often not fully developed, regardless of his chronological maturity and physical size. His life performance frequently does not match his age and stature; he matures in a patchy, irregular way; he achieves only a limited power of choice; he is still critically dependent upon his environment. His level of functioning and adaptation to significant life roles varies accordingly. He may perform adequately in his job and do poorly within his family. The quality of this adaptation, adequate in some roles, failing in others, is deeply influenced by his on-going family relationships. Within certain disordered families, the attainment of full emotional maturity is hardly possible. The psychosocial configuration of the family group is such that it rigidly binds the individual to a few limited roles from which he cannot escape, and within which it is extremely difficult to accommodate to change, to learn, and to grow. Psychotherapists who pursue their professional work with members of families and communities in which persons are, in effect, trapped to limited, stereotyped roles know how difficult it is to achieve a cure of such persons. This is notably the case in the suburbs of New York or in such special communities as Hollywood. But such persons are extraordinarily sensitive to critical shifts in the prevailing pattern of role relations within the family.

Bearing in mind such considerations, it is necessary to qualify the traditional conception that adult personality is fixed and static in its organization and no longer subject to significant change by the social environment. Such a point of view underplays both the potential plasticity and vulnerability of adult personality, as is clearly illustrated in many kinds of clinical situations. For example, we find that following divorce, one of the partners may suffer a breakdown as a result of the loss of the emotional support of the marital partner. It is this characteristic of adult personality that makes it advantageous to apply to the adult the theoretical model of a child's relations with environment, while respecting the essential differences between child and adult.

But this traditional misconception can be changed, indeed revolutionized, by the intervention of a family psychiatrist. Operating with a full knowledge of the original, disturbed family pattern and cognizant of each and every shift in family relationships, he is able to guide these individuals to a new and healthier identity and stability pattern by treating them as individuals and, at the same time, as members of the family group.

Breakdown

Psychoanalytic theory underscores the principle that the seeds of mental illness are sowed in the family of childhood; but the growth of these bad seeds into emotionally twisted adult persons becomes meaningful only as we study the relations of individual and family in adolescence and adult life as thoroughly as we have studied these relations in the family of childhood.

Psychiatrists have acquired adeptness in the retrospective study of mental illness, in the minute examination of family histories. But they have not yet cultivated an equivalent skill in the study of family process here and now. This is the next step. It would add a new dimension to our insights into mental illness as an on-going process that changes with time and the conditions of group adaptation.

Psychiatric disorders are neither static nor isolated entities. While the patterns of vulnerability to illness are laid down in childhood, the fate of this vulnerability is determined by the interpersonal experiences of later life. Adolescence is notoriously a phase of transitional development within which the vulnerability to breakdown is intensified. Predispositions to illness are brought into sharp relief. The struggle to entrench personal identity and to integrate personal drives with the conditions of social living, and the tension of harmonizing the requirements of family roles with those of extrafamilial roles play a tremendous part in dictating the destiny of these predispositions to illness.

Moving a step further, when an individual reaches adult age, marries and creates a new family, the pattern of his adult family may be similar to or differ from the family of his childhood. In adulthood the individual may perpetuate an old and familiar family pattern or defensively take flight to a radically different one. In choosing a marital partner and raising children, he initiates a new set of close relationships which may either give him added protection against mental illness or aggravate his inclination toward it. Thus vulnerability to illness is lessened or magnified. A circular process is involved. Conflict internalized at earlier phases of family integration influences the present patterns of conflict in family relationships, and contemporary conflict in family relations influences the expression and fate of the older levels of conflict.

Thus far studies of the ongoing process of mental illness have emphasized one-sidedly the effects of specific psychiatric treatment. But we must examine with equal care the concurrent environmental factors that influence the course of illness, in particular the matrix of ongoing family processes. We do not understand well enough why certain apparently hopeful psychiatric patients receiving the best kind of therapy nonetheless fail to get well. Nor do we know exactly why it is that certain other patients, though untreated, achieve a "spontaneous recovery." Cured cases are more frequently reported than uncured cases. We know too little about the failures in psychiatric treatment. It would be illuminating to investigate more fully how it is that certain seemingly favorable cases of illness fail to recover despite optimal psychiatric therapy, whereas certain untreated cases spontaneously heal themselves. There are instances on record of dramatic and remarkable recovery from both psychoses and neuroses, despite a complete lack of systematic psychiatric therapy. In mysterious fashion catatonia and acute states of hysterical, phobic, obsessional, and hypochondriacal disorder seem sometimes suddenly to be relieved. But what looks like a miracle is not really so. Such occurrences in all probability represent a peculiarly fortunate set of interpersonal circumstances which favor the movement toward recovery. Were it possible to trace step by step the interpersonal experiences of patient and family or equivalent group relationships, we might have a better measure of environmental forces which are conducive to the perpetuation of illness or a spontaneous return to health.

The importance of this line of investigation is a growing one. In the psychiatry of children it is amply reflected in a trend which emphasizes mother-child interaction as a two-way process and the need to examine mother-child interaction within the frame of the total psychological life of the family. Within this broader matrix the behavioral reactions of the child are checked against all combinations of family relationships which affect one another in a circular manner—parent-child, inter-parent, parent-sibling, and inter-sibling pairs and related triads. In the psychiatry of adults a similar emphasis is emerging. Numerous studies are under way which focus on the family processes which influence mentally sick persons. At the present time much attention is paid to the families of schizophrenic patients. What is really needed, however, is an across-the-board program for the investigation of the relations of individual and family as these affect the life history of all major types of psychiatric disorder, the neuroses, character disorders, psychosomatic disorders as well as the psychoses.

The relations of family environment and schizophrenic illness are presently being explored in a variety of ways. There is the work of Jackson and Bateson[1] on family homeostasis and communication processes as related to schizophrenia, and the studies of the schizophrenic patient and family at the National Institute of Mental Health by Bowen, Wynne, and Hamburg.[2] There is the project of the Boston Psychiatric Home Treatment Service, which provides emergency treatment of mental patients within their own homes. There are also the special family studies of Lindemann[3] on bereavement, the research of Caplan[4] on the effects of crisis situations on family mental health, the studies of well and sick families and the role of cultural values by Spiegel and Kluckhohn,[5] the investigations of family theme by Mendell,[6] family image by Hess and Handel,[7] the clinical investigations of family diagnosis and therapy by Ackerman, Gomberg, etc.[8] The schizophrenic child and family are the focus of a number of special investigations by Goldfarb, Szurek, and Behrens.[9]

Of special significance in relation to the contemporary rise of juvenile delinquency is the investigation of psychopathic tendencies as these are influenced by the phenomena of family life. Johnson and Szurek[10] have illuminated some aspects of this problem, with special emphasis on the induction of delinquent behavior in a child as a response to the unconscious expectations of the parents.

Systematic elucidation of the major categories of mental illness as a family process is clearly a matter for the future. Not too much can yet be said definitively because thus far so little has been done. But the investigative work that should be undertaken is now clearly marked out. (See Chapter 20, Problems of Family Research.)

Mental illness limited to a single member of a family group is a rarity. More often than not there are multiple illnesses. The question then arises as to how these illnesses are phenomenologically related one to another. Are the relations of several illnesses within a given family fortuitous, accidental? Is it that the course of illness in one family member proceeds independently of the course of illness of another family member, or is it that the two illnesses interact and affect one another? Clinical observation brings to life dramatic examples of interlocking psychopathology in family relationships. Such observation underscores the importance of such interlocking processes as *folie à deux,* cases of mutually dependent psychosis in husband and wife, mother and child, or a sibling pair. There are, too, the striking phenomena of sado-masochistic marital partnerships, the coupling in marriage of a psychopathic drinking man and an obsessionally conscientious child-wife. Moving further there are instances of homosexual behavior linked to a domineering, possessive mother and a remote, reticent, inaccessible father. Then there are the many cases of psychopathic personality with criminal tendencies influenced profoundly by a disorganized, chaotic family pattern.

It is the growing recognition of these principles that has influenced the development of "open" hospitals and day and night hospital programs for the care of the mentally ill. The community at large is not yet tuned to the idea of viewing emotional illness as a problem of the entire family group. Families as families do not yet present themselves, therefore, to community clinics or mental health practitioners as sick units. They follow rather the traditional habit of referring one member of the family with emotional difficulties for study and treatment, but this first referral calls attention to the psychopathological disturbances of the entire family group.

Such phenomena of interlocking psychiatric disturbances in family relationships can readily be illustrated by a typical neurotic family. The first person referred represented a link in a long chain of interconnected family events revealing the multiple disturbances in the family group. The story of this family serves to pinpoint the special role of the family-oriented psychiatrist.

Here is a middle-class family, newly rich within one generation, dedicated to the goals of security, conspicuous consumption, and entrenchment of a favored position in the community. Every member of this family is plagued with a sense of inferiority and fear of rejection by the socially elite.

The family group consists of five people, the parents and three children. The parents are in their mid-fifties. The oldest child is a daughter, twenty-four years old, married, with one child. The second, a daughter, is twenty-one years old and single. The third is a son, fifteen years old. The son-in-law is assimilated to the pattern of this family, is deferential to the symbols of paternal authority, and is incorporated into the father's business. The father is an aggressive, hard-driving, self-made businessman, who strives mightily to fortify and aggrandize his power position in the community. In the wider community he is a "big man," a V.I.P. Within the family he is both king and slave. He is given to irascible temper outbursts. He has prudish, stereotyped, exacting standards. He asserts a rigid, arbitrary, but impotent control over the family. At the same time he is trapped to the role of serving his family with lavish indulgences. The mother and children are intimidated by his loud dictatorship but are frequently able to evade its worst aspects while exploiting the father for his material services. The mother is a childlike person whose sole concern is her looks and social status. She plays the role of the helpless but charming baby doll. She is continuously absorbed in enhancing her status through her dress and appearance. She has a history of asthma and an acute psychotic depression. The older daughter is much like her mother, a spoiled child, pervasively harassed by anxiety. She is a demanding, greedy person, wrapped up in her looks and intensely competitive for social recognition. The younger daughter is much like her father, aggressive, hard-hitting, agitated, fretful, and grandiose. The youngest child is the only son, nervous, restless, provocative, nagged and pushed by his family. He is the whipping boy for his father and fulfills a significant role as the family nuisance.

The parents absorb themselves with aggrandizing social activities and expensive, though boring, vacations. They buy the allegiance and servile respect of the daughters with costly gifts. Occasionally, the sisters are solicitous of the younger brother but are mainly preoccupied with their own pursuits.

Here is a frightened and tyrannical man married to a child-wife. He aggrandizes himself as a family god, but he is a tin god. He demands adoration from his wife and children, but he is imprisoned in his self-imposed role as idol. He is both master and slave. He dictates, but he also caters to the ceaseless, exorbitant demands of his baby-doll wife and spoiled children. The mother plays the part of the grand dame, exquisitely clothed, unassailably the prettiest girl in the family, who intimidates husband and children with the threat of another nervous breakdown. The father is seductive with the older daughter, who with tongue in cheek plays up to her father-god. She flatters him with her show of warmth and adulation while picking his pocketbook. The middle child develops into a fiercely aggressive person like her father. She has a mortal dread of her father, but she becomes locked in a life and death competitive war with him. She rebels against his domination in a desperate, panicky way, but she fails to break free of his control. Her mother admires her for her show of gusty strength and "brilliance." The mother looks to her to act as her protector in quarrels with the father, a kind of second husband. This daughter shies away from competing with the feminine wiles of her mother and sister. She retreats from the field when her sister is seductive with the father. She is unable to fulfill herself in a love relationship with a man. She entices men into a competitive, teasing struggle, only to reduce them to rubble. The boy, unwanted, neglected, becomes the family clown. The children cater to the mother's demands, do not compete with her role as the pretty baby doll, but feel no closeness to her and are secretly contemptuous of her as a useless, empty, unimportant person. It can be seen from this description that the emotional disturbances of the parental relationship are parceled out in a special way among the children.

The clinical diagnoses on each of these persons are as follows: The son is a severe neurotic with pre-delinquent tendencies; the mother is a socially integrated infantile character, somewhat paranoid with borderline psychotic tendencies; the father is a phobic person with deep castration fears cloaked by powerful counterphobic reaction formations. He has concealed inferiority feelings and pervasive anxieties concerning his physical health. The older daughter is a hysteric with intense fears of illness and death. The younger daughter is a deeply alienated person with a compulsion neurosis, a deep core of depression, and death anxiety.

The first person referred from this family group for psychiatric treatment is the son. The spur for referral comes from the boy's school: he is failing academically. This first referral initiates a chain of events which ultimately brings the entire family to the psychiatrist. In sequence, first comes the boy, then the parents, then the younger daughter, and, finally, the older daughter. Over a period of years, every family member except the father receives psychotherapy. The father, though closely invested in the therapy of other family members, maintains a defensive denial as to his personal need for therapy.

The boy is a confused, unhappy, lost child, picked on by every member of his family and battered from pillar to post. He serves as the scapegoat for his father's violent outbursts. He is treated with indifference by his narcissistic mother. He is alternately harangued by his parents and ignored. Despite his acute fright of his father, he feels closer to father than to mother. He forces attention from his father with his provocative, irresponsible, passively disobedient behavior. He also entertains and disarms his parents of hostile punitive power with his clownish antics. He eludes the worst of his father's attacks. Despite horrifying phantasies of violent assault he has the urge to defy his father; he wants to "get away with murder."

With six months of psychotherapy, the boy shows substantial improvement. In periodic interviews arranged for both boy and father and focused on father-son conflict, the boy is able eventually to stand up to his father with some show of self-respect. Gradually, the father, with increasing confidence in the therapist, surrenders some of his rigid dogma, curbs his tyrannical abuse, and tries to understand his son better. As the father gives ground to the therapist and the relations of son and father improve, the mother responds to this change in a special way. She shifts some of her deference from the father to the psychiatrist and alters her previous family role. She competes with her own son to get the psychiatrist's attention for herself. She is encouraged in this direction by the recognition of her son's greater assertiveness with his father. She begins to imitate the boy. She takes sides with him in defying the father's authority. She proceeds to accuse the father of neglecting both herself and the boy. This precipitates critical quarrels between the parents, which culminate in unfounded accusations of infidelity. She exploits these accusations as a weapon by which to coerce the father into catering to more of her demands. She torments him with her bitter reproaches, imprisons him in the home, and for a time virtually makes his life unbearable. The mother's behavior has the effect, of course, of diverting attention from the boy to herself. It shifts the focus of overt conflict from the father-son pair to the parental pair. The movement of the critical zone of conflict away from the son to the mother-father relationship is so sharp as to necessitate a new level of psychiatric intervention into the pathology of this family. The psychiatrist proceeds at this point to treat mother and father together. After a period of therapy for the conflict of the parental pair, the psychiatrist engages the mother in individual therapy. The crisis in the parental relationship is brought under control. Parental relations improve very much.

In the meantime, with one or another pretext, the boy is withdrawn from treatment. He is sufficiently well advanced in his progress to hold his own.

During the period of acute conflict between mother and father, their relations with the two daughters also shift. As the mother pursues her campaign of villification of the father, she recruits the sympathy and support of the second daughter. She presses this daughter for more and more devotion to herself as she builds up the barrier between herself and her husband. But the daughter, alerted to the change in her brother and vigilant against further exploitation by her mother in this critical exacerbation of parental conflict, appeals to the psychiatrist on her own behalf. This begins for her a long period of analytic therapy, which brings about a fundamental reorientation of personality. She removes herself from the family to begin a new life in an apartment of her own. Ultimately, the older daughter, standing on the sidelines and watching the remarkable therapeutic transformation in the younger daughter, becomes envious, faces her own problems more honestly, and she too requests analytic treatment.

Here we have an example of an emotionally sick family. The identity of this family is epitomized in a value orientation that emphasizes material security, acquisitiveness, competition, conspicuous consumption, and aggressive mastery. The mother is a hungry parasite, the father a glorified, power-driven slave. The children are caught in the whirlpool of the parental conflict and accommodate to family positions required of them by the distortions of the parental relationship. The personality disorders of the various family members are structured according to the dynamic interplay of these persons acting out their respective, mutually interdependent family roles.

Part 2

CLINICAL
ASPECTS

CHAPTER 7

CLINICAL ASPECTS OF FAMILY DIAGNOSIS

MOST PEOPLE believe that there is an easy distinction between mentally healthy and mentally sick families. On closer inspection, however, the clinician finds that such is not the case in our society. The distinction is relative rather than absolute. There is no ideally healthy family. Families are either predominantly healthy or predominantly sick, psychiatrically speaking. Moving one step further, it is possible to distinguish in a given family some components of family functioning that are mainly healthy and others that are mainly disabled. If for practical, clinical purposes it is useful and necessary to distinguish between well and sick families, let us think of sick families as those which progressively fail to carry out their essential family functions.

It is possible to conceptualize along a single continuum degrees of success and failure in the fulfillment of essential family functions. From one point of view, we may grade the depth and malignancy of failure of family adaptation in accordance with the level at which the family deals with its problems.

1. The family confronts, accurately defines, and achieves a realistic solution of its problems.
2. Though unable to achieve a realistic solution, the family can nevertheless contain the problem and control the potentially noxious effects, while giving itself a longer period within which to find a solution.
3. Unable to find an effective solution or to contain the destructive effects of conflict, the family responds to the tension of failure with an "acting out"

pattern of impulsive, ill-judged, self-defeating, harmful behavior. Sometimes the family as a group seeks a scapegoat, either within the family or outside. In this condition the family as family cannot long maintain its defenses.

4. With persistent failure at the preceding three levels, the family shows increasing signs of emotional disintegration, which in some circumstances may culminate in disorganization of family ties.

Within this scheme, it becomes possible to specify quantitatively any degree of failure of a family to solve its problems, maintain unity and balanced role relations, execute its necessary functions, and learn and grow in a creative direction.

Whatever its degree of failure, the disordered family may show a predominance of social pathology or of psychopathology. Social pathology and psychopathology may coexist or they may not. Severe disorder of both kinds overlap in some families. Other families, superficially integrated as a social unit, are marked by severe psychopathology; they seem able to maintain the surface semblance of unity and conformity to community requirements, while consisting inwardly of seriously disturbed, alienated persons. In other family types, the opposite pattern may prevail and in response to a family crisis, the social pathology for a time may be serious, although one cannot immediately detect signs of psychopathology.

It is of considerable clinical importance that the means by which a given family copes with its problems and conflicts varies with its social status and cultural position. In a poor family, the primary pressure to maintain family organization is economic. For this reason, the wage-earning role of the father is of paramount importance. In upper class families, the father need not escape to the corner saloon and return home drunk. He is more likely to seek release in an extramarital love affair. In some sections of society, one finds progressively malignant forms of social pathology in the structure of the family group. Such families may be broken by divorce or desertion, or they may disintegrate because they are economically insolvent. In some families one or both parents may be dead. Occasionally, the social disorganization of the family is related to an absentee father, one who is in the armed services, unemployed, alcoholic, critically ill, or crippled. Some of these become "fringe" families, or the so-called "hard core" families, who live on the edge of the community economically, socially or both. Often, they are underprivileged families and members of minority groups. Where social disorganization of the family persists and turns chronic, it leads ultimately to psychopathological distortion. Such families, socially deviant and unintegrated with the community, breed nonconforming and sick behavior. The adolescents frequently become delinquent. In these socially chaotic family situations, multiple forms of psychiatric illness and social maladjustment emerge.

When the social pathology is severe and the disorganization of family relationships has progressed to the extreme, clinical experience suggests that members of such families are frequently not amenable to individual psychotherapy as it has been traditionally practiced. Often, such persons are labeled by the clinician as uncooperative and untreatable. This indictment is sometimes prejudiced and unwarranted. It derives in part from an unconscious tendency in the psychotherapist to reject a patient who does not submit to his conditions for therapy. But this reaction reveals a deficiency in understanding. One cannot administer psychotherapy to a starving person or to one who is in danger of freezing to death.

In these socially and economically maimed families, the human situation is critical and demands emergency measures. There is real danger, not merely neurotically imagined danger; and the danger is a shared one. It is only natural that members of such families should resist individual psychotherapy. They feel impelled to mobilize their energies for neutralizing the real threats in their environment before they can consider attending to their inner emotional conflicts. Food and warmth come before psychotherapy. The first priority for such an unfortunate family is emergency help, an all-out effort to save the life of the family through social therapy, to neutralize the real threats to its security, integrity and continuity. First come support and reinforcement for all the failing family functions, food, housing, and opportunity for work, the restoration of the central relationships within the family, particularly the bonds of man and wife, father and mother, parent and child. In some instances, without help in the way of housing, employment, nursing of the sick, etc., the restoration of family unity cannot be established even minimally. When some semblance of social integrity for the family group is restored and the family is again a "going concern," it then becomes possible to achieve access to significant levels of family conflict and to the disturbances internalized in the personalities of individual members.

Classical examples of such difficult situations are to be found in instances of adolescents of disintegrated families who erupt into psychopathic behavior, or of Negro children from underprivileged families who react with isolation and depression and develop learning blocks in school. Often it is not possible to induce such persons into a psychotherapeutic experience until first steps are taken to deal with the emergency status of the entire family. The psychopathic adolescent who is sorely in need of psychiatric therapy may prove incorrigibly resistant when he feels he alone is to be made over. He will often prove more accessible if he and his family together become the unit of diagnosis and therapy. So also with the emotionally disturbed children of underprivileged, minority families, Negroes or newly immigrated Puerto Ricans.

Indeed, whatever the social and economic level, it is clearly recognized that family life acts as a kind of conveyor belt for pathogenic conflict and anxiety. In other words, the family becomes a source of sick emotional contagion. The link of individual and family identity is so basic, so pervasive, as to preclude completely the possibility of any one member's being immune to the effect of emotional contagion.

It is true, of course, that the greatest intensity of the destructive effects of anxiety may concentrate now in one, now in another part of the family. It may shift erratically from one person to another, from one family pair to another, or a family member may be helplessly sucked up in the swirl of uncontrolled violent conflict in another family pair. One family member may achieve a partial immunity through victimizing one or several other members of the family; that is, one member of the family may save himself from the more injurious aspects of psychopathological contagion by keeping another member of the family sick. Time and time again, we see families in which the psychiatric illness of one member represents a symptomatic result of the need of several other family members to protect themselves; in other words, one part of the family holds itself in one piece at the expense of another part.

There are, on the other hand, families in which the immunity to the destructive effects of emotional contagion is virtually nil and just about every member of the family breaks down. Each of them shows some effect of emotional disintegration, and each breaks down in a different way. Because the personal history of each family member is in some part unique, the corresponding patterns of vulnerability are different. And when the family breakdown finally comes, the symptoms of illness necessarily differ from person to person.

We need not go far to identify manifestations of family breakdown. There are unmistakable indications of emotional alienation, isolation of family members from one another, the building up of critical barriers to communication, the emergence of family factions and splits. There is clear evidence of a pattern of conflict and hostility that disintegrates family unity. Often the family breaks up into separate camps, and one part of the family is pitted against another. Such trends demoralize the members so that the family as a group can no longer fulfill even its minimal functions. Familiar symptoms of family disintegration in young children are disturbances of social development and learning difficulties; the avoidance of association with peers; in adolescents there are signs of disorganization, confusion, and alternating waves of conformity and rebellious, delinquent conduct.

Total breakdown presents a bleak picture, but breakdown in the psychological operations of the family group does not occur all at once. Initially, evidence of a family breakdown may be relatively localized and impair ability to confront and correctly define problems only in certain spheres; that is, at first, the family's capacity for problem-solving and decision-making is impaired in a circumscribed way. The disintegrative effects of such breakdown may therefore be relatively subtle in the beginning, but by degrees they spread progressively to affect more and more of the family's basic functions.

Clinically, we must also take into account the varying capacity of families to contain those problems for which they cannot find a solution, while endeavoring to make some tolerable restitution. Such compensatory behavior in certain families is possible only when, despite conflict and alienation, some family pairs are able to maintain a satisfying pattern of complementarity. This means that the members of a family pair (husband and wife or parent and child) may damage one another in one way and yet in another provide some degree of mutual support and complementation of one another's needs. It is on this basis that it becomes possible for one member, though distressed and maladjusted, to complement the needs arising out of the emotional illness of another family member. Sometimes such complementary behavior is buttressed by an unconscious conspiracy of two members of the family to displace their hostility onto a scapegoat, who may be another member of the family or a person outside.

From the psychiatric point of view, it is imperative to trace clearly the dynamic relations between specific trends of family conflict and the intrapsychic conflicts within an individual member. This relationship is basic to the question of individual and family stability, and the stability of individual personality is partly contingent upon the stability of the family. Critical tensions are apt to emerge from family situations in which the integrative patterns of both individual and family group lean toward a rigid, static form of equilibrium, sharply constricting the possible range of reciprocal family role adaptations. The pattern of reciprocity in family role relations, man to wife, father to mother, parent to child, influences in a fundamental way the vicissitudes of personal conflict and the fate of individual psychopathological symptoms.

The pathology of some families is such that it makes much the same kind of person of all members and produces essential similarities in the manifestations of psychiatric illness. In other families, the opposite is true. Perhaps the family pathology is such that the children divide into "good" and "bad"; one child is a conforming, socially acceptable person and the other the "black sheep." Or in another family, composed of the parents and three daughters, each daughter fulfills a special destiny, predetermined by the mother's expectations: one fulfills the role of the intellectual genius; the second becomes the "body beautiful," who turns into a respectable prostitute by marrying a rich man whom she does not love; and the third cultivates the career of a social deviant, a renegade, a bohemian artist.

The family as a group develops a major pattern; individual members or family pairs may echo this pattern, inject opposing ones or act out minor patterns. In some, the major area of stress centers in the marital relations; in others, in parent-child relations; in still others, it centers in a struggle entailed in reconciling the requirements of multiple roles, or in entrenching the position of the family in the wider community. Stress and conflict emerge when the behavior of a member in one family role fails to complement the needs of the member in the reciprocal role.

But whatever the pattern—and we recognize countless patterns of family behavior—it is useful in a basic sense to think of the family as a kind of carrier of elements predisposing both to mental illness and mental health. Degrees of success or failure of adaptation in the paired family roles of husband and wife, father and mother, parent and child, child and sibling, bear directly on the question of staying well or getting sick. This is a function of the individual and the family group environment, not of the individual alone. What are the clinical psychodynamic and social features which distinguish predominantly sick from relatively healthy types of families? Why does one type, generation after generation, multiply the crop of mentally sick people? Why does the other produce a sturdy lot?

It is not the individual personality of the parent alone, mother or father. It is a paradox that certain pairs of neurotic parents, despite distortions of individual personality, interact in such a way as to create emotionally healthy children. Other pairs, in which the man and woman are apparently healthy persons, produce disturbed children. We do not claim this to be the rule, but it does occur. How does this come about?

Certain persons, fairly stable prior to marriage, break down afterwards. Certain others, critically unbalanced prior to marriage, attain following marriage a remarkable degree of stability. Some marital pairs maintain emotional balance just so long as they are without offspring. The advent of a child disrupts the pre-existing marital balance. To contrast with this, there are those other parental combinations that hang together only as long as they are absorbed in rearing children. When the children are grown, the parents move apart. One can multiply many times relevant empirical observations such as these.

We have said that psychiatric patients come from disordered families and that the first family member referred for psychiatric care may prove to be the most or the least sick member of the group. If the psychiatrist exerts himself to inspect the relations of the primary patient with other family members, he will be rewarded with some cogent information. The primary patient, whether he be child or adult, proves often to be an emissary in disguise of an emotionally warped family group. Frequently, one factor in the motivation for this first referral is that another family member seeks to control and make over the primary patient's behavior to better suit his or the family's needs; or to discipline and punish him; or to relieve an excessive burden of guilt; or to use the primary patient as a scapegoat behind whom other family members may hide their own psychiatric warp. Occasionally, the tendency is to send first to the psychiatrist the weakest and most defenseless member of the family, a child or the more docile of the marital partners.

For example, a man of middle age, successful and holding a position of prestige in the community but severely neurotic, confused, and unhappy in his family life, refers for consultation first his niece, then his second wife, using these persons as scouts to test the psychiatrist's benign intentions. Then, reassured against his fear of harm, he requests psychiatric help for himself. Such an individual often proves to be the most sick family member and the center of destructive force in family relations. To a varying extent the initial psychiatric referral may reflect the unseen purpose of restoring a pre-existing emotional balance or power alignment in family relations. Thus, the first contact with the psychiatrist may be a symptom of pathological family equilibrium.

A close inspection of the inner emotional life of the family reveals other things. Each family tends to be characterized by typical foci of anxiety and conflict. These foci come sharply into view when the family relations fail to meet the emotional expectations of its members. Sometimes the patterns of anxiety and conflict are well established and stable, sometimes erratic and shifting in their expression.

In one such pattern, the main conflict is contained and reflected in the personality of a particular family member; the personality of this member becomes, so to say, the dramatic expression of the pattern of stress that characterizes the particular family group. For example, the emerging personality of an only child epitomizes the chronic conflict and unhappiness of his parents; or one child in a group of three becomes laden with guilt and repeatedly provokes punishment because his birth induced a long illness in a martyred, hypochondrical mother.

In other patterns, the central conflict is fixed in the interactional pattern of a particular family pair and continuously lived out in the relationship of these two people. Let us say, a man with inferiority feelings and fears of exploitation comes to feel that all he is good for in the family is to provide money. The wife's dependence on his earnings and his habitual resentment of her demands create persistent conflict between them.

Sometimes, the typical conflict is reflected in a threesome in which, for example, father and mother vie for first place in the affections of an only child. Or perhaps it is a foursome, illustrated by a family group in which father and son team up against mother and daughter in order to exhibit the superiority of male over female; naturally mother and daughter join aggressively in self-defense.

When a person shows the first signs of falling ill emotionally, the initial disturbance is not simultaneously manifested in all areas of adaptation. The initial failure of adaptation may be relatively localized; it may occur only in the context of one particular family role. If, over the span of time, conflict and anxiety exceed the integrative resources that the individual can mobilize within his family group, the processes of disorganization and disablement spread to invade a progressively widening segment of adaptation. In intermediate stages, the individual may behave in a sick way in some roles and maintain a tolerable adaptation in others. Gradually, as the decompensation of defense against anxiety strikes deeper, adaptive performance fails in all the family roles and in the entire range of life activity.

During this process, it is possible to trace the individual's breakdown to a failure to find support within the family group for his personal need, for the solution of conflict, for the affirmation of a favored self-image, and for the maintenance of necessary forms of defense against anxiety. When on occasion the failure in adaptation seems to emerge first in an extrafamilial role, it is almost always the case that a needed role within the family has not found the required emotional support from the members in reciprocal family roles. For example, if a man demonstrates his masculinity as a tycoon in business but is a flabby bed partner to his wife, it is partly because his wife prefers it that way. Or if masculinity in business and masculinity in sexual relations are linked in the minds of the marital pair, failure in business and failure in bed are apt to occur together. On the other hand, sexual impotence is frequently selective in its expression: the same man may be a feeble lover with his wife and be joyously potent with another woman. If a man is crushed by castration fear, it is partly the man's personality, to be sure, but it is also the consquence of what a particular woman does to him.

Such expressions as "That woman makes me sick," "She'll be the death of me yet," or "She'll make a man of me" carry more than casual meaning. If a man is locked in chronic, competitive conflict with his boss, his relations with his wife may make the difference between successful working through this conflict and a depressive reaction and may also make the difference between success and failure on the job. If a boy is dominated and emasculated by an aggressive mother, the relations between the parents and the relations of father and son may make the difference between a final achievement of masculine strength and confidence or a movement toward homosexuality and delinquency.

Moving along a different path, we find that failure of integration in one family role may have the paradoxical effect of facilitating adequate performance in another family role. In certain personality types and family groups, it is possible on a selective basis to meet the requirements of some roles while proving inadequate to others. A woman on vacation with her husband may be an exciting sexual companion but revert to frigidity when she returns home to be with her children. A woman may be an effective marital partner and yet prove a total failure in the mother role or vice versa. Depending upon the personality make-up, the strivings and value orientation of the individual, and the psychological structure of his family, adaptation to one role may conflict sharply with the requirements of another or the two roles may have a mutually enhancing effect on adaptation.

Certain individuals may be observed to accommodate easily to the demands of several roles, others fit themselves only to the conditions of a single role while experiencing unbearable conflict in other roles. To illustrate, one woman feels deeply fulfilled as mother but feels acutely anxious when called upon to meet her husband's sexual needs. Another woman adapts well as mother and also as marital partner, yet she cannot play her part as hostess. Or she retreats from participation in social events, at which her husband looms as the important figure. Or a man richly meets his needs for self-esteem in his professional activity but grows insecure and irritable when he is expected to be more of a father to his children. Certain individuals with a detached temperament hold themselves aloof from involvement in any family role. The degree of success and failure in adaptation to family role is determined partly by individual personality, partly by interpersonal processes in the family that either support or clash with the individual's strivings.

The primary patient must therefore be viewed both as an individual in distress and as a symptomatic expression of family pathology. In this context the disturbances of the individual person may become the fulcrum or entering wedge for the further investigation of family pathology and intervention with suitable forms of family therapy.

The subtle and complex weave of relations of individual to family group and the accommodation of personality to role requirements play a large part in the maintenance of mental health or precipitation of breakdown. Where there is a failure to compensate family conflict or to restore balance of family roles following a disturbance, there is an inevitable aftermath in terms of dissension, breakdown of communication, frustration of need, and interpersonal alienation.

The relative ability of the individual to meet the requirements of multiple family roles and the effect on mental health of conflicting requirements in these roles applies not only to the child but to the adult member as well. Thus the relatedness of individual to group plays a potent role in the stabilization of the mental health of the adult.

The clinical importance of this problem is reflected in still another way. More often than not, the incentive for referral of a patient for psychotherapy is the outbreak of a disabling conflict in family relations, rather than the recognition of the existence of specific psychopathological symptoms in one family member. Such tends to be the case whether the individual patient refers himself or is sent by some other family member. Sometimes the existence of neurotic symptoms is not even known until the psychiatrist identifies them as such. Surely there is a relation between psychoneurotic personality and the occurrence of conflict in family relations. And this relation is a circular one. Conflict in family relations often precedes the emergence of psychoneurotic symptoms, and, at a later point in time, further conflict in family relations influences the fate of these symptoms or plays a role in the induction of new ones. Nonetheless, it is significant clinically that the main impetus toward psychiatric referral frequently comes from the suffering caused by family conflict rather than from the existence of mental symptoms per se.

In many families there is no thought of psychiatric referral as long as the neurotic tendencies of the family members are moderately well compensated within the pattern of reciprocal family role relations. The timing of the demand for professional help tends very strongly to coincide with the immediate, dramatic impact of a decompensation in the previous state of balance, which brings in its wake a distressing family conflict. Critical upsets of the emotional equilibrium of a family group thus become a significant mental health phenomenon.

Initially, the first point of reference is the disturbance of the individual patient. We move from this to the pattern of conflict in which this patient is locked with other family members. We seek to make clear the extent to which this family conflict is controlled, compensated, or decompensated and the extent to which it induces progressive damage of the relationship, impairs reciprocity in role relations, and therefore frustrates individual need. We then try to discern the extent to which the perpetuation of this family conflict intensifies the internal stress of the primary patient, and through this stress, predisposes to progressive disablement of functioning and the fixation of symptoms. Often it appears that prolonged family conflict tends to disintegrate a relationship, alienating the partners and promoting regressive behavior.

The crucial question is this: Is the integration of the family relationship preserved despite conflict, or does conflict tend to destroy the family tie, the link of individual and family identity, and thus cause an intensification of individual pathology?

It is within this broader frame that we try to establish the correlations of intrapsychic and interpersonal functioning. Within the frame of family interaction, we endeavor to determine the vicissitudes of the individual's capacity to resolve or at least mitigate the destructive effects of intrapsychic conflict. In this way we can correlate the dynamics of individual conflict with family conflict and relate the efficacy or failure of the individual's defenses against anxiety with the adequacy or decompensation of control mechanisms operating in conflicted family relationships. Within this same conceptual frame, it becomes possible to weigh the balance between areas of residually healthy adaptation and areas of unhealthy adaptation.

Does this point of view subordinate the significance of individual differences? I think not. If anything it tends rather to promote a more accurate appreciation of these very differences. The significance of difference is measured less by the objective nature of the difference and more by the meaning put upon it in interpersonal relations. In a similar sense, examination of the pattern of relatedness to family group provides a clearer understanding of the adaptive mechanisms by which the individual controls, defends against, and displaces his conflicts and anxieties. The processes of regulation and balancing of emotion and impulse, the neutralization of anxiety, are functions partly of individual personality, partly of role adaptation to the family group. Clinical diagnosis is perforce only partial unless all these elements—individual, role, family group, and their interrelationships—are taken fully into account.

CHAPTER 8

BEHAVIORAL DISTURBANCES OF THE CONTEMPORARY FAMILY

THE BEHAVIOR PATTERNS of the "contemporary family" cover a vast territory open to exploration. Reliable landmarks are few; much of the area is only vaguely mapped or entirely uncharted. What is really going on in the American family today? Judging by the newspapers, periodicals, and other mass media, we have a plethora of self-styled family experts who espouse every conceivable shade of opinion regarding family problems. Occasionally their pronouncements show true sincerity and wisdom. More frequently these diagnoses and the suggested remedies veer far from the mark. They tend to oversimplify complex problems, offer quick and ready nostrums that stir false hopes but bring in the end only deeper disillusionment. Often they harm rather than help, and they snare many victims. In them, we find no useful evidence about the American family except what we already know: the contemporary American family needs and wants help in these troubled times.

The design for family living in America is undergoing a remarkable transformation. Although there is no single type of contemporary American family, most observers would agree on a few basic characteristics of the contemporary family. First of all, the underlying direction of change, regardless of class of origin, is toward the standards and expectations of the middle class. The contemporary family is economically more secure; it enjoys more of the material things of life, though it is none the happier for it. It is responding to the inexorable effects of industrialization, urbanization, the advance of technology, and the corresponding clash of life values.

Familiar to all is the trend toward removal from the family of the traditional functions of work, religious worship, the nursing of the sick, and education. We also recognize the greater mobility of the family, the tendency to family breakdown, the rise in divorce, the change in sex morality, and the periodic surges of delinquency. But all these are expressions of the process of change.

According to Galdston,[1] the nineteenth century witnessed the family's adaptive response to the economic effects of the industrial revolution, but only now in the twentieth century are we confronted with the delayed social and psychological effects. Mowrer[2] alludes to the "loss of family consciousness." Parsons[3] speaks of the "disintegration of transition," a parallel process of disorganization and reorganization of family patterns. Burgess[4] summarizes the change as characterized by a downgrading of the authority of parents; a trend toward equalitarianism in the relations between male and female, with a relative decrease in the authority of the father; parental uncertainty; decline in the importance of grandparents; and the irresponsibility of children. According to Burgess, these trends spell a shift toward a new companionship form of family. Mead,[5] pointing to the recent trends toward an earlier age of marriage and a rise in birth rate, suggests that "the American family is flourishing"; she states at the same time, however, that fathers, being so well tamed domestically, are in danger of losing their sense of adventure and so may cripple their creativity.

Here we see a group of scholars ostensibly confronting the same family facts and yet reaching different conclusions. They differ among themselves and sometimes even differ with themselves. Clearly, we do not yet have the true or full answer. Perhaps the current features of fluidity, turmoil, and realignment of family parts are the harbinger of good things to come. We cannot be sure, however, whether the change augurs better or worse for the family's future. Yet, cognizant that the interrelations of the individual and the family group determine dispositions to illness and health, we cannot wait for final answers if we are truly concerned with the mental health problems of our time.

Let us first of all look at the contemporary American family, paying special attention to the middle-class, white, urban group that tends by and large to come most often into contact with mental health workers and with psychiatrists in particular. My account will necessarily be generalized and will emphasize emotional weaknesses and vulnerabilities so that the problems and conflicts of family here described out of context must appear stark and severe. But it should be remembered that problems and conflicts do not in themselves constitute pathology. What we are concerned with is the question of the family's resources for dealing with them and the measure of the family's basic health pitted against its stresses and strains.

The mark of our time is the peculiar disharmony of the individual's relations with wider society. A variety of hypotheses come to mind: Durkheim's[6] concept of anomie, Fromm's[7] emphasis on the trend to alienation, Riesman's[8] theory of the other-directed man. Whatever the term, all are agreed on a trend toward a sense of lostness, aloneness, and confusion of personal identity. One effect of this trend toward disorientation is that each person is thrown back upon his family group for the restoration of a sense of security, belongingness, dignity, and worth. The family is called upon to make up to its individual members in affection and closeness for the anxiety and distress that is the result of failure to find a safe place in the wider world. Individuals pitch themselves back on their families for reassurance as to their lovableness and worth. This pressure to compensate individual members with special security and affection imposes upon the family an extra psychic load. Is the contemporary family equipped to carry this extra load? No—not very well! The family tries but at best it achieves a precarious success and often it fails.

"Togetherness" is a family theme that currently draws wide acclaim. It is propagandized everywhere. It is so extremely popular precisely because there is not enough of it. When the family gets together on Sunday, the tension is sometimes unbearable; it gives rise to the "Sunday neurosis." Togetherness is a grand and wonderful thing, but as families are now constructed mere physical togetherness may be worse than none at all. There is a marked discontinuity in relations of individual, family, and wider society—an incongruence, a lack of fit. Perhaps Durkheim's concept of anomie applies to families as well as individuals.

The anxiety stirred by loss of horizontal support in the community seeps deeply into the heart of family and upsets the equilibrium of family relations. Imbalance with environment induces imbalance within the family. External conflict and internal conflict reinforce one another, with consequent impairment of basic family functions. Thus the family is plagued with insecurity both inside and outside.

Some families seek stability in a static pattern of conformity, but to which of the shifting community standards shall it conform? Those families that cling to a static stability soon find themselves out of step. Others make quick impulsive choices and find themselves in the wrong place. Some families move in wavelike fashion between periods of attempted static adaptation and sudden shifts, but they find themselves frustrated and disoriented in both phases. Some families console themselves with dreams of aggrandizement. Others plunge hectically into a ceaseless round of social activity, amusement, and play. Others retreat to the small comfort of "happiness drugs." Still others gravitate to a condition of passive resignation; in response to shared feelings of inferiority and powerlessness, the members of the family group slip into a routine. A family that fails to solve its conflict with the community cannot maintain a secure identity. It hangs suspended in mid-air and loses its capacity for harmonious functioning.

Today people are chronically unsure of what their family stands for, its strivings, standards and values. Mother, father, and child each perceive differently what the family is or ought to be. Parents do not perceive correctly their turbulent relations with the environment. They feel thwarted, confused, depressed, lonely, and irritable. They resort to scapegoating. They fall prey to petty bickering, argue over the wrong things, and tear each other down in a picky, fault-finding way. They either hit out blindly or seek surcease in inappropriate forms of escape. This anxiousness and confusion permeates all aspects of family living. In a vicious circle, external problems aggravate internal disturbances, and internal tensions intensify the hardships of external adaptation. This unbalances the relations of the parents, complicates questions of choice, and spills over to affect all problems having to do with the care and education of the children.

Parents are notorious doubters. They feel chronically uncertain. They try desperately to be independent, to make responsible decisions on their own. But the striving for independence and self-sufficiency is often spurious, exaggerated, and defensive in nature. And it comes at a high emotional cost. Young parents renounce the guidance of grandparents whose authority and wisdom they no longer respect. Often they deem their advice to be misleading, damaging, even treacherous. But the rejection of grandparents backfires. Young parents attach to themselves the same doubt and disrespect they project onto the grandparents.

When confused parents turn to friends, they are again thwarted because friends are equally unsure of themselves. They seek guidance from all quarters, pit one person's advice against another's, but really trust no one. Amid this turmoil, they turn hopefully to the experts, professionals in the fields of social work, education, religion, medicine, and psychiatry. They seek the omniscient; they grope for secure symbols of authority; but in the end, they grow chary of and cynical toward the advice of experts as well.

Everywhere in family relations, there is an undercurrent of unease, guilt, and fear, as though one member may betray another. The family standards, lines of loyalty, and allegiance are not clear. The relations of the parents themselves are full of these currents of suspicion, doubt, and indecision. Neither partner feels safe enough to take the allegiance of the other for granted. Sexual union is a fundamental bond; in it each tests the love of the other. But sex tends sometimes to become mechanized and depersonalized, a physical release that leaves the partners even lonelier after the act than before. The expression of tender sentiment shrinks. Sex becomes the arena for the struggle for dominance and control. Or it becomes a drab, hollow routine, carried out on schedule. Sometimes the man, harassed by his anxiety over the daily competitive battle, returns home to his wife to use sex as a way of sharpening his aggressive weapon for the next day's warfare. Sometimes sex simply dies a slow, withering death. And with impressive frequency there is a reversal of traditional sexual roles.

Moreover, delineation of the expected family role functions of male and female is often unclear. Issues of cooperation, division of labor, and sharing of authority are consequently confused. Each parent competes with the other and fears being bested. Neither is sure, yet each pretends to superior competence. Paradoxically each passes the buck to the other for the responsibility of decisions. The strife of competition reduces empathic sympathy, distorts communication, impairs the mutuality of support and sharing and decreases satisfaction of personal need. In effect, intelligent cooperation lessens, and bickering and recrimination mount. The inevitable consequence is progressive emotional alienation in parental relations.

With the father absent much of the day, the mother assumes the dominant position in the home. The isolated pattern of living of the nuclear family group, cut off from the larger extensions of the family, focuses responsibility for family affairs sharply and exclusively on the mother. The father strives mightily to show success as a man. He pursues what has been called "the suicidal cult of manliness." To prove his merit, it is not enough to be a man; he must be a superman. In his daily work, he serves some giant industrial organization, or he is a lone wolf in the jungle warfare of modern competitive enterprise. The more he succeeds, the more he dreads failure. He brings his work worries home. Depleted by his exertions, he has little emotional stamina left over to give freely of his love to wife and children. From his wife, he seeks comfort and solace. He needs some mothering for himself and so competes with his children. He wants to be buttressed for the war of tomorrow, but he finds his wife absorbed in her own busy life. He feels deserted and alone and angry that his wife gives him so little understanding. She reproaches him for not taking a more responsible role in the family. She demands more consideration for herself and the children. For the difficulties with the children she feels guilty. But she denies this guilt and projects it to father. Father takes it. He thinks it must really be his fault. Though confused and angry, he appeases mother because of his need for her. He tries to be useful to win her favor. He washes dishes, minds the baby, becomes mother's "little helper." He submits to this role but silently begrudges his wife's dictates. He feels alien as parent, shut out of the relations of children and mother, or at least relegated to the far corner. In all this he feels self-conscious, unnatural, and somewhat lost.

The mother, in turn, pretends to a degree of strength and sureness she does not at all possess. Because she cannot feel safe in leaning on her husband's strength, she takes to herself the powers of regulating the family. She demonstrates her worth through imitating the stereotype of male strength. She tries to be omnipotent but succeeds only in being detached, impersonal, and alienated from the spontaneous sentiments of a mother. She strives intensely to do the right thing with the children but plagues herself with fear of making mistakes. Nonetheless, she pretends to know, acts strong, superior, and self-sufficient, and with this façade often deceives her husband. Fundamentally, however, she remains insecure and dependent, wanting mothering for herself, though she is loathe to confess it.

Both parents therefore act unnatural. They are suspicious of any open show of emotion, which they regard as weakness. A free flow of emotion is felt to be dangerous, as if all emotion were equated with something bad and destructive. Therefore it must be curbed. Anxiety over loss of control is constant. Tender sentiment is avoided or, if expressed, is ignored; it spells weakness and the threat of loss of control. Thus the behavior of both parents becomes overcontrolled, unspontaneous, and reduced in vitality. Both parents are burdened with anxiety, guilt and doubt. They are afraid of life and have lost their zest for play and sense of adventure. They settle down to a stereotyped way of living, a safe, conforming routine. They strive to live up to the Jones' with all the external accoutrements of conventional success—a home, a new car, the latest gadgets.

In this family frame, there are, in the final showdown, only two possible roles: the role of the child, dependent, exposed, vulnerable; and the role of the superman, self-sufficient, infinitely strong and not needing anyone. Neither parent wants to be in the role of the defenseless child, exposed to attack. Each prefers the role of omnipotent master and the phantasy of total immunity to hurt. The parents may in actual fact alternate these roles. An inevitable effect of this is to blur the essential, ineradicable differences between male and female, differences which in nature should lead to a true joining and completion in one another. The striving for the position of omnipotent supremacy leads ultimately to a sense of aloneness and emotional deadness.

Like his parents, the adolescent of today is scared and worried. If his parents are fearful, he is doubly fearful. If his parents are confused and lash out blindly, he is himself plunged into confusion and panic. Currently, the "anarchy of youth" and the tendency to delinquency is made much of in news-papers and magazines. But far less is said of the adolescent who simply gets lost amid the crowded and hurried events of modern family and community life. It is the obligation of the adolescent moving to maturity to find himself, but it is incredibly easy for him to lose himself instead. If he is to emancipate himself from parental authority and cultivate his autonomy, he must preserve lines of healthy identification with parents and family. If these lines of identi-fication are warped, he may fail to find himself in the wider world. Healthy togetherness with family means healthy separation of self. But here comes the hitch: how can the adolescent emancipate himself from parents whose own identity is vague, contradictory, and fragmented?

The behavior of adolescents today is bipolar. They tend to seek identity at one of two poles: conformity or delinquency. At one extreme occur the weird explosive acts that lean toward crime. At the other extreme emerges a kind of caricature of cautious, monotonous, conforming behavior. In some groups the static, unadventuresome spirit of adolescents is a painful thing to see. They no longer dream of great things, an exciting foray into the unknown of life, but rather of a safe haven, a secure job in a big industry, a pension. Early marriage is often an escape from the confrontation of the adolescent's responsibil-ity for achieving a mature personal identity. Max Lerner quipped, "This is the age of 'unflaming youth.'" Justice William Douglas spoke of youth as having lost its dissenting voice, having lapsed into a kind of "conspiracy of silence."

The sexual behavior of the adolescent is itself symptomatic. He has greater freedom sexually, but he does not know what to do with it. He takes pride in the thrill of the act, the single exploit, but is careful to stay detached and un-involved, to avoid feeling. He fears losing himself in love. His prime concern is with the assertion of competitive dominance, fear of loss of control, and the maintenance of his emotional isolation.

With this family background, it is little wonder that parents experience anguish in their rearing of children. The naturalness of the joy of children is often suppressed. Parental attitudes tend to be intellectualized. Parents have children not for the sheer satisfaction of creating new life, but for ulterior reasons: to conform to society's expectations, to pacify grandparents, to assure companionship and security in old age, to neutralize marital unhappiness, to assuage loneliness, to aggrandize the self, to show off, to counter a wide range of neurotic fears such as sterility and doubt of sexual adequacy.

Parents displace onto their children anxieties and hostile urges which be-long to their disturbed relations with their own parents and with wider society. Being preoccupied with their own needs, they do not make adequate emo-tional room for their children's needs. They react to the children's needs as if exorbitant and menacing. They do not love fully or freely. What they give to their children means to them that much less for themselves. Out of a sense of guilt they try to pacify their children, overindulge them inappropriately in material things, and accord them disproportionate power within the home. Out of their own insecurity, doubt, and impotence, parents find themselves governed by their own children. The absence of confidence and natural pleasure in parenthood is expressed in attitudes of rejection, cruelty, overindulgence, anxious overprotection, inconsistent and inappropriate discipline.

Can we now draw together the meaning of these behavioral configurations in the contemporary middle-class, urban, white family? I shall endeavor to do so by clustering the observations around the dimensions of behavior to which I previously alluded: psychological identity, stability, patterns of conflict and restitution, and, finally, role adaptation and capacity for new learning and further adaptive development.

Psychological Identity: The psychological identity of the contemporary family is affected by a variety of forces that disturb its unity. It is weakly integrated; it is confused and conflicted, sometimes split and fragmented; in varying measure it is disoriented to the surrounding social realities. The family is emotionally isolated. There is discrepancy between what the family believes it is or ought to be compared with what it actually is. Emotional sharing and identification is thinned, and effective communication is reduced. Emotional dependence is feared. Tender sentiment is suspect and renounced as weakness. Mutual satisfaction of needs is deficient. Individual members are detached from their own basic emotions and alienated from the emotions of other family members. Undue emphasis is placed on competitive superiority, aggressive mastery, and self-sufficiency. Competitive and alienating trends erode the matrix of essential family togetherness. Sexual relations are often mutually frustrating; love-making tends to become mechanized and impersonal. It fails as an antidote for loneliness.

The family shrinks away from events in the wider community which it cannot understand and assimilate. It tries unsuccessfully to compensate by a concentration of the satisfaction of emotional needs of its individual members within the fold of family. Thus the family bears an extra psychic load; it endeavors to make up to its members in closeness and affection for the failure to achieve goals and satisfactions in the wider community. This intensifies mutual dependence and hostility among family members, and aggravates internal conflict. The family seeks compensatory stability in a static pattern, but this is maladaptive and predisposes to episodes of unreal, impulsive behavior.

These trends seem not to signify a true shift toward a companionship family, as Burgess[9] believes. It is as if the fear of life impels a defensive need for compensatory closeness in family relations. The urge for intimacy and a safe haven at home is to some extent a flight from life rather than a positive striving, a quest for a special complementarity at home to neutralize the sense of danger in the wider world.

The problem of the contemporary family is not simply a question of conflict within the family, it is also a question of imbalance, confusion, and disorientation in the relations of family with wider society. Perhaps Erikson's[10] concept of "ego diffusion" can be applied to the problem of family identity as well as individual identity.

Stability: The equilibrium of the family is not maintained. The stability patterns are unsteady and vulnerable. Precisely because control patterns are weak, erratic, and undependable, there is exaggerated concern with issues of control and discipline. There is a failure to understand that matters of control and discipline cannot be mediated apart from the related issues of basic security, satisfaction, and unity.

The instability of the family favors implementation of such pathological defenses against anxiety as substitution of aggression for anxiety, scapegoating, magic doing and undoing, projection, isolation and the tendency to externalize conflict, *i.e.*, to act out. Episodically, these families may turn "delinquent."

Conflict and Restitution: Conflict and restitution devices in family functioning may be conceived as occurring at several levels, each overlapping the other: conflict and imbalance between the family and surrounding community; intrafamilial conflict among members; conflict within the personalities of individual members. In the contemporary family there is conflict at all three levels. Conflict with society arising from its unsteady external adaptation spills over to aggravate intrafamilial conflict and in turn affects the vicissitudes of control of intrapersonality conflict. Failure of control of intrapsychic conflict increases interpersonal conflict and in turn hampers the family's adaptive performance in the community. The restitutive devices for conflict, such as isolation, compensatory togetherness, obsessive devotion to children, geographical shift, moving to the suburbs, escape into anxious forms of amusement and drinking, are inefficient operations. They do not effectively neutralize conflict, anxiety, emotional alienation, and the tendency to disorganization.

Role Adaptation, Capacity for New Learning and Further Adaptive Development: In the contemporary family, disturbance of integration into the required family roles is prominent. Parents experience shame and anguish in their default as parents. They are equally troubled with their sense of inadequacy in the male and female sexual roles. There is a varying measure of disturbance in complementarity in the family pairs of husband-wife, father-mother, parent-child, child-sibling. In some families, there is rigidification of roles, or members are imprisoned to the requirements of a single role. There is insufficient resiliency to achieve a new and improved level of role reciprocity. When role reciprocity breaks down, disorganization of family relations ensues and hampers the capacity to learn from new experience and achieve further growth.

A Contemporary Family Study

Having examined the broad outlines and the general patterns of the contemporary family, let us now look at a sample family which emerges out of a relatively poor background but achieves some upward social mobility and reaches the standards of the middle class. This family illustrates well the stresses and psychological disturbances that we have outlined.

PRESENTING PROBLEMS

John Cohn, four and a half, was brought to a psychiatrist by his mother because he was troubled by many fears. These began early, at about six months, and rapidly increased. He was afraid of sirens, foghorns, and other loud noises. He had nightmares. He was extensively absorbed in phantasies with a strong tinge of magic, and did not clearly distinguish what was real and imaginary.

John was a well-built, bright child, restless, distractible, and evasive. His facial grimaces were peculiar. He was testy and belittling toward his mother. He expressed with baby-like relish his feeling that his mother was a "duty" (bowel movement) face. He handled his penis with some show of agitation.

It was later learned that John's sister Betty, two and a half, also feared loud noises. She had a vacant expression on her face, sucked her thumb, and was late in talking. The mother talked loudly and continuously and exerted a belligerent control over the household.

IDENTIFYING INFORMATION ON FAMILY AT REFERRAL

John's parents were American-born children of poor Jewish immigrants. They were in their early thirties. Both were college graduates. The father was a pediatrician who pursued his practice within the home. He earned about $13,000 a year. The Cohns did not practice their religion, although the family background was orthodox on the maternal side.

They owned a house in a typical suburban middle-class community, in which Dr. Cohn developed his practice. The home was highly prized by both parents. Much effort was invested in making it warm and attractive. Although they could afford a maid, Mrs. Cohn found it difficult to tolerate another woman in her home.

DESCRIPTION OF PARENTS AND HISTORY

Mrs. Cohn was a big woman, childlike, naive, hostile and domineering in an overwhelming way. She was obese and alternated bouts of overeating and dieting. She imposed a rigid routine on the household. Her approach to family problems was a compulsive, omnisciently intellectual one. She suffered from mood swings. When depressed and irritable she became explosively argumentative. But she was frightened of her own power and felt a guilty pressure to undue any damage she might inflict on family members. She was afraid of dogs and squeamish about bugs. She tended to bang herself on doors. She feared she was hurting her children with poor rearing. She felt that reading psychiatric literature kept her on an even keel.

Mrs. Cohn was the oldest of three children. She said her parents quarreled and frequently threatened separation at which times the children sided with their mother. Her father was an unresponsive person, her mother, a martyr. Mrs. Cohn did not feel close to any part of her original family.

Diagnostic study of her personality raised a question as to a latent weakness toward schizophrenic disorganization. She had a bestial image of sex. She feared loss of control over her destructive urges. She felt estranged. She had an overlying layer of obsessive defenses which were only partly compensated. Her striving for magic, omnipotent power, covered her basic infantile needs. She was intensely competitive, demanding and exhibitionistic. She reacted to crises of anxiety with explosive outbursts.

Dr. Cohn was a big man who spoke in a stiff, expressionless way. He was rigid, compulsive, controlled. He had periodic psychosomatic disorders, migraine, and ulcer.

Dr. Cohn was one of four children. His parents ran a small store, worked long hours, and left the children largely on their own. His father was the disciplinarian of the family, a silent, intellectual man. His mother was a superstitious woman, headstrong, forceful, and energetic. She nagged at the children and was overprotective with respect to clothes and health. While Dr. Cohn was at high school, the family went bankrupt and had to go on relief. They were ashamed of this and tried to hide it from outsiders. Dr. Cohn was close to his one brother but not his sisters. He continued to be a detached, withdrawn person.

Though his family could ill afford it, he went to college and isolated himself with his studies. He felt he could not afford to go out on dates. At school he experienced an active anti-Semitism which reinforced his view of the world as a dangerous place. He feared hunger and humiliation. Building up his position and fortifying it with money became a principal goal.

Diagnostic study revealed a fearful, withdrawn man with rigid controls and defenses. His personality was poorly integrated. His sense of self was vague. He was deeply inhibited. He reacted to anxiety with body fears and psychosomatic disturbance.

Marital relationship and fulfillment of marital roles

The Cohns met while he was at medical school and she held a job. She continued working for several years after marriage in order to help support them. They were drawn to each other through a mutual sense of deprivation, loneliness, and fear of the dangers of life. Dr. Cohn came to marriage with no prior sex experience and an intense fear of venereal disease. He looked upon his future wife as a mothering person and as a sexual outlet. He liked her vivacity but did not recognize it as anxious aggressiveness. She was attracted by his intellectual ability, his pliability and passivity. She wanted to escape from an unhappy home, the domination of her mother, and the oppressive religious atmosphere. Both partners shared a fervent desire for economic security and a home which would be a safe haven. Their ideal for marriage was a strong mutually dependent bond, which would exclude all intruders. Within this bond they sought a position of respect and approval in the community. Both wanted to give their children the home and advantages of which they had been deprived.

The early part of their married life was marked by an active sexual and social life, mainly patterned by Mrs. Cohn. Dr. Cohn needed sex to ease his tensions, but Mrs. Cohn after the initial period began to resent his use of her body. She felt degraded, and this induced bitter conflict. They did not want children until after Dr. Cohn had established his professional position. Mrs. Cohn wanted children to reassure herself against a fear of sterility but on the other hand was afraid a child would separate her from her husband. Decisions were made by Mrs. Cohn, who would interpret her husband's silence as compliance.

During courtship and early marriage they formed a mutually protective alliance. They verbally shared feelings and interests. After establishment of their home and his professional practice and the arrival of children, they became preoccupied with amassing monetary security and the problems of the children. Emotional communication between the parents deteriorated. They were perpetually embroiled in argument and became estranged. Yet on an intellectual level compatibility was maintained. At certain other levels they complemented one another's needs. Mrs. Cohn appreciated her husband's earning power.

Dr. Cohn depended on Mrs. Cohn's cooking and sexual services. With this division of labor, each tried to do a good job. They cooperated in seeking approval and respect in the community. But the children assumed special importance in engendering a growing barrier between the parents. Mrs. Cohn tied herself anxiously to the children to the point where her husband was excluded. Despite the anxieties and weaknesses and conflicts of the parents, they shared a strong mutual incentive for improvement. The basic need to cling to each other emphasized the importance of maintaining unity in their marriage and family. They both required the close protective embrace of the family to counteract feelings of inferiority, rejection, and vulnerability to external threat.

Mrs. Cohn contributed greatly to the tension in the marital relationship by her aggressive pressure for compliance on her husband's part. She demanded self-sacrificial submission as proof of his considerateness and devotion to her. She required that he buttress her defenses against anxiety. But her omnipotent domination, denials, and rationalizations engulfed husband and children.

Dr. Cohn expressed his sex drives compulsively to prove his masculinity and counteract his tendency toward emotional isolation.

Social relationships shared by the parents became sharply reduced after the first years of John's entry into the family. Each, however, found some compensation in developing individual friends of the same sex, from whom each sought approval and reinforcement of self-esteem. Elements of masculinity in the wife and femininity in the husband found disguised expression in these platonic relationships outside the family.

Both partners were confused about their sexual and marital roles. The wife controlled the sexual relationship by rationing the satisfactions she provided for her husband. It became an instrument to enforce compliance. She also used excessive eating and resulting obesity to repel him. In phantasy she linked food and sex, took pride in her large breasts, but feared being eaten. She spoke of her husband's sexual behavior as crude, animal-like, impersonal, and lacking in tenderness. She was anxious to exact proof that her body was attractive and lovable rather than disgusting. She had fears of body mutilation. She used her physical bigness as a symbol of her power, which she could use to intimidate her husband and children.

Dr. Cohn saw himself as both boy and man. Underlying his sexual activity were fears of sexual deficiency and the need to counteract hypochondriacal worries and death anxieties. He complied grudgingly with his wife's dictates in order to obtain sexual service.

A measure of emotional reciprocity was expressed in the balance of the wife's masculine power drives and her husband's underlying feminine passivity.

In spite of all this, a superficial atmosphere of harmony and rapport was maintained as a safeguard against disorganization. Both partners recognized their childlike qualities, their insistent demands of each other, but Dr. Cohn was more realistic and mature than his wife. They agreed there was a basic union between them and wanted to work out their conflicts. The stability of their relationship rested in this desire to cooperate and better their family life. The striving for improvement was impeded by the narrowness of their aims and the rigidity of their defenses against anxiety. Devices to control conflict became progressively less workable.

PARENTAL RELATIONSHIP AND FULFILLMENT OF PARENTAL ROLES

The ability of this couple to adapt to their parental roles was poor and a source of stress for both parents, especially the mother. Each of the parents competed with the children in their need for parental protection. The childlike dependency of the parents impaired their marital adjustment.

The lack of unity as a marital pair was carried over into the interaction of husband and wife as a parental pair. Dr. Cohn escaped into his professional work but was otherwise friendly toward his son. Dr. and Mrs. Cohn were in sharp conflict with regard to their children. Mrs. Cohn was excessively anxious to avoid the mistakes of her own rearing and had difficulty in disciplining the children. Dr. Cohn felt she was too permissive, allowed the children to walk all over her, but then became excited and angry. Mrs. Cohn depended on articles on child-rearing as a guide for her parental behavior.

In spite of the conscientious struggle of both parents to pull together, they were caught in continuous quarrels, were mutually critical, and guilty, and retreated from one another. Mrs. Cohn perceived herself as a dedicated mother but was disappointed in herself, worried and guilty over her failure. The children were extensions of herself. If her control over them was menaced (as by her husband), she became hostile and withdrew. She was obsessed with the idea of being a better mother than her own. The factors in her personality that impaired her mothering were her tendency to panic, low self-esteem, magical thinking, and fear of abandonment and death.

Dr. Cohn saw himself as a conscientious parent but felt the need for keeping something for himself. His importance as a parent was reduced by the mother's competitiveness, her criticisms, and her need for absolute control. He resented this and felt impelled to retreat. The factors in his personality that influenced his parental behavior were his immaturity, his own need of mothering, his competitiveness with the children, his fears of hostility, and his tendency to emotional isolation.

Mrs. Cohn's attitude toward her husband at the time of referral was that he could do no right. She severely criticized his behavior and attitudes toward the children. She felt that his importance to her was as a husband only. She negated his role as father.

The effect of these trends on the parental relationship and role fulfillment was a tendency toward enslavement to duty with underlying resentment of sacrifice and guilt over failure.

FAMILY AS A GROUP

Internal Organization: The value of family unity, although pursued especially by Mrs. Cohn, was only achieved in a surface way by an overcalm and controlled atmosphere. The father's success in establishing himself in the community and ability to buy material things was the one area in which the family strivings had been fulfilled.

Stability of the group was sharply affected by the mother's inability to continue her early empathy with her husband as a child over whom she exercised control. As he grew into a person in his own right and achieved some partial separation from her, difficulties in communication mounted with increasing misunderstanding and alienation. The day-to-day functioning of parents and children was maintained by superficial verbal communication and intellectual discipline. John's preoccupation with himself and Betty's inability to talk tended to push the children toward the fringe of the group. The unity that was forced by the mother and her rigid conceptions of family life tended to make the other three members pull away from her. Her tendency to go into panic states pervaded the atmosphere. Family life was therefore characterized by some degree of disorganization, confusion, and efforts to prevent explosion. Family roles— parents' and children's—fitted mainly into the mother's concept of what they should be. The mother's regressive pattern tended to hold back the whole family and prevent learning and further development. Progressive alienation in the marital and parental relationship led to compensatory efforts on the part of each parent to achieve closeness with the children, causing them to withdraw in turn and feel torn between the parents.

Again, on a superficial level, the family enjoyed joint activities and shared an appreciation of their home and economic advancement.

The group could not grow and adapt to changing needs in the face of the constrictions introduced largely by the mother. Spontaneity in family roles became effectively blocked. The fit of family roles was dependent on the mother's dictation.

Adaptation to the Community: Interaction of the family with community became progressively diminished after John was a year old. Contacts with families of origin decreased. Neighborhood friends dropped off. Mrs. Cohn became increasingly worried lest the use of a baby-sitter injure the development of the children. She therefore gave up social life except for occasional family get-to-gethers. She compensated, however, by forming an excessively intimate relationship with a woman next door whose approval she craved. Dr. Cohn went to professional meetings, fished with friends occasionally on Sundays. Mrs. Cohn objected strenuously to her husband's extrafamilial activities. She could not allow him these outside pleasures because of her own inability to accept pleasure.

On the whole this family conformed to community middleclass expectations for achievement and economic security. In its external façade, it met community requirements for status, home, and children. But Mrs. Cohn choked off the natural interests of father and children for associations outside the family. The earlier patterns of social participation melted under the pressure of Mrs. Cohn's obsessive, panicky devotion to the care of the children. Even Dr. Cohn's desire to train in a professional specialty was crushed by Mrs. Cohn's violent insistence that duty to family came first.

JOHN'S DEVELOPMENTAL HISTORY: EVALUATION OF HIS DISORDER

Despite Mrs. Cohn's fears of emotional separation from her husband, she had a child immediately after her husband became established professionally. She felt physically well during pregnancy. She resisted breast feeding so as to be able to continue being close to her husband. She sustained the companionship with her husband and her social life until John was one year of age, when she became acutely anxious about damaging the child's development through lack of devotion. Dr. Cohn, preoccupied with building a practice, saw little of the child. He also feared to touch him.

Mrs. Cohn allowed the child to suck at her dry breast after bottles. She said there were no problems and she enjoyed him. Toilet training started at ten months, but John became scared and Mrs. Cohn gave it up for awhile. Between one and a half and two John learned to control his urine and at three was bowel trained. Mrs. Cohn said she frequently became excited, said "don't," and smacked him. She was afraid to allow John in bed with his parents for fear of crushing him. As he grew older, he was not comfortable with other children, and his mother pushed him out to play. John reacted with extreme jealousy when his sister was born. Dr. Cohn's principal concern with John was that he should eat the proper foods. He treated John as if he were much older.

The dynamic content of John's disorder can be summarized as follows: His mother failed to establish a close emotional contact with him, especially during the first year. She then became guilty in the face of his anxieties and frantically tried to compensate for the damage. She dominated the child while treating him as an extension of herself, conveying to him a fear that he would carry out her own catastrophic urges. She was inconsistent, overindulged him, deprived him, and thwarted his individuality. John came to feel that he could neither do with nor do without his mother. He made a frightened retreat from her oral, devouring attitude.

John was unable to achieve satisfaction or identification with his father because his father was too preoccupied with himself. Intermittently, his father gave him warmth and affection, but it was part of his competition with his wife. His retreat from his paternal role in the face of his wife's angry accusations made it progressively more difficult for John to relate to him.

John was basically withdrawn from the family group but continued obedience to his mother's control. He retreated from symbols of hostility between his parents and between himself and his parents. It was impossible for him to understand the parental relationship because of its confused, disintegrative trends.

BETTY'S DEVELOPMENTAL HISTORY: EVALUATION OF HER DISORDER

Pregnancy and delivery were uneventful with nothing unusual in development, except for speech retardation. Betty was bottle fed. After the bottle, Mrs. Cohn let the child suck at her dry breast as she had done with John. She was concerned about Betty's thumbsucking and tried in many ways to stop it but finally gave up. Betty was partially toilet trained at referral and only wet her bed if her mother did not get to her in time in the morning. During Betty's first year, Mrs. Cohn was very concerned about the child's loose bowel movements and her refusal to consume starches. Mrs. Cohn finally withheld other foods and forced the starches. Betty weaned herself after a tonsillectomy at eight months.

At seven months she said a few words but soon ceased and subsequently made herself understood by grunts and gestures. Mrs. Cohn tried to teach her to speak, used punishment, and finally checked with the doctor. He was not concerned and suggested that Mrs. Cohn leave her alone, which Mrs. Cohn was partially able to do.

Here then is a family that corresponds at many points to the outline of the contemporary family that we have already seen. And here it becomes apparent that the issue for those of us interested in mental health problems is not so much the problems and conflicts of this family or any specific family in the changing world but the resources of the family for dealing with them. The realities of progressive revolutionary change in social patterns and the lag in the family's capacity to accommodate to them, which gives rise to a varying lack of fit between family structure and wider society, are not in themselves psychological problems. We cannot psychoanalyze reality; we can only seek out an accurate definition of it and act appropriately. But we can learn to deal with mental health problems in and through the family. We can establish the essential links between individual and family behavior. By conceptualizing the issues of family diagnosis and correlating individual and family disturbance, we can build a program of family-life education and family therapy that is specifically suited to the problem of the family in our time. In this context, it is important to support parents in their own efforts to educate themselves to a correct definition of the realities of their changing world. We can relieve them of a burden of shame and guilt over family tensions that are not solely of their own creation but are a symptom of the stress of modern life. In so doing, we may help them resolve the discrepancy between unreal family ideals and the actualities of current family life and so, perhaps, facilitate their adaptation to family roles and family functions. A more effective process of reality testing would do two important things: it would make possible a dissolution of inappropriate and distorted perceptions of prevailing social realities and thus open the way to better utilization of actual opportunities for obtaining community support for the family; it would also provide more efficient avenues of access to the intrinsic psychological problems of the family group. At this second level, it becomes necessary to clarify the psychotherapeutic challenge of fitting persons more suitably to their family roles, heightening the quality of complementarity in family pairs, and promoting family unity. This clarification can, it seems to me, result only from a family approach to diagnosis, education, social treatment, and psychotherapy. Only by working through and with the family can we hope to meet the challenge of our changing society.

CHAPTER 9

SOME SPECIAL TECHNIQUES
OF FAMILY DIAGNOSIS

THE FIRST PROBLEM that confronts the mental health worker as he attempts to meet the challenge of family disturbance is one of obtaining sufficient and dependable data to enable him to make correct diagnoses and to plan intelligently for successful treatment. The gathering of data has always been of great importance in any type of diagnostic and therapeutic work, but the immeasurably greater scope and comprehension of the data necessary to family diagnosis raises problems peculiarly its own. It is not a task to be carried out easily by one person alone. When necessary, a clinician working by himself may, of course, follow the general principles of family diagnosis. Within limits he may integrate his observations of the relations of family members and usefully apply these insights to the purposes of psychotherapy. In most instances, however, it would seem too large a burden for one person.

Under optimum conditions, the collection of the relevant information for family diagnosis is treated as the responsibility of a small group of professionals collaborating as a mental health team. Not only is the burden lessened but the results seem to be more effective. The team may be made up of a psychiatrist, a psychologist, and a social worker, as is the traditional guidance team. But it is possible to vary the membership in all sorts of ways, either from necessity or in order to meet particular interests and goals. Sometimes, for example, the family physician or a nurse is a helpful teammate; sometimes a psychoanalytically oriented sociologist proves invaluable. But whatever the composition of the group, the purpose remains unchanged.

The process of collecting data takes many forms. Useful, of course, are the usual initial exploratory interviews and history-taking from the primary patient. In family diagnosis, this procedure is often supplemented by history-taking from other members of the family, still in the more or less conventional manner so thoroughly developed by psychiatric workers in the past. But the further step of interrelating these histories, clarifying apparent discrepancies, bridging gaps, and the like is made possible by the combined efforts of the clinical team.

In the same way, direct observation of family interaction during office interviews yields not only information about the immediate situation but when pooled with observations made by other members of the team may produce illuminating insights and material of inestimable value. (In later chapters, I shall discuss the office interview in connection with specific disturbances of family living.)

In the effort to explore the mental health problems of family life, with the goal of relating the behavior of the family as a group to the behavior of a family member, the home visit becomes a valuable tool. Not always regarded with favor in the past, the home visit must be reassessed in the light of recent shifts in conceptual orientation to the nature of emotional and mental illness and the tasks of psychotherapy. And because of the special applicability of the home visit to the diagnosis and treatment of the family as a group, I should like to spell out in some detail the techniques that I have found most useful.

The home visit is unstructured, informal, and without notetaking. The primary focus must be on family interaction patterns and family role adaptation. Of special interest is the emotional climate of the home, the psychosocial identity of the family, and its specific expression in a defined environment. The visit is arranged when all or most members of the family are at home. The best time to visit is at mealtime when the family is normally together. If the visit is begun before the father gets home from work, the behavior of family members before and after he enters provides valuable clues to family group organization, attitudes, and feelings. A visit may last two to three hours and is usually written up in detail after its completion.

The visit is most profitable from the clinical point of view when the observer is a participant in the activities and emotional interaction of family members. This encourages a maximum of spontaneity of family behavior and interferes least with its "normal" functioning. The fact of participant observation inevitably introduces an element of bias in the observations, but such bias can be explicitly taken into account in interpreting the observations. The live quality of the information far outweighs the risks of biased observation. The observer makes his report from memory, since notetaking on the spot would damage the spontaneity of the experience. The danger of error from selectivity of impression is more than compensated by the positive gains.

The insights into family interaction thus acquired are derived from the level of communication between observer and family members. The kind of information obtained depends on the emotional quality of the observer's participation and will differ enormously if the contact of the observer with the family is mainly verbal or deeply emotional. If the observer can win his way fully into the family experience, his insight will be more profound. The aim in observations of family life is a true picture of the essence of the relations between family members. Both positive and negative aspects of these relations are recorded.

The written report is divided into five parts:

1. a summary of chronological events of the visit;
2. the family as a group, which covers the visitor's impression of interaction patterns and role behaviors;
3. a short description of each member of the household;
4. the physical and community environment;
5. miscellaneous information.

This data may be integrated with other information leading to family diagnosis (see Guide for Data Leading to Family Diagnosis, p. 138).

The member of the clinical team designated to make the home visit is more a matter of practical choice than theoretical preference. A trained, sensitive and astute observer at ease with strangers in a social setting and oriented toward the concepts and goals of the visit, whether therapist, case worker, or other professional, whether known or unknown to the family, will be equally effective. If the visitor is the child's or parent's therapist, the visit need not interfere with the therapeutic relationship. The emotional tone of the visit is set by the visitor and mutual interaction of visitor and family. In any case the visit should not be on a question-and-answer interview level. One advantage of using someone other than the therapist is the possibility of checking impressions.

Visits may be made with and without foreknowledge of the family problem or background. A certain emotional neutrality, lack of selectivity, and avoidance of bias is achieved when the clinical history is not known. But there are advantages to prior knowledge. It helps the visitor to feel less a stranger and assists the therapist by ensuring that central problems are sufficiently noted. Whether the observer meets the parents before the visit is not a matter of critical importance, although this may ease the initial part of the visit.

Often the insecurity of psychotherapists and their apprehension of invasion of their control of their patient seems to be a source of resistance to visiting.

The visit is conceived as a threat to the family, an invasion of privacy, or a possible complication of the response to psychotherapy. I have never found these objections valid. If key family members are prepared for the visit by the therapist, who presents it to them as a clinical procedure necessary for understanding the primary patient, child or adult, and related problems, any resultant anxiety of the parent can be handled before the visit. If the therapist does not convey his own anxiety, the parents usually will not be anxious. More often, the visit is interpreted as proof of the therapist's interest and devotion, and the observer is perceived as part of a clinic team, a helping agent of the therapist who energizes expectations of more and better help. Actually, the idea of observing a child patient in the home seems quite logical to the family. The social level of the visit puts the family at ease and feelings of being "spied on" are reduced to a minimum. Absence of anxiety in the therapist and the visitor is quickly reflected in family reactions.

The most frequent concern about home visits is that the family may not behave normally, that they may be on their "best behavior," and that the interjection of a stranger in the home creates an atypical situation. Such contentions are not pertinent to the basic purposes of the visits. The home visit is only one means of evaluation of the family and must be integrated with other findings. Discrepancies with clinical impressions are evaluated by therapist, visitor, and sometimes the parents. Sometimes differences provide additional insights. In practice, however, family behavior during a visit deviates from usual behavior only in degree, not in quality. We may not see the mother lose her temper with the child in either home or office, but, whether her behavior is strictly typical or not, we can observe the quality of her attitudes and relatedness to the child. We may not see open conflict between two parents, but, to the astute observer, feelings and attitudes will be betrayed. Often, parents are anxious to show their own and their child's "worst side," as if they wished to prove the existence of their problems and justify their need for help.

The introduction of an outsider into the home must of course be considered, but, the observer is a stranger only in a very special sense because he is identified with the helping therapist. Differing reactions of family members to the visitor can be quite significant. Sometimes the visitor is sought as an ally; his approval is required and his attention vied for. At other times, he is noticeably excluded. In many families, the visitor becomes a vector or catalyzer of family interactions and disclosures. Usually a good deal of interest is shown by the parents in the observer's impressions. The therapist, of course, must use his judgment as to what part of the conclusions to reveal to the family and how to utilize the observations therapeutically.

The earlier the visit is made in the therapist's contact with the family, the more value it has for diagnosis and for treatment plans. It may also be used during the course of treatment to evaluate family functioning, to measure therapeutic progress, to check perceptions and reports of the family, or to assess special problem situations that arise. As a means of follow-up, the visit is indispensable.

Let us, however, take as our example a home visit made early in the diagnostic process, in order to see the ways in which it facilitated both diagnosis and the planning of treatment.

Seven year old Bobby was referred by his father for fears of physical injury and bleeding, anxiety when his parents went out, bedtime rituals, nightmares, and sibling rivalry. He was the oldest of three children in a wealthy, upper-middle-class family. The father was a successful businessman, who tended to be hypochondriacal and ritualistic. His manner was intelligent, poised, and affable, but discussing the boy, he was anxious and tense. He worried because the boy was much like him. The mother was ten years younger than her husband, attractive, tense, compulsive, and mildly euphoric. She said her main concern was her children. She felt more relaxed with them when her husband was not present. Each parent claimed to admire the other and maintained that their family life was ideal. In the early days of marriage, however, there had been severe tension between the father's mother and his wife. The couple had always led an active social life.

Bobby was born the first year of marriage. Both parents wanted a child as early as possible because the father was already in his thirties. During Bobby's early infancy, the parents were severely frightened by a medical report that Bobby had an enlarged heart. They became anxious, overprotective and panicked at any signs of illness. Although when Bobby was a year old they were reassured he was normal, their anxiety continued and carried over to the other children. Nurses had always been employed, and, currently, one shared the care of the children with the mother.

Regular contacts with the parents and therapy for the child were initiated. A home visit was arranged for a Saturday morning when the father could be present. The following is a condensed report of the visit.

Physical Environment: The Temples live in an eight-room apartment in an upper-middle-class residential section. Their home is ample in size, suitable and comfortable for family needs. It is decorated plainly, without evidence of any particular concern for appearance or tasteful result. Bobby and his sister Alice, five, share a bedroom. Another room is used by the nurse and baby John, seventeen months old. The Temples' bedroom is adjacent to the baby's room. The family expect to move so that Bobby and Alice can have separate rooms. The Temples employ a full-time maid in addition to the baby's nurse.

Details of Visit: I was greeted very cordially by all family members. Mrs. Temple said the children were terribly excited by my visit. She immediately asked if there was any particular situation in which I would like to see the family. I told her I was interested in whatever they did normally. We went into the children's bedroom. Mr. Temple asked if I wanted him and Mrs. Temple to stay in the room. He remained most of the time, but Mrs. Temple was in and out because she had to dress the baby. Bobby asked his father to help him sort some foreign coins and sat down at his typewriter to record the amounts and names of the countries. Several times during the visit, Bobby went back to his coins, always asking for help, mine or his parents', whoever was available. Mr. Temple asked Alice if she would dance for me. She was eager to do so and followed her father's suggestions for little dances. From time to time, Mr. Temple would unsuccessfully suggest to Bobby that he stop the coin play and do something else. Whenever Mrs. Temple came into the room, Bobby would ask her help and she would assist him.

Mr. Temple suggested we all go into the living room. He asked Bobby if he wanted to play the piano, and Bobby did immediately. Mr. Temple would look at me and beam with pride at everything his children did. Alice played patiently by herself, waiting for her father's attention. John was brought in by the nurse, and Mrs. Temple followed. Alice took John over, watching over him, etc. Bobby asked his mother to help him with the music and she did. After Bobby exhausted the pieces he knew, he played with John's punching balloon. He then told Alice to lie on the floor so he could jump over her. She jumped over him also, and they both jumped over John. After this they jumped over the couch. When they got a little rough, Mrs. Temple told them to stop and they did. The two older children competed for John when they were all playing together, but it was Alice who gave in and let Bobby have his way. John went to both parents from time to time, and each picked him up and hugged him. Mr. Temple left the room to telephone. When he returned, Mrs. Temple left. Alice wanted to play the piano. Mrs. Temple has been teaching her, whereas Bobby takes lessons. Mr. Temple loudly praised Alice.

Mr. Temple told me that they control the children with respect to TV. They play with the children, suggest other amusement, and provide substitute entertainment. Whenever he told me anything in relation to the children, he always asked for my approval and advice. When the children heard "TV," they asked for it, but both parents said no. Mr. Temple suggested we all go back to the children's room so that they would have more room to play. Bobby immediately returned to his typewriter and coins. Both parents, particularly Mr. Temple, again tried to dissuade him. Bobby showed me his collection of pieces of coal and bottle caps. Alice then took out her bag of coal to show me. As soon as John came in the room, Alice went to him, but Bobby returned to typing.

The Temples had planned on a boat ride for that afternoon. Several times Mrs. Temple came in and told one or the other of the children that an invited friend could not come. She told Alice that she had asked another child, to which Alice did not respond. She asked Bobby if he wanted a certain friend. He said yes. She returned saying the friend was sick, but she had asked someone else. Later she told Bobby he was to go to this child's house for supper and would be walked home by his friend's brother. Bobby said he did not want to go for supper. When asked why by his father, he said they might have a hot meal there. Mrs. Temple said he knew he did not have to eat it. Then Bobby said he did not like the dog, and his parents discussed this with him. Mr. Temple told Bobby he should chase the dog instead of letting the dog chase him. Finally, Bobby repeated that he did not want to go. Mrs. Temple said he would like it when he got there and tried to persuade him. Then Mr. Temple told his wife that it was all right if Bobby did not want to go, and she immediately agreed. Bobby replied that he did not tell them where to go and not to go and he didn't want them to tell him either. The Temples both agreed that this was right.

Mr. Temple pointed out to me that Bobby collects things and tries to be perfect. Mrs. Temple said difficulties arose because Bobby was very neat and Alice was disorderly. Also, Alice learns faster with little effort. Both parents made it plain that they try to build up Bobby and help him to get attention, as they did with me. (It is easy to be diverted by Alice, who is a very appealing child.) Mrs. Temple asked me if I needed John anymore. Since I did not, John left for the park with the nurse. Repeatedly both parents tried to dissuade Bobby from playing with the coins but to no avail. Mr. Temple put on a victrola record and Alice played some drums. When I said goodbye Bobby left his coins to come to the door to say goodbye.

Family as a Group: The Temples appear to be an excessively, almost exaggeratedly, integrated group. Rapport between the parents seemed good. Neither appeared to dominate the other and no hostility was shown. They seemed overtly warm and affectionate when talking to each other, which was exclusively on the subject of the children. Neither one appeared to favor any one child, nor did the children show overt preference. There seems to be more sharing of the care of the children than in most families, with Mr. Temple playing a more prominent role. In speaking of themselves in relation to the children, both parents used "we" rather than "I." Children and parents all were very close and intimately related to each other. Both parents seemed overanxious to do well with their children, were overinvolved with them, participated too much in the children's activities, gave too much direction, and overstimulated them. Mr. Temple constantly suggested changes in play activities, always being careful that each child had his share of attention. The result was both unnatural and unreal, the concern being more Mr. Temple's than the children's. Mrs. Temple is more relaxed than her husband, less directive, and, apparently, less anxious to see the children make a good showing. But she goes to exaggerated lengths to obtain companionship and arrange activities for them. Both parents lean over backward to build up Bobby because of Alice's charm and aptitudes. The older children constantly but independently ask for attention.

The children get along well with each other and occasionally played together. There was no fighting. Alice doted on the baby and was very maternal with him. There was some evidence of competitiveness between Alice and Bobby for the baby's attention.

Both parents were cordial and friendly to me, but Mr. Temple frequently sat very close, was confiding, anxiously sought my approval, and made some attempts to take me over for himself. He tried to impress me with the children's positive qualities. The mother maintained some distance. In both parents, there was a hint of covering up in their marked resistance to conversation on any subject other than their children. Alice was friendly and accepting with me. Bobby related easily but only in terms of getting something he wanted.

Mrs. Temple: Mrs. Temple seemed warm, affectionate, interested, but overconscientious and manipulative with the children. She told me that for one year they had carefully thought about taking Bobby to a psychiatrist, because they were fearful that his problems would be blown up too much. This seems typical in that careful thought and planning leave little room for spontaneity in their behavior.

Mr. Temple: Mr. Temple is similar to his wife in behavior but more so in all respects. He seems to be much more concerned about his children's behavior and less sure of himself as a parent. He appears to drive himself to be a good father, and is very anxious about each thing they do as parents. He asked repeatedly if I was getting what I wanted from the visit and seemed anxious to give me information on the children. Although outwardly he gave the impression of being relaxed, I felt he was really quite tense.

Bobby: The contrast between Bobby and Alice is quite striking. Bobby is detached and preoccupied. He does not seem sufficiently aware or related to what is going on around him and seeks refuge in compulsive activities. He can assert himself but is usually amenable to his parents' suggestions. He obviously resented his mother's planning for him but made it known only in an indirect way.

Alice: Alice is not pretty but has a great deal of charm. In some ways she acts beyond her years, in poise, physical ability, and ease of relating. She is affectionate and warm in her contacts and related in a most understanding manner to the baby. It is easy for her to monopolize attention, but she is tolerant of allowing Bobby to get his share. An outsider could easily allow her to shut Bobby out because he readily withdraws.

John: The baby walks well and speaks a few words sufficiently clearly to be understood. He reacts appropriately, is responsive and affectionate, and likes to play with the older children. He showed no preference for any one family member, including the nurse.

Nurse: She is a genial and pleasant woman in her thirties. She seemed equally interested in all three children and was flexible and warm in her behavior. She adapted easily to the parents' involvement with the children.

The visit highlighted some of the family patterns. The intimate relatedness between children and parents indicated an exaggerated, strained, and unnatural cohesiveness and a child-centeredness atypical for a family of this socio-economic status. Although the parents appeared to be harmonious in their attitudes and behavior toward the children, there was an overemphasis on sharing between the parents both in decision making and in the care of and activities with children. The father, especially, overinvolved himself in their play, wanted to show them off, and was concerned about dividing his attention. The mother, although more relaxed and distant, was overconscientious and manipulative. Although both parents seemed genuinely fond and proud of the children, they also seemed to need attention from them. Activities were carefully planned and overorganized and involved excessive efforts at joint family activities and being together. Spontaneity in the parents and in Bobby was conspicuously absent.

The parents appeared to relate to each other only through their common concern with the children. Both parents were overtly warm but controlled and somewhat formal with each other.

The children were competitive among themselves for parental attention. They also vied for attention from the visitor, strongly encouraged by the father. Bobby's ritualistic play, self-isolation, and preoccupation were in sharp contrast

SOME SPECIAL TECHNIQUES · 137

to the lively outgoing behavior of his sister. At times both children competed for the attention of the youngest child.

The home was comfortable and appropriate to the family's socio-economic status, but furnishings and decoration of the home did not reflect much concern or interest.

The home visit gave an immediate clue to the atypical child-centeredness of the family group. (1) The parents exaggerated their parental solicitousness as a way of denying the emotional and marital barrier between them. (2) Exploitation of the children was highlighted in terms of the father's exhibitionistic needs. (3) The emotional immaturity of both parents could be seen in their need to live vicariously through the children. (4) There were hints of reversal of the usual sex roles in terms of the mother's allowing the father to assume a position of dominance in relation to the children.

The home visit was evaluated in terms of the child patient and his clinical interviews. For example, the child sensed that the mother was really the supreme power. He resented her manipulation and thus empathized with his father. In such ways, the social interaction patterns of the family had become absorbed into the child's pathology and internalized in his disturbance.

The mother was curious about the observation, and the therapist acquainted her with the gist of the report. She admitted the accuracy of the report and went on to reveal dissatisfaction with her husband and marriage from its inception. She was unable to respond sexually, found her husband's rituals and hypochondriasis unbearable, but felt that she had been successful in maintaining a façade of satisfaction. She said this was the best solution and insisted that the children were her first concern.

The home observation added to clinical data verified judgments and added to understanding the structure and functioning of this family. In addition, the visit performed the unlooked-for function of removing the façade of happiness that had been originally presented and made it possible to deal more directly with some of the main issues. The visit indicated the degree to which the parents were compensating for their own and their marital deficiencies by channeling through the children their quest for love, affection, attention, etc. Bobby's early "physical disability" and subsequent behavior played into this pattern. As long as the parents could evade the basic issues in their own relationship in a common concern for some "real" difficulties in Bobby and the other children, they could successfully escape facing up to their own dissatisfaction and disappointment in each other and the potential explosion both feared.

The clinical team felt that if Bobby's behavior improved and the parents were guided to involve themselves less with the children, it could be expected that sooner or later they would need to deal with each other on a more realistic level. This did occur several months later when Bobby began to show improvement. Subsequently, the marital relationship itself was treated and the mother entered analysis. Thus the home visit can bring into sharp relief the significant dynamic forces in the life of the family and be of tremendous service in planning treatment and evaluating expectations of success.

But once data have been collected by means of history-taking, home visits, and office observation, the clinical team is faced with the problem of organizing this mass of material in a workable form. The guides that follow have been found helpful if used flexibly and with discrimination. Included are a guide for data leading to family diagnosis, a guide for the evaluation of marital and parental interaction, a guide for the evaluation of the personality of a child here and now, and a guide for the sequential stages of child development. It is self-evident that the guide for marital interaction may be used independently and serves a special purpose when the pair under consideration has no children or other family connections. The evaluation of a parental pair should be made in the context of a comprehensive family diagnosis insofar as children or grandparents affect parental interaction. In both instances provision is made for the evaluation of individual personality and formulation of the dynamic interrelations of personality and family role adaptation. Of special importance in family psychiatry is the evaluation of the personality of a child here and now, the determination of the child's level of emotional maturation, and the correlation of this data on child behavior with the diagnosis of the family group. The last two guides are intended to serve this purpose.

Guide for Data Leading to Family Diagnosis

Note: For each category of information provide the relevant historical background.

I. A. Presenting problem
   B. Level of entry
      1. Disturbance of family member
      2. Disturbance of family relationships
      3. Impaired family functions
      4. A special stress situation which precipitates the referral, inside or outside the family
   C. Attitudes toward the family problem and toward professional intervention

II. Identifying data
   A. Composition of family: age, sex of family members and other persons in the home

B. Physical setting: home, neighborhood, geographical mobility

C. Social and cultural pattern: occupation, income, education, ethnic and religious status, social mobility

D. Special features: *e.g.*, previous marriages, separations, pregnancies, health problems (mental or physical), significant deaths

III. Family as a group

  A. Internal organization

    1. Describe emotional climate, communication, shared goals, activities, pleasures, lines of authority, division of labor, child-rearing attitudes, problems, etc.

    2. Evaluate:

      a. Identity of the family group: strivings, expectations, and values

      b. Stability of the family (identity and stability as imaged from within)

        (1) Continuity of family identity in time

        (2) Conflict in family relations, mechanisms of control and interplay of defenses

        (3) Capacity for change, learning, development; complementarity in family role relations

  B. External adaptation of the family to community

    1. Describe associations and transactions of the family with the community as a group, as marital and parental pairs, and as individuals

    2. Evaluate identity and stability as above (as perceived from without)

    3. Conflict and complementarity in the requirements of intra- and extra-familial roles

IV. Current family functioning:

  A. Current marital relationship

    1. Describe interaction as marital partners; perception of own and partner's role adaptation; describe components of marital role relations at sexual, social and emotional levels: quality of love and related satisfactions, image of future relationship, including children

    2. Evaluate identity and stability of marital relationship as above

  B. Current parental relationship

    1. Describe interaction as parents and with children; describe perception of own and partner's role adaptation

    2. Evaluate identity and stability of parental relationship as above

  C. Current parent-child relationship

    1. Describe relations of parental pair and each parent with child, influence of parental pair and of each parent on the child, and vice versa

    2. Evaluate identity and stability of parent-child relationship as above

  D. Sibling pair relationship, as in IV C.

V. Personality make-up of each individual member
   A. Appearance, attitudes, behavior
   B. Personality structure: evaluate identity and stability as above
   C. Evaluate pathogenic conflict, anxiety, symptoms and patterns of control in the frame of total functioning and integration into the family group
VI. Relations with primary parental families
VII. Developmental history of the primary patient; problems in relation to mother, father and family group
VIII. Summary interpretation of the mental health of the family group and interrelations between individual and family mental health

Criteria for Evaluation of Marital and Parental Interaction

I. Past interaction
   A. Origin and development of relationship during courtship
   B. After marriage, but before children
   C. After children
   For each historical phase:
   1. Shared identity: strivings, values, expectations
   2. Stability, realism, maturity
   3. Reciprocal role adaptation
      (a) Levels of complementarity
         (1) Non-sexual aspects of complementarity
             Emotional:
                 Capacity for affection, empathy, intimacy, communication and mutual support
             Social and economic:
                 Companionship, balance of authority, sharing of activities, resources, division of labor, and problems
         (2) Sexual aspects of complementarity
             Sexual satisfaction or frustration
         (3) Family aspects of complementarity:
             Interdependence and reciprocity of marital and parental role function
      (b) Levels of conflict and patterns of restitution
      Areas of shared functioning most involved in conflict; patterns of conflict, intensity, degree of spread; controlled or acted out; patterns of restitution. Mutuality of support as husband and wife, father and mother.
         (4) Interaction of marital and parental partners as couple with external environment

(5) Specific trends toward isolation, regression or disintegration

II. Current interaction (use criteria under Past interaction)
III. Achievement (measured according to family's expectations and also according to an ideal of healthy marital and parental interaction in our culture)
   A. Relation between strivings, values, and actual performance
   B. Fulfillment of goals for relationship and each partner as individual
IV. Interrelations of individual personality and marital and parental roles
   A. Individual personality structure
      1. Symptoms and character structure of husband (psychiatric diagnosis)
      2. Symptoms and character structure of wife (psychiatric diagnosis)
   B. Integration of personality into family roles (husband and wife, father and mother)
      1. Goals for relationship
      2. Image of relationship
      3. Self-image projected into relationship
      4. Need and conflict projected into relationship
      5. Emotional control of relationship
      6. Control of anxiety—specific defenses
   C. Interdependence and reciprocity of family roles
   D. The effects of ancillary roles, in own family, as children of own parents, as employee, friend, member of the community
V. Neurotic component of relationship
   A. Specific pattern of neurotic interaction
   B. Intensity and depth
   C. Spread of involvement
   D. Degree of deviation from healthy marital and parental interaction
   E. Failure of personality of each partner to integrate into family role
   F. Degree of symbiosis in the pathology of the relationship
   G. Specify the pathology of the relationship in the following terms:
      1. The unrealness and inappropriateness of strivings and expectations for the relationship
      2. The distortions of perception of the relationship
      3. The conflicted, confused images of self projected into the relationship
      4. The specific neurotic needs and conflicts involved
      5. The pathological techniques for control of the relationship
      6. The pathological mechanisms of control of anxiety
VI. The consequences of neurotic conflict. (Impairment of marital and parental role adaptation evaluated)
   A. Distortions of strivings, values, and expectations

    B. Breakdown of complementarity in special areas of shared functioning

    C. Intensification of conflict, pathological defenses against anxiety

    D. Trends toward isolation, disintegration

VII. Patterns of restitution

    A. Increased tolerance or support of immature or regressed emotional needs in the partner

    B. Increased tolerance of distorted perceptions of the relationship; tolerance of irrational projections, one partner onto the other

    C. Tolerance of inappropriate (irrational) patterns of control of relationship

    D. Tolerance and reinforcement of pathological defenses against anxiety

    E. Or, in each of the above categories, effective control of the neurotic tendencies of one partner by the other, or the facilitation of healthier forms of defense

When the specific component of neurotic conflict has been differentiated, a careful estimate of the balance between the pathology and the residual health of the relationship is of the utmost clinical importance. The following questions may be helpful in making such an estimate:

1. Appraisal of the damage to the relationship, resulting from neurotic conflict:
    a. Does it threaten to engulf all major aspects of the marital and parental interaction, or are its effects relatively circumscribed?
    b. Do the conflicted urges, irrational projections, and inappropriate, rigid defenses of one partner threaten to overwhelm the other?
    c. Are there clear signs of a push toward isolation, disintegration, or regression in the relationship?
2. Appraisal of the residual health of the relationship:
    a. What areas of marital and parental interaction and shared functioning are least damaged?
    b. What is their importance relative to the critically impaired areas?
    c. What degree of mutual trust and acceptance prevails despite the existence of neurotic conflict?
    d. What is the motivation for reconstruction of the relationship in each partner?

If we estimate in this manner the assets and liabilities with regard to the mental health of a marital relationship, it begins to be possible to institute a realistic program of therapy. We may then erect goals for the psychotherapy of husband and wife in the context of a clear awareness of the reciprocity of the marital roles, rather than operating psychotherapeutically with an abstract goal of cure of neurosis in one individual partner, while giving insufficient attention to the features of the total marital relationship. One must take into account, too, what is residually healthy in the personality of each partner and the positive factors preserved in the relationship over and above the content of its neurotic component. Adequate diagnosis of the marital relationship makes it possible not only to focus therapy on the damaged areas of functioning but also to reinforce and strengthen the relatively healthy areas of functioning, and so fortify the whole relationship.

The Child Here and Now

Intelligence
Physical status: height, weight, general health
A. General appearance and behavior (the child patient as a living person)
B. Symptoms
    1. Structured psychiatric symptoms, if any: organic, psychotic, psychoneurotic, psychosomatic
    2. Enumerate the child's disturbances in:
        a. Attitudes toward other people: family, siblings, etc.
        b. Attitudes toward self
            (1) Motor activity
            (2) Eating, sleeping, elimination, sex
        c. Mood
C. Diagnostic evaluation of the family group
D. Adaptation to external reality
    1. Perception of real experience; range, quality, capacity to discriminate
    2. Distortion of real experience: degree and kind
    3. Mastery of real experience: degree and kind
        a. Use of the body in mastery: active, passive, coordination, control, play, speech, etc.
        b. Use of phantasy as bridge of contact to reality
E. Interpersonal relations
    1. Attitude toward others:
        a. Contact with others, adults and children: degree and kind; closeness or emotional separation
        b. Dependence on adults: degree and kind
        c. Control of other persons: degree and kind
        d. Capacity for identification, for sharing experience
            (1) The role of fear, aggression and love in these relationships
            (2) The role of ambivalence in these relationships
            (3) Patterns of submission and rebellion
            (4) Evidences of fear of injury
    2. Attitude toward self:
        a. The image of self and own body; changes in this image at reality and phantasy levels

    b. The stability or instability of the self-image

    c. Self-esteem and self-confidence; strivings and reactions to frustration and failure

F. Quality of affects

    1. Quality of affects according to criteria of:

       a. Richness and depth of emotion

       b. Spontaneity

       c. Stability

       d. Appropriateness

       e. Flexibility

    2. Capacity for rapport and range of emotional interests

    3. Relation of the affective responses to general activity pattern

G. Anxiety reactions

    1. Quantity

    2. Quality

    3. Localization (diffuse or bound in symptom formation)

    4. Control of anxiety (stable or unstable)

    5. Panic reactions

    6. Adequacy of defenses

H. Patterns of control

    1. General capacity for control of emotion: adequate or deficient

    2. Degree of impulsiveness

    3. Control of impulses at the periphery of the personality (control of impulse through conscious suppression)

    4. Control of impulses within the core of the personality (through repression)

       a. normal

       b. deficient

       c. excessive

    5. Capacity for spontaneous self-expression: adequate or deficient

    6. Capacity for pleasure experience: In what life situations, roles and activities is this found?

    7. Tolerance for frustration and pain: In what life situations, roles and activities is this found?

    8. Functioning of conscience

       a. Guilt

       b. Inhibition or expression

       c. Fear of retaliation; defenses against retaliation

       d. Punishment pattern: self-punishing attitude, self-destructive behavior, depression, suicide

I. Defense patterns

    1. Quality

       a. Range of defenses against anxiety

    b. Stability and variability of defenses
    c. Rigidity or flexibility of defenses
    d. Reliability of defenses
    e. Occurrence of panic reactions with emotional disorganization
J. Central conflicts
    1. Formulate the salient conflicts of the patient:
        a. At conscious level
        b. At unconscious level
        c. Contradiction between conscious and unconscious levels of conflict
    2. Define role of conflicts and associated symptoms within the frame of total
        functioning of personality and prevailing modes of interpersonal adaptation
    3. Specific relation of conflicts to self-image and choice of defenses
    4. The interrelations of child's disturbance with personal development and
        family experience

For such purposes of correlation of child and family behavior the child's emotional development is divided into stages. Each stage is conditioned by the previous stage and merges imperceptibly into and overlaps with the next stage. With movement from one stage to the next, the processes intrinsic to the previous stage do not cease but become less prominent and are differently integrated into the dominant patterns of the succeeding stage. These stages of development, loosely ordered on a temporal scale, are best identified in terms of the characteristic trends of adaptation.

The Developmental Stages of Childhood

    1. The intrauterine stage: foetal symbiosis.
    2. The neonatal stage: the immediate postbirth period reflects mainly a phase of vegetative readaptation, from existence in the womb to the conditions of life in the outside world. The physiological balance of the organism is profoundly altered. The infant becomes active in satisfying basic life needs; he must breathe, suck, and swallow. Since the vegetative nervous system is not fully organized, physiological responses are characteristically unstable. Irregularities of respiration, episodes of regurgitation, vomiting, and startle reactions are common. Among the newborn there are marked differences in activity pattern which are apparent in the rhythm of feeding, movement, sleeping, and waking; differences in responses to sound, smell, touch, and taste are less conspicuous.
    3. The stage of primary identification: This is the phase of primary emotional union with mother. Though physically separated

from the mother by birth, the infant is totally dependent for survival and development on the integrity and continuity of the union with mother. The infant requires nourishment, tender warmth, touch contact, and other stimulation, and also protection from danger. The taking in of nourishment from the mother's breast is the model for psychic incorporation of the mother's image. It is the basis for the process of primary identification. A feeling of confident expectation strengthens the unity of child and mother. It acts as an emotional shelter. It protects the infant from an excess of external stimuli. It facilitates learning. But the process of primary identification with mother is influenced not only by a stimulation of oral needs but also by sensations of smell, touch, taste, hearing, and vision. A sustained flow of gratifications leads to a feeling of body pleasure and self-esteem. Failure of this sense of trust and confidence disrupts unity, disturbs empathy and communication. This stage of child-mother union is characterized by complete dependence and by a tendency to omnipotent behavior. The omnipotent attitudes may be understood not as the unfolding of the child's individuality but rather as an expression of the symbiotic union of infant and mother. The child commands; the mother obeys. The mother commands; the child obeys. The child does not yet distinguish the mother self from the own self. The mother functions not only as the source of love and security but also as the perceptive and executive agent of the child. She conveys through her own behavior her affective interpretation of the prevailing realities and also devices for dealing with them. In this stage premature withdrawal of the mother induces in the child feelings of helplessness, panic, retreat, and apathy.

4. *The stage of individuation:* The fourth stage is one of gradual separation of the infant's self from the mother self. This occurs in a healthy manner only as the continuity of primary union is preserved. As the infant's needs are met, his curiosity and exploration of the environment expands. Thwarting of basic needs blunts the learning process. As he learns to walk and talk, he expands his mastery over the environment. With the acquisition of speech, he substitutes verbal communication for the pre-verbal body language. As the symbiotic union of child and mother lessens, omnipotent behavior gives way to progressive reality and an increasing measure of realistic control. Social discipline of the child grows in importance. The child must come to terms with the social standards of his parents. These standards vary, of course, with family structure and social and culture pattern. The mother's care controls the socialization of the child. It is influenced by her relations with father and other family members. As the child submits to parental discipline, he begins to internalize the standards of

parents and family. At first this takes the form of depending upon the parents as an external conscience, but he gradually incorporates these standards into his emerging personality. The child learns to pursue pleasure within the frame of reality. He learns to avoid pain and to postpone the need for immediate satisfactions. His emotional integration into the family group is influenced by his perception of those actions that bring the mother's love and approval.

5. *The stage of sexual differentiation (oedipal stage)*: The fifth stage reflects the changing expressions of the child's love needs to the two parents according to sex, a differentiation of self in accordance with recognition of sex differences, and the pattern of relations between the two parents. In close association with this trend is the emergence of distinct identification with each parent. There is deeper internalization of the functions of conscience now influenced by the distinction between male and female parent and the emerging sexual identity of the child. The further stages of assimilation of parental standards and control are differentiated accordingly.

6. *The stage of extrafamilial development*: The sixth stage is one of expansion of the emotional and social spheres of the child's interaction with his environment beyond the confines of his immediate family, testing of social reality, and learning in the context of wider contact with peers and parent substitutes. This is a period of broadened social growth, education, and preparation for adolescent maturation.

7. *The stage of adolescence*: This is the stage of pubescent growth bringing in its wake the struggles of adolescent adaptation to society. Differentiated sex drives emerge and there is reorganization of the lines of identification, realignment of group allegiances and roles, anticipation of and preparation for tasks of adult life.

8. *The stage of entry into adulthood.*

Certainly it should be apparent that the complexities of family diagnosis are such that any technique for the collection of diagnostic information must be used with clinical discretion and judgment and with due attention to the special problems inherent in the individual situation. No technique can be considered fixed and unchangeable, and no opportunity for utilizing or developing other techniques can be ignored.

CHAPTER 10

DISTURBANCES OF MARITAL PAIRS

THE SPECIAL PROBLEMS of marital and parental pairs can best be understood in terms of the mutuality and interdependence of the respective family role adaptations, the complementarity of sexual behavior, the reciprocity of emotional and social companionship, the sharing of authority, and the division of labor. As the marital pair moves on to parenthood, the problems of shared parental responsibility add another level of complexity to family relations, and conflict in parental role relations is superimposed upon any conflict which may already exist in marital role relations. Only by means of accurate diagnostic assessment of the functioning of these family pairs can we hope to evolve a therapy for such disturbances that is psychologically specific. The concept of diagnosis is not a mere label but a definitive evaluation that absorbs within itself the dynamics of the disorder. Diagnosis is the beginning of a plan of action, the strategy of therapeutic intervention.

In this era of transition, characterized by widespread value conflict and confusion of aims and expectations, the goals of marriage and home and the aspirations of parenthood have changed. Whereas the earlier emphasis in marital relationships rested on issues having to do with security and survival, now increasing importance is placed upon the values of companionship and love. There is reason to believe, despite lack of scientific data, that the choice of mate represents the merging of many motives: love feeling and sexual need pointing ordinarily toward members of the same or similar social class; an image of self related to a family image; corresponding values; strivings for security, stability, and prestige. In the main, when a person expresses the need of love by entry into marriage, he is apt to select a person who reciprocates his sexual make-up, character, group allegiances, and corresponding aims and values. In other words, he is practical and realistic even in the act of falling in love. In this sense, love is not as blind as it seems. There are exceptions, to be sure. The romantic version of love which so dominates the phantasy life of the young people of Western society is tempered under ordinary circumstances, however, by the person's respect for reality. Often the importance of social position and the sharing of common interests, security, and economic advancement play a subtle but important role.

Particularly significant is the disguised motivational element of searching out a mate who is likely to assuage or counteract one's personal anxiety. In this sense, marriage is approached as a potential cure for whatever psychic ails a man may suffer. The choice of a marital partner thus incorporates much of reality and much of common sense. It must prove to be a practical and working partnership or it fails. When the marital relationship does not fulfill these several interwoven purposes, the reciprocity of the partnership breaks down and there is a heightened risk of emotional alienation or divorce. With considerable frequency early expectations are not fulfilled by the actualities of marriage and family. The resulting disillusionment accentuates the tendency to divorce.

The divorce rate in our present society is high, roughly one divorce for every three or four marriages. The frequency of divorce of childless parents is of no great consequence to the evolution of society and family. Divorce involving the fate of offspring is the more vital question. In the latter instance, marital conflict is of significance not only of itself but also as the epitome and the very core of disintegrative trends in family life and the harbinger of distorted emotional development in the offspring. Ultimately this distortion adds to the burden of mental illness in the community. It is to be remembered too that there can be no effective divorce for parents. Though permanently divided as a sexual couple, they remain permanently tied by their joined responsibility for the care of their children, and in some instances this tie becomes a source of suffering for many years.

At the same time, we recognize the fact that, for every marriage that eventuates in divorce, there are many in which the partners stay together but are emotionally alienated from one another. They stay joined not out of reasons of love, but out of economic need, duty to children, personal dependency, fear of loneliness, or simply because there is no place else to go. The family unit remains together physically, but there is, in effect, an emotional divorce of the parents. These are the situations that call for the most careful scrutiny in terms of their effect on the personality development of the children and their final fate in terms of illness or health.

The disturbances of marital and parental couples need first of all to be viewed against the backdrop of the profound social changes that are part of the contemporary scene. We have reason to believe that the intrinsic value conflicts of our changing culture have a direct bearing on the fate of family life and family relationships. It requires no great stretch of the imagination to realize that the survival or destruction of our kind of civilization will depend in no small part on how these value conflicts are resolved and what happens concurrently to the mental health of the family. It is the clear and present threat to our traditional values in family living which challenge us. Our anxiety is for ourselves; it impels us to take a stand.

Of the first importance is a clear-cut recognition of the general category into which this problem falls. In undertaking to diagnose marital and parental relationships, we are not concerned in the first instance with the autonomous functions and pathology of individual personalities but rather with the dynamics of the relationship, that is, with the reciprocal role adaptations that define the relations of man and wife. This is, by its very nature, a problem that belongs to the sphere of social psychopathology.[1]

A marital relationship is something beyond the sum of the personalities that make it up. The relationship itself tends to influence and change each partner and this in turn influences the relationship anew. In confronting problems in this particular area, we shift our traditional focus of interest as psychiatrists from the pathology of individual personality to the pathology of a human relationship as a social unit. And we have to admit that the efficacy of our diagnostic and therapeutic tools for dealing with the pathology of relationships lags behind our ability to deal with the intrapsychic disorders of the individual.

This raises an interesting problem of definition: Does the term "neurotic" as it refers to marital relations have precisely the same connotation as the term "neurotic" when it applies to fixed forms of conflict within individual personality? I might offer two definitions of neurosis to elucidate the point. For example: Oberndorf defines a neurosis as "a compromise formation showing itself repetitively in thinking (mentally) or performance (bodily), caused by a preponderant intrapsychic conflict, and the compromise is incapacitating and ineffectual, *i.e.*, the compromise does not accomplish what it sets out to do." Freud describes the structure of neurosis as resulting from chronic repression of a specific internal conflict between id and superego, in which the repressed instinctual impulses are displaced and disguised and reappear in the form of disabling symptoms.

Is conflict between persons to be conceived in the same terms as conflict within a person? Is neurotic conflict in a marital pair to be conceived as having dynamic connotations identical with neurosis of individual personality? Even when we take full cognizance of the principle that neurosis in the individual implies a particular set of propensities in interpersonal adaptation, we must nevertheless draw a distinction between interpersonal conflict, real or neurotic, and conflict within the individual; although they overlap, the two are not identical. The proof is readily available in empirical observations unequivocally demonstrating that a given individual with a fixed neurosis will interact in significantly different ways with different partners. For example, a psychoneurotic male with strong castration fears may be totally impotent with his wife and strong as a bull with another woman. In other words, though he is affected by, or, we might say, enjoys, the same neurosis in both relationships, he is, as a person, differently integrated in the two situations, and the psychosocial consequences of neurotic conflict are correspondingly different.

The recent developments in the behavioral sciences are immediately relevant to the task of evaluating the mental health problems of marital relationships and family life: the emphasis on multi-disciplinary research; the growing partnership of psychoanalysis and the social sciences; the increased influence of the anthropological principle of relativity of behavior; the effort to move beyond Freud in linking the phenomena of biological maturation with the processes of social participation; the correlation of ego dynamics with social interaction; the rediscovery of the ancient principle that behavior is determined not only by a person's view of his past, but also by his view of the future; and so on. There are indications that we are on the brink of a new revolution in the integration of the behavioral sciences and this revolution is an essential step in coping with hitherto unsolved problems. Only when we can correctly merge the dynamics of individual and group behavior does it begin to be possible to deal effectively with the mental health problems of family and marital relationships.

A relationship represents more than the sum of two personalities. A new level of organization creates new qualities. A marital relationship, like a chemical compound, has unique properties of its own, over and above the characteristics of the elements that merge to form the compound. It is an entity, new and different, but its properties although unique preserve a specific dynamic relation to the elements that have joined in its creation. In other words, the psychological principles that govern the behavior of an individual and those that govern the behavior of a relationship are not the same. We cannot directly extrapolate from our knowledge of individual personality to behavior of a relationship or a group; the psychological processes involved at the relationship or group level must be viewed in a different dimension because a different level of biosocial organization is represented. The dynamics of the two situations, individual and group, are therefore not interchangeable, and the integrative processes appropriate to the one level of biosocial organization cannot be superimposed on the other.

By way of pointing more sharply to the nature of this problem let us consider the mental health implications of some common empirical observations. Some neurotics are nice people, in fact, extraordinarily likeable people, despite their neuroses, or occasionally because of them. Other neurotics are disagreeable persons. People with the same neurosis may be extraordinarily different in their personal values and in the social manifestations of such values. Depending upon our own values, we either like them or find them offensive.

It is often said that one neurotic marries another. But what a neurotic person seeks out is not primarily a partner afflicted with neurosis, but rather an individual who, hopefully, will complement his idiosyncratic emotional needs. The outcome, in mental health terms, of a particular marriage is not contingent exclusively on the character of the neuroses of the individual partners. The ultimate effects on mental health are determined rather by the part that neurotic conflict plays in the complex process of integration of the personalities of the partners into the reciprocal roles of husband and wife. The factors that shape this process are multiple; we shall consider them at a later point.

In some instances neurotic conflict destroys the marriage; in others it seems to save the marriage. It is common knowledge that the neurotic tendency of one marital partner often complements that of the other. Sometimes the traits of one partner reinforce in the other healthy defenses against neurotic conflict, so that its destructive effects are mitigated. Sometimes this form of complementarity decompensates and the marital relationship disintegrates. The issue is a question not merely of the effect of individual neurotic conflict on the marital functioning but also of the interplay of the two persons sharing one life. The bad marriages that some neurotic individuals make are notorious, but what enables some to make good ones? The wonder is not so much that one neurotic marries another, but rather that some neurotics marry persons who strengthen them against regression and also provide support so that they can function as reasonably good parents.

The potentially hopeful aspect of this whole problem is that some neurotics, despite traumatic childhoods, make fine marriages and fine parents. These are the well-intentioned people who pit a fundamentally sound set of personal values against the destructive expressions of their neurosis. Neurosis in individual personality is not, therefore, the sole factor that predetermines the fate of marriage, family life, and a new crop of children. Were it so there would be little hope for the world. The saving grace is that in certain neurotic marital partnerships the effect each partner exerts upon the other is a favorable one and neutralizes the injurious results of their neuroses. Within this matrix the character of each partner improves.

It is a common observation that neurotic disturbance of a marital relationship is rarely, if ever, the creation of just one of the partners. In marital pairs ambivalently bound in neurotic love and neurotic competition, when one partner exhibits pathological anxiety responses, the other usually does too. Being immature and unready for a full love union, the partners tend to parentify each other. Seeking the love and protection of a parent figure in the marital partner, each pushes the relationship toward the needed form of child-parent relationship. In this context, the marital relationship is forced to assume a compensatory and curative function for the anxiety-provoking features of the original child-parent experience. Insofar as the marital relationship is coerced into satisfying conflicted and regressed childhood needs or compensating for the lack of emotional fulfillment, the relationship is burdened with an extra and an inappropriate psychic load. It should be remembered, however, that some marriage relationships are so patterned as to bear this extra load with minimum damage to mental health.

Let us, for example, consider the young wife, married only six months, who consulted a psychiatrist because she was considering a separation. Initially, the psychiatrist was hard put to discover the reason. He felt puzzled because it proved so difficult to uncover the significant area of conflict. In many ways she seemed satisfied with the relationship. Finally, he asked this young woman if she had a sexual problem with her husband. She said: "Oh, no! Sexual intercourse is perfect; it couldn't be better." "Then what in the world is really the trouble?" asked the psychiatrist. The woman then blurted out her true complaint. "When we have sex, there's just no verbal intercourse at all." Her basic unhappiness was simply that her husband didn't talk enough.

A corrective approach to marital disturbance cannot be a simple undertaking. It must be recognized as therapy for the disturbances of "husbanding and wifing" rather than straight therapy for an individual neurosis. Neurotic interaction, therefore, is a new, dynamic entity, not to be defined merely as the separate and distinct neuroses of the two individuals who join in the relationship. If we agree to the proposition that neurotic interaction is a part, perhaps central, but nevertheless a part, of total interaction, it is necessary first to find criteria appropriate for evaluating the total process of marital interaction and then to differentiate the neurotic component of that interaction.

If we are motivated to rehabilitate the mental health of a disturbed marital relationship, we must take into account not only the pathological elements of behavior but also the malleable aspects of personality in both partners, their residual strengths, their capacity for realism, for new learning, and for emotional integration, the positive features of the marital relationship and of the family life, and the motivation of both partners for change; all these are needed to counterbalance pathological tendencies. Toward this end, it is necessary to make a systematic evaluation of all aspects of the marital relationship: its history, its path of motivation, and the past and current patterns of marital interaction. The diagnostic appraisal of the mental health of marital and parental role relations is central to the objectives of "family diagnosis."

Disturbances of marital relationships are characterized by two salient elements: (1) failure of reciprocity of satisfactions and (2) conflict. These central features are influenced by several processes: disturbance of empathic union and identification; defective communication; the failure of devices of restitution following an upset in the balance of the relationship; and a failure of complementarity in which the one partner no longer derives from the other satisfaction of needs, support of personal identity and buttressing of necessary defenses against anxiety.

For clinicians, conflict in marital relationships and the lessening of mutual satisfactions present a particularly knotty problem. The relevant factors are multiple and complex; they overlap and interact to such an extent that a clear and communicable definition of the problem is difficult to achieve. The task is to reduce the salient characteristics to a clear-cut formulation, but this is more easily said than done.

In marital disorders, as elsewhere, conflict may be overt or covert, real or unreal, conscious or unconscious, in varying mixtures. Moreover, the conflict between the partners bears a special relationship to the structure of intrapsychic conflict in each partner. Marital conflict may aggravate or serve to obscure the real nature of these internalized conflicts. Such internalized individual conflicts may move into the center of the stage of the disorder of marital relations or occupy only a peripheral position; thus, the irrational content of individual neurosis may represent a component of the marital conflict or appear at the very center of the whole relationship.

The question is: What part of the marital conflict is real, what part unreal and determined by neurotic perception and motivation? Further, how does the unreal part secondarily distort the relatively more real aspects of marital interaction? Because we cannot psychoanalyze realistic components of experience, all that is needed is accurate awareness of the realistic levels of marital interaction, and a plan of action appropriate to this awareness. The unreal part, structured by neurotic interaction, calls for a different program—definitive diagnostic evaluation and suitable psychotherapeutic correction.

It is important, then, to see the neurotic component of conflict in the context of total marital interaction. Although it is easy to detect the more pathological types of neurotic marital relationships, the task of evaluating the partial significance of specific patterns of neurotic conflict in the context of the total relationship and the prevailing social realities is a complex one. The effects of neurotic motivation may be variably diffuse or localized both in individual personality and in a relationship. Just as in the individual some areas of adaptive functioning may be heavily disabled and other areas relatively conflict-free and less disabled, so in a marital relationship some levels of interaction may be critically impaired whereas others are relatively conflict-free and less impaired.

It is surely easier in our time to spot the more obviously pathological marital relationships than it is to be definitive regarding standards for healthy marital relations. Nevertheless, the goal of erecting a model for a healthy marriage, elusive and changing as this may be in our culture, is an essential one. Presumably, such a relationship would be characterized by a relatively clear awareness of strivings and values, positive in emphasis rather than defensive. Strivings and values would be shared to a reasonable degree by both partners and would be relatively realistic, stable, and flexible. There would be a reasonable degree of compatibility in the main areas of shared experiences—the emotional, social, sexual, economic, and parental areas. Conflict would not be excessive, would be under control, and would have mainly a realistic, rather than an irrational, content. There would be empathic tolerance of differences based on mutual understanding and equality and tolerance as well of residual immaturities of need that might be present in either partner. There would be sharing of pleasure, responsibility, and authority. There would be reasonable fulfillment of goals both for the relationship and for the further development of each partner as an individual. Each would be as much concerned for the welfare and development of the partner as for the self. Where differences exist, the mutual, unreserved acceptance of each partner by the other would make of these differences a stimulus for growth, both for the relationship and for each partner as an individual, rather than a basis for conflict or alienation. Actual performance in marriage would reasonably approximate goals. There would be a relatively high complementarity on a positive basis as husband and wife and as father and mother. There would be no significant trends toward isolation, disintegration, or regression.

Unfortunately, however, the clinician sees a large number of family patterns that bear little resemblance to this ideal. Mr. and Mrs. Owen illustrate a common form of marital conflict in contemporary society. Married four years, they had reached an impasse in their relationship. They had become trapped in conflict from which they saw no way out except divorce. The tension between them was severe. They expressed it in torrents of mutual abuse or morose silence.

Mrs. Owen's complaints were several: she blamed her recurrent depressions on her husband because he was too busy to take her away with him on vacation. He persistently found fault and heaped abusive, insulting epithets upon her. He accused her of being childish, stupid, and irresponsible. Mr. Owen alleged that his wife was too demanding, extravagant, and inconsiderate of him; she was a sloppy, disorganized housekeeper, had no respect for money, and disrespected him as a man.

Mr. Owen was fourteen years older than his wife. He was an intelligent and successful professional man, punctilious, perfectionist, self-righteous, and compulsive. He scolded and preached to his wife. Mrs. Owen was an attractive, stylishly dressed young woman, emotionally immature, exhibitionistic, and needing a continuous flow of flattering attentions. She experienced flurries of hysterical symptoms and had obsessive fears of contamination. She fitted herself distinctly into the role as child-wife.

Both of these people were plagued with an underlying sense of inferiority but compensated for it in quite different ways. Mr. Owen denied and concealed his inferiority behind a mask of pompous dignity. In the marriage he assumed the unchallenged position of superiority. Mrs. Owen was his exact counterpart in taking the outwardly dependent, inferior role, while secretly treating her husband as a captive prisoner and exacting a ransom. She provoked her husband's insults but was adroitly devastating in her devices of retaliation. She drained him financially with her extravagances. Mr. Owen tried to save money. She showed off by spending it. She sabotaged her husband by procrastinating in the carrying out of household responsibilities. She undercut him as a man with her sexual coldness. In these several ways she made it impossible for her husband to rely upon her. With all this these partners in marriage had much in common. They shared similar goals for security, affection, social position, and a beautifully decorated home. They complemented one another most successfully in their shared social life; in the company of others they got along exceedingly well. He was proud of her attractive appearance. She was proud of his professional attainment. In their private relationship, however, their competitive hostilities emerged sharply. Sexually neither of them felt satisfied. She regarded sexual submission as an obligation to her husband for his support of her, while he felt that she gave him too little pleasure. Emotionally they slid into a mutually disparaging relationship which obscured their underlying fondness and need of one another.

In a marital disorder of this type, the conflict and failure of complementarity are, first, functions of the peculiar character of the relationship and, second, an expression of the unresolved dependency needs of each partner. The need of each to be indulged and served in a special way drove them into a competitive war.

Mr. and Mrs. Roberts represent a different type of marital conflict. They have been married for twelve years. Each of them holds a responsible position in the advertising industry. They have no children. For nine years the marital relationship was sustained in a condition of tolerable neurotic balance. The relationship was an immature, mutually dependent one. Each partner played the role of parent and mentor to the other. Ostensibly, the status of the husband was dominant, while the wife occupied the submissive position. In the husband's mind, this first phase of the marriage was heaven. Three years ago, however, "all hell broke loose." The pre-existing marital balance was acutely disrupted.

As the husband sees it, this crisis had its origin in the office of his wife's psychoanalyst. He accused this analyst of being a home breaker. As the wife sees it, were it not for her psychoanalyst, she might not be alive today. Her chronic distress with ulcerative colitis was relieved by psychoanalytic treatment. She had been in analysis for five years. For the first three years, she lay dormant. Two years ago, she experienced a deep and radical change of her emotional life. Instead of pouring out her conflicted emotions by way of bloody diarrhea, she turned her hostile feelings outward against her husband. She became provocative; she withdrew affection from him and defiantly altered their domestic habits. For example, she now refused provocatively to respect her husband's longtime aversion to certain foods, such as crabmeat. She also turned cold and inaccessible. This incited her husband to fury. It precipitated recurrent episodes of explosive conflict. The marital crisis went from bad to worse. Each partner made emotional demands the other could not fulfill. They could neither revert to their old pattern of marital balance nor discover a new level of complementary relations. They became trapped in a war to the death. The wife feared her husband's abuse and physical attacks; she feared actual body injury. The husband felt rejected, demeaned, unmanned; he felt a deep humiliation in his position as the man of the family. Each demanded a pound of flesh.

Originally, Mr. Roberts had married a "soft, sweet girl." The only trouble was that she was sick. She had frequent bloody stools, was depleted in energy, weak, depressed, and barely managed to drag herself through the day's work. The husband played the role of the boy genius, and the wife was the devoted, servile admirer. She now believes the contentment of the first nine years was a neurotic illusion. As long as she was the adoring slave, she made her husband happy. But his happiness came at the cost of her health and personal freedom. She took out her tensions on her own body. Then, she believes, her psychoanalytic therapy liberated her. She vigorously asserted her new-found freedom. But this change in her attitude clashed severely with her husband's expectations. To him, it seemed that his sweet wife had turned into a shrew, under the influence of "Svengali," as he called his wife's analyst.

Mrs. Roberts is an intelligent person, outwardly calm, placid, and controlled. Inwardly she is a cauldron of disturbed emotion. She is quiet on the outside, noisy on the inside. It is her inner agitation that threw her bowels into an uproar. She tends now to overvalue the results of her psychotherapy. She continues to be vulnerable to a recurrence of colitis and is still plagued by obsessive doubts and fears. By contrast, Mr. Roberts is noisy on the outside, soft and weak on the inside. He roars like a lion but turns into a mouse. Mrs. Roberts looks like a mouse but bites like a lion. Mr. Roberts is rigid, arbitrary-minded, arrogant, possessive, and jealous. He is intensely emotional, agitated, and explosive. He is a boy trying to sell himself to the world as a big man. When his wife revolted against her dependent position, he fought like a cornered animal to protect his masculine façade. He feared that if his wife ripened into a full-blooded woman, she might find herself a better man.

A special complication in this marital crisis is the wife's emotional misuse of her analysis to wreak vengeance on her husband. She behaved as if it were a matter of her husband's life or her own, as if she might become a whole woman only over her husband's prostrate body. This pitched her husband into a state of critical turmoil. His pride and his defenses against anxiety were thrown into jeopardy.

It becomes apparent in these two cases that the clinician faced with an unhappy husband and an unhappy wife must look beyond the neurosis of the individual to the disturbance within the relationship itself. (See Criteria for Evaluation of Marital and Parental Interaction, p. 140.) Diagnosis of one without the other is impossible, and treatment of one without the other can multiply problems rather than alleviate them. Marital crisis is seldom the result of one partner's disturbance.

CHAPTER 11

DISTURBANCES OF PARENTAL PAIRS

MOST PEOPLE feel that they know very well what a good mother is, but they do not know nearly so well what a good father is. They recognize a good mother immediately when they see one but they cannot identify a good father with anything like the same ease and sureness. In general, the image of the ideal parent, whether male or female, is a continuously changing one; like the image of the family itself it shifts with time and place. A characteristic picture of the ideal parent emerges with each successive phase of history, in different parts of the world, and in different societies.

There are, however, a few basic elements which within limits are fairly constant, though extremely difficult to pin down. These elements derive from the biological differences and the complementary relations of man and woman, and from the long dependency of the child. The mother protects the child, gives it food and care, assures its survival. The father protects mother and child, provides them with the necessities of life, and in some situations he confronts the dangers of the outer world and fights for the safety of the mother and child. He trains the male child for the masculine roles in the community. The father is often but not always the link of family with wider society. If for any reason the parents become separated, the child generally remains with the mother.

This pithy picture of the family group attempts to penetrate to the biological matrix, undercutting the extensive, multitudinous, time-conditioned effects of social influence. But such an attempt, however careful, inevitably fails.

It is this very failure that forces home the realization that the biological and social processes in family life cannot be separated.

Consider, for example, two aspects of this statement: the father provides mother and child with the necessities of life; the father is the link with wider society. It requires but a moment of thought to reach the instantaneous conclusion that these are not universal features of family life. There are too many exceptions to the uniformity of this pattern. In many types of family, the provision of the necessities of life is the shared responsibility of both parents. Although it is true much of the time that the father is the link with the wider society, it is by no means always so; in some types of social organization, the woman has the greater prestige and provides the more important link. In still other family types, there is an elaborate sharing between male and female parent of the significant connections with the community. The origins of fathering and mothering are both biological and social.

Despite the complexity of the problem, there is nevertheless some pragmatic value in the attempt to build a theoretical model for the basic biological configuration of the family group. Although any attempt to strip away the endless layers of social influence is foredoomed (since this can never be done in real life), it is theoretically useful in the difficult task of conceptualizing the family phenomenon. Bearing in mind this principle, let us consider the few elemental qualities in the relations of mother and child, father and mother, father, mother, and child that seem biologically irrevocable. The relations of mother and child are in some basic respects distinct from the relations of father and child. The mother's biological contribution to the life of the child is overt and obvious. The father's biological contribution is less overt, less obvious; it is, in fact, cryptic.

Historically, the discovery of the specific male function of impregnation came late. The direct connection of copulation and fertilization of the ovum was not known in the primitive phase of human history. Currently, the recognition of the biological role of the male in impregnation is almost universal. There are, however, a few places in the world, as for example in the Trobriand Islands, where this fact is still not known.

But fathering and mothering are both special functions in life, specific family roles to which man and woman dedicate themselves. When they do so, they act not only for themselves but also for the species, the family, and the entire community. The acceptance of the parental role carries with it certain intrinsic satisfactions and social rewards.

Parenthood is the natural eventuation of the involvement of a man and woman in the love act out of which the woman becomes a mother, the man a father. The biological contributions of male and female to the creation of offspring are each of them unique and indispensable. But this very uniqueness in the biological functions of the two sexes creates potential conditions for a different structuring of the emotional and social relations of mother with child on the one hand, and father with child on the other.

There is one fundamental difference which has direct bearing on the social patterning of these relations. A man can sire an infant without knowing it. A woman can not bear a child without knowing it. A man may impregnate a woman and leave the scene, being none the wiser for his paternity. A woman may interrupt a pregnancy and leave; she may deliver a baby, surrender it to others, and leave; but at no point in the proceedings can she do any of these things and still deny consciousness of her connection with the baby. The emotional significance of being an unmarried mother is surely different from that of being an unmarried father. A man may be unaware of his connection with pregnancy or, if aware of it, may more easily disown it. The mother herself may be unsure of the paternity of the child, but there can be no equivalent uncertainty as to her maternity. The woman's pregnancy cannot be concealed. Pregnancy and childbirth are visible to the naked eye. The growth of a baby cannot be private; of necessity it becomes a public affair.

It is this hidden quality of the male's role in impregnation which explains the long historical delay in the discovery of fatherhood. It may also play a subtle part in a woman's resentment of the man who tries to evade paternal responsibility. It is this special feature that Margaret Mead had in mind when she characterized fatherhood as a social invention. The conflicting theories of Westermark and Briffault about the historical origin of the father's position in the family have been mentioned in an earlier chapter.

The epitome of the family phenomenon is the birth of a child. It is the woman who visibly creates the baby. She cannot do this without the man, but the man's contribution to the act of creation comes early and is in no way visible. It is this irrevocable biological difference between male and female that preconditions in some degree the emotional and social relations of mother and child and father, mother and child.

In the first phase of the infant's life after birth, it is clearly recognized that the mother is the prime parent. Through her breast-feeding function, she is the first source of nutrition, and the child's security, comfort, and survival depend upon the mother's care. During this vegetative phase of the infant's development, the father is clearly the secondary figure. He is an auxilliary parent, needed as the mother's protector and the mother's helper in the care of the infant. The special role of the mother reflects, therefore, a factor of biological indispensability in the life of the child. The need of the father is neither so immediate nor so urgent. Mother and infant may survive without the father, not conveniently or securely perhaps, but they can nevertheless survive. It is in this biological setting that we tend to think so much more of the existence of a maternal instinct and so much less of a parental instinct. Although many people believe that women are endowed constitutionally with different intensities of maternal instinct, it is virtually impossible to measure such endowment in real life, because mothering behavior cannot readily be broken up into its biological and social components.

Is there in the man something analogous, something parallel to maternal instinct? Fathers show parental feeling as well as mothers. Is paternal emotion clear, identifiable, and distinct from maternal emotion? The evidence is scanty and inconclusive, but there is remarkably little to support the notion of a separate fathering instinct. Yet the warmth and passion of some fathers is a striking thing. How shall we interpret it?

Direct observation of paternal behavior leads to some interesting speculations. First, we often see in men, as in women, a tender, solicitous, protective attitude toward a helpless child. A father may act "maternal" too. In his family role as mother's helper, he facilitates the maternal function. In the absence of the mother, he may take over exclusively the maternal responsibility.

Let us examine the man's family behavior at still another level. From one point of view, as the mother mothers the child, so the father mothers the mother. The mother, while caring for the young infant, needs care for herself. In essence, although she is a mother, she still has inside herself something of the dependent child. She requires the solicitous protection of the father, as she previously required the care of her own mother. In actual fact, we may often observe that the protective care of the young mother is divided between her husband and her mother. This view of the father as showing some maternal feeling is admittedly conjectural, but it is the kind of conjecture that receives convincing documentation from direct observation of processes of family interaction.

According to this theory, then, the father, too, is capable of mothering behavior. He may share the parental care of the infant with the mother. He may share the parental care of the young mother with her mother. From these observations we might perhaps evolve the tentative hypothesis that there are biological roots for something like a *basic family feeling,* epitomized in maternal behavior but shared by the father and also by the older child who gives parental care to a younger sibling.

I am inclined to believe that there is no separate fathering instinct. If we speak of something like a maternal instinct, it can be supposed that the father shares this, but his protective parental feeling is organized on a different level by the structure of the family and the structure of society. In this context, "maternal instinct" becomes a theoretical model for a broader form of protective parental urge, a *family emotion,* which may be expressed by man or child as well as by woman. In essence, mothering behavior epitomizes family togetherness, family care, and family loyalty. It expresses the social core of the human species. In this broader sense, maternal feeling is shared with the mother by the father and other siblings. But the mothering behavior of the man is expressed in a different way and at different phases of the child's development.

It should not be forgotten, however, that the young father has within him too a concealed child. He too needs to be cared for; he too seeks mothering from the mother of his child, or from a grandparent. Thus it seems everyone, child, woman, and man, needs mothering. It is the warm embrace of the family group, the essential emotional unity of family, that answers this need. It is only as this need is satisfactorily met that persons may be gradually and wholesomely weaned, that they can grow in strength and face the problems of the larger world with courage and conviction.

In the first phase of the infant's growth, the mother and child are one. The father is a subsidiary figure. He is in the background and serves to facilitate the primary maternal function. His importance as a parent becomes enhanced as the child matures, learns to walk and talk, achieves increasing physical mastery, acquires greater control of his environmental experience, and takes on the characteristics of a social being. The child's interaction with father epitomizes the child's earliest separation from mother and his first adaptation to the "stranger." It symbolizes the child's readiness for expanding his relationships with other family members, including siblings. It prepares the child for progressively wider impact with the outer world, the social universe that extends beyond family. Contact with the first "stranger," the father, personifies the challenge of adaptation to the wider community. The child who fears father also fears the stranger.

The development of an emotional bond with father is the first step in weaning from mother, the first step in integrating an expanding self into the complexities of social organization. Fathers often allude to this transitional phase in a remarkably simple way. They say they feel indifferent or only mildly interested in the infant while he merely feeds and sleeps, but they become vigorously interested when the baby "becomes a person," *i.e.,* after the infant has passed through the vegetative phase, begins to walk and talk, and asserts a place in the family as a social citizen. It is then that the father becomes a more significant parental figure and assumes a role of increasing importance in training of the growing child into society.

Both parental roles are, of course, profoundly influenced by surrounding social patterns, but the functions of the father are perhaps more sensitized and more immediately responsive to the vicissitudes of the broader social fabric. Another way of saying the same thing is to say that the mother-baby union is, to begin with, a symbiosis, two persons living as one. It is biologically more intimate and slightly more immune to the impingement of social force than the father-infant pair.

In a special sense then mothering in its origins may be said to be relatively more biological, whereas fathering is relatively more social. As the infant matures, the significance of this difference tends to dissolve. When the child is grown, the mother-child pair and father-child pair are equally vulnerable to the larger social pattern.

The unique biological features of male and female parent dictate a certain difference in the social patterning of the roles of mother and father that is especially pertinent to the first phase of life: the creation of the offspring and the early symbiotic union of infant and mother during which time the infant is not yet a social being. After that the biological difference of male and female parent becomes progressively less significant and the social structuring of these roles more crucial. In fundamental terms, fathering *as* a life function is less rigidly anchored to fixed anatomical and physiological characteristics than mothering. This difference paves the way to a greater flexibility and a range of molding by social influence of the role of father.

By nature the functions of mothering and fathering are interdependent. The reciprocity of the two sets of parental functions is so basic that any change in the carrying out of the functions of one parent must immediately be echoed in a corresponding change in the functions of the other parent. Therefore it is not possible in any way to consider the roles of mothering and fathering in isolation, rather each of these parental functions must be continuously related to the other. Furthermore, the complementary relations of man and woman are so fundamental that the interaction of male and female as a parental couple is inevitably influenced in the most sensitive manner by the interaction of male and female in other roles—marital, sexual, occupational, social. The relations of mother with child and father with child must therefore be weighed constantly within the frame of the relations of mother and father in roles other than the parental one and at other levels of shared experience.

Disturbances of Mothering

It is a curious paradox that, although the mother's role in the child's emotional life is universally recognized as being fundamental, the conceptual formulation of the psychotherapy of mothers of disturbed children remains in many respects an unsolved problem. Up to the present time the challenge of what to do with "problem mothers of problem children" has not been met satisfactorily. It is the purpose here to try to clarify the factors that contribute to disturbances of mothering. Only in this way does it become possible to work toward specificity in the therapy of deviant patterns of mothering behavior. The importance of this special phase of mental health work cannot be overstated. A clear understanding of the factors that determine disturbances of mothering and specific criteria for the therapy of such disturbances are of the utmost importance.

The mother is with rare exceptions the most significant adult in the child's life. But the mother is given to the child. No child can choose his mother or change her for another. Nor can the child control the threats to his security which are intrinsic to certain forms of maternal behavior, except to the most limited extent. The younger the child, the longer the period of enforced dependence upon maternal care and the weaker his powers to counteract or even mitigate any destructive tendencies the mother may show. It is these immutable features of the mother-child relationship that predetermine the overweening importance of the mother in shaping the child's fate. It is this which establishes the principle in child guidance of concomitant therapy of child and mother.

It has become axiomatic that where one undertakes to study and treat an emotionally disturbed child, it is essential in a parallel procedure to attempt to evaluate and modify the pathogenic elements of the child's daily personal environment. It is usually the mother in whom these pathogenic stimuli are sought. It is self-evident, however, that, although the maternal influence is pivotal in the child's experience, it does not encompass his total environment. There is no one-to-one correlation of pathogenic environmental stimuli and mother; they are not identical, though they often significantly overlap.

The length and breadth of the child's personal environment embraces much more than the mother; it includes the entire family group—father, siblings, other significant relatives, as well as mother. It is in the very nature of family life that its members are interdependent, that they reciprocate one another's behavior, that a change in the attitudes and conduct of one brings a change in the other. There is no true autonomy, therefore, in the behavior of a mother, because her performance in that role is continually influenced by the role of the father and the transactional patterns that characterize the family as a whole. The only clinically significant exceptions to this principle are those unusual situations in which a child is raised exclusively by the mother, the father being dead, or absent, or those in which the isolation of parental partners is so extreme that in effect there is no parental interaction.

EMOTIONAL INTERACTION WITH CHILD

The relationship of mother and child is a two-way process. Not only does the behavior of the mother affect the child; the behavior of the child also affects the mother. In some family situations, a mother may build up a tremendous anticipation of pleasure from the child and be very ready to love him, but because of unforeseen and uncontrollable events, she is painfully disillusioned by the child and his behavior. For example, the child may be born defective from a birth injury, may be maimed early in life by encephalitis or epilepsy, or may fail to reciprocate the mother's initial show of warmth, as happens in the case of a child with a constitutionally defective affective response, such as occurs in some forms of childhood schizophrenia. In such unfortunate situations, a mother, initially able and desirous of loving a child, experiences a painful disappointment and is induced by the child's unresponsive behavior to react against it.

At the other pole, a mother, emotionally set to reject a particular child for reasons extraneous to the child, is impelled to reverse her emotional response to it because of the beaming warmth of the child's first smile. The natural appeal of the child is irresistible and melts away the hardness of the mother's initial rejecting attitude.

In estimating the quality of interaction between mother and child and its effects on the mother's acceptance or rejection, we would be concerned with several phases of the interaction: the closeness of the relationship; the pleasure the mother derives from it; the sense of fulfillment it offers her; the harmony or conflict of the relationship; the specific oppositional patterns that emerge.

Is the relationship a close or distant one emotionally? Is there empathy, communication, and a growing identification of the two persons? Is there mutual satisfaction and pleasure? In the context of this relationship, what is the woman's image of herself as a mother, a pleasing or a conflicted one? Does she have a self-sacrificial image of herself as mother? Does she enjoy the child? Is there an easy perception of the child's demands? Do they appear too great? Do they evoke anxiety in the mother? Does she react to this anxiety with rage? Is the child provocative, destructive? What reactions does this evoke in the mother? Does the mother isolate herself emotionally from the child? What conflicts emerge? What patterns of opposition? How does the mother deal with these? To what extent is the conflict externalized, acted out, suppressed?

The hostile, destructive content of the mother's attitudes is of special clinical interest. Does this primarily derive from intrapsychic disorders of her personality, from conflict and anxiety that antedate the advent of the child? Or is the mother's destructiveness in some part a reciprocal response to the child's destructiveness? Is the mother's destructiveness a response to fear of being en-nervated or depleted by the child's demands?

Or is the mother's destructiveness a response to other factors or persons in the environment? Is it intended primarily for the child or is it displaced sec-ondarily from some other family member to the child? From, for example, the father, maternal grandmother, or mother-in-law? Is the mother's destructive motivation superficial or deep? If the child's provocativeness subsides, does the mother's reciprocal hostility also diminish? What effect does the child's response to discipline have on the mother's attitudes?

THE WOMAN'S MOTIVATION FOR MARRIAGE AND CHILDREN

A woman may desire marriage and yet not desire children or vice versa. The motivation for marriage may be quite complex and need not encompass a desire for children. Along the broad spectrum of a woman's responses to a child are every variety of feeling, every variety of desire and motivation.

Some women have an intense desire for a child, some crave many, some few, some do not want any. Or the desire for the child may be activated only after he arrives. There are mothers who want a child other than the one they have. Some feel the capacity for boundless love; some are detached and ex-perience little if any feeling. Some want a child not for the love of the child but for some ulterior motive: to neutralize anxiety concerning frigidity or steril-ity; to please or punish the husband; to use as a pawn in the parental conflict; to keep a marriage "off the rocks"; to win the approval of other persons, grand-parents or women friends; to fulfill a conventional idealized image of family life; to make into a parent figure; to use as a symbol of the suffering of the fe-male; to mold into a more perfect edition of self; to live vicariously through the child; to make the child into a masculine, aggressive extension of oneself; or to give the child what the mother herself never had in her childhood. In general, one needs to discern the extent to which the desire is not for the child himself but results from the need to exploit the child as a defense against the woman's feeling of inadequacy or as a defense against the break-up of the fam-ily.

Because of its clinical importance, maternal rejection and its relation to motivation merit particular consideration. Needless to say, there is no one-to-one correlation, no exclusive identity of maternal failure and maternal rejec-tion. There are some causes for failure which do not derive solely or even in part from maternal rejection. There are such traumatic and situational factors as illness or death in the family, loss of employment for the father, a crisis in housing.

Where maternal failure coincides with the existence of a rejecting motive in the mother, the rejection may be influenced in diverse ways. It is important in clinical work to qualify the rejection of the child in several respects: (a) its intensity, (b) its form of expression, (c) its relative specificity or non-specificity for the given child, (d) the role of the motive of rejection in the economy of the mother's personality, (e) the role of the rejecting behavior in the psychosocial economy of the family life, (f) the mother's emotional reactions to the rejecting motive.

Maternal rejection of course varies tremendously in intensity. It is rarely total. When on occasion it is, there is little to be done. In most cases, it is partial and its relative intensity is influenced by many factors.

It is likewise important to appraise rejection in relation to the form of its expression; whether it is open or disguised has different emotional consequences for the child. It is rarely expressed in nude form, though occasionally, when maternal guilt is absent, a mother will forthrightly exclaim: "I simply can't stand looking at that child. I hate him. I wish I could be rid of him." Generally, the expression of feelings of rejection is not nearly so overt. The hostility of mother to child is more often disguised, rationalized, or expressed in many subtle forms. Not infrequently, a mother completely denies consciousness of such feelings.

Perhaps the most significant qualifying factor in maternal rejecton is the relative specificity or nonspecificity of the motivation for rejection. It is essential to assay this aspect of rejection, because its effects on the child are often profound. Specificity in this sense means the degree to which the mother specifically rejects the child for himself, i.e., the mother responds specifically to the child's unique identity, as opposed to an accidental or incidental rejection of the child promoted by tangential factors having little or no direct bearing on his identity. To judge of the relative specificity or nonspecificity of the woman's feelings of maternal rejection, it is important to trace the history beginning with the original craving for a baby, when this was a pure phantasy desire, a gleam in her eye, through the events of a pregnancy and childbirth to the subsequent quality of her emotional "give and take" with the child.

There are kinds of rejection that come directly out of a mother's response to a particular child. For example, a mother rejects a hairy child because she has had a life-long anxiety about excess hair on her legs and breasts. Or another, feeling that her own buttocks are big and unattractive, cannot bear to cleanse her child after a bowel movement. Or a mother with anxiety about childbirth sustains an injury in the act of birth and forever after blames the child for it. Then there is the mother, very vain about her figure, who never forgives the child for the change after birth in the contour of her breasts.

These are kinds of rejection that are relatively specific because the mother associates threat, pain, or injury specifically with this child. In the main, such specific rejections of a child revolve around experiences or associations that menace the mother's idealized image of herself, threaten her specific personal goals or values, or impose upon her some forced sacrifice that carries relatively specific emotional connotations.

Somewhat less specific is the rejection of the mother who bore her child mainly to counteract anxiety about sterility. There are still other instances in which the child's birth and continued existence only incidentally create some threat to the mother. The threat to the mother actually derives from another source and is only peripherally associated with the child. In such instances, the content of the threat to the mother usually antedates the birth of the child. The advent of the child serves as a more or less accidental precipitant of the threat. For example, a mother has unresolved guilt toward her own mother. She gives birth to a child shortly after her mother's death. The two events become associated in her mind. Her mother's death induces a crisis of guilt. She reacts with a hostile effort to deny it. She displaces this hostility to the child. Or a woman is married to a man who fervently desires a son to carry his family name. She gives birth to a female child. This causes guilt feeling toward her husband. She feels that she has let him down. She deals with her guilt by becoming hostile to the innocent female child. Another woman is unhappy with her husband. She feels miserable about sex relations with him and secretly wants to separate. She becomes pregnant. Foiled in her secret intention to break with her husband, she blames and rejects the child.

To be contrasted with these forms of rejection are those in which the particular child's identity or his existence has little or no dynamic relation to the origin of the rejection. The relation of the child to the rejecting motive in the mother is rather more tenuous and incidental. A few illustrations may serve to clarify the difference: maternal rejection based on an accidental pregnancy; partial rejection bearing little or no specific relation to the identity of the child because the child was unwanted at the time; or rejection resulting from a pregnancy coming at a time when there is an unfortunate turn in the family finances, father is drafted into the army, or the like. In many instances of nonspecific rejection, the mother's feeling of hostility may be transitory and gradually replaced by love feeling as the intimacy between child and mother ripens.

In dealing with whatever is wrong with a mother's attitude toward a child, it is important to make an accurate appraisal of the content of that rejection because the feelings of remorse that the mother experiences in her failure to carry out her maternal duties bear a direct relation to the nature and content of her rejection. Such appraisals will affect the psychotherapy of the child and of the mother and will affect also the lines of cooperation that the mother may establish with the teacher, nurse, or doctor. The probability is that the pathogenic potential for the child is greater for the relatively specific forms of rejection.

MATERNAL BEHAVIOR INFLUENCED BY FAMILY ROLE

At another distinct level, it is essential to appraise the role of the rejecting behavior of the mother in the psychosocial economy of the family. Pertinent here is the interplay between the parents in their respective maternal and paternal roles, the factors of harmony or conflict, the pattern of sexual adaptation, the trend toward seduction of the child by a sexually disappointed parent, and also the displacement of hostility from the area of conflict between the parents to conflict between parent and child. In some degree, renunciation of feminine and maternal functions may be influenced by the processes of family life as well as by the intrapsychic structure of the mother's personality disorder.

All too obviously, the quality of the intimate relationship of mother and father exerts a pervasive influence on the mother role. Here we are concerned with the quality of protection and emotional support the father gives to the mother and the effect of this on the mother's view of herself as a mother and on the execution of her maternal duties. Is this aspect of the relationship positive or negative? Or is he carping and critical? Does he show up the mother's faults? Do the parents hold the same values for children or do they clash sharply in their concepts of child-rearing? Is there a conflict of authority? Do they disagree concerning discipline of the child?

The basic adequacy of the sexual union of the two parents exerts a tremendous influence on the mother's concept of herself as mother. If she is sexually frustrated, frigid, or unfulfilled or if she reproaches herself for coldness to the father, her maternal attitudes and behavior may be significantly affected. Where there is a sexual barrier between the parents, the sexually unfulfilled parent will frequently seek compensatory love from the child. This in turn leads to seduction of the child and intensifies the barrier between the parents. Complications of this type inevitably affect the mother's feeling and behavior.

It is clear that a definition of the integration of the woman's personality into the maternal role must be attempted in the context of a psychosocial evaluation of the family as a whole, taking fully into account the effects of the significant multiple relationships.

MATERNAL BEHAVIOR INFLUENCED BY THE WOMAN'S PERSONALITY

Closely related is the question of the role of the rejecting motivation in the economy of the mother's personality. Is the relationship between child and mother intimate or distant? Is the rejecting motive in the very center of the mother's conflicts or in the periphery? This determines the extent and depth to which the mother involves her child in her personal pathology and explains those profound symbiotic disturbances in which child and mother share their pathology. When the relationship between the mother's pathology and the child's is an intimate one, the two disorders may be dynamically reciprocal, as in *folie à deux*. Just as the mother may occupy the central role in the child's pathology, so the child may occupy the central role in the mother's pathology.

Of course, the established personality patterns of the woman are a potent determinant of mothering behavior. But evaluation of psychopathological symptoms or a psychiatric diagnosis by itself constitutes inadequate data. On the one hand, systematic criteria are needed for the appraisal of the functions of total personality, with special emphasis on the main character patterns, but it is also necessary to develop a conceptual frame within which it is possible to discern how the relevant aspects of personality are integrated into the maternal role. In evaluating personality, we are concerned with the ego-integrative aspects of personality, with assets as well as liabilities, strengths as well as weaknesses.

Some of the relevant criteria for evaluating the mother's personality are intellectual endowment, reality perception, capacity for emotional relationships, image of self and personal goals, image of other persons, emotional reactivity, control of emotion, the specific characteristics of anxiety response, the conflict patterns and associated defenses, the relations of current and past conflict. A clinical appraisal of these behavioral trends sheds light on the mother's rigidity or flexibility, her emotional capacity for loving, her dependency need, her aggressive drive, her need for control, her capacity for pleasure, her guilt and self-punishment tendency, her acceptance or rejection of sex, femininity, and maternity. It also offers an approximation of the degree of social maturity and the balance between strengths and weaknesses of personality.

The next step is to try to discern how these personality characteristics are integrated into the requirements of the maternal role. The criteria suggested in Chapter 4, "Social Role and Personality," can be used to define the dynamic relations between personality and role in relation to the following: the mother's goals and standards as mother; her perception of and responses to surrounding interpersonal influences (father, family, and community, as they bear on the function of mothering); her techniques of emotional control of interaction with child and other family members; the assertion of a particular image of self as mother; the conflicts experienced in this role, with special reference to discrepancies in conscious and unconscious motivation; the effort to find gratification of personal need in this role; the anxiety experienced and the defenses mobilized against it.

MATERNAL BEHAVIOR INFLUENCED BY A CONSTITUTIONAL FACTOR

The constitutional factors influencing mothering are difficult to estimate in and of themselves, insofar as their manifestations can never be observed in pure form; their influence can only be inferred because their effects are always clothed in socially structured patterns. A variety of attempts have been made to study differences in constitutional endowment of "maternal instinct" with concern for such items as general body configuration, intensity of mating urge, craving for offspring, menstrual behavior, breast development, pregnancy, and breast feeding. It is difficult to draw definitive conclusions, however, because it is not readily possible, for the purpose of experimental study, to dissociate the biological component from the socially conditioned patterns. Nevertheless, the weight of empirical observations leans strongly toward recognition of significant individual differences in such constitutional endowment.

MATERNAL BEHAVIOR INFLUENCED BY CULTURE PATTERNS

At the level of the cultural influences that shape maternal behavior, we want to know the child-rearing standards of the family and the small groups to which the mother belongs as well as the over-all cultural standards. Are they consistent? Are they contradictory? Are they in a state of flux? Are the standards that prevail today different from those of yesterday? Is there a sharp clash between the mother's childhood training experience and the current standards? Is she clear as to what is expected of her by grandparents, pediatrician, teachers? Does she conform, rebel? Are her child-rearing attitudes culturally deviant?

We have already seen that it simply is not possible to dissociate the two aspects of mothering—biological and social. But we have also seen that women in our society are highly confused about their roles as women and as mothers. What has happened to their image of themselves? They are in danger of losing their identity as women. They tend too often to envy the male, to deny their femininity, and to derogate the time-honored function of mothering. They become frigid and are plagued with anxieties about their incompleteness as women.

In the fields of clinical psychiatry and child and family guidance, it is a common observation that in certain families there is a reversal of sexual roles. The woman dominates and makes the decisions; she "wears the pants." The father is passive and submits to avoid argument. The mother pushes the father toward many of the maternal duties. Today's society tends to confuse parents not only in their sexual identity but in their social and occupational lives as well. Such trends as these have had an immeasurable effect in distorting the functions of mothering and in confusing the sexual and emotional development of the child.

If a woman is to be a good mother, she must have a true understanding of her female body. She must not have a distorted image of the way in which her body differs from that of a man. She cannot with impunity deny these differences. Naive and trite as this may sound, no woman can be clear in her sexual and social position unless she is able first to dissolve some basic misconceptions concerning her female body and its relations to the male body.

It is unfortunately true that women who deny their femaleness, who have "penis envy," build up extensive illusions about their body that warp their self-image and play no small part in maintaining their maladapted role in society. If a woman can clear away those cobwebs of confusion concerning the nature of her body, she is in a better position to improve not only her sexual functioning and her performance as a mother, but also her integration as a whole person in the community at large. Changes in the social position of the woman, however desirable otherwise, must not be permitted to induce a warped image of the physical being of a woman. It is understandable that a woman should defend her changed position and vigorously assert her new prerogatives, but she cannot at the same time deny her physical uniqueness without serious consequences. This is going too far.

The anatomical and biological uniqueness of the woman must be respected. When a woman demands equality with men, does she mean equality or superiority? When she demands as much respect as men, does she want the same kind of respect a man gets, or a unique respect for herself as a woman? Men and women can receive an equal measure of respect for what they give to family life and society, but they must be differently respected.

The competitive aspect of the relations between the sexes has become a virtual battleground because of the associated connotations of superiority and inferiority. This is superfluous and harmful. Each of the sexes has its special place and merits respect in its own right. Looking to the future, there is no intrinsic necessity whatever for the battle of the sexes. The basic principle of life has been shown to be cooperation rather than competition.

In another large area, the cultural patterns of our society have imposed an additional burden on mothers. In all work with children, whether in medical practice, psychotherapy, or education, a functional standard of what constitutes normal behavior, normal functioning of personality, normal learning, normal emotional contact with other persons is indispensable. Whatever we do in therapy and in education hinges on our ability to estimate the pattern and degree of deviation from normal. Gesell provided a statistical guide for expected performances in children at each stage of maturation, but a reliable set of norms for the development of personality is still critically lacking. Many of us make our appraisals automatically and unconsciously. We evaluate a child's development in relation to our inner intuitive notions of what is normal and what is healthy. But where does this sort of assessment leave mothers today? The intensity of a mother's sense of responsibility is qualified by her subjective conviction as to how far her child's behavior deviates from normal. To whatever extent the child deviates, she is apt to feel the deviation as a disparaging reflection on herself. The present lack of clear-cut standards leaves her feeling lost and confused.

In addition, she is still subjected to an earlier trend in clinical work in the mental health field that focused excessive attention on the responsibility of mothers for disturbances in the emotional development of their children. For a number of years, wherever the mother turned for advice, help, or treatment, she was confronted as if by a ghost with the haunting and taunting image of her failure. Other people always seemed to know better than she what she as a mother should be doing, was not doing, was doing improperly, and on and on. As soon as her child showed some deviation from the presumed norms of personality development, educators and child guidance personnel immediately became concerned with her maternal attitudes. Wittingly or unwittingly they pointed an accusing finger at her. In their haste to prove the guilt of failing mothers, they sometimes launched a crusade that had the quality of a witch hunt.

Fortunately this trend has abated considerably in recent years, but its effects still linger on. Surely, the responsibility and remedy for disturbances in child personality involve the mother as a central figure but never exclusively. Both the causation and the correction of such disturbances must be shared by the father, by the family as a whole, and by the doctor, teacher, and community as well. Yet, when we consider the disturbances of mothering, we must not forget the large part that this sense of responsibility can play, and we must examine carefully the degree and kind of distortion of what should be a healthy care of and concern for the child.

For further clarification, it is useful to remind ourselves that there are three terms that are commonly applied to failing mothers—responsibility, blame, and guilt. Descriptively, these terms are sometimes applied loosely and interchangeably. There are some important distinctions, however, for they refer to three different levels of relatedness of mother to child, and the social connotations of each are different. In cases of disturbed mother-child relationships and failing mothers, it is one thing for a mother to deny responsibility for her influence on the child, another for her to refuse blame, and still another for her to blunt the guilt, even if she accepts the blame.

It is conceivable that a mother will accept a good measure of responsibility for her child and yet reject the accusation that she has exerted a baneful influence. It is also possible that a mother will feel an intense guilt on an irrational basis and yet carry in reality only a small responsibility. She may feel profoundly guilty and yet justifiably direct much blame to the child's father.

In child guidance practice it is useful to keep these shaded but significant distinctions in mind. In what measure does a mother feel her sense of responsibility? In what degree does she feel accused or blamed. If she feels guilty, what is the depth and content of her guilt?

In a recent monograph, Gerhart Piers and Milton Singer[1] distinguish between the two kinds of psychic tension, guilt and shame. They believe the term "guilt" should be reserved for the mainly unconscious sense of wrongdoing related to the infliction of harm on another person, a painful internal tension which brings a concomitant anxiety into consciousness. With this anxiety goes an inner conviction of inevitable punishment. The Law of the Talion is the dynamic source for this conviction of punishment.

Shame is by contrast an emotion epitomized in the urge to "bury one's face," to "sink out of sight," a kind of rage turned against the self, when one has failed to achieve one's own goal. One feels one's "shortcoming" and is painfully embarrassed by it.

The Law of the Talion applies less to shame. Guilt derives more strongly from the inner quality of the person's conscience. Shame relates more closely to what society expects of one. From the point of view of this distinction, is the mother's response to her sense of failure one of genuine guilt and conviction of punishment? Or in equating the community's standard of ideal maternal behavior with her personal goal, does she react with shame rather than guilt and with a need to hide her sense of failure, inferiority, and shortcomings?

According to Piers, guilt feeling produces a true psychic need for self-punishment, whereas shame leads to a fear of condemnation, ridicule, and social ostracism. In this sense, is the mother's reaction to failure shame or guilt or a mixture of both? In any case, there are differences in intensity of the reaction and differences in degrees of awareness. Some mothers are acutely aware of this painful tension and are constantly plagued with self-reproach. Others are only mildly conscious of it. Still others deny it to consciousness altogether.

How do mothers defend against these painful tensions? One way in which a mother may react to her sense of failure, whether it be guilt or shame or both, is to build up the conviction that the child was born bad and she can do nothing about it. Still another way is to run away from the whole problem. She may do so by detaching herself emotionally from the child or by developing driven interests in other directions outside the family. The adjective "driven" is used advisedly, in the sense of compulsion. Many such mothers in their anxiety concerning failure take frantic flight. They feel driven at all costs to get away from their child, to cultivate all sorts of external interests, to keep their minds and energies so busy somehow that they can shut out the painful awareness of failure with the child.

Still another way to react to the tension is to "take it out on the child." The mother substitutes an aggressive attitude for her anxiety and punishes her child for her own failure; she "beats the hell" out of the child. Still another way is to project blame for failure onto the child's father and "take it out on him" or to blame the teacher and scold her. Or the mother may retreat from the maternal responsibilities and demand that the father take over many of these duties, or she may turn these responsibilities over to grandmother, maid, teacher, etc.

Another way of overreacting to feelings of guilty self-reproach is along the path of inordinate submission to the child, thus allowing the child the power of complete domination. Frequently, this encouages in the child a false sense of omnipotence and invites an accentuation of destructive behavior. Another such path is taken by the mother who appeases her guilt by accentuating the physical care of the child while ignoring it emotionally. This trend is especially evident in those families in which a child wins the mother's interest and care only when he is ill.

These are just a few of the varied channels along which a mother may react to her sense of maternal failure and inadequacy. It is all too obvious that the fate of these tendencies is deeply influenced by the reciprocal attitudes and behavior of the father and by the vicissitudes of other significant relationships in the family. Such trends may be encouraged, discouraged, accentuated, or effectively counteracted, depending upon other factors in the behavior of the father, the family as a whole, the teacher, the family doctor, etc. In any case, pathological reactions to failure in the mother will have destructive effects on the mother's personality and on the family harmony, even beyond their effects on the child.

Shared Responsibilities for Child-Rearing

It is only necessary to pause for a split second to realize the profound responsibility of everyone who is potentially in a position to influence a mother's reaction to her sense of failure as a mother. It is easy to realize the intensity of the temptation of fathers, teachers, doctors, and others, to ease their own conscience by placing all the guilt at the mother's door. All too often the tendency to show up a mother in her failure reflects a defense against anxiety in the very person who does the showing up. A pediatrician, teacher, or psychiatric social worker may be impelled to prove his superiority by inciting guilt in a mother. Sometimes unresolved resentment in these persons toward their own mothers may motivate them to punish any mother who comes along. Not infrequently, professional persons get involved in competitive feelings with a mother because of their own need to be loved by the child. Such inappropriate motives and emotional involvement jeopardize the execution of professional responsibility.

Whenever a helpless child is hurt we all feel responsible, individually and collectively. The community must bear its load of guilt, but to avoid the pain of doing so it seems easier sometimes to put everything off on the mother. This is exactly what must not be done.

Fortunately the tide has changed in recent years. People have come to look on troubled mothers with greater compassion. Child guidance literature has come to the defense of mother and shaved the top off the veritable mountain of guilt that towered menacingly over her. (One article, for example, has the catchy title, "Unmarried Fathers.") There has been a sharper trend toward examining father's responsibilities for the disturbance of the child, and there is now more pressure to draw him into the center of corrective child guidance procedures. More and more it is recognized that child-rearing is a joint venture, that the responsibilities are shared responsibilities.

Disturbances of Fathering

The functions of fathering are complex and influenced by a great multitude of factors. Disturbances of paternal behavior are in general overdetermined; in no way are they likely to be brought about by the single cause but rather by a number of overlapping factors.

The disturbances of fathering in our society are greatly varied. In broad terms we may consider two main categories of influence, past and present. The historical factor is represented in the progressive differentiation of maleness in the personality of the father as conditioned by his life history and in a corresponding type of emotional preparation for the specific tasks of fatherhood. Contemporary influences are reflected in (a) the reciprocity of paired family roles; the emotional integration of the man in the relations of man and wife, father and mother, father and child; and the adaptational response of the man to the psychosocial configuration of his family as a unit; (b) the integration of masculine capacities in the extramarital roles of work and other role functions in the wider community.

With regard to the historical factor, we are especially concerned with the particular features of the personality development of the man that have shaped his emotioal preparation for carrying out the masculine prerogatives in sexual relations, marriage, parenthood, and work responsibility. Of special importance in the emotional conditioning of childhood is the father's image of his original family, the kind of man his own father was, the manner in which the father expressed his masculinity in marital relations and in the sharing of parental duties, and the way in which he brought into the family his image of the man's role in the outside world. It is clearly the young father's emotional identity with his own father in the years of his childhood that profoundly patterns his image of his masculine self as he moves into adult life. A weakness in his emotional preparation for masculine functioning in any of the several significant spheres—sexual relations, marriage, parenthood, career—will, of course, be echoed in all other spheres.

It may be useful to schematize the range of contemporary influences which may mold the conduct of a man in the role of father as follows: (1) the cultural patterning of the father role; (2) the man's motivation for marriage and offspring; (3) the father's relationship with his child; (4) the relationship of father and mother as a parental couple and a marital couple; (5) the integration of the man's personality into the family as a group (which involves his interaction with other family members: children, parents-in-law, grandparents, family maid, etc.); (6) the father's specific emotional reactions to success and failure in the paternal role.

It is self-evident that the special problems of fathering in our society must be viewed against the backdrop of the progressive changes in the organization of family relationships that we have reviewed before. Because fathering as a life function is relatively more sensitive to the vicissitudes of social change than is mothering, we must pay special attention to the cultural factor in the molding of fathering behavior.

The cultural shift in the image of the father is extraordinary. He has been stripped of all semblance of arbitrary authority in the family. He is no longer the unquestioned ruler, to be feared, respected, and obeyed. His power to discipline and punish family offenders, whether wife or child, has been sharply undercut. In place of this we see several other trends. The father is seen on the periphery. The mother comes first; she is the important parent. In effect, the father sits in the shadow; he is the "forgotten man." The significance of the father's role is played down; the mother's role is dramatized.

There is a strong tendency in the broader community to atomize the members of the family group, approaching each as an individual and viewing the family members as separate and relatively isolated from one another. This tendency has special importance insofar as it sets the mother and father apart, treating them as separate beings rather than as a parental couple.

Our earlier examination of the contemporary American family disclosed a father who is regarded as weak, inferior, frightened, continuously in dread of defeat in his competitive struggle with other men. This is the image that other people have built up of the father and the image that he holds of himself. It is this image that has nourished an opposite image of the mother's role in the family. In her reciprocal position, the mother becomes more aggressive and dominating and reduces the father's position to a subordinate one. And so we reach a point in time where father and mother reflect complementary images: the father weak, immature, dependent, frightened of competitive injury by stronger men; the mother strong, self-sufficient, aggressive, and shaping the fate of the family.

Surely this image of the man of the family in our society stands in striking contrast to the equivalent image of a century ago, when the father was depicted as a man of vigor, strength and courage, the unchallenged leader and governor of his family. Wife and child deferred to his superior wisdom. He exercised his authority firmly but fairly. His discipline was strict but not abusive. He was consistent both in his role as protector and in his meting out of punishments for offensive behavior. Sometimes he became the tyrant; if so, in the end he suffered for the abuse of his power. Echoes of this older image still persist, but they have grown dim.

On the other hand, as we have seen, woman's aggressiveness and mastery are really a façade. Her façade of self-sufficiency and strength represents an effort at compensation, an effort to console herself for her inability to depend safely on the man. Thus the cultural patterns tend to alienate not only man from man but also man from woman. In the end both the man and the woman are left with a feeling of aloneness, fright, and loss of love.

In this machine-dominated age, there is a movement toward even greater concentration of power. The "small man" is hemmed in, sometimes cornered.

There is sound reason for the competitive insecurity of the man. He fights powers that are vast and beyond his reach. The odds are against him and he knows it.

An interesting question arises in this connection: In our kind of society and family structure are men permitted to be men at all? Implied here is the thought that the ruthless competitive struggle between men in our society is such that every man fears defeat and failure, as if the only criterion of manhood were the achievement of the status of superman. Perhaps that is why the myth of superman in comics is so exceedingly popular with our generation of boys— their idealized conception of masculinity. It reflects the distortion of the present ideal of manhood, almost implying that no man can ever hope to be a man. The inference is clear: a growing boy can hope to be a man only by becoming a superman; only by achieving omnipotent destructive power can he kill off all rivals so as to remain the sole survivor. So we have the curious contradiction of living in a democracy in which the boy worships the superman and aspires emotionally to be king. But in such a world he would be a king without an empire. The phantasy aspiration to become superman is foredoomed. Inevitably, it tosses every growing male back to a conviction of masculine weakness and deficiency.

It has sometimes been said that no man becomes a father until his own father dies. This is a catchy and psychologically fascinating thought. Like all other pithy statements that dramatize a piece of human behavior, this one has the ring of truth; it has a valid core but unless interpreted in context it can be misleading, a dangerous half-truth. It implies first that there is room in the family and in the world at large only for one real man. This is perhaps true in some families and in some communities in which the psychological constellation requires that there be a ruler or king. If a father is equated with autocratic authority, this statement is true and the son becomes the whole man only over the dead body of his father. However, if the family group or community structure has a different configuration, it can allow not only for two men but for any number of men who respect one another, accept equality, and cooperate for the common good.

In essence, this qualification carries the connotation that the role of father needs to be defined in relative terms, that this basic family role must always be qualified by the character of the group into which the man is integrated. Some groups demand a king or dictator, whereas others have no tolerance for dictators and destroy them as soon as they rise. The latter type of group insists that all males grow to be men. This is the democratic value, as contrasted with the reverence for and fear of an autocratic power.

From such considerations as these we can only draw the conclusion that there exists in our contemporary culture a deep distortion in the ideal of manhood so that no man matures to the full estate of adult masculinity. In a reciprocal pattern the woman who appears outwardly to be aggressive, self-sufficient, and masterful is mistrustful, competes with the man, is derailed in her feminine development, does not learn what it is to be a woman, and remains a secretly scared child, craving, in phantasy, to retreat from marriage and go back to being her own mother's child. Not a very happy state of affairs!

Motivation for offspring is in itself very complicated. In mature, happy marital pairs, if the man feels a genuine love of the woman, he desires that this love be expressed in procreation. He will love the child in the same measure as he loves his wife. To whatever degree there is failure in the reciprocity of roles of man and wife, in sexual relations, in the sharing of pleasure and responsibility, in the division of authority, there will inevitably be some disturbance in the man's motivation for a child. To whatever extent the man feels threatened in his maleness within the family or in his competitive relations at work and in wider society, he will have mixed feeling about a child. In fact, anxiety in excess proportions, regardless of its source, will complicate the motivation for offspring.

In the ideal sense, if a man and wife love one another, it will be expected that they will together love their child. In other words, the child is the tangible flesh and blood expression of a love experience between the man and woman. The deepest mortification that can be inflicted upon the child is the discovery that he was not born out of love. In this context, when a man loves his child, he is extending and enriching his love for the child's mother. This is what might be called normal narcissism, a healthy kind of pride in the man for his wife as his sexual mate and for his child as an extension of that love relationship.

But the child plays many roles in the emotional life of the father. He is an object of the father's love, an object of the father's teaching and training. In accordance with the father's emotional need, the child may be used as living proof of the father's manliness, potency, and success; or, at the opposite pole, the child may reflect the father's fear of adult responsibility, his fear of failure as a man first and as a father after that. The child may also be viewed as a rival for the father, as an intruder who usurps some of the mother's affection. The father may feel that the mother's devotion to the child robs him of some maternal attention or of some part of his sexual pleasure. Finally, the child serves the father as a significant link to the community. The performance of a child in the wider community casts a reflection on his father and family and thus influences the social status of both father and family.

It is self-evident that to whatever extent the father feels threatened, insecure, and anxious about his adequacy in any of his several significant masculine roles in life, to that same extent will his functioning as a father be impaired. Throughout life the male person strives to demonstrate his worth as a man and thereby win a certain status. Failure in proving sexual adequacy, in earning prestige and authority in the family or a position of merit in the work world, any measure of failure in any of these roles will arouse anxiety and so interfere with the man's fulfillment of the paternal function. To be a good father a man must be sure of himself in all these spheres. To whatever extent he becomes plagued with doubt, he will wrap his energies in the task of neutralizing this doubt and thereby be unfree emotionally to derive positive value and pleasure from fatherhood.

In our times, we encounter many men who make a grand pretense of fulfilling the ideal of fatherhood. They put on a loud show of fatherly concern because of their intense need to exhibit themselves favorably, to win approval in other people's eyes. Fundamentally, however, these men "crave the name but not the game." They are motivated less by the positive pleasure of being a father and more by the ulterior motive of winning family prestige in the eyes of the community. They are not primarily interested in the paternal relation with the child but seek rather to bolster themselves through an aggrandized social position. In so doing they are climbing on their children's backs. They exploit their children for their own vicarious gains. It is therefore important to distinguish between pseudo or noisy fathering and genuine fathering. A good father is the man whose primary incentive is the thing itself, the development and welfare of his child, rather than a spurious glorification of his maleness in the eyes of other people.

We meet other men, however, who express their unsureness as men in a different way. They endeavor to demonstrate their worth at work, in business, in a profession but pay little attention to their responsibilities as father. They take the stand that children are the woman's responsibility. If the woman does a good job as mother and the child adds glory to the father, so much to the good. If the mother does poorly, makes serious blunders in her rearing of the child, then the father is innocent; the mother is solely to blame. We see here a kind of man who is only too willing to pass the buck to mother. He considers himself important in other spheres. The care of the children is too trivial. He aggrandizes his position by his hard work outside the home, and, if anything goes wrong with the child, it is entirely the mother's fault. Here we have an instance of a rigid pattern of separation between the man and the woman, the man driving himself to achieve success in the outer world, the woman looking after the home. This is a kind of man who needs the home as a symbol of security and who feels his wife more as a mother than as a full partner in life. There is little equality and little sharing in the relations of such parental couples.

We come now to a special aspect of the father's relation with his child, namely, paternal rejection. In the light of the kind of distinction we have already drawn between mothering and fathering, a rejection of a child by a father carries a connotation different from a rejection of a child by a mother. In other words, paternal and maternal rejection are different psychological entities and therefore have different emotional and social consequences for the child. This is deeply affected by the way in which the child gradually builds up his image of his two parents and the contrasting qualities of masculinity and femininity. If in the child's emotional development the images of masculinity and femininity have been clearly and definitively separated through the contrasting roles in life of his maternal and paternal parents, the effects of rejection by mother and rejection by father will be very distinct. If by contrast the images of masculinity and femininity have been intermingled and blurred in the child's emotional development because the traditional male and female functions in life have been carried out by both parents, then the effects of rejection by mother and rejection by father will be less distinct.

The motives for a father's rejection of the child may be psychologically specific or nonspecific. There are forms of paternal rejection that are accidental or incidental and have little relation to the father's feeling toward a particular child. There are also forms of paternal rejection that reflect a high order of psychological specificity for the particular child.

For example, a man may be incapacitated in the paternal function because he suffers from physical illness, is emotionally ill, is a drinker. He may be driven through personal need to concentrate his feeling in other relationships. Or his emotional neglect of the child may be occasioned by the demands of work; he may be a migratory worker, traveling salesman, etc. His absence from home and separation from the child may be unavoidable. Even when this is not the case, however, a man's work may be of such a nature that it never ends. The work day of some men is from nine to five; for many others, however, the man must carry his work home literally or figuratively. In any case, it matters little to the child whether the father must work at home in the evening after the formal end of the day's labors or whether the father simply carries his business headaches home with him after work hours. If the father continues to worry in the evening, he is not, so far as the child is concerned, accessible as a parent. He is physically present but paternally absent.

When the father gets home, strained and anxious as a result of the day's work, he may have an inordinate need to be mothered by his wife, to unload the day's tension, to get emotional support from his wife for the struggle of his work world. The father's own need to be mothered may result in irritable rejection of the child. The daily work anxieties of the father may stir up a greater need for sexual indulgence, which may at times have the effect of excluding the child. The father, in answering his own needs, may compete with his own child and thereby reject the call of paternity.

In another direction, if the father feels unfulfilled in his marital relations, his rejection of his wife may be displaced upon the child. He rejects wife and child together. He may escape to the men's club, to the barroom, to gambling, to extramarital adventures. In all this, he rejects the entire family, including the child. Or, alienated from his wife, he may be seductive with his daughter. At another level, feeling unfulfilled, he may lean back on his own original family; he may desert his close position with wife and child, in order once again to restore the shadowy, dependent security of his own childhood.

In all this the rejection of the child by the father is relatively nonspecific in its emotional content. It is either accidental or incidental. But the rejection does not derive directly from the father's emotional experience with the particular child.

In contrast, there are those instances where the father's rejection of the child is a highly personal one. It is the child himself, rather than something tangential, that arouses the father's anxiety and provokes an attitude of hostile rejection. A few short illustrations of specific rejection will serve to distinguish this quality of rejection from the nonspecific form. A father may identify his son with his own father, toward whom he was bitterly competitive. He therefore rejects both his father and his child. A father has felt cheated of his birthright by his own father and therefore follows suit in his paternal attitude toward his own child. Or a father identifies his son with a rivalrous younger brother toward whom he is deeply embittered; he tends to take out his anger on this son. In another instance, a male child who is innocently assertive will inadvertently show up the father's sense of masculine deficiency and induce in the father an attitude of hostile rejection. A trend of this sort may easily be intensified if the child fails to defer to the father's authority. In still other cases, a father who feels lacking in virility and is overanxious concerning some feminine tendency in his make-up will reject a girl child because she is too painful a reminder of his own masculine weakness.

A paternal rejection of a psychologically specific type can only be understood if the motive for the rejection is related to the economy of the father's personality and to specific emotional conflicts for which the father has found no effective solution. In this context, the son becomes the carrier of the father's unhealed neurosis. This may be reflected in a correlation between the father's rejection of himself and his rejection of his child. Self-hate breeds hatred of the child. A focus of vulnerability in the father's personality that is manifested in feelings of inferiority and injured self-esteem will often rebound on the child in the form of rejection. Insecurity in the father that assumes the form of a need to be reassured as to his importance or a need to be the number-one person in the family will filter off as neglect of the child.

A particularly common form of disturbance is that which is dramatically expressed in the biblical quotation: "The sins of the father shall be visited upon the son." The son begins to behave as if he carried the burden for the father's "crime." The son assumes the guilt for his father's bad deeds. By the simple process of extension, a father who identifies his child as part of himself will carry over to the child hypochondriacal anxieties, omnipotence attitudes, obsessional rigidities, fears of dirt and contamination, a compensatory need for aggrandizement, etc. Or in a different situation, a father who in his own original family was too good, too obedient out of fear, will derive a vicarious thrill out of encouraging his child's rebelliousness. In these various ways, neurotic anxieties in the father may become overtly expressed in terms of overprotective or rivalrous attitudes or in an unconscious alliance with the child in the direction of rewarding rebellious, destructive behavior. This kind of paternal conduct bears in it an element of disguised rejection of the child insofar as the father does not allow the child to be a separate being but uses him as a pawn for the release of his own conflicted emotional needs.

Paternal rejection may be molded by a variety of elements in the psychosocial configuration of the family. Already mentioned is the rejection of the child born of the father's bitterness toward the mother for his sense of sexual frustration, impelling in the father a vindictive neglect of both wife and child or a secret stirring of the child's rejection of the mother. Disappointment in the love experience with the wife may cause the father to require from the child an exaggerated compensatory show of affection. He may demand from the child the love that he cannot get from his wife. He therefore becomes actively seductive toward his child. The child is then neither respected nor valued as a separate being but becomes the object of the father's unsatisfied love needs. Such situations often involve triangular relationships in which tremendous tension is aroused because of the patterns of jealousy and competitiveness. In all this the issue is whether the child fortifies and enhances the father's self-esteem, whether the child adds to the father's feeling of being loved or detracts from it, and whether the father's alliance with the child arouses the mother's jealousy or the mother's alliance with the child mobilizes the father's rivalry and rage.

The disturbances of fathering may be influenced in further ways by the father's emotional response to a second or third child or by his relations with his own parents or wife's parents. This sort of disturbance is best illustrated in several examples. A man may establish a close, mutually defensive alliance with his wife, which entails a hostile exclusion of both his parents and his wife's parents. Thus the marital partners express a shared antagonism to the older generation, isolating themselves from the extended representations of family. The behavior of the man as a father in such families may become distorted if the child is used as a pawn in the battle of the young married couple with their own parents. Husband and wife may deprive the grandparents of contact with the child, or the child may be used in a variety of ways to provoke or irritate the grandparents. In some instances, the father unconsciously identifies his child with one of the hated grandparents and accordingly assumes a rejecting or punishing attitude toward the child.

There are infinite variations of this same theme. The father may severely reject his in-laws while remaining attached to his own parents. The dependent clinging of the man to his own parents can remove him from his paternal interest in his own child. If the father is fearful of the authority of his own parents and identifies his child with one or the other of his parents, he may submit excessively to the child's aggressive demands and inordinately appease the child out of motives of unconscious guilt toward the grandparent. Still another angle of the same problem is the kind of father who, irritated by his own parent's demands for his personal devotion, pushes his child toward the grandparents in lieu of himself. At the other end of the same scale, a pair of young parents may be emotionally immature and excessively dependent on their respective pairs of parents. An insecure young couple of this kind may curry favor with the grandparents and unfold a resentful rivalry with their own child.

In our times, young people tend to be extraordinarily self-conscious in their role as parents. They are continually bombarded from all quarters with advice as to how to behave as parents. They receive guidance in lectures, P.T.A. meetings, magazine articles, radio, and TV. Because many American families are child-centered, sometimes child-dominated, many parents become uneasy and defensive about their performance, continuously measure their success or failure as parents and seek all kinds of reassurance to mitigate their anxiety. The inevitable sequel is the emergence of elaborate secondary emotional reactions to feelings of success or failure. These secondary elaborations must be taken into account in understanding the attitudes of men toward their particular brand of fathering.

We can only hint here at some of the manifestations of such reactions. In some instances, the fathers show inordinate pride in being good fathers. They become excessively dependent for their self-esteem on the measure of success they demonstrate in being good fathers. If a man feels secretly inadequate or secretly ashamed of failure in some other aspect of his adult activity, he may compensate overstrongly through his pride in being a good father. If he is disappointed in his marital relationship, if he is disillusioned in his sexual life, if he feels he has let himself down in his profession or business by an inferior performance, he may console himself by making an inordinate display of his good work as a father. Some men who show this exaggerated form of vanity compete strongly with their wives to prove they are better fathers than their wives are mothers. They may become carping, critical, and self-righteous and may try to show up the deficiencies of the wife in seeking the approval of the child or of a grandparent.

The secondary emotional reactions to failure and unimportance as a family man may move in a great variety of directions. One response is to try to deny the failure, to provide alibis for being an indaequate parent, and to place all the blame on the mother. Still another reaction may be to withdraw from the family scene, to shrink down to a minimum the interest projected toward the child. Sometimes such men deal with their shame and guilt for being a bad parent by removing themselves extensively from the center of family life. They may seek a consoling retreat through concentrating their entire vigor on their job or take flight into a preoccupation with competitive sports or plunge into an extramarital adventure.

Of particular importance in the secondary reactions to feelings of failure in the role of father is the behavior of those men who show exaggerated feelings of disappointment in the child. The child has failed to fulfill the high expectations of the father, who has thus failed in his need to achieve a vicarious success through the outstanding performance of his child. In such instances, mere association with the child will arouse discomfort, tension, anxiety, irritability; the father flees or becomes vindictive toward the child. Thus a vicious cycle is set up in which the child suffers and the pain of the father's failure is magnified.

We must indeed remember that in all these areas there is a circular movement, full of currents and cross-currents. Disturbances of fathering can no more be separated from disturbances of family than can disturbances of mothering. The interrelation of father and child necessarily has its effect on relations with mother and siblings. Once again we are forced to return to recognition of the total pattern of family relationships, both for good and for harm. In a very real sense, we can make no valid diagnosis of disturbances of mothering or fathering as separate entities. The very nature of the parental pair as an interacting unit and their shared responsibilities for child-rearing indicate once again the urgent need for family diagnosis.

CHAPTER 12

DISTURBANCES OF CHILDHOOD

A MOTHER COMPLAINS that her four-year-old boy steals. The clinician discovers upon further inquiry that the boy took food from the refrigerator without first asking the mother's consent, or that he took a toy from his sister, or that he pocketed a coin that he found on the dresser at home. Another young mother complains that her little girl is excessively demanding, in fact, insatiable, that she is disobedient and destructive. Yet direct psychiatric examination reveals an essentially normal child. It is quite apparent that the clinician faces a special problem when he confronts the child patient for the first time. Unlike the adult, the child has not come voluntarily to the psychiatrist. He may or may not be abnormal or emotionally ill. At the outset only one thing is certain: he has somehow failed to live up to the expectations of his surroundings; he has somewhere violated the norms of his personal community. Surely there is something wrong, but what is wrong may be within the child, or outside the child, or both in varying combinations. Therefore, the evaluative procedures used in child diagnosis are of particular importance.

Evaluation begins, of course, with the initial referral of a child patient. It may be mediated through a letter, a phone call, or the personal appearance of the patient, usually accompanied by another member of the family, but whatever its form, the information it produces depends upon the person who is its source and upon the character of his connection with the child. Ordinarily such preliminary data are sparse, fragmentary, selective, and arbitrary, serving mainly the purposes of initial orientation. Such information may be valid, or it may represent misinformation. It is, naturally, apt to be influenced by the prejudices of the person offering it. The clinician must sift, test, and judge its validity in further study.

But it would be a grave mistake to ignore, cast aside, or in any way belittle such information, regardless of its subjective nature. It may have value in several directions: it may be revealing of the child himself, or of his family environment, or both. It may point directly or indirectly to certain kinds of distortion of the child's personality or to specific pathogenic elements in parental attitudes and the emotional climate of the family as a whole. It may suggest the deviant levels of adaptation of child to family. If it tells little about the child himself, it may nonetheless provide some immediate insights into family trends. If the data are subjectively distorted, the discerning clinician will still learn something of value. He will be able to trace the path of distortion back to its origin within the family.

For example, a mother's story of her child's difficulties need not be entirely true or false. Some parts of her account may be remarkably accurate and perceptive and other parts distorted. Often what impresses a mother most about her child may be extremely revealing about both mother and child. If a clinician tries to separate the valid from the inaccurate parts of the child's history and endeavors to understand the subjective source of certain distortions, he will add to his insights into the relations of child and family. Misinformation at the point of referral of the case often provides significant clues. The clinician's attitude in receiving such communications determines their potential value in his study of the problem. The skillful interpretation of false information is as important in unraveling the case as true information. To say this is simply to stress the principle that from the very beginning the clinician should be concerned with both what is inside and what is outside the child's mind.

Once the initial referral has been assessed, most clinicians depend mainly on the history of the child obtained from his parents and on direct clinical examination of the child in an office interview. It must be remembered, however, that child behavior shifts significantly in relation to the person to whom he is adapting. He is one kind of person alone with his parents, another with others. In a clinical interview, he is apt to show only certain parts of himself. To appraise the whole range of potentials of behavior, it is helpful to observe him in various interpersonal situations: at home, in the office with his parents, and in the office alone.

And this observation is of a special kind—participant observation—for the clinician fulfills the dual role of participant and observer. He and the patient enter into a live relationship that involves an emotional give and take, an on-going process of communication in which there is a two-way exchange of feeling. It is this back and forth flow of emotion that defines the quality of com-munication. The emotional climate of the relationship molds the entire process of fact-gathering, and the verbal interchange is secondary to the flow of emo-tions. Thus, there are three facets of the clinician's role in examinational in-terviews: (1) his participation in an evolving emotional relationship with the patient; (2) his trained observation of the dynamic processes of the relation-ship; (3) his organization and evaluation of the data to arrive at a diagnostic judgment.

The data sought in these interviews with child and with parents and in home visits falls into four categories: (1) the organization of the child's personality here and now; (2) the child's relations with his family; (3) the char-acter of the child's environment, with special reference to the psychological make-up of the family as a group; (4) the onset of the clinical aspects of the child's difficulty (his "emotional illness") and the history of the develop-ment of his personality. But the first emphasis must remain on obtaining a definitive picture of the present status of the child's personality. The child functioning as a whole person—the living child here and now—must be the basis of any understanding of his clinical disturbance, his symptoms, conflicts, and deviations in adaptation to other persons. Without this basis, the most care-ful history-taking in the world is of little clinical use.

It should also be emphasized that because child and family are part of one another it is in no way possible in a clinical estimate to dissociate child from family. The tasks of obtaining an image of the live child and an image of his family must be pursued concurrently.

These two tasks necessitate a whole series of complex judgments by the clinician. Whom shall he interview first? Shall he see the mother or both par-ents to obtain a history? Or would he prefer to initiate the proceedings with a direct examination of the child? Or the child with his parents? In the office or in the home? There can be no set rules and formulae. Procedures must be ad-justed to the unique features and needs of each unit of child and family. But in making his decisions, he does not act unilaterally; he shares them with child and family. He divides responsibility for them with the parents. He takes into account the actions and expressions of all the persons involved and gives due consideration to their feelings and preferences. He may choose to respect these feelings, or, for sound clinical reasons, he may suggest an alternative set of procedures. In other words, he gives full weight to the emotions of family members who invest themselves in the experience but reserves for himself the powers of ultimate professional decision.

The majority of parents are in deep earnest in their striving to do right by the child, despite their personal conflicts. The clinician must give this full respect. There are, of course, certain situations that require the clinician to act firmly and forthrightly, despite the risk of conflict with parents. Such situations arise when the clinician becomes aware of destructive motivations in one or both parents or perhaps in the child. He must be alert to the possible harmful intrusion of such motives and be prepared to counteract them. For example, if he detects evidence of insincerity and manipulative tactics on the part of the parents, he is obligated instantly to take a firm stand and to refuse any part of this. Fundamental to all else is the sincerity of the clinician's position with the child patient. He must in no way compromise in his dealings with the parents.

The parents of disturbed children are conflicted people. They are concerned for the welfare of the child and yet are ambivalent and guilty. At times their feelings of guilt are covered with a solicitousness that does not ring true. Their actions toward the child will reflect divided emotions. The conflict of the parents reveals itself in inappropriate behavior in the initial interviews. The parents may be coercive. They may force the child to submit to interview in a way that is traumatic. They may frighten the child or in some way communicate to the child a menacing image of the clinician. Sometimes they offer false reassurances to the child, which only intensify his fears. To cover their hostile feelings, parents may engage in various manipulations. They may wheedle and coax the child or engage in deceptive tricks in an effort to win his cooperation. They may banter with the child or offer subtle forms of soothing or even direct bribes. In all such machinations of hostile and guilty parents, the clinician must promptly intervene to neutralize the potentially destructive effects on the child. Such parents are prone to appeal to the clinician to join in a tacit conspiracy against the child. This the clinician must not do. He must in no case jeopardize the integrity of his role with the child. At the opposite pole, however, where a child's behavior is potentially harmful, the clinician may be called upon to take sides with the parents openly, lending his professional weight to their authority, in order to protect the child from himself.

Generally, it is advantageous for the clinician to observe the child and parents together on the first occasion. This is a natural thing to do. For a young child to be immediately separated from his parents and deal with a clinician all alone is an experience that is alien to the child's nature. An interview with the child and parents together gives the clinician a quick glimpse into the relations of the child and parents, the areas of tension and conflict. It reveals at another level the characteristics of the parents as a couple and the tensions that emerge between them concerning the child's problems. It also provides some hint as to the interconnection between certain patterns of parental conflict and the child's internal emotional state.

In the multiple interview situation, the clinician acts as a catalyzer for free emotional interchange between child and parents and also between the parents. In the beginning the absence of free expression is common. There may at first be a period of restraint and self-consciousness. Sometimes the mother may wait for the father to begin or vice versa, or both parents may sit back and expect the child to do the talking. Frequently parents are initially inhibited; they do not know quite how to behave; they are not sure what is expected of them. They defer to the initiative of the clinician. They may feel that the clinician's primary interest is in the child and that they are only there to provide background information. Or, influenced by a feeling of guilt about competing with the child, they may constrain the urge to call attention to themselves.

In another variation, the parents may be distrustful of the clinician. They may be guarded about revealing themselves, and yet paradoxically they may be very willing to push the child into an exposed position. In this early phase, the child usually has little real understanding of the purpose of the interview and no incentive for disclosing his difficulties to a stranger. Sensing danger, he balks. At this awkward moment, the child may look to his parents, the parents may look to the child, or each parent may look to the other, to make the first move. Each clinician finds his own way to activate movement in such interpersonal situations. Soon the initial block is overcome and the interview rolls along at a fast clip. One or another member of the family group makes the first move. Not uncommonly, one or another parent, being anxious, "gets out on a limb," from the point of view of the child. The parent makes a wrong move, says the wrong thing, and begins an account of the child's behavior that the child feels is incorrect, critical, unfair. Often a child in conflict with his parents lies in wait to catch the parents in the wrong move. Or the parents themselves may disagree about the child's difficulty and argue out their differences.

Throughout these early interviews, the clinician acts as neutral arbitrator as well as catalyzer. He stirs the process by leading questions, by challenging the behavior of one member, by checking with another, and at the same time he makes certain that each member has a chance to be heard and understood.

Occasionally, a child will refuse to be interviewed together with his parents, particularly in cases in which the relations are characterized by deep mistrust and defensive isolation of child from parents. If the situation has proceeded to the point at which there is a serious barrier to communication, the child may be emotionally unable and unwilling to be part of the proceedings. Usually, however, the child accepts the family interview as more natural than an isolated interview with him alone. He derives a feeling of acceptance and satisfaction from the opportunity of having his case heard. He also wants to hear directly what his parents have against him, the basis of their disapproval and criticism.

Of course, certain complexities that may bear directly on the diagnosis of the child cannot be dealt with in the child's presence. This is particularly the case when the child's difficulties have been influenced by persistent conflict between the parents. Some levels of conflict between parents are of a relatively private nature and require discussion alone with the parents. The child should have his say; so should the parents.

None of these interviews is in any sense a stereotyped question and answer procedure. The spontaneity of the situation and the emotional currents and cross-currents that prevail from moment to moment in the family relationships will provide the cues and ultimately the ordered and comprehensive history that the clinician needs for diagnosis.

The child himself, in private interviews with the clinician, has special problems of his own and presents these to the clinician in a special way. The child does not have the adult's conception of what constitutes appropriate or inappropriate behavior or of what emotional illness is, nor does he have any idea about receiving psychological help. He comes because he must. He is told to come or is brought to the clinician's office. The clinician is a total stranger, and the child is apt to be perplexed, even bewildered. Because there is no familiar frame of past experience into which he can put this new event, his initial attitude will, of course, be influenced somewhat by the kind of preparation he has had for the interview. If he has had any at all, he may have been told the simple truth. He may have been reassured that there was no reason for fear. He may have been threatened or warned. He may have been deceived or even bribed with false and inappropriate promises. For example, a parent may tell a child, "You're just going to play with the doctor. He is not going to examine you physically. You are going to have fun." Or "The doctor is going to advise you about camp or school." Or, if the parent is so motivated as to try to intimidate the child, he may say, "If you don't behave, the doctor is going to send you away." It is no wonder that the child is bewildered when he actually faces the new experience.

The professional person is an adult and a stranger, and he must give due consideration to these facts as he meets a child patient for the first time. He must also be aware of his personal need to be important to the child. In his role as a professional helper, he has the urge to make his powers felt; he has the need to accomplish his therapeutic purposes. Excessive self-consciousness in the therapist as a professional person can readily get in the way of achieving a natural and useful quality of contact with the child. If he is too concerned with his professional dignity, he will arouse the child's resentment. Like the parent, the professional person wants the child's respect, but he must not expect it in the beginning; he must be willing to earn it.

The challenge that faces the clinician is to establish a relationship with a quality of emotional rapport and communication that will best favor his purpose in understanding the child and in preparing the child for psychotherapy if it is indicated. His immediate purpose, however, is to foster a quality of contact with the child that will enable him to conduct a useful examination of the child's personality. Just as the clinician, at the outset, is a total stranger to the child so the child is at the outset a stranger to the clinician. He must get acquainted. In order to achieve this purpose, it is best for the clinician initially to leave the relationship between the child and himself relatively unstructured, undefined. This will provide the widest possible range of freedom for the child's own initiative and self-expression.

At the outset, the child may for his own security require some sense of distance, both physical and emotional, between himself and this stranger. It is certainly not desirable for the clinician to be too forward or even to touch the child physically unless he derives some cue from the child's behavior that such action would be welcome. On the other hand, the child's total behavior, his emotional attitudes, facial expression, and body mobility—his nonverbal as well as his verbal behavior—provide all sorts of valuable data for the alert clinician. In accordance with his preparation and expectations, the child may anticipate pleasure or hurt or may have some predetermined notion about the clinician's intentions toward him. Usually, in a short time the clinician is able to discern through his observations whether the child feels trust or mistrust, expects satisfaction or is apprehensive of pain, or seems motivated to escape the situation altogether. The child may want something of the therapist or he may fear what the therapist wants of him. He may have totally inappropriate inner phantasies as to the clinician's purpose with him. His immediate incentive may be to reduce the contact to an absolute minimum and get away as fast as is possible.

The clinician is concerned with getting some initial impressions as to whether the child shows interest and responds to or ignores the clinician. Does the child move toward him or away? Is the child disposed to keep a safe distance or move toward the clinician with some of his personal needs? Is the child disposed mainly to talk or to act? Sometimes the child will shrink from the contact as much as possible, show extreme attitudes of avoidance or withdrawal, occasionally seem even to freeze on the spot. An inhibited child may seem paralyzed, rooted to one place in the room, and fearful of making any move. Another child may immediately launch into motor activity, rove about the room, and explore its contents. Still another child may show a minimum of movement and engage only in talk. One child will talk too much and play hardly at all; another child may choose exclusively to play while refusing to talk.

The clinician observes and records in his mind these preferred modes of reception of this new experience. He searches out the emotional levels at which the child is willing to engage in a relationship with him. At one extreme, a child may refuse any form of contact with the clinician. The immediate question is whether the child, in terms of his personality make-up, possesses the capacity to form an emotional relationship or does not. On occasion a child's voluntary refusal of emotional contact is misinterpreted as the absence of capacity for relationship. This may not be the case at all. If one takes into account the child's initial perceptions of the situation and the mistrust and fear that are associated with these perceptions, it may well be that a child is able to form an emotional relationship but that consciously he is not so motivated. His immediate incentive is rather to escape. Excluding this possibility, the child may be dormantly motivated to make contact and reveal his needs to the clinician but may be too frightened and inhibited to do so. He may fear attack and injury.

It is important for the clinician at this point to estimate the quality of communication that is activated between the child and himself. Does the child reveal himself or conceal himself? Does he use his play and talk to disclose something of his inner emotion or is his paramount purpose one of defense? As he talks and plays does he refer to himself as "I" or does he use the third person, does he vicariously expose something personal by talking of another person in order to avoid any direct allusion to himself? Is his activity in the interview realistic or dominated by phantasy? What part of his activity is symbolic?

As the child feels out the possibilities of the new situation, he proceeds to test the therapist in a variety of different ways: that is, in an exploratory way he watches the clinician's every reaction closely in order to try to discern what the clinician is up to with him. The child proceeds step by step to test the reality of this new experience. Is this a situation in which he may expect pleasure or is it dangerous? What is the risk of retaliation for this or that move on his own part? In the meantime, the clinician tries to glean from the child's behavior how the child sees himself in the situation and how the child sees the clinician. What needs does the child assert? How does he endeavor to control the relationship? What are the expressions of conflict and anxiety, and what kind of defense behavior does the patient display?

Gradually, then, the clinician is able to build up the body of information about child and family necessary for diagnosis. But, having reached this stage, he is faced with other special problems that arise in connection with the disturbances of children. Foremost among these problems is the understanding of the developmental features of child behavior. It seems self-evident that the child is a human being, immature, and in a state of rapid growth. Yet all too often these simple facts are ignored when diagnoses are made.

The child is a human being with a specific biological capacity, endowed by heredity with a particular physique and temperament. He has a characteristic nervous, motor, and metabolic pattern and a certain potential for intellectual development. But he is immature—physically, sexually, emotionally, socially, and intellectually. He shows a level of curiosity and motor activity and a rate of metabolic exchange generally higher than that of an adult. His mentation is nonlogical, egocentric, magically toned, and primarily related to affective states and personal needs. To a large extent he communicates at nonverbal levels through somatic reactions and motor expression; much less than an adult does he rely on verbal communication. His behavior is less influenced by memory, and he responds sharply to the perception of present experience. But the child is in a state of rapid growth. Therefore his nonverbal communication changes with the acquisition of new motor skills, his verbal communication increases with new learning, his memory expands with time, and so forth. A diagnosis made two months ago may be found to need reconsideration today.

Likewise, it may seem self-evident that the child is almost totally dependent on his environment, at least to a greater extent than the adult. What happens to this immature human being, the ways in which he grows, are to a degree the product of his heredity; thereafter, they are the product of the care and socialization, the emotional conditioning and learning, of a specific family environment. Because the child is in a state of becoming, his personality is incomplete in its individuation, changeable in its structure and function, uniquely vulnerable to inner tension and environmental pressures. Yet, diagnostic systems have, in the past, failed to place the clinical evaluation of the child in the broader frame of the family group. Despite the most painstaking attempts to improve their usefulness, they seem to move into a dead end, in large part because they have not taken into consideration the seemingly self-evident differences between child and adult.

In principle, in the adult, there is a more fixed organization of basic drives and adaptive reactions, more intactness of personality, more individuality, more internalization of conflict; in the child, by contrast, a less complete, less stable, less intact personality, with less individuality, a more fluid personality organization and more externalization of conflict.

The adult is conceived as being responsible for his behavior; the child is not. The adult constrains his impulses; the child characteristically acts out. The adult acquires some insight into the social and personal implications of his emotional illness; the child ordinarily has little such insight or perhaps none at all. The sick adult takes his own suffering; the sick child tends to impose his suffering onto his environment. The adult holds some power to control his environment and within limits to change it; he can take himself voluntarily out of one situation and place himself in another; the child cannot. In the adult the line of demarcation between normal and abnormal behavior is more sharply defined than in the child.

Granting all these differences and seeking a new system of psychiatric classification that will take them into account, let us examine the patterns of behavior that may emerge from the clinician's initial evaluative procedures. A child attempting to cope with a depriving and threatening environment may react in one of several ways:

1. The child can attack his family and attempt thereby to coerce gratification of basic needs. In this category fall the aggressive conduct disorders and the psychopathic forms of behavior.

2. The child can narrow or withdraw from contact with his family. In this category fall recessive personality developments and trends toward excessive preoccupation with self and own body.

3. Finally the child may react to conflict with his family with excessive anxiety, internalization of conflict and with the production of one and another structured form of psychopathology: (a) excessive anxiety with internalization and encapsulation of specific conflicts, as in the production of psychoneurotic reactions; (b) excessive anxiety, defective emotional control, decompensation of defenses against anxiety, paralysis or disorganization of adaptive functions, which may induce psychopathic tendencies or psychosomatic dysfunctions; (c) excessive anxiety, disorganization of adaptive behavior, arrest of development and/or regression and reintegration at a primitive psychic level as in psychotic forms of reaction.

To judge the normality or abnormality of the given piece of behavior, it is necessary to appraise the behavior in two ways: is it congruous or incongruous with the adaptational requirements of the child's interaction with his environment? Is it congruous or incongruous with the child's total pattern of emotional reactivity? In general, there is strong suspicion of pathology when behavior becomes fixed and repetitive, loses its plasticity and adaptive value, and becomes less responsive to internal stimuli and pressures from the environment.

As we have seen, the characteristics of clinical disturbances in children are shaped by a variety of component factors: chronological age, rate of growth, level of personality integration, and the dynamic equilibrium between child and environment. Because the personality organization of the child is continuously changing, the dominant behavior reactions are prone to shift with the integrative patterns of personality and the quality of the child's interaction with the environment at a given time.

Pathological offshoots may arise at any stage of emergence of the personality. At each such stage, the deviational patterns may become fixated and persistent. As the child moves to the next stage, new deviational patterns may be superimposed and added to the clinical picture. Thus multiple types of pathological response and mixed symptoms may emerge, referrable to different stages of development. Because the processes of development are often patchy and uneven, especially so in disturbed children, there is a tendency to produce multiple and mixed forms of pathological response. It is only as the personality organization of the child congeals and stabilizes toward its adult form that one gets a crystallization of specific patterns and a corresponding consistency in symptom expression. In relation to children, therefore, it is perhaps more accurate to think in terms of component behavior reactions that are related to specific developmental stages than in the more static terms of personality type.

Close study of clinical syndromes in children underscores these specific features of child personality and corresponding differences between child and adult adaptation. The common symptom pictures of children do not display anything like the fixity and consistency that are characteristic of adult symptom pictures. In the young child, acute anxiety reactions with temporary disorganization of adaptive behavior may be dramatic and yet completely reversible. The younger the child and the less formed his personality, the more difficult it is to discriminate between a normal response to stress and pathological anxiety. The manifestations of psychopathology in children show sensitive changes with shifts in time, social setting, and total life situation. A set of symptoms which dominates the clinical picture at one age may be replaced by a new set at a later age. The child changes as the family changes. If the child is moved from one environment to another, the adaptive reactions and symptoms may change radically.

In view of these qualities of emotional reactivity in children, it can hardly be surprising that a multiplicity of diagnostic systems has emerged. Up to now, no one of these systems has gained universal acceptance. At different times one or another of these systems has found transient favor only to be discarded as its weaknesses are revealed. Each has reflected a particular etiological bias and emphasized a distinct set of differential criteria. One gave priority to the constitutional determinants, another to the organ systems whose function is involved in the pathology; another emphasized the descriptive approach to overt deviational behavior; and the psychoanalytic school stressed unconscious motivation and the genetic patterns of development. No one of these diagnostic classifications was satisfactory insofar as it emphasized single phases rather than the totality of child experience and adaptation.

Furthermore, child psychiatry has been a Tower of Babel. Diagnostic terms have been used loosely and ambiguously. Scientific communication between different psychiatric institutions working with children has been difficult because of lack of a common language. What is diagnosed primary behavior disorder in one child center is diagnosed psychoneurosis in another. Within a single child clinic, the same diagnostic terms may be used differently by different psychiatrists.

In fact, the difficulties of finding a workable set of diagnostic criteria for child personality have been so great as to induce a widespread custom of casting aside altogether the responsibility for clinical diagnosis. It has proved easy to rationalize this renunciation. It is said such diagnoses are futile, useless, descriptive rather than dynamic, lacking in precision, and in no way helpful in planning and carrying out the therapy of the child. It is as if the reference points for and the approach to therapy are somehow distinct and belong to a different conceptual frame. The reason for this tendency for diagnosis to lose its meaning is not difficult to find. The gap that has grown between diagnosis and therapy is the failure to relate the clinical estimate of the individual child to a diagnosis of the family group.

This difficulty is sharply reflected in the field of child therapy. Child therapists are often impelled to undertake treatment of a child without a clearly defined clinical diagnosis and without a dynamic appraisal of the total functioning of the child's personality within the frame of a defined family environment. At the least, this is bad practice. How can one presume to correct what is wrong with the functioning of a child personality without first establishing what is wrong? Too often, therapists treat without knowing what they treat.

The factors that have thus far hindered the development of a satisfactory system of psychiatric diagnosis for children are several: the historical tendency to transpose to child psychiatry the conventional, and sometimes biased, principles of the psychiatry of adults, the incompleteness of present-day knowledge of child development and of the group dynamics of family life. Although child psychiatry is rapidly emerging as a respectable specialty, it is still an exceedingly young science, with a history far shorter and more recent than that of adult psychiatry. The scientific weaknesses of these early systems of diagnosis are therefore understandable.

The disadvantages of traditional systems are mainly the following: they tend to carry over into childhood those conceptual trends of structured individual psychopathology which are familiar from the sphere of adult psychiatry but are less specifically suited to child behavior. They tend to conceive the child too strongly as a separate individual and do not provide sufficiently for child's interaction with family environment. They tend to carry over into childhood the concepts of difference between normal and abnormal which prevail in adult psychiatry but again are less specifically appropriate to the phenomenology of child life. They relegate disturbances of character development and the broader problems of social adaptation to the sphere of normal experience and tend therefore to disassociate artificially the study of sick and healthy behavior. Finally, their orientation is largely descriptive rather than dynamic, and as a result, too great a stress is placed on manifest behavior while insufficient consideration is given to motivation, unconscious conflict, and the developmental trends of personality. A given piece of behavior cannot be accurately diagnosed simply in terms of its overt form; its dynamic and developmental basis must be understood—that is, its relation to the total emotional functioning of the child and its meaning in the matrix of the child's adaptive position in the family. For example, it is very difficult in such diagnostic systems to classify properly such forms of behavior as enuresis, masturbation, and tics.

The foundations of diagnosis must consider differences in heredity and constitution, differences in temperament and reactivity at birth, in body structure and function, in rate of growth, and in social development. It is necessary to take into account abnormalities both of body equipment and of family environment. Body equipment and physiological response may be impaired before birth or after birth by heredity, disturbance in embryo, abnormalities of physical development, disease, or accident. A general distinction must be drawn between deviations of development and behavior influenced by organic conditions, in which there is impairment of body structure and function, and deviations of behavior and development in which the body structure and function are normal. The organic conditions include deviant behavior patterns associated with hereditary conditions, disorders of the central nervous system, mental deficiency, the convulsive states, post-infectional disorders, and conditions associated with other forms of somatic disease or defect. Some types of disturbance, behavior disorders, neurotic and psychotic reactions are secondary to and engrafted upon an organic defect.

The functional disorders divide themselves mainly into primary behavior disorders, psychoneurotic and psychotic reactions.* Psychoses are rare. If we concern ourselves for the moment with the nonpsychotic disorders, what do we find? The clinical manifestations are varied, unstable, and tend to change with time. They rarely appear in a pure form. The clinical syndromes of behavior disorder and psychoneurosis are generally neither typical nor pure. Commonly children show a mixture of varied types of deviant behavior, frequently a combination of behavior disorders and psychoneurotic reactions. Even in the case of deep-seated phobic or obsessional neuroses, behavior disorders are present as well. The disturbances of children are patterned responses to stress in a child's

---

* See *Diagnostic and Statistical Manual: Mental Disorders* (Washington: American Psychiatric Assn., 1952).

relation to his inner and outer environment. All types—behavior disorders, psychoneurotic and psychotic reactions—are profoundly affected by the experiences of interaction of child and family. In behavior disorders, conflict is focused on the child's relations with parents; the conflict is largely externalized. In psychoneurotic reactions, the tendency is toward the containment and internalization of conflict with resulting symptom formation. In different children, one or another form of deviant behavior may become the dominant mode of adaptation. When behavior disorders and psychoneurotic reactions coexist in the same child, one of these ways of expressing conflict with family may appear in the center of the child's evolving personality and the other may show itself at the periphery.

The broad grouping of primary behavior disorders embraces the subgroupings of habit disorders, conduct disorders, and neurotic traits. Habit disorders tend to arise at an earlier stage of development than conduct disorders. Habit disorders emerge in a child-parent relationship in which the child cannot project his affective needs with satisfaction. They are tension-reducing forms of behavior that appear before the psychomotor maturity of the child is sufficiently advanced to enable the child to coerce the parental environment into more indulgence. Habit disorders occur on a background of emotional deprivation and are usually expressed as one or another form of autoerotic activity, the purpose of which is to reduce disagreeable inner tension derived from accumulated aggression and to provide pleasure from one's own body.

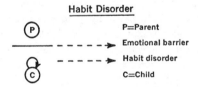

Habit Disorder

P=Parent
Emotional barrier
Habit disorder
C=Child

Conduct disorders require the psychomotor maturity essential to the motive of attacking the family environment. They are found universally on a background of failure of parental responsibility. The parents are inadequate, hostile, or rejecting. To whatever extent the parents withhold love and approval or fail to give their child security, they fail in the goal of socializing the child. The child simply does not get the needed emotional acceptance and the usual social rewards for submitting to restraint. It does not, therefore, pay the child to inhibit his infantile impulses. The child's reaction to parental denial is revolt, and he defends himself against parental hostility with egocentric aggression. He attempts with infantile omnipotent attitudes to coerce the parents into more indulgence. The parents' standards of social conduct and control are not internalized, and there is a corresponding failure of or impediment to the process of identification with the parents. The energy of the child's aggressiveness remains externally oriented. The level of conflict continues to be focused in the zone between the child and the environment.

In this setting, the child's aggression fails to turn inward and contribute to the establishment of internal mechanisms of self-control and the functions of conscience. Thus, the child's emotional life remains egocentrically oriented, and conflict is externalized, between child and parent.

Conduct Disorder

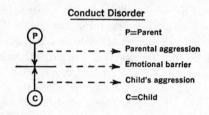

P=Parent
Parental aggression
Emotional barrier
Child's aggression
C=Child

From the developmental point of view, neurotic traits are transitional between the personality organization represented in primary behavior disorders on the one hand, and organized psychoneuroses on the other. Structurally and functionally, neurotic traits are related to that phase of personality development in which the processes of identification with parents and internalization of parental standards to form the inner functions of conscience are only partly completed. Infantile urges are not fully restrained. Fear of parental hostility and retaliation is displaced from the parent figure to some symbol such as an animal or thunder. The dynamic pattern is not one of internal guilt and self-punishment but anticipation of punishment from without. Some external object becomes the symbol of an external conscience. This level of structuring of personality implies partial internalization and partial externalization of conflict and some degree of "acting out."

Neurotic Trait

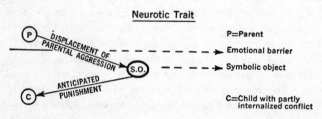

P=Parent
DISPLACEMENT OF PARENTAL AGGRESSION
Emotional barrier
S.O.
Symbolic object
ANTICIPATED PUNISHMENT
C=Child with partly internalized conflict

Organized psychoneuroses represent a more differentiated form of pathology. They cannot come into being except in the context of a higher degree of organization of personality. The ego structure of the child must have achieved sufficient differentiation to accomplish the internalization of the functions of conscience. The psychodynamics of an organized psychoneurosis implies the repression of a specific conflict, which becomes circumscribed and localized. The repressed and socially prohibited urge is displaced and disguised and emerges in symbolic form in the neurotic symptom. The symptom itself is therefore composed of three basic elements: (1) the repressed craving and the associated aggressive urges; (2) the unconscious guilt feeling and the need for punishment; (3) the ego elements which serve to preserve the repression and the symbolic disguise of a socially disapproved, unconscious urge.

A fourth element is often variably present but is not specific to the psychodynamics of symptom production. This is the element of secondary emotional gain which the personality may elaborate in connection with the suffering and disability accompanying the symptom itself. Most often the secondary emotional gain is expressed in behavior motivated by the wish to be relieved of responsibility and to win more attention, indulgence, and special privilege.

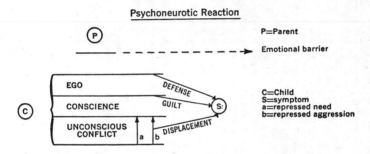

Psychoneurotic Reaction

In organized psychoneurosis, the psychodynamic processes are such as tend to circumscribe the conflict. The conflict is contained and localized, and its impairing influence on the more general functions of the personality is restricted. An apt analogy for this process is the way in which pus is drawn out of the blood and lymph system and confined in a local abcess. This is a natural self-protective device which can be observed to operate at the psychic as well as the physiological level, and its obvious purpose is to render as many of the personality operations as possible relatively free of anxiety.

In contrast to the primary behavior disorders, the conflict in psychoneurotic reactions is internalized. The child is absorbed mainly in conflict with himself. This is why in the primary behavior disorders it is the environment that suffers most, whereas in psychoneurosis the child suffers most.

Some comments are in order with regard to the more common problem of differential diagnosis. The syndrome of psychopathic personality implies the

PSYCHIATRIC DISORDERS IN CHILDREN

FUNCTIONAL DISORDERS

Environment	Primary Behavior Disorders			Character Disorders	Psychosomatic Disorders	Psychoneurotic Disorders	Psychotic Disorders
	Habit Disorder	Conduct Disorder	Neurotic Traits				

A. Favorable
B. Unfavorable
1. physical
2. social
  a. familial
  b. extra-familial
	feeding disorders, sucking, biting, vomiting, crying, picking, scratching, masturbation, enuresis, rocking, head-banging	defiance, rebellion, tantrums, destructiveness, cruelty, overactivity, negativism, lying, stealing, withdrawal, asocial behavior, deviant sex activity	jealousy, inhibition of play, imagination, curiosity, inhibition of aggression, sleep disorders, night terrors, sleep walking, enuresis, masturbation, disturbances of body attitudes, speech disorders, fear of animals, darkness, thunder	infantile, isolated, schizoid, inhibited, narcissistic, neurotic, paranoid, psychopathic, psychotic	colic, vomiting, constipation, diarrhea, enuresis, skin eruptions, asthma, hay fever	hysteria, phobia, obsessive, compulsive, hypochondriacal	undifferentiated psychosis, schizophrenia, affective psychosis

Conflict with Environment ⟷ Conflict with Self

DISORDERS WITH ORGANIC BASE

Body Structure and Function	Mental Retardation (Structural Type)	Secondary Behavior Disorders	Organic Syndromes
A. Normal B. Impaired 1. disorders C.N.S. 2. endocrine imbalance 3. body defects 4. abnormal body functions 5. physical illness	weakness of intelligence, poverty of association, impairment of perception, defect of judgment, disturbance of memory (variable), inadequacy of motor coordination, "stigmata" of degeneration	behavior disorders secondary to defect, deformity, illness, deviant physiology, etc.	cortical impairment, defect of intellect, memory, or judgment, poverty of association, inadequacy of concept formation, limitation of imaginative powers, undue generalization, defective organization of emotions, emotional instability and inadequacy, psychotic disorders engrafted on organic base.

presence of a fixed character defect. The idea that this defect is constitutional in origin is rapidly giving way. In childhood, the "true psychopathic syndrome" is found rarely if at all. It has been assumed in this condition that the classical symptoms of impulsiveness, shallow emotionality, intolerance for authority, poor judgment, antisocial conduct, inability to postpone gratifications, inability to learn from experience, lack of capacity for emotional rapport, and absence of genuine guilt feelings assert themselves consistently, regardless of the quality of the family environment and life experience. The validity of this conception is very much in doubt. In terms of overt clinical symptomatology, it is often impossible to distinguish between a "true psychopathic syndrome," a severe primary behavior disorder, and schizophrenia. Some cases of "affect hunger" are diagnosed psychopathic personality. In another theoretical frame, Partridge, impressed with the social origin of this pattern of deviancy, suggested the term "sociopath."

One word, in passing, concerning psychosomatic disturbances in children. Again, it is more useful to regard these as reactions rather than distinct diagnostic types. The vulnerability to such reactions is highly contingent on the maturational level of the personality. Psychosomatic disorders tend to appear when the child, immature and adaptively ill-equipped, is overwhelmed by situational danger and reacts with diffuse anxiety, rage, temporary loss of emotional control, decompensation of defenses against anxiety, and disorganization of the adaptive functions of personality. In such circumstances, the organism is apt to respond with evidences of psychosomatic dysfunction. In early childhood, acute psychosomatic disturbances frequently appear in evanescent form—colic, nausea and vomiting, breath-holding, constipation, diarrhea, skin eruptions, asthma, etc. They are less apt to become established patterns as the personality matures and achieves a higher degree of integration.

Psychoses in children do occur but are rare. The manifestations do not assume the same organized form as in adults. The criteria for psychotic adaptation in a child must be distinct from those which are appropriate to such diagnoses in adults. In adults the manifestations of psychosis are largely conceived as a panicky disorganization of previously achieved levels of adaptation and regression to primitive affective behavior. In children, the factor of arrest or failure of development of personality is more significant. Psychotic trends in children are less organized and more fragmentary and can often be related to arrest or sheer failure of the processes of ego development and differentiation. Disturbances of coordination are frequently found. Whether childhood schizophrenia is to be conceived as an illness identical with schizophrenia emerging in later life is a moot question. The evidence for organicity in childhood psychosis is more convincing; the prognosis is usually worse.

In recent years the diagnosis of childhood schizophrenia has become rather too popular. The diagnosis is sometimes offered too lightly and carelessly; occasionally this has insidiously harmful effect on the general management and the therapy of the child. The mere presence of autistic, withdrawn behavior is not in itself evidence of the existence of a schizophrenia. Often severe behavior disorders, in which the overt behavior shows some degree of disorganization, are misdiagnosed as schizophrenia.

Often fragmentary psychotic reactions are engrafted on a primary mental defect. In this instance, the primary diagnosis is mental deficiency; the superimposition of fragmentary psychotic responses is secondary.

In the attempt to classify childhood disorders, it becomes apparent that the first need is a set of criteria for the evaluation of the functioning of the particular child here and now. Only when we have such criteria and a corresponding clinical evaluation can we properly diagnose, in the more formal sense of the word. It becomes apparent also that an understanding of the functioning of the child here and now is dependent on a view of the child not as an isolated entity but rather as a part of a defined family system operating in specific life situations. (See The Child Here and Now, p. 143.) Hence the need for clinicians to look beyond the narrow limits of clinical definitions at the total life pattern of a disturbed child.

CHAPTER 13

DISTURBANCES OF ADOLESCENCE

ALTHOUGH the understanding of adolescent behavior is crucial to the entire theory of personality maturation, some aspects of the problem remain to this day a mystery. Adolescent behavior is ever-changing. It is unstable, elusive, and evanescent; its true meaning occasionally escapes even the most astute observer.

The social conduct of adolescents can be most trying. It can impose the severest test on family and community. It is common knowledge that parents often fail to understand such behavior. Sometimes they fear the worst—the beginning of a hardened criminal career or a psychosis—when actually the child is experiencing a temporary adolescent storm from which he will emerge intact, unscarred, and with reasonably good emotional health. Or sometimes parents come to the psychiatrist with a mentally sick adolescent but are grudging and suspicious of the professional consultation. They insist that the disturbed boy is "normal," that he is just "adolescing" and will "grow out of it."

To misjudge the fleeting shifts of adolescent behavior may have serious consequences. A parent who vacillates, who alternatingly imagines the worst and dismisses the problem as trivial, may do permanent harm to the unfolding of adolescent personality. Why is it in this era of life that the danger of confusion and misinterpretation is so great?

Adolescence is a critical phase in growth. During this phase the personality undergoes a deep transformation. There is a basic shift in equilibrium, characterized by simultaneous tendencies toward emotional disorganization and reorganization. Out of these processes is finally precipitated the permanent structure of adult personality. Conflict emerges at all levels of emotional experience. Earlier phases of psychic distress are reactivated; latent weaknesses are exposed. In those who are so predisposed, a major mental illness may emerge.

The typical manifestations of adolescent change are familiar: insecurity; instability of mood and action; egocentricity; the sexual drives; exhibitionism; shifting images of self and emotional disorientation; lack of ease with one's own body; preoccupation with physique and health; self-consciousness and fear of exposure; feeling of difference; conflict with authority; rebelliousness; craving for independence; hero worship; suggestibility to outside influence; fear of inadequacy and failure; finally, aspiration to be big in some field of human achievement.

Underlying these typical adolescent manifestations are the fundamental biological processes of pubescence. Changes in glandular function produce changes in physique, in physiological balance; with these changes, the sex drives emerge. The growth processes tend to be asymmetrical. In girls there is the onset of menses, the change in contour of the body, the development of breasts and hips, changes in skin texture. In boys there is the growth of the genitals, the onset of ejaculation, change in voice, hair growth, change in skin texture, and acne.

The elements of physical change are accompanied by a shift in emotional, social, sexual, and intellectual behavior. Inequalities of development in these various spheres tend to intensify the usual instability. Not only are there tremendous variations from one individual to the next, but, perhaps even more important, every conceivable type of imbalance may occur within the one individual, a factor that sharply stimulates anxiety, self-consciousness, and feelings of difference and inferiority.

Overt sexual desire emerges in both sexes. Masturbation is more easily stimulated in boys than in girls. Girls develop earlier their secondary sexual characteristics but are slower in their sexual awakening. To boys sex offers its own intrinsic pleasure. To girls sex traditionally represents a means to an end rather than an end in itself; that is, the sexual behavior of girls is closely linked to strivings for security and status. But this pattern is changing and in our culture girls also are coming to think of sex for sex's sake.

Yet sexual maturation is the positive feature of adolescence. In other areas, all sorts of transitional adaptation between childhood and adulthood appear. Adolescents show in their behavior both the child and the adult. They are indeed "tween-agers," as Lawson Lowrey said. Their complex adaptation is the product of two sets of forces: physical changes associated with rapid growth and sexual development and group pressure, familial and cultural. This two-way pressure inexorably forces a profound shift in the equilibrium of personality. The emergence of an unbalanced mixture of childhood and adult traits is, therefore, to be expected. The adolescent does not mature in a consistent forward movement; instead, anxiety induces an irregular movement, alternately forward and backward. The adolescent loses the protection of childhood but does not yet have the strength and privileges of the adult. The realities of adult living represent an unknown and undefined threat. Fear of being a child pushes the adolescent forward. Fear of being an adult pushes him backward. Dangers loom large either in moving toward maturity or in regressing to childhood forms of adaptation, but the adventure, the challenge and satisfaction of adult life is a potent force.

The closeness of the adolescent to his group is a significant molding force during this transitional adaptation. Often, the interchange between the adolescent and his group is so fluid and rich that their respective identities can hardly be separated. The distinction between what is inside and outside the adolescent mind cannot, therefore, always be clear. Within the family circle, the adolescent rebels. Outside the family, the urge to conform to group standards is often extreme. The adolescent seeks to "find himself." There is just as great a danger, however, of losing himself in his unreasoned rebellions and conformities. The adolescent may merge his personality with the activities of his group or isolate himself. He may entrench a positive group identification or show a negative effort toward self-preservation through isolation. Thus, in the end, the adolescent may solidify his individuality or submerge it behind defensive conformity.

The cultural pattern plays a large role in dictating the adolescent's place in the social scheme and in shaping adolescent personality. The adolescent moves out to make contact with an expanding series of groups bound by common religious, recreational, intellectual, and economic interests.

In all societies, adolescents achieve new privileges, but they must also assume new responsibilities. They must prove their worth sexually, socially, economically. They are expected to pursue and control their sexual drives according to modes predetermined by the given culture. They must evolve into approved versions of men and women. Beyond this point generalizations become difficult. Each society imposes a distinct set of standards. Moreover within any single large culture such as our own there are infinite numbers of subcultures which in turn differ among themselves. Let us look first at the influences of our culture on these young people and consider its special relevance to the larger questions of mental health.

The Adolescent in Our Changing World

It should be immediately apparent that grave problems may arise when a human being in a state of transition is faced with a society in a state of transition. The adolescent of our day is a scared and worried youngster, and with ample reason. His parents are worried too. So are the leaders of the community and the leaders of the nation. No one can predict the events of tomorrow; therefore, everyone fears for the future. The insecurity of the adolescent is intense. He cannot easily see ahead and cannot safely plan his future. It is his job to grow up, to develop strength and confidence, to achieve a clear view of himself as an emerging man, a clear view of the surrounding world, and to equip himself for the tasks of adult living. What chance has he in our kind of world?

In our country today, the adolescent is neither master of himself nor master of his surrounding world. He is neither sure of the conquest of his own emotions nor sure of his ability to counter the dangers of his environment. As he looks inside himself, he perceives dimly the mysterious, pervasive changes produced by his physical and sexual maturation. These biological forces have a profound impact on his psychic being. But he has only a vague understanding of their meaning. He is frightened by their autonomous power and by his helplessness to control them. As he looks outside himself, he is impressed by the momentous events in the outer world, events that alter his world with amazing speed, almost from day to day. Yet again the profound implications of these social changes elude him. And over these processes, too, he has negligible control.

At the same time, he cannot help but be aware that this social instability is a continuing menace to his parents' sense of security and to their efforts to plan the family's future. Inevitably, if his parents react with fright, he must be doubly frightened.

Adolescents maintain an alert, vigilant watch on the behavior of the older generation in this crisis. Can it muster the strength and wisdom to protect civilization from total devastation? The adolescents of our time shoulder a huge responsibility, for it is their job to provide a "loyal opposition" to their elders, to challenge their goals, judgments, decisions and actions. The universal pattern of the son's fundamental loyalty to his father becomes in our day even more crucial. The son rebels against his father, but his very rebellion adds to his father's maturity and deepens his wisdom. And the father must also be loyal to his son; he cannot betray his son's trust. The authority and the superior understanding of the older generation must be proved over and over again in the eyes of youth. Youth watches—and watches closely, for theirs will be the responsibility of shaping the world of tomorrow.

In this time of crisis, there is the temptation to react to fear and worry with the tendency to deny fear and attack a scapegoat, to intimidate minorities, to suppress freedom of expression, to spread the contagion of mistrust and suspicion, to engage in witchhunting or character assassination. These are all signs of weakness, confusion, regression, and self-destruction. To deny one's own fear and doubt and to substitute intimidation and bullying of one's neighbor is not the way, for it is merely to confess fear and mistrust of oneself, to confess spiritual bankruptcy. The situation calls for honest self-examination, not panic and indiscriminate lashing out. But if grown persons deal badly with their fear and yield to such temptations, what can we expect of our adolescents? If the adolescent sees his father frightened, confused, and lashing out blindly, the adolescent is himself plunged into confusion and panic. The example set by the older man must profoundly affect the adolescent's view of himself and the dangers that beset him in our day. It is a great threat to the maturation of our young men if they react to their own anxiety with irrational aggression and regression.

Yet, we are all familiar with the fact that some of them plunge blindly and pathologically into playboy activities and live only for the pleasure of the moment. Some resort to alcohol, narcotics, and delinquency. Some pitch themselves feverishly and fanatically into political movements. Many become disillusioned, embittered, cynical, and weakened in their ability to meet the responsibilities of maturity.

A common reaction is to build a defensive layer of callousness and cynicism. The contemporary adolescent has a shaken faith in the older generation. He feels that he has been let down, that the adult offers a poor example. He scoffs at the problems of ethics; he is little concerned with the welfare of other human beings. In his own brief lifetime, he has witnessed the elders grow callous to war, callous to the destruction of life and property on a stupendous scale; he has seen them turn cold to the suffering and mutilation of other human beings. The social ideals of the previous era have become unreal and meaningless. Perhaps the cynicism and callousness of the adolescent is a surface response, a defense against experiencing the pain of such occurrences at too close a range.

On the other hand, the adolescent discovers that the moral code with which he as a child was indoctrinated is not the same as that which dominates society. Children who are taught to share, to cooperate, to be considerate of the rights of other persons, are ill prepared for the code of ruthless, competitive aggression that prevails in the adult world.

Present-day society places an inordinately high premium on success, success in conventional prestige tones, success at any price. The unrestrained, crude use of aggression proves often to be a sheer necessity for the achievement of conventional success. One must ruthlessly stamp out rivals. With the loss of ethical values and ideals, the emphasis moves toward a goal of "success" through sheer power and self-aggrandizement. The orientation is egocentric: "To hell with the other fellow." The childhood conscience reacts to such aggression with anxiety, fear of retaliation, and ostracization. Thus, the adolescent's struggle for acceptance and for establishment of a firm personal identity is made still more difficult.

One other feature of our culture compounds the difficulties of adolescent adaptation: the highly developed technology and the trend toward specialization. The necessity for long apprenticeship and training and the prolonged dependence on family in preparation for the special tasks of adult life impose on the adolescent an added strain. They tend to hamper his sexual development and aggravate his feelings of inadequacy.

In contrast with earlier forms of society, the relations between the adolescent and contemporary culture today are extraordinarily complex. The adolescent has little security with surrounding groups. The lines of contact with society are muddled; the future is unclear. It is difficult for the adolescent to bring his personal goals into harmony with a society that does not clearly know its aims. And there is always the lurking fear that the issue may be sheer survival, that there may be no future.

As a result, adolescents, as planners for the future, fall into three groups: There are those rigid persons who plan inflexibly on a long term basis, refusing to believe their lives will be touched by the world struggle. They blithely ignore the larger threats, phantasy themselves omnipotent and immune to outside interferences. Then there are those who refuse to plan. Either they are crushed by their anxiety or, at the opposite pole, they indulge in a hectic "flight into reality," keeping busy with their day-by-day pleasures, so as not to think. Finally, there are those of more flexible temperament, who admit the realities of their world and therefore plan their futures on a contingent basis. This last is the most healthy group.

One particular aspect of today's culture affects the future of every adolescent, and each one must come to his own terms with it. Compulsory military training is in this country a relatively new facet of adolescence and one to which we see a great diversity of reactions. Some adolescents regard their military service in terms of adventure, the glamour of the uniform, the opportunity to be a hero and to prove masculine strength and courage. Others, particularly those who have little hope of making a place for themselves in civilian life or who have no family ties, see service as a way of life; they "join the Navy and see the world." Some find it a means to free training for jobs in civilian life; they "join the Navy and get a free training for a career." For some, the military is an escape, a way of avoiding other problems, disappointments in family or love, or fear of failure.

But attitudes of welcome anticipation toward military service are by no means the rule. Many young men see this period merely as an interference with life plans, career, marriage, and family. They dread the loss of time and feel that they are being placed at a disadvantage in the competitive pursuits of civilian life. They react with homesickness, fear of separation from family, mother, and fiancée, and anxiety concerning exclusive restriction of contacts to males. Military service is a compulsory duty, and quite striking are the lack of enthusiasm, the inability to idealize the aims of war, and the cynicism about the emotions of patriotism. Many become resigned to the inevitable but with apathy and loss of hope. Others hate it in the extreme and, like so many who regarded the fighting in Korea as an unwarranted interruption of their civilian lives for political causes they could not easily understand, live only for the day when they can resume their normal places at home.

The psychological implications of military service are many, for the military takes over some of the protective and educational functions of parents in preparing young males for adulthood. At the same time, it may create certain conflicts in the adolescent, divided allegiance between parental authority and the authority of the military, conflict between the standards of the family and the standards of the peer group in the military unit, which may involve a temporary renunciation of personal responsibility for sexual aggression and for violence. There may also arise conflict over the necessity for automatic and uncritical obedience to superior officers and the surrender of individual responsibility to the dictates of the military.

In some cases, the threat of injury or death produces reactions of acute anxiety. There are fears of mutilation and death, conflict about the violence of war and the command to kill, conflict with childhood conscience, and phantasies of world annihilation. The military can act as a precipitating influence in mental illness, producing pathological anxieties about the body and about health, phantasies of being maimed as a punishment for masturbation or other sexual offenses, and countless other manifestations of personality disturbance. Compensatory preoccupation with body-building, sports, and other forms of vicarious release of aggressive drives may result.

It is certain, however, that changes in the character of the adolescent male result from this societally imposed period of transition. These changes may be in the direction of strength and maturity, or they may lead to regression, sometimes in extreme form. Eventually the adolescent returns from the military to his civilian community and feels the full impact of the conflict of values that dominates it, all too often ill prepared to deal with its problems.

The feminine half of the adolescent community, although not directly involved in compulsory military service, reacts to its influences on the males. If the serviceman, feeling the urge to live while he can, fast and furiously, indulges himself totally in the appetites of the body, the girl responds. If, as soon as he gets by the hurdle of the military, he turns cautious and seeks out a safe niche in the community, a steady job, a home, a car, she responds. She too is out to get what she can while she can, particularly the security of marriage, home, and a respected place in the community. But today's young woman cannot easily trust herself to the man. He may be gone tomorrow. Girls are forced to shift their security leanings away from the man himself to the more impersonal symbols of a home, family, children, and steady income. When necessary, they work too. They are thus committed to the sentiments of domestication and the practical affairs of everyday living.

The Adolescent and His Changing Self

Although, as we have seen earlier, it is difficult to separate the inner and outer aspects of experience, there are certain areas of adolescent development that lie closer to the center and core of the self and farther from the influences and pressures of the surrounding society. If we keep clearly in mind the continuous interplay of the inner and outer components of development, we may move for a time "inside" the adolescent, examining his "internal" processes, and from them draw information that is relevant to the adolescent's significant relations with his family.

As the child grows and moves out from the dominance of the family circle, one of his major concerns is a clear orientation of his personal self to the outside world. The adolescent struggles to resolve his identification with his two parents and to build from this identification a personal identity uniquely his own. The manner in which he solves the oedipal struggle and builds his personal identity influences basic aspects of his behavior: his self-assertive pattern, his sexual tendency, his attitude toward his own nature and the nature of the world around him. In the meantime, the uncertainty and confusion that characterize his sense of his own self radiate outward to affect all of his attitudes toward life.

Adolescence is a groping, questioning stage, a phase in which the adolescent condenses the values that will guide his social perspective for the major part of his life. It is exactly here that he confronts the challenge of bringing into harmony his view of self and his view of the world. He must now link his life striving with a personal philosophy. The adolescent asks: "What is life? Who am I? What am I good for? Where do I fit? Who are my real friends? Who are my enemies? What must I fight? With whom? Against whom? For what life goals?" And finally: "Is life really worth the struggle?"

This kind of feverish, anxious searching for identity, values, and social orientation is paralleled by an expanding interest in social and economic conflicts, in religion and philosophy. In the service of this search, the adolescent mobilizes his intellect and exploits it as a defense against his anxiety. Such struggles deeply affect the adolescent's choice of group associations. In a time of testing of parental images and temporary dissolution of self, the adolescent seeks to identify with something larger than himself. His urge is to ally with a cause greater than his own.

Economic and religious affiliations offer such an opportunity. The allegiance to a group characterized by a special economic philosophy, especially one advocating rebellion or social reform, serves to conceal disappointment in parents and to reinforce the unstable repression of hostility to parental authority. It also buttresses the unstable repression of adolescent sexual drives.

The excessive religiosity of adolescents or, on the other hand, their radical turn away from it to atheism is sometimes interpreted as a defense against unconscious tendencies to passivity. A symbolic parallel may be drawn between the fervor of submission to a new religion and the emotion of submission to homosexual seduction. Conversion to a new religion or a new social ideal is thus conceived as a disguised expression of passive homosexual leanings. It may sometimes be. But more important may be the search for a more secure symbol of parental authority, a new protective ideal, a new personal identity. Can we not view the adolescent's concern with religion and social philosophy as a stage in the expansion of the adolescent's sense of self, a legitimate quest for union with the larger world?

A nineteen-year-old boy was referred after he had ignominiously flunked out of the first year of college. When asked why he wanted to go to college, he gave the vague reply: "I suppose, to do good for others." Further questioning failed to elicit any more concrete explanation of his motivation or life goal. This same quality of vagueness characterized all his actions and relationships. If nothing better showed up, he thought he would finally enter his father's business. His guiding principle was to do things "the easy way." He disliked exertion.

This young man was detached, passive; he wore a peculiar grin. His mother was a social worker of the old vintage; his father, a business man. The family was Jewish, assimilated, strongly conformist, high in the economic scale.

But the emotional atmosphere at home was drab, colorless, lacking in solidarity and substance. The mother, nominally a Jew, attended a Protestant church. She encouraged the boy to do likewise. At thirteen, feeling already converted, he joined a Christian church.

Since early childhood he had felt the compulsion to conform in order to insure social acceptance. In fact, he leaned over backward to the extent of deliberately shunning Jewish circles for fear that Christian groups would exclude him. Acceptance by a Christian group provided gratification for his need for companionship but enabled him at the same time to reject his Jewish father.

The boy had a long, hooked nose, which he disliked and associated with Jewishness. Three times, between the ages of eleven and fifteen years, in apparent accidents, he broke his nose. He planned to have plastic surgical repair at nineteen but could hardly wait until then to change his nose.

This boy's sense of masculine adequacy was damaged; he had some unconscious homosexual leaning. He was deeply confused in his concept of self and equally confused as to what his parents represented. Beset with inner doubts about himself and troubled with violent, repressed hostility against both parents, he resorted to the game of "playing dumb."

Though very intelligent, he wore a mask with people; he acted as though he were dull and uncomprehending. This was his defense against extreme hostility to his parents. He concealed his real emotions behind a façade of empty compliance and inconspicuous politeness. Unconsciously he equated exertion with hostility and therefore assumed a defensive guise of extreme passivity and lack of initiative. He had made no real progress toward orienting self to his outer world.

Another adolescent, faced with the same basic problem, may take refuge in the contrary but typical addiction to excitement and danger, in the thrill of daring the representatives of authority to catch and punish his excesses. He matches his urge for omnipotent power against authority. He craves the satisfaction of outwitting and triumphing over authority, but beneath this façade lurks the fear of retribution. Often this type of motivation finds expression in bizarre, irrational, and delinquent acts, e.g., walking a narrow roof ledge or stealing automobiles.

But most often this period of unstable transformation is characterized by lightning shifts of behavior, characterized alternately by restraint and self-indulgence. Strivings that represent elements of unconscious conflict are released impulsively. Inevitably such acting out is followed by a resurgence of guilt and anxiety, and this in turn impels the reimposition, temporarily at least, of childhood patterns of restraint. In a single individual, therefore, one may see cyclic behavior: periods of inhibition, followed by periods of impulsive discharge, followed again by inhibition. The fluidity of both the self-system and conscience structure in the adolescent personality favors the outbreak of disturbances of social conduct.

Another conspicuous area of conflict in adolescence centers around real or fancied injury to self-esteem. Adolescents show extraordinary sensitiveness concerning their concept of self. They react with triggerlike responsiveness to what they think of themselves and what others think of them. Because their image of self is in a state of flux, they are especially vulnerable to other persons' judgments. The issue of being approved or disapproved by others assumes a critical importance.

Earlier discussion has already hinted at adolescent sensitiveness about feelings of difference, not only from others, but also from themselves, because the rapid transformation of personality gives them little opportunity to gain familiarity with one stage of self before it is replaced by a new one. All this is a necessary reflection of the fluidity of the self-structure. Not only in the present is their self-esteem exposed to attack; past assaults on their feelings of self-worth are dramatically laid bare.

Adolescents often disclose, with astonishing vividness, memories of deep, early injuries to their pride. They painfully relive these childhood hurts. They dread renewed assaults on these old but still exposed wounds. Not infrequently, they perceive them consciously as new, fresh wounds. Of importance in this connection are the adolescents' fears of bodily attack and physical pain. Extraordinarily sensitized to their bodies, they often feel irreversibly damaged. Although in some part these attitudes may represent fear of castration, they frequently mean something deeper: the threat of total destruction. In this context, fears of being dominated, engulfed, crushed, even killed, find their appropriate place. Masochistic phantasies are frequently woven into the context of such anxieties.

Anxiety associated with lack of confidence and fear of failure releases a host of secondary defensive attitudes: timidity, submissiveness, gullibility, or, at the other extreme, excessive rebellion, belligerence, tactics of intimidation, and a variety of other compensatory tendencies. Adolescents characteristically have a difficult time organizing their aggressive impulses. They do not quite know how to handle their aggressiveness, when to be assertive, or when to be yielding.

A sixteen-year-old boy with superior native endowment showed a striking discrepancy between his potential abilities and actual achievement. His achievement was practically nil. He frankly confessed he had no ambition except to be a bum. His father was an outstanding success professionally, but the patient did not expect to accomplish anything in life. He insisted that he was interested only in the fun he could have now. He claimed this choice as his own prerogative; so long as he stayed by himself and hurt no one else, why couldn't he simply be a bum if he so preferred.

This boy persistently evaded responsibility, dissipated his energies, refused any and all exertions, and fortified a pattern of passive resistance to authority. At school he was a chronic failure academically and socially. He was strongly disliked by his peers because of his supercilious, patronizing, sarcastic attitudes. He seized any opportunity to ridicule his schoolmates. This was his defense, his quick alibi for failure.

He attempted in every way to fortify this perverseness. Although loathe to admit it, he was unable to get pleasure from the more usual activities. Beneath his overt defensive attitudes, he was extremely tense, depressed, and despairing and had death fears and a profound sense of defeat.

His self-esteem had been deeply hurt years back by his recognition that his successful, ambitious, vain father did not prize him for himself but wished merely to pad his own vanity by exhibiting the boy's intellectual superiority. He insisted that the boy be twice as smart as any other boy. At the same time, the father never really got close to him emotionally. He was detached and more absorbed in his professional activity than in his children. In this background the boy built up his pattern of spite and negativism. His self-esteem had not survived the blow.

In the "tween-age," intricately interwoven with the struggle for identity, orientation, and self-esteem, is the problem of moving from the standards of right and wrong the adolescent absorbed as a child to a set of moral standards appropriate to adult life. This aspect of maturing is made more difficult by the instability and confusion that characterizes the values of adults. There is no dependable model in adult society.

This feature of the problem must be considered from several different angles: the transformation of childhood to adult conscience, the struggle for control of sexual need, aggression, and tendencies to self-punishment, and, finally, the tendency to externalize the functions of conscience during adolescence, with the resulting urges to act out. These phases are not really distinct but are interrelated aspects of a single process.

Always lurking behind the scene and shaping both his sexual behavior and his self-image are the adolescent's struggles with the symbols of authority. His feelings toward authority are loaded with ambivalence. His need of parental protection continues. His emotional dependence upon them is unresolved. Simultaneously, however, he has a strong need to live his own life, to demonstrate his self-sufficiency, and to make his own decisions. But always the question returns: would his parents approve or disapprove? He feels guilty over his sex urges, guilty over his aggressive impulses. He feels shame for his desire to exhibit himself, shame for his physical idiosyncrasies and his imagined differences, and shame for his failure to perform up to his idealized expectations. He defends against his guilt and shame by denying it, by inviting minor punishments, by overcompensating through his belligerency and boastfulness. But his underlying weaknesses show as through glass.

A fifteen-year-old girl, large for her age, inhibited, shy, socially withdrawn, was unable to make friends. She had a beautiful face that clashed cruelly with her figure. In physique, she alternated in appearance between something like a cadaver and the fat woman of the circus. At one time she weighed eighty-eight pounds and looked like a walking corpse. Another time she weighed 220 pounds and looked like a freak. Either she nibbled food constantly and insatiably, or she put herself on a starvation diet.

She feared sex and strictly avoided boys. She was at the same time intensely anxious, even greedy, in her sex interests. In phantasy she characterized certain foods as feminine, others as masculine. She alternated between devouring one or the other type of food. She was confused as to how much she wanted to be a girl and attractive to boys or to be strong, independent, and aggressive like boys.

She was not secure in her dependence on either parent. She had cannibalistic phantasies of eating her father's genital; then, overwhelmed with guilt, she punished herself with a starvation diet. But her basic hostility against her mother distorted this relationship too. She repressed this hostility and intensified her dependence on her mother in order to be protected from her sexual cravings. She made her mother serve as an external conscience. Her conception of herself was so confused that she did not dare let herself grow up; she avoided the issues of maturity and clung tenaciously to the status of child.

Even in less extreme cases, the guilt reactions are peculiarly labile. They tend at first to be rather rigid and derive from the pattern of moral standards laid down in childhood through parental approval or disapproval. The temptation to transgress this code is accompanied by fear of punishment and loss of love of the parents.

As the adolescent detaches himself from his parents, he shifts his dependency to persons and groups outside the family, occasionally to other adults but more conspicuously to peers and older adolescents who symbolize a big brother or sister. In a parallel process, he experiences a shift in ideals and standards. New patterns of aspiration emerge, based on these new associations. Persons other than parents are now made to personify ideals and conscience. The adolescent tends to externalize his conflict and control his behavior in accordance with his need of approval by particular persons and groups outside the family. For a time, the standards laid down by peers and "big brothers" may completely dominate the adolescent's attitudes and bring about a sharp clash with the parents' ideas about life. The subjective struggle over standards is often bitter because of the adolescent's fear of losing control over his sexual and aggressive urges.

The temptation to release these drives is intense, but the adolescent, dreading the loss of control, clings tenaciously to his childhood conscience and the parents from whom it was derived. These symbols represent for him a safe haven. This is the expression of adolescent conservatism and caution. But adolescents vacillate; they swing from one extreme to the other; they tend either to be overcautious and rigid or positively rash.

A central area of adolescent development, one in which these ambivalences and confusions are very marked, is of course the area of sexual maturation. The emergence of the sexual functions and related emotional needs is at the very core of adolescent development, and the related problems of adaptation to our culture are enormous.

The adolescent male's all-encompassing drive to complete his incomplete self is by far his most dramatic feature. He feels far from whole, and a gnawing tension accompanies this feeling. All too obvious is his striving, day in and day out, to extract from life, from people, from his personal experiences that which he feels he lacks, so that he may edge a bit further up the ladder of superiority and in his own and other's eyes approximate more closely his ideal image of himself.

The adolescent male has a tender skin, but nowhere is this sense of vulnerability expressed more vividly than in his relations with the other sex. In one way, he watches with a hawk's eye for the outcroppings of acne, which will make him less attractive to the female. In another way, his skin is so tender that he feels that everybody can see through it, that anything he feels and thinks is completely transparent. Toward the female, he is indescribably sensitive, sensitive to her as to his own incompleteness. She is a mirror into which he gazes anxiously to measure his defects and to confess his masculine unfulfillment. His need of her is acute; his fear of her is critical. Sometimes it reaches immense proportions. He yearns to complete himself in her but fears instead to lose himself in her.

He watches with hypertrophied alertness her slightest move, her merest gesture. Will she be receptive, will she rebuff him, will she strike out in anger? If he dares approach her, his movements are awkward and fumbling. He is eternally vigilant and with the first sign of danger is poised for an instantaneous leap to his own defense or for complete retreat. His urge is to show himself to her, but the moment danger looms, he flees for cover.

His exhibitionist urge turns into a dread of exposure, betrayal, injury. He reacts by going into hiding. He yearns to complete himself through union with the female; to be master of her is to triumph, but what if she masters him? The urge to complete himself through union with her becomes transformed through his insecurity and fright into a battle between the sexes, waged on a grand scale and in a domination-submission frame.

In this battle, he is constantly matching his image of himself against what he imagines the girl expects of him. The ambivalence in the relationship is extreme. To strengthen himself and make his position safer, he strikes up mutually protective alliances with other males. He seeks refuge in the precepts of his older brothers. The drama of the sexes is tense, thrilling, full of suspense, sometimes fierce, sometimes painful, but it always offers the anticipation of pleasure and fulfillment.

But if such is his inner experience, what is the affect of his outside world? Certainly, attitudes toward sex are changing, and although there are large disparities from one social group to another, the over-all picture is one of increased permissiveness.

Significant sexual contacts occur earlier than they did two generations back. Minor sex stimulations are sanctioned. Chastity is less valued. Sexual intercourse before marriage is on the increase. The adolescent enjoys more freedom, but does he know what to do with it? He wants his fun, but he seeks to measure the cost in the social consequences.

Parents, confused themselves, often shift erratically from moods of cheerful permissiveness to moods of irritable, dogmatic assertion of authority. The adolescent cannot know where he stands; he gets little from his parents in terms of protection and positive guidance. Knowing that he can have no increased freedom without a corresponding increase in responsibility, his anxiousness is intensified, his disillusionment in his parents that much greater.

In religious groups, in educational institutions, in the community at large, the situation with regard to sexual standards is not much better. The conflict of ideas, the confusion of values, places these representations of community life in a relatively weak position to offer helpful guidance.

The problems that beset his parents, problems of sexual identity, the role of man and woman, etc., do not make his own solution any easier to come by. He must deal with prolongation of adolescent dependence on "Mom," fear of "Mom's" bossy aggressiveness, distrust of father's strength, conflict in identifying with the father's maleness, and confusion over the struggle for dominance between male and female parent. He carries over into his relations with girl friends an image of feminine aggressiveness, fears being unmanned, protects himself from genuine intimacy with a girl, and seeks out protective alliances with boy friends.

Thus having erected a protective barrier against emotional closeness with a female, the adolescent is likely to find actual sexual experience, when it comes, a painful disillusionment. It is a physical release, unaccompanied by spontaneous tenderness or a conviction of togetherness; frequently, it brings afterward a feeling of repulsion and loneliness.

A psychic split emerges between the need for tender feelings and genuine closeness and the need for physical release of the sex urge. The mutual competitiveness and mistrust of the sexes make for a growing isolation between them; if anything, the experience of physical release intensifies the pain of loneliness. The need for dominance and the fear of being hurt prevents the capacity for genuine loving.

But in many instances and despite increased permissiveness, even physical release is not possible, as is clearly demonstrated in the phantasies of adolescents. In daydreams or in the so-called "wet dreams" of boys, sex contact is not usually carried to completion. Boys will frequently allege thoughts of intercourse, but close questioning usually reveals that the phantasy has stopped short of it.

Similar considerations hold for the waking and sleeping dreams of girls. In phantasy, girls preserve the protection of clothes or interpose some other symbolic barrier that effectively foils a completed sex act. Careful study of dream content will disclose signs of anxiety and symbols of prohibition of a fulfilled sex act.

Closely related to this phenomenon is another tendency, having much the same significance. Confused and contradictory concepts of sexual organs and functions may exist side by side in the mental life of adolescents. One set of concepts usually represents the unrealistic images of sex derived from childhood phantasy; the other set represents the more realistic, factual notions of sex obtained in later years. These two contradictory systems often carry on a parallel existence, occupying in some adolescents dissociated compartments of the mind. The infantile, distorted concepts of sex persist because they are protected from impact with reality. They continue to significantly influence the adolescent's behavior. In other adolescents, the contradictory concepts of sex clash openly, with the result that the adolescent is overtly confused.

The anxiety that is activated by an awareness of the mature aspects of sex impels the adolescent to cling to childhood notions that are less threatening to his defensive attitudes. Repression of sexual anxiety in adolescence is unstable, incomplete, and impels the mobilization of auxilliary defenses.

These trends hold obvious relevance for matters pertaining to sex education. Regrettably, sex education is not a simple procedure. One may readily wonder whether there really is such a thing as "sex education." In a deeper sense, true sex education begins at birth and is an inseparable part of the total education and rearing of the child. Many of the superficial forms of sex education fail utterly and, at times, do more harm than good because information and advice is given without relation to the specific nature of the individual adolescent's conflicts and defenses against sexual anxiety. For example, an adolescent may preserve the phantasy that his parents are too decent to indulge in the degrading experience of sexual relations or, if they have, it was only once or twice, for the purpose of having children. Or a girl who has received repeated instruction as to the nature of sexual intercourse and childbirth may continue to have the phantasy that if she gazes directly at a boy she can be impregnated through atmosphere. Or a boy whose mother deliberately exhibited herself to prove that the female genital differs from the male may nevertheless preserve the phantasy that a woman has a penis.

It is frequently observed that adolescents have a tendency to dissociate temporarily the emotional expressions of hostility and sex. Hostile feeling and sexual drives become temporarily dissociated in the adolescent's relationship to his parents. Often the full hostility is directed against the parents while the sexual needs are directed away from the parents and toward outside persons. Later this defensive trend is reversed. When the adolescent's conflicts have subsided, and the hostility is less, feelings of affection for the parents return.

The transformation of personal identity and the relation of this to parental and family identity is a critically important phenomenon in adolescence. Oedipal conflict of every shade is prominent in adolescence. The patterns of relationship to the parents which prevailed at the age of five or six years are reactivated. The emotional tendencies inherent in these relationships are affected now, however, by overt sexual pressures and the increased maturity of the adolescent. The oedipal configuration rarely shows itself in pure, unadulterated form. Instead, its manifestations are heavily tinged with the influence of pre-oedipal character traits. The partial components of the sexual drive are conditioned in their expression by the basic character structure.

Incestuous phantasies may appear in adolescence, often just below the surface of consciousness, sometimes fully conscious. They often involve both the parent and sibling of the opposite sex. The content of the phantasy often discloses the specific parts of the parent's body to which the adolescent has a special attachment—breasts, legs, buttocks, etc. This in turn illuminates the concrete content of the repressed sexual urges, all highly patterned by the basic character patterns. The degree of oral, dependent craving and the degree of sadistic possessiveness which characterize the adolescent's attitude toward the parent are clearly reflected in the specific content of sexual phantasies.

The striving for a stable sexual identity, sensitively influenced by the vicissitudes of oedipal conflict, frequently reflects some degree of confusion. The partial identification with each parent may result in some measure of bisexual identity, the boy having some feminine quality, the girl having some masculine quality. The so-called "inverted oedipal attachment" and unconscious homosexual leanings represent part of this same picture. Homosexual fear is much more common than is imagined and is usually indicative of some confusion and fragmentation of the development of personal identity. It is not generally a sign of sexual deviancy but rather a reflection of the adolescent's struggle to draw pieces of self-image into an integrated picture of the whole person. In this culture, during the process of maturation, some degree of injury to masculinity is common, and passive, dependent tendencies in the male are reinforced. In the development of female children, the necessity for shifting the love interest from mother to father and also the culturally conditioned competition between the sexes tend to encourage some degree of persistent dependence on mother figures and envy of men. Attachments to persons of the same sex are used as a protection against the dangers of heterosexual intimacy. Thus, there is the tenacious clinging of girls to mother or girl friend and the tendency of boys to form themselves into a mutually protective gang when they go seeking heterosexual adventures. The residual narcissism of adolescents also plays a significant role in the preservation of friendships with those of the same sex and those most like themselves.

For example, a sixteen-year-old girl, intelligent but confused, unstable, and disorganized, was preoccupied with sexual phantasies. Although a very attractive girl, she was unpopular with both sexes. Her social attitude was biting, spiteful, belligerently destructive. Consciously she was "boy crazy." Actually, she was in dire need of a girl friend whom she could really trust.

She was absorbed with phantasies of being raped. She liked the idea of exciting boys sexually but conceived of contacts with boys as a struggle for physical supremacy. She imagined wrestling or fist fights with boys; she seized all opportunities to humiliate members of the male sex. Beneath this aggression, she had an intense fear of being trapped in a dependent, submissive, childlike position in which she might be forced to confess defeat. Overtly she was cocky, proud, and boastful and attempted to deny her fears. Underlying all this was a profound disillusionment in not being wanted or loved as a girl and deep feelings of guilt and worthlessness. She was excessively dependent upon her mother, violently hated her father, but could not trust either parent. She concealed her fear of abandonment beneath her aggressiveness.

She pretended to like her dominant role, to enjoy to the fullest her tactics of revenge against males. Behind all this, lurked a helpless child, weak, dependent, lonely, wishing she could trust someone enough to curl up in his arms and go to sleep. She did not dare surrender her vigilance, however, because of her fears of being hurt or being exploited sexually.

We have here a strong tendency to social and sexual delinquency based on primary emotional deprivation and confusion of sexual identity.

The Adolescent and His Defenses

Defenses against anxiety in adolescence reflect the fluid, exposed quality of the whole being. The control of anxiety operates inefficiently. The typical adolescent defenses emerge in dramatic and extreme form; they are readily transparent; there are rapid shifts from one pattern of defense to another. The vicissitudes of defense are reflected in the patterning of group alliances.

Inevitably disillusioned in the standards of his parents and society, the adolescent searches for new and more satisfying standards. From among these diverse extrafamilial groups, he makes a choice. He does so in accordance with the vicissitudes of his changing concept of self and the outer world. To replace the shattered ideal of his parents, he seeks a new one.

The unusual features of modern society render the adolescent's problem of choice of an ideal more difficult. Adolescent groups in the present-day community frequently show a woeful lack of real substance. They are loosely organized, drift aimlessly from one activity to another. There is an atmosphere of goallessness and ensuing tension and a search for easy distractions. The temptation to relieve boredom with bursts of delinquency is strong. Neighborhood centers for youth are deficient in inspired leadership; the emotional climate of such places only too often is conspicuously colorless and void of appeal. By contrast, the atmosphere of the bowling alley or the neighborhood poolroom, balefully regarded as breeding places for adolescent crime, sometimes provides a better understanding of their emotional strivings. Such places could well be exploited as neighborhood clubs with community interests and a social code suited to adolescent needs. The natural formation of adolescent groups into so-called "cellar clubs," usefully exploited by well-trained leaders, might easily be a significant cultural force for good. There is great advantage in preserving spontaneous groupings of adolescents wherever one finds them. The possibilities for constructive guidance of adolescents utilizing these natural groups have hardly been touched.

The poverty of opportunity for gratifying self-expression in group life is responsible for another significant trend in adolescent behavior: namely, the adolescent's striving to create his own culture, to mold his social environment to his own liking. Adolescents create within their own group a small world of their own, with unique standards and values, carefully suited to their needs. Some features of contemporary community life accentuate this trend. The young people make a place for themselves insofar as the larger community fails them. To whatever extent they do not feel understood, they will withdraw and create their own separate subculture within the larger community. This trend is similar to the behavior of eccentrics, Utopians, artists, and writers who, feeling misunderstood and exiled from the larger community, tend to withdraw and create their special group. Here is the effort to lock off a smaller world within a larger one, to fence off an "island culture."

Such efforts are at best only partly or temporarily successful. In the end, interpenetration between the "island culture" and the parent culture inevitably occurs. The pressure toward "one world" is inevitable. The defensive walling-off of adolescents in their own group is a symptom of the failure of the parent culture to provide an adequate place for them at home and in the community.

Culture molds the adolescent, but the adolescent also molds the culture. The process is circular. The interaction of the adolescent with his environment shapes his drive for emancipation from authority, sexual success, and achievement in the intellectual, social, and economic spheres. Even under favorable circumstances, this struggle is characterized by conflict, confusion, and insecurity. From it finally emerges the more stable adult pattern of interpersonal relations. Some adolescents recoil from meeting the issues of life; others take a headlong plunge into them. Such a plunge, on occasion, means no more than a panicky "flight into reality."

Against this background and in a culture that places extreme stress on "success," the compensatory drives of contemporary adolescents can easily be understood—the urge to be big and powerful, to be "top dog," to obliterate all possible rivals, and to rely for such purposes on fantasies of omnipotence. Of special significance clinically are the narcissism, the vanity, and the exhibition-istic urges of these adolescents. The neurotic among them are often im-pelled by the misplaced assertion of these compensatory drives to acts of de-linquency.

One of the latter was an intelligent eighteen-year-old boy, reared in an

Orthodox Jewish home, who was on the brink of expulsion from college for two reasons: poor academic work and chronic lateness. Much of the time he appeared painfully bored, under constant strain, dirty, and degraded in his dress. He was confused and depressed, afflicted with obsessive rituals, and fearful of death.

He felt imprisoned by his rituals and the monotony of his daily obligations. He hated all routines; his resistance took the form of chronic lateness to all commitments in time: classes, appointments, the hour of retiring to bed, etc. His whole struggle in life was to push backward against the clock. His primary tendency was to be submissive, but he fought against this with morose defiance, insolence, and belligerent argumentation.

He found it impossible to go to sleep before 1 or 2 A.M. and in the morning could hardly be roused from sleep. Weekends he slept until 2 or 3 P.M. Sleeping was for him an experience of stupor—symbolic death. He had an obsessive anxiety about lying down and resisted going to bed.

For a time he did not dare to kiss a girl. He clung parasitically to boy friends but covered up by assuming a leader's role. In the company of his group, he engaged in delinquencies: truancy, stealing money, running away from home, etc.

At one extreme, he treated himself like dirt; he felt profoundly degraded and worthless. At the other extreme, he assumed an arrogant, grandiose, contemptuous air and was devastating in his criticism of others. He was guilty about his sexual interests in his mother and sister yet was bullishly aggressive to both. He tormented them. At the same time, he had thinly disguised homosexual anxieties.

This boy was the product of an overprotective, controlling, and seductive mother and an obstinate, domineering father. He hated asking his father for anything. In his early years he was an unusually good boy, submissive to mother, fearful of father. Later, he rebelled against his mother and found himself trapped in a violently ambivalent struggle for supremacy with his father.

He showed marked confusion in his sexual identity. His ambitions in life were confused by his negativism, his injured self-esteem, his self-degradation, and his compensatory grandiosity.

Other adolescents take refuge in extreme privacy. At no period in life do human beings feels so exposed and defenseless. The fluidity of the adolescent's self-image, his changing aims and aspirations, his sex drives, his unstable powers of repression, his struggle to readapt his childhood standards of right and wrong to the needs of maturity bring into sharp focus every conflict, past and present, that he has failed to solve. The protective coloring of the personality is stripped off, and the deeper emotional currents are laid bare.

This feeling of vulnerability nourishes the adolescent's belligerent defense of his privacy.

For example, a boy of fifteen, the only son of a scientist, was confused about sexual matters and had feelings of inferiority about his physique and some submerged anxiety about homosexuality. He had a soft feminine face. His manner was detached. He treated people with an air of aloofness and constraint.

His parents separated when he was seven years old. His mother then made adamant demands that he make his home with her. He bitterly rejected these demands and insisted on living with his father. But he allowed neither parent to intrude into any aspect of his personal life. He was Sphinx-like in his obstinate determination to shut out both of them. He exercised, literally, a twenty-four-hour vigilance over his privacy; his parents knew almost nothing of his personal feelings, interests, and activities.

At home with his father, his facial expression was a mask; he was reticent, maintained a strict isolation. When his father made an effort to show interest in his private affairs, he reacted with insolence. He visited his mother occasionally, when he could not avoid it, and maintained the same silent guard with her. Outside his family, his manner was distinctly less suspicious, more agreeable and friendly.

Adolescent defenses against guilt are numerous and varied. Quantitatively viewed, the guilt related to sex drives and the corresponding aggression is often intense. In this connection, one important point must be made: adolescents are not guilty about the sex act per se but only about the psychic representations of the act as being injurious to another person. In oedipal conflict, the guilt does not derive from the wish to possess the mother's love but rather from the uge to inflict injury on the rival for her love. In the effort to allay the guilt, a variety of defensive devices are brought into play.

One means for evading guilt is the mechanism of "externalizing" it. This is a device for displacing the responsibility of conscience to another person. In essence, "let so-and-so do the worrying for me." Still another device for dealing with guilt is the assumption of a defensively passive attitude in an effort to avoid responsibility for the initiative. "Let the other person do it first" is the means of shifting the burden of guilt.

Another defense, closely related, is the avoidance of completion of an act that will incite guilt. The act may be begun, and it may be carried to near-completion, but, by magical thinking, so long as the act falls short of actual completion there need be no guilt. This mechanism is conspicuously demonstrated in attitudes toward masturbation and sexual aggression. Masturbation and other sex acts, except genital intercourse, may be freely indulged, but guilt is avoided if the full act is aborted, if it falls a little short of completion. The concrete symbol of completion varies from one adolescent to the next. This trend of behavior is clearly exemplified in those cases in which actual orgasm must be avoided at all costs, both in masturbation and in sexual play. Or it may be demonstrated in cases of so-called mental masturbation, where pleasure is experienced at a phantasy level but is not permitted in reality. Such adolescents may indulge in the wildest kind of sexual phantasies and yet not permit themselves to touch the genital.

An inevitable corollary of this defensive behavior is, of course, the incompleteness of the pleasure experience. The measure of actual indulgence varies, but the sexual pleasure is never fulfilled. The feelings are numbed; boys may react with disappointment or disgust to masturbation and may suppress it altogether. In such instances, orgasm sometimes occurs without erection and even without pleasure. The girls may feel excitation close to orgasm, then experience a sudden and complete cessation of pleasurable feeling. In minor contacts, the girls may say that kissing gives them no feeling whatever.

A sixteen-year-old boy, the only child of two highly intelligent parents, was referred allegedly because he was "adolescing too rapidly." His parents were especially alarmed one time when he shot off his father's hunting rifle right in their home. They were also worried because he insisted on climbing across the ledge of the roof just for fun.

This boy was intellectually far advanced. He talked freely with his mother about his sexual preoccupations. In fact she relished it. He was extremely close to his mother. She took an obvious pleasure in reliving his adolescent sexual experiences with him, kidded him about his wish to exhibit his penis to her, etc. At the same time, she was an alarmist, exaggerating his illnesses, encouraging him to nurse himself carefully with each cold. This boy had no conscious worries about masturbation, indulged in it regularly, experienced intense pleasure in "mental masturbation," but felt completely numb if he attempted full manual masturbation. Although he had masturbated for years, he was completely unable to carry it to the point of ejaculation. This changed only after he received psychotherapy. Firing his father's gun at home was a symbolic substitute act, indicative of his frustrated wish to experience actual ejaculation.

When the quantity of guilt is large, there is a strong trend toward masochistic motivation. Sado-masochistic behavior is especially prominent in adolescence. The pleasure element may be mostly or entirely concealed, and in its place we see the experiencing of suffering, which reflects the need for self-punishment. Sometimes, the suffering clearly outweighs the pleasure; sometimes the pleasure is highly significant and is merely covered up by the more obvious suffering.

Depending on the degree of guilt and the basic character structure, every variety of self-punishment appears: castration phantasies of all sorts, impotence, sterility, incapacitating fatigue, pain associated with menstruation and masturbation, fears of illness and death. To counteract such anxieties, there are compensatory phantasies of magical omnipotence, immunity to hurt, and immortality.

A sixteen-year-old boy was referred from school after taunting a female teacher with obscene drawings and lewd suggestions of intimacy. On examination, this boy was found to be suffering from acute panicky fears of death, which came on suddenly at night and horrified him to the point that he felt he was losing his mind.

He was the only child of professional, middle-class parents, the father a teacher, the mother a social worker. As a child he suffered from nightmares. For years he carried on an active phantasy life in which he inflicted cruel sexual tortures on a loose type of woman or rescued a pure, ideal type of woman from attack by other men and then himself had sexual relations with her.

In these phantasies he was always the hero. In his usual, everyday behavior, he was well controlled, respectful of his parents, cooperative. In his mind, women fell sharply into two groups: those like his mother, with whom he might have a real friendship, but with whom sex was completely excluded; and, in contrast, the sexually promiscuous type of woman, on whom he might freely release his sexual urges but whom he regarded as a low, dirty creature who inevitably made him feel disgust with himself. He had an active social and athletic life but was basically very lonely.

During childhood his mother was frequently out of the home. She was immersed in social welfare activities. Her attitude toward the patient was well-meaning, but she had little real understanding of his needs. His father was naïve and felt it to be his moral duty to warn the boy vigorously against masturbation and the dangers of venereal infection. Both parents were over-zealous in their ambitions for this only child and extolled his virtues to the skies.

The Clinical Diagnosis of Adolescents

Adolescent conflict and instability may be precipitating factors for any form of psychiatric disorder. There are a few categories, however, that merit special attention. The one condition most clearly precipitated in adolescence is schizophrenia. The fragility of personality, the weakness of repression, the inefficiency of defenses, the closeness to basic drives tend strongly to push into an overt state any latent schizophrenic trends that exist. It is true that in some instances schizophrenia may become clinically manifest only in later years—in the third, fourth, and occasionally even the fifth decade—but when this occurs the individual's fate has already been decided by the exposure of vulnerable areas of personality during the adolescent phase.

Only occasionally is manic-depressive psychosis precipitated. Fairly commonly, psychoneurotic depression breaks out in adolescence. Of considerable dynamic relevance in this connection is the deflection back on the self of hostility intended for the parents. Self-depreciatory trends are inevitably related to the adolescent's hostile need to destroy the idealized image of his parents, by which he feels he has been betrayed.

The occurrence of the classical forms of psychoneuroses represent simply the reactivation of neurotic patterns already evidenced in earlier years but now highly colored by the dynamic events of adolescence. Regardless of the type of pathology that emerges in adolescence, the typical symptoms of each psychiatric entity are significantly affected by the total dynamic movement characteristic of adolescence. It is, therefore, an imperative necessity to discern the course and ultimate destination of such movement. Without such discernment, reliable diagnosis is not possible.

But differential diagnosis in the adolescent era presents great difficulties. It is highly complicated by the infinitely changing façades of personality that are characteristic of this period. When is adolescent behavior, with its inevitable accompaniment of anxiety, conflict, confusion, and multi-colored disturbances, "normal?" When is it "abnormal," and for what specific reasons?

During adolescence, anxiety, emotional confusion, erratic social behavior, shifting concepts of self and the outer world, weaknesses of reality perception, vacillating moral standards, instability and irregularity of impulse control, and fickle, ambivalent interpersonal relations may all be part of a "normal" transitional adaptation. Transitory mild disturbances of these types may not constitute clinical pathology. Clinical diagnosis can in no way be based on intrinsic adolescent phenomena. Often adolescent disturbance per se is mistakenly interpreted as representing clinical pathology. Or, conversely, actual psychiatric disorders are missed because they lie concealed behind the overlying facade of adolescent instability. How then to differentiate the abnormal?

Accurate differential diagnosis is possible only when the subtle interplay of basic pathology and adolescent dynamics is clearly discerned. Specific forms of psychopathological illness underlie and subtly interact with intrinsic adolescent phenomena. It is this dynamic interrelationship that must be disclosed by comprehensive examination. Correct appraisal of total personality functioning during adolescence requires close study in several dimensions: (1) current adaptation of adolescent personality; intrapersonal, familial, and in the wider community; (2) early conditioning of personality; (3) pattern of movement of personality up to the present time; (4) potential future course of personality, in a given life situation.

Accurate evaluation is possible only through a careful integration of knowledge of current personality functioning with knowledge of developmental influences, from which is derived an evaluation of the pattern of movement of personality through current experience into adult patterns of integration.

The intrinsic phenomena of adolescence must be thoroughly deeply understood in themselves and in their over-all effect on basic character so that behind this facade one can glimpse the underlying pathological trends. One needs always to bear in mind the manner in which a disposition to a specific psychiatric disability is affected by the intrinsic phenomena of adolescence. The task of diagnosis is complicated by the essential fluidity of adolescent personality which imparts relatively ambiguous outlines to all psychiatric entities. In the final analysis, the test of the relative accuracy of clinical diagnosis is the ability to predict successfully the course of future behavior.

All aspects of clinical study depend on comprehensive assessment of current adaptation, which must include careful appraisal of the role of family, surrounding culture, and the pattern of group integration. Without this exact picture of current behavior patterns, one cannot know clearly what one is trying to explain by way of the history of personality. The tendency to grope for developmental explanations before achieving a correct formulation of present behavior proves often to be a significant source of error in clinical judgment. If one makes this error, one surely cannot visualize the path of future behavior.

A useful guide to evaluation are the following questions:

1. What part of the behavior represents intrinsic adolescent change?
2. What part represents the reaction to current environmental stimuli?
3. What part, if any, is constitutional?

4. What part is the product of fixed intrapsychic patterns conditioned in early family life?
5. How do the intrinsic adolescent phenomena influence the basic personality trends?
6. How do the basic personality trends influence the adolescent phenomena?
7. What is the dynamic interplay of adaptation to contemporary familial roles and extrafamilial roles?
8. What is the probable future course of personality?

In drawing this picture of the adaptational processes of adolescent personality, we must give a special place to the significance of the adolescent's emotional integration into his family group. In expanding his relations with the wider world and preparing to fulfill his roles as a responsible adult in society, the adolescent has a unique need to preserve the security of his basic bond with family. Even as he asserts his increasing individuality in the ever-growing network of extrafamilial associations, the adolescent requires the support of a preserved link of personal and family identity. Disturbances of adaptation point irrevocably to conflicts experienced in the striving to reconcile the requirements of familial and extrafamilial roles. For the adolescent, the family is a protective envelope, a buffer between his raw skin and the venturesome, though unpredictable experiences of contact with the larger world. In the diagnosis and treatment of emotional disturbances in adolescence, a parallel approach to the individual adolescent and his family is strongly indicated.

CHAPTER 14

ADOLESCENT "PSYCHOPATHIC" CONDUCT AND FAMILY DISTURBANCE

WE MUST GIVE special attention to that elusive, hard-to-pin down syndrome identified as "psychopathic" conduct in adolescence. The rude shock of juvenile delinquency comes to us with every glaring news report of a new wave of stabbings, beatings, and killings. Such psychopathic conduct has become a crucial problem for mental health workers, as parents, community officials—indeed everyone—call out to us for help.

I believe that the unsolved problems in this one sphere of psychopathology raise implications for the entire system of clinical evaluation of deviant forms of behavior, not merely those we label "psychopathic." If we could fully plumb the depths of this particular psychiatric phenomenon, we would undoubtedly also shed light on other processes which reflect a component of shared psychopathology in individual, family, and community.

On the one hand, we are confronted by the global proportions of the challenge to deal with the antisocial, destructive tendencies of adolescents in a radically changing society. On the other hand, we face the specific psychiatric problem: what is a psychopathic personality? I do not believe psychopathic personality is a valid diagnostic entity. The evidence for a specific constitutional factor is slim. I hope to make out a convincing case for the hypothesis that psychopathy of this type is a social disease, that it is contagious and virulent. It seems that psychopathy is endemic to some component parts of our culture.

When the social climate favors it, it can become epidemic. It is a form of perversion of human relations away from love to purposes of destruction.

Immunity against contaminating invasion by this social disease differs from one person to the next. The "disease" is a dormant danger for all of us. Any one of us may be afflicted—some more, some less. It is in the atmosphere. The more vulnerable among us pick up the contamination first, and there is no age grouping more vulnerable than that of adolescence. Just as the infectious agents, bacteria and viruses, related to tuberculosis and rheumatic fever are everywhere about us but strike down only those with the weakest immunity, so too is the "psychopathic germ" ever present but mows down only those with the weakest defense.

Insofar as psychopathic conduct can become entrenched as a habitual pattern of interpersonal adaptation, it is most apt to occur during adolescent maturation. We once believed that adolescence was universally a phase of critical turmoil and instability preceding entry into adulthood, the same in all cultures. We can no longer assume an inevitable one-to-one association between the crisis in growth and the crisis in social adaptation. It behooves us, therefore, to recall everything we have said thus far about the effects of our particular culture not only on today's adolescents but on their families and communities, on the kinds of childhood they have known and the mothering and fathering they have received; inversely, also, the effects of the dominant patterns of adolescent behavior on family, community, and culture.

It is my belief that "psychopathic" conduct among adolescents, male and female, is understood only superficially if we do not join our evaluation of these troubled adolescents to the evidences of social psychological distortion in the family and community group structure. I have learned from personal experience that psychopathic conduct in adolescents cannot be treated effectively if we try exclusively to treat the adolescent as a separate individual. In common with my psychiatric colleagues, I have been taught that psychopathic personality is an untreatable condition. And so it is if one undertakes to treat a psychopathic adolescent in isolation from his family and community. I have also discovered, however, that I could successfully alleviate psychopathic behavior in adolescents when I was oriented to it as a family process, with the adolescent representing a symptom of the psychopathological warp of his family group.

Let us now critically review what is meant dynamically by the designation "psychopathic personality." I have expressed the conviction that this is not a valid diagnostic category. There is perhaps no other behavior disorder upon which has been pinned so many names: constitutional inferiority, moral insanity, moral imbecility, perverse personality, sociopath, etc. They are all ill-sounding names. They connote offense to the ideals of society. The one feature they hold in common is the suggestion of something evil, destructive, Machiavellian.

The symptoms of the disorder may be summed up in the following traits: impulsiveness, antisocial conduct, defective control and judgment, lack of foresight, shallow emotionality, egocentricity, magic omnipotent thinking, power striving, grandiosity, inability to empathize with others, a failure to respect the rights of others, a lack of genuine guilt, failure to learn from experience, and deviant sexual behavior. And in addition, words are said to be without their usual meaning for such persons, a condition that has somewhere been characterized as a "semantic dementia."

Even in their most benign sense, both the labels and the symptoms pointedly suggest a trend toward ethical deterioration. But can there be ethical deterioration without the threat of disintegration of the total structure of personality. As Harry Stack Sullivan once said, "For the life of me, I can't tell the difference between psychopathic personality and psychosis." The evaluation of the basic process by other experts varies: defective constitution, pathological immaturity, deformed maturation, diffusion of the instincts, adolescent group influence, and the effect of clashing culture patterns. Clearly, the clinical diagnosis is hazardous and subject to error. When the case cannot be proven for another diagnosis, psychopathic personality becomes the diagnosis by exclusion, a trash basket category. Kraepelin divided his classification into seven groups, Herman Adler suggested four groups, and Eugene Kahn described as many as sixteen. This by itself sharply underscores our present confusion concerning the definition of this psychiatric syndrome.

Basically, this form of behavior reflects an arrest in the processes of socialization, a deformation in the patterns of identification. The individual remains fixed at an infantile, egocentric, omnipotent, manipulative level of adaptation to his human environment. He is the master mind who redesigns his world to suit himself. He does not experience persons as persons but rather as things. People are to him not human beings but objects, agents, and tools. In social relations he perpetually asserts the "I," never the "me." Consciously he denies that he is ever the object of other persons. Because he does not admit the "me," there can be only one "I" in the world: himself. Yet, without being aware of it, he may be used as a tool by other persons. I raise here a crucial question: Is it not probable that the ethical distortion which is internalized in the psychopathic person echoes a corresponding distortion in the ethos of family and community?

Such behavior is observed clinically in all degrees of intensity. Some such conditions are mild, others malignant. In whatever degree, the characteristic trends are found in a variety of personality types: behavior disorder, character deviation, neurosis, sexual perversion, paranoid personality, and psychosis. In the latter condition, psychopathic conduct is often observed both before and after the acute phase of psychosis. With striking frequency in the phase of remission or partial social recovery, a schizophrenic will show exactly this form of behavior, as will also manic-depressives. Furthermore, psychopathic conduct is to be seen in persons subjected to an abrupt shift of physical and cultural environment for which they are in no way prepared: for example, soldiers suddenly plunged into combat, or persons torn away from the lifelong bonds of family and locked in concentration camps.

Some experts argue strongly for the unique features of this condition, attempting to cut beneath its superficial manifestations to a characteristic underlying psychological mechanism. But this is more easily said than done. The specific behavior mechanisms may be viewed as a component trend, more conspicuous in some persons, less so in others. In some individuals, the psychopathic distortion is the core of their mode of adaptation; it persists throughout their entire lives. In others, however, the same traits rise to a dominant position only in intermittent episodes of acute disturbance; otherwise, their behavior trends fall mainly into one of the other diagnostic categories. There is real doubt as I see it that psychopathy represents a distinctive personality type or a distinct form of illness.

It seems more logical to conceptualize this behavior form as a component reaction, which under some conditions occupies the center of the individual's character and under other conditions appears only at the periphery. According to these variations, the reaction may be relatively reversible or irreversible. The phenomenon is in some ways analogous to the paranoid defect. Paranoid reactions also occur in all degrees of intensity, are reversible or irreversible, benign or malignant, and appear in a variety of personality types, including the so-called "normal person." In fact, from the point of view of genetic development, psychopathic and paranoid trends are close relatives and often coexist in the same person.

It may be assumed that psychopathic behavior, whether at the core of character or at the periphery, is correlated to a corresponding configuration of group integration. I mean by this that the traits that represent the social identity of the psychopathic person are correlated to a group structure with an analogous identity configuration. The psychopathic response at the core of character must be related to a family structure, or a component of family structure that has a central orientation to destructive power motives in human relations; and, in turn, the psychopathic response at the periphery of character must be related to a family structure in which the orientation to destructive power motives in human relations is more superficial. Also, it is likely that the psychopathic response at the core of the character is related to an earlier and deeper group conditioning in the family of childhood, whereas psychopathic response at the periphery of character is likely to be related to group integration at a later and more superficial phase of development.

For a full understanding of this phenomenon, it is essential to examine it in both longitudinal and cross-sectional terms, that is, in the dimension of both time and space. The longitudinal dimension defines the degree of vulnerability or immunity to this condition. The cross-sectional dimension determines its overt expression. In the longitudinal dimension, it is possible to trace the levels of maturation at which the pathogenic elements of the family environment were incorporated into the personality. Once these pathogenic features have been internalized, they may at any later time be reprojected according to the perceptive stimuli inherent in later patterns of group experience.

In discussions of this phenomenon, psychopathic conduct has been interpreted in innumerable ways. Each interpreter has a vested interest of his own, largely dependent on his own needs and position. If he is a parent, he may be protecting the prestige of his family. If he is a policeman, he may be guarding the sanctity of the law. If he is a local official, he may represent the chauvinistic sentiments of his community. If he is a psychiatrist, he may be jealously upholding the status and cryptic wisdom of his profession.

Even among professionals who are attempting to discuss the problem objectively, some emphasize the intrapsychic expressions, others stress its social manifestations. But the intrapsychic and interpersonal aspects are not mutually exclusive. They are simply different ways of looking at the same reaction.

The tendency to emphasize exclusively either the intrapsychic or the social manifestations gives rise to a varying confusion as to what causative factors are inside the mind and what factors are outside, that is, in the environment. For example, there is the difficulty inherent in the loose use of the terms "psychopathic and "delinquent." Most people agree that anyone who goes persistently against the law must somehow me "touched in the head," must have a "screw loose" somewhere.

On the other hand, it has been repeatedly argued that a sharp distinction should be drawn between psychopathy and delinquency. Delinquency is a social diagnosis. It describes merely the action of a person who comes afoul of the law. It is clinically nonspecific. It is also a form of conduct which occurs in a variety of personality types. By contrast, psychopathy is interpreted as a specific endopsychic disorder of personality. Psychopaths often do clash with the law, but they may not. "Psychopathy" stresses what is inside the mind; "delinquency" stresses what is outside. The one view emphasizes predisposition or vulnerability, the other overt action. One focuses on the individual, the other on the group aspects of the phenomenon.

A kind of semantic confusion perplexes the parents of psychopathically acting adolescents. They are often unsure as to how far to hold their own child personally to blame and how far to place the responsibility on bad companions. Parents are prone privately to blame their child, publicly to place blame on unfortunate group associations. To keep the approval of family friends, they say it was just bad luck; their son joined bad companions. The clinician, however, asserts the opposite: it is not the bad companions that cause the psychopathy; rather the psychopathy invites the bad companions. But is this an either-or proposition? Is it not often the confluence of a certain pattern of vulnerability and the effect of a particular disturbance of group integration? As I have said earlier, "acting out" requires a partner. Certainly, the root of the disorder is a failure of healthy social integration, and the condition expresses itself as a warp in the ethical behavior of the person. It is an incapacity to feel human and to respect the humanness of other persons. This ability either is never developed or is somewhere impaired enroute. It is a distortion fundamentally tied to the dynamic interrelations of individual and group, beginning at an early age and continuing into the present.

Two terms which have been applied to this condition seem most apt: "perverse personality" and "sociopath." The term "perverse personality," suggested by Karl Menninger, perhaps comes close to identifying the essence of this condition. It is perverse in the sense of being not merely antiauthority but antihuman. Human relationships are perverted away from the purpose of love to the purpose of hate and destruction. Psychopaths are the true human perverts. They may engage in deviant sexual behavior or they may not. But, as I see it, a perverted person cannot be defined exclusively in terms of a sexual pattern nor in terms of a single sex act. The determining factor is not what is done, but how it is done. When a human relationship is shunted away from love toward a dedication to power for its own sake and cruelty and destruction of the partner, this is perversion. And there can be no perversion except as it expresses the entire fabric of the individual and his values. The value problem provides the appropriate bridge to Partridge's term "sociopath" which implies the internalization of specific distortions in social relations.

Basically the issue is one of dominant orientation to life and human relations. It is an issue of values; a potential development toward love and creativity in human relations moves full circle to power, cruelty, and destruction for its own sake. The end result is the experiencing of human beings as things rather than as people. This, in my opinion, is the heart and core of the psychopathic orientation.

The relevance of these dynamic considerations for the special problems of the adolescent in contemporary society must now be self-evident. We have earlier mentioned the unique vulnerability of personality in this age group; the tender quality of adolescent identity, the fragility of the borders of the adolescent self and with this, the extraordinary sensitivity to group pressures arising both within the family and in the wider community. The adolescent is readily torn by the conflicting requirements of his familial and extra-familial roles. This makes of him a ready victim of the special form of social contagion which we characterize here as the "psychopathic germ."

Clinical Illustration

The patient Jim is a young male, nineteen years old, over whose conduct both parents had lost control. At the time of the first interview with this young man's mother, neither parent knew where he was or what he was doing. Both parents were alarmed and yet helpless. It was later learned that Jim was in another state, indulging in his habitual irresponsible ways, while living financially on his parents' bounty.

Over a period of several years the boy's behavior had been an uninterrupted nightmare for his parents. He flunked out of college. He ran up bills on his parents' charge accounts or used their names to get merchandise from stores at which they had no accounts. He took family cars without permission and drove them without a license and without legal registration papers. He lied freely to cover his tracks; he manipulated parents and grandparents and wheedled from them a constant flow of money. Despite this and because of his extravagance, he was constantly in debt. He managed, however, to jockey his position cleverly, borrowing from Peter to pay Paul. While placating one end of the family, he was terrorizing and blackmailing the other. He was a past master at knocking his parents heads together in order to get his way. He pitted one parent against another, parents against grandparents, friends against friends, etc. He was adroit in playing both ends against the middle. At the very moment of infuriating one of his parents, he was seducing the other to feel sorry for him. His manipulative genius operated in high gear. He moved unpredictably from one group to another depending on personal convenience. He played the game of being in love with love and tripped from one romance to another. With each girl in turn he aggrandized himself, exploiting to the hilt the social status of his family. He nourished in these girls a precious deference toward his superiority and importance. Then, as soon as he got what he wanted, he was on his way.

He did not pursue this path in life with impunity, however. Periodically he took a dive into states of panic. He had episodes of depression and withdrawal. At such times he would sleep for sixteen hours at a stretch. Bouts of depression were frequently followed by outbursts of hectic impulsive action, such as driving across the country in five days, alone and without sleep. But these episodes were intermittent and short-lived. For the most part he was devilishly effective in turning his destructive, manipulative motivations against his environment.

In relating this tragic story, the mother was concerned first of all about how to get Jim to the psychiatrist. She was confident that she could do so if she took recourse to her usual tactic of bribery. But she vacillated. She feared that he would demand a huge bribe and that as soon as there was no further material profit forthcoming, he would quit. The mother feared also that his father and grandparents might intervene and foil her plan for psychiatric therapy.

I shall not dwell on the early history except to highlight the more important features. Through the years, Jim's relations with both of his parents were characterized by the prime motivation to make a deal. His contact with them consisted mostly of high-level negotiations, and he did business with them only in terms of what he could extract from them. He maneuvered one parent at a time. He and the parent alternated with one another in laying down ultimatums. Each yielded momentarily, offered a minor concession, and then promptly turned about to usurp once more the dominant, threatening position. Such was the characteristic diplomacy that prevailed in the relations of mother and son and father and son. Sooner or later, a compromise was struck, a temporary bargain was reached, but no issue was ever settled.

The behavior of the parents served as a prime example for the pattern of Jim's power-oriented, competitive, exploitive strategy. Between themselves, they characteristically engaged in high level diplomacy. They dealt with one another in much the same way that they dealt with their son. They maneuvered shrewdly, each striving to outsmart the other so as to get the best of the bargain.

The parents were divorced. The father had remarried and he now had a young wife, with whom he had three small children. Jim had one full sibling, a sister three years younger than himself. She was an angel child, well-behaved, ingratiating, very much the conformist. Recently, however, she showed signs of a beginning "crack up." Her concentration in school failed; she became depressed and entered psychiatric therapy.

Jim's family was socially prominent. The parents were highly endowed persons. Each of them in their own fashion had achieved conventional success as an artist. Each of them drove hard to prove their worth. Each felt the pressure to live up to the high expectations of the older generation. In their surface behavior, the parents were clever, skillful conformists. Underneath, however, they were hostile, manipulative, destructive persons. Despite the touch of glamour in their lives they were neither satisfied nor happy. Secretly each of them suffered a layer of self-contempt because of the inner conviction of ethical corruption and a wasted life. They had sold themselves down the river for the trappings of conventional social success, and, in so doing, they had betrayed a deeper ideal of genuine creativity. Privately they blamed this on their parents, and on their compulsive obedience to family standards. Despite their secret shame over their failure to be true artists, they continued nonetheless to stand in awe of the older generation. Perhaps for this reason, they harbored a secret admiration for their delinquent son, who rebelled in a way which they never dared.

The divorce of the parents was the culmination of a long history of friction, competitiveness, mutual recrimination, and failure of sexual satisfaction. Especially important were the complications created by each parent's pursuit of an independent career. There was mutual blame and undermining of one another's position. This pattern of reciprocal sabotage did not cease with divorce. After the breakup, the competitive clash, the mutual accusations and Trojan horse tactics continued unabated, particularly in their handling of their children.

The conflict between the parents had a long history that began with the grandparents. The older generation kept the young parents strictly in tow. Each of the parents continued in a dependent position despite a secret sense of humiliation. Their marriage was partly an arranged one. It was an expression of the orientation of the families on both sides to smart manipulation on the social scene. But the rivalry, jealousy, manipulation, and hypocrisy that characterized the behavior of all sections of the family is beyond the power of words to communicate.

Jim and his sister were raised by governesses. They were seen for limited periods during the day by their parents, and there were prearranged times of visitation with the grandparents. The grandparents were critical, at times contemptuous, of the parents' management of these children. They expressed this contempt through unrealistic, excessive indulgence of the children in material gifts, money, special privileges, etc. The attitudes of the grandparents on both sides undermined critically the authority of the parents. This was impaired in two ways: by the persistent pattern of conflict and alienation in the parental relationship, and by the tendency of the grandparents to usurp the parents' position with the children. In some measure, the grandparents' tactics of buying the allegiance of the grandchildren alienated the children from their parents.

Both parents feared that their psychopathic son would heap disgrace on the family and irrevocably ruin their status in the community. Jim fully exploited his parents' fears; by sly innuendo he terrorized them with threats of publicly smearing the whole family.

When the mother first presented this story, the outlook was discouraging. There seemed to be no point of entry. The psychiatrist discussed with her the possibility that Jim might become accessible for therapy at some future time if he were plunged into a deep depression or should actually crack up in a full blown psychosis. Therapy might then be initiated by having him under lock and key in a sanitarium. Of course, the patient's mother would have no part in hospitalizing the boy. This would be too great a shock and an insufferable blow to the family pride.

The mother mobilized her resources, however, and maneuvered the boy to the psychiatrist by the usual means of bribery. She was determined to use this strategy as "the least of all evils." With the mother's deliberate connivance Jim extorted from her a promise of his own apartment and a generous monthly allowance. At the same time the mother neutralized possible interference from his father and grandparents by slyly encouraging the boy to provoke their fury against him, to the point where they were about ready to wash their hands of the whole matter. In this way, for the time being, she seized exclusive control.

This is the background in which the patient first arrived at the psychiatrist's office. His behavior in the first interview was as expected. He was detached, impersonal, ritually courteous and at the same time armed to the teeth. His mood was one of negotiating a deal. He used the psychiatrist as a convenient instrument for arranging a profitable family bribe. The psychiatrist accepted the pattern of relations between the boy and mother exactly where it stood at the moment.

The boy's attitude was crystal clear. He was a sharp dealer. He would play the game if it paid him to do so. He was chary, guarded, suspicious, watchful of every move for signs of possible treachery. He was instantly ready to renege on the entire deal with the slightest show of failure on the mother's part to fulfill her end of the bargain. Boy and mother behaved similarly. Each of them attempted to jockey the psychiatrist in exactly the way they had maneuvered relationships within their own family. Such was the emotional climate that prevailed at the beginning of this boy's treatment.

With a careful survey of the relations of this boy with his family, it seemed clear that psychotherapy was foredoomed unless it were first possible to restore a positive affectional bond between him and his parents. The immediate challenge was not intensive individual psychotherapy for the boy but rather a form of family therapy. Effective therapeutic intervention on the family scene constituted an indispensable preparation of the emotional attitudes of this patient for psychotherapy. The roots of a healthy link between Jim's personal identity and the identity of his parents had been torn up. Unless this link could be restored, there could be no hope for his treatment. Somehow, a minimum of mutual respect and sincerity had to be re-established in his relations with parents; otherwise, individual therapy would be just a futile gesture. Access to the family conflict and the associated value distortion were sine qua non to access to the boy's internalized conflict. The psychiatrist therefore focused initially on this effort to bring some emotional health back into the family relationships. Fortunately, beneath all the distortion, there were rudiments of an old sentimental love attachment between mother and son. Over a period of time, the psychiatrist was able to reach these roots and nourish them to good advantage.

It proved necessary at all stages of Jim's treatment to carry on concurrently an appropriate level of family treatment. This involved a complicated series of therapeutic contacts with the relevant family pairs, son and mother, son and father, and separate dealings with each parent. Through this level of family therapy, the interpersonal levels of conflict were kept under control, not always, but at least part of the time. Whenever the psychiatrist felt he had lost effective control of destructive forms of family conflict he interrupted systematic individual therapy to concentrate on the family level of treatment. Each time a crisis of family conflict developed it was instantly discernible as a threat to the continuity of Jim's treatment. As soon as this threat was brought under control and a workable measure of emotional complementarity had been restored to the significant family pairs, it proved possible once more to resume the task of individual therapy for the internalized conflicts of the boy. It must already be clear, then, that there was no smooth sailing. Time and time again, there were interruptions for short periods, induced by family crises. Maintenance of the continuity of therapy was possible only by means of effective neutralization of family conflict.

The psychiatrist began work with the relationship of son and mother exactly where it stood initially. It was war, nothing short. His first task was to make rules for the war. He asserted strongly the conditions under which he would intervene. If either party failed these conditions, he would promptly withdraw.

But both son and mother basically wanted to achieve at least a truce. This level of mutuality of motivation played into the psychiatrist's hands. It was his task to influence the negotiations so as to impel both parties to make a square deal instead of a crooked one. This took hard work, but in the end it was rewarding. He made clear, too, that he would not be a party to manipulation, trickery or deception on either side. He informed both son and mother that each would know of the other's contacts with the psychiatrist, in person or by telephone. The psychiatrist had to integrate several roles: he had to be an arbitrator in a bitter family battle; he had to induce the contestants to abide faithfully by an ethical set of rules of battle; he had to function as therapist for family conflict and protect the family from a debacle; and, finally, he had to function as therapist for the boy as an individual. A crooked war had to be transformed into an honest one. He had to parlay the mother's efforts to use money as a club over the boy's head and do likewise in counteracting the boy's tactics of blackmail. He had to energize in both parties the dormant incentive for a restoration of a love union between them.

It was strenuous work. There were repeated episodes in which son and mother tested the psychiatrist's mettle. What stood him in good stead was the sure conviction that no other approach would have the remotest chance. After long and arduous effort, son and mother, each basically wanting union, became convinced that the psychiatrist meant exactly what he said; he would instantly withdraw if they did not keep fairly to the rules. Later similar therapeutic tactics were employed in dealing with the son's relations with father and the relations between the parents.

The family conferences continued because it was in the interest of both boy and mother to carry through. Neither wanted really to sever relations. Beneath all the fighting there was an essential bond, which neither wished to admit because it seemed to signify giving in, complete surrender of defenses, and loss of personal power for either person to confess a need of the other's affections.

As contact with this family continued, there were therapeutic conferences with the boy and mother, individual regular sessions with the boy, intermittent sessions with the mother alone, and at a later stage treatment sessions with the boy and father together. Inevitably there were periodic crises from time to time, induced by the pressure of destructive motivation. Similar complications were faced later when the father made an effort to interfere. Each of these crises was met in the same way by group sessions with the family pairs locked in conflict. Much time was spent with the mother alone as well as with the boy. In this family, it was not possible to deal with both parents together; circumstances precluded this approach.

The treatment of Jim and his family took several years. Over the long view, however, there was clear progress. The high-level manipulations radically lessened. There was much more frankness and open expression of family sentiment, more mutual acceptance and trust. Jim proved to be increasingly responsible in his work life and in his dealings with money and women. Mother and son developed a warm friendship which was sustained.

Thus, in the case of Jim and his family, we see how psychopathic tendencies in adolescents reflect a component of psychopathic behavior in the family structure. Psychopathic behavior cannot be treated as an isolated phenomenon, expressing only the inner psychic life of one member of the family. It is a projection of distorted relations of the personal identity of the adolescent and the group identity of his family and, at the same time, a warp of values toward a perverse pattern of human relations. For these reasons, the individual and family must be the unit of clinical evaluation and treatment, not the individual alone.

PSYCHOSOMATIC ILLNESS AND FAMILY DISTURBANCE

THE ROLE OF FAMILY in psychosomatic illness poses some special difficulties. Some students of the problem emphasize the concept of family diathesis, a specific familial constitutional vulnerability toward breakdown of the functioning of particular organ systems. Others emphasize the role of emotional tension in interpersonal relationships, especially within the family group. The significance of the emotional factor in such conditions as hypertension, ulcer, colitis, asthma, and skin disorder is widely recognized. In the psychodynamic study of such conditions attention has been paid mainly to disturbances of balanced functioning of the internal forces of personality. The intrapsychic components of conflict have received the first emphasis; the external aspect of conflict between the individual and his surrounding group environment, while the subject of considerable speculation, has nonetheless only rarely been the subject of systematic investigation. Clinical studies of the problem generally focus on the manifestations of illness within the individual but omit systematic consideration of environmental forces. On the other hand, sociological and cross cultural approaches to psychosomatic disorders generally exclude or at least minimize the factor of individual personality.

The study of psychosomatic illness taking family relationships and conflict between person and environment as the main point of reference constitutes a significant emphasis for future research.

Psychosomatic illness needs to be examined from four points of view: (1)

the constitutional factor, if any; (2) the special factor influencing organ choice; that is, the problem of organ specificity; (3) the factor of vulnerability toward psychosomatic breakdown which is established in the family of childhood; (4) the influence of the individual's adaptation to familial and extrafamilial roles in adolescence and adulthood; (5) pathogenic factors in the interpersonal patterns of the group, family, community, and culture.

The clinical investigation of these conditions introduces some critical problems: the sharp differences in accuracy as between physiological and psychological measurement; the inadequacy of present-day knowledge concerning the relevant neural and hormonal patterns, especially the mechanism by which tension is shunted from the striped muscle system into the pathways of the autonomic nervous system and the internal organs; the special difficulties of carrying out physiological measurements on patients undergoing psychotherapy; the problem of studying the families of patients suffering psychosomatic illness; finally, the differences in psychosomatic response between the child and the adult.

While much remains unknown, there is some suggestive evidence that psychosomatic dysfunction has some dynamic features in common with traumatic disorders of personality. The outbreak of psychosomatic symptoms reflects damage to the integrative capacities of personality, manifested in diminished mastery of the environment and weakened control of basic emotional drives. The psychological disturbances associated with psychosomatic dysfunction seem in fact to represent a regressed, ineffectual effort to compensate for this failure of control. The homeostatic potential of the individual organism is variably disabled. The organism is faced with an excessive barrage of stimuli both from without and from within, with which it cannot adequately cope. The psychic aspect of the psychosomatic response suggests a miscarried effort to re-establish control of the overflow of emotion and to restore mastery of the dangers in the external environment at an infantile level of omnipotence. It is the external component of conflict, that is, the conflict focused in the zone between organism and environment which seems to bear the prior relation to the psychosomatic response, rather than the internal component of conflict. Naturally, this extrapsychic aspect of conflict, unresolved, feeds back into the personality and aggravates the older patterns of internal conflict. Thus, the psychosomatic reaction is conceived as an ineffectual and regressed substitute device for the discharge of impulse into overt action; its implied purpose is to restore control over an environmental threat by re-establishing magic mastery.

As indicated, there is thus far available only a small body of documented knowledge regarding the possible correlation of psychosomatic illness and family dynamics. What does exist in this field is mostly in the realm of conjecture.* The following clinical discussions illustrate some of these problems.

Hypertension and Family

The elevation of blood pressure in this patient was first observed when he was nineteen years old. He was nervous, perspired easily, had palpitations and cold feet. He looked paradoxically young and old at the same time. He had a keen, articulate intelligence but was suspicious and alternately ingratiating and sarcastic. He showed a tendency to depression and despair.

This patient pictures himself as follows:

Because I simulated illness in childhood, I ask myself if I'm simulating it now. I blamed myself for it. When I look at the experiences of my life as the cause of these symptoms, I'm afraid I'll fall to pieces. I have had too many shocks and crises in my life. I always expect the worst, and when the worst comes I am never prepared to cope with it. Now I feel like a shell only, like an empty hull without a motor; the machinery just isn't there. I never felt able to take care of myself, yet I never wanted to be dependent on anyone. I was always afraid to be refused. I felt guilty; it might hurt the other person. I wanted someone to wave a magic wand and give me what I wanted. A minimum of trouble and a maximum of help is what I needed. Yet, I realized I couldn't live on borrowed resources. I know I could have made a successful son of a rich man. I never wanted to admit frustration or weakness to myself, otherwise I would be in despair. I was afraid my feelings would overwhelm me. When I raged inwardly, I sensed great danger. I immediately had the phantasy of being beaten. I was afraid I'd go insane.

When I was out of a job I felt crushed, useless, submissive like a jellyfish. I had no backbone. I never wanted to see myself as I really was because if I did, I couldn't stand it. I might want to commit suicide. As I know myself, there's a lot I don't like. I'm afraid not of what I know, but what I might find out. All my life I have avoided a reckoning with myself.

I always felt oppressed, humiliated like a slave. I wanted to be

---

* In the chapter on Social Role and Personality some partial hypotheses were suggested as to the dynamic connections between psychosomatic illness and specific failures in role adaptation, both within the family and outside. These hypotheses and other ideas of a similar nature need to be substantiated through definitive studies.

free. I didn't like to be ridden as a horse is by a master. Yet I was like a little dog running around licking the master's boots. I wanted to make money so that I could be free. I didn't like to work for its own sake. To work just for a living is to half starve—to starve spiritually.

My main goal in life was not to seek pleasure but to avoid pain. I felt exposed, vulnerable. I was afraid to fight. I might get killed. Sometimes nothing hurt me, yet I moaned and whimpered. I feared a major disaster but I had a terrific urge to stave it off a little longer. If I fought openly, I'd be killed immediately. But if I fight unconsciously I kill myself slowly. I stew in my own protesting juice. I'm not afraid of every fight, only those fights that threaten my existence, but my existence seems to be threatened by every fight. I have a profound sense of defeat; I feel like a walking corpse with the major part of me sitting, stalling and refusing to move.

In some ways I feel too young, in other ways I feel too old—old in the sense of having failed to achieve anything. My future is bleak. It makes me feel limp and exhausted. Where I am now I have to raise myself by my own bootstraps. I don't know if I have any bootstraps.

This patient was the youngest of four children and the only boy. His mother died of cancer when he was seventeen years of age. His father died when he was thirty. The second eldest sister died of tuberculosis. The two surviving sisters, married, lived in another state.

"By the time I came along my mother was already used up by too many children. I felt impoverished so far as mother's love was concerned. Mother was an aloof, shadowy presence, over-burdened with neurotic worries about illness." He was the "baby" of the family and was cared for mainly by his sisters.

Up to the age of six years he was his father's favorite. He showed no active rebellion against his sister's domination but was often stubborn. He had a terror of asserting himself with other boys and men. At six years of age he remembered lying in bed holding his father's erect penis. He felt it was wrong but liked it. He feared being attacked by a strange man coming in through the window.

He felt like a little girl among men, rather than like a boy. At about this same age, five or six, a Gentile boy attacked him for being a Jew. His parents told him it was better for a Jew not to fight back. Sometimes a Jew could get more by humbling himself than by fighting. He felt himself to be an object of contempt. He remembered a compulsion to spit whenever he saw another man spit.

When he saw his mother and father in bed together, he felt a violent antagonism toward his father. He imagined his father was inflicting pain on his mother. Yet he also felt his mother was enjoying it.

The sixth year of his life marked a significant turning point. Between the ages of six and ten, he lived through the World War and, since the family dwelt on the Russian-Austrian-Polish border, they suffered seriously from the ravages of the war. Privation was severe and more than once they were on the brink of starvation. Frequently, his family was forced to evacuate their home in the face of advancing armies. When he was seven years of age, his father was conscripted into the Army, and was absent from home for four years. His mother continued to be ill and the home was governed by his sisters.

He was deeply affected by this separation from his father, and yearned for his return. He wrote a secret diary of grievances against his sisters, which he saved against the time when his father would be home from the war. He regarded his sisters as his enemies. They fed and cared for him—in fact they made a baby of him—yet he felt a bitter hatred because they humiliated him. He was especially jealous of one sister because she was competent and resourceful—"she was everything I wanted to be."

To him to be poverty-stricken, without food, without clothes, to be Jewish, was a profound humiliation. The patient's feeling of degradation, his feminine identification and his longing for a rich father who could provide abundantly for him were closely associated. "If there must be two classes, why should I be in the lower class? If one is born a cobbler's son, one can't hope to be a favored rabbi's son. If one is born a Jew, one can't hope to become a Christian."

Between the ages of eight and ten years, influenced by his ailing mother, he feigned illness "because a sick person gets the best crumbs."

During the war years, he played up to soldiers in the hope of getting some favor. "I flirted with them." At about the age of ten he began the habit of masturbation. At first he masturbated to keep warm when there was no heat in the house. He masturbated only to the extent of producing erection, never to the point of ejaculation. Only in his sleep, did he ejaculate. Often he lulled himself to sleep with his hand on his penis while having phantasies of love.

At the age of eleven years, his father returned from the Army. To the patient he seemed to be a totally different person. He was ill with malaria and unable to find employment. His whole attitude seemed changed, especially toward the patient. He was less affectionate and more critical. The patient felt bereft of his last friend and protector. He felt a deep despair. He believed he must now be on his guard with everyone.

He threw a knife at one of his sisters when he was eleven. At twelve years of age, he became enraged at a cousin and attacked him with the intent to kill. This transitory outbreak of near-criminal aggression was associated with the loss of his father's love and the feeling of abandonment.

From that time on he was caught between several conflicting tendencies: a fierce drive for individual success, for wealth and power; a tendency to avoid exertion, "to take it easy" and to indulge himself; and a tendency to be a revolutionary. These three apparently conflicting tendencies represent unconsciously: (1) a compensatory aggressive drive for power and success; (2) a desire for passive parasitic existence; (3) the unrestrained expression of his criminal hostilities. The patient could not successfully pursue any one of these goals.

At thirteen the patient came to the United States with his family. He experienced acute disillusionment. For two years he was one of five people in two families, living in one small room in the slums. This was a new blow to his pride. "Coming to America was no improvement except that there was more to eat."

Physically, he felt inferior to other boys but he felt this was compensated for by his intellectual superiority, his ambitious drive, and his administrative talent. He found, however, that this feverish activity was too much for him. It exhausted him. He had glowing phantasies of being a great engineer, going to West Point and becoming an Army Officer, being a Rockefeller or the President of the United States. In high school he became a "big shot." "I must have looked like John D. Rockefeller to my classmates. Someone said I was the kind of foreigner who allowed nothing to stand in the way of his success."

Beginning at eighteen, he had disturbing phantasies about men. He felt a magnetic attraction to them. Whenever he found himself in a men's lavatory and saw other men's penises, he felt he didn't belong there. The phantasy of a man's penis in his mouth gave him a bad taste. He said to himself, "Hell, you're not a girl, why are you so prudish? I wanted to shave the man down to my size." He associated these phantasies with "getting the dirty end of things."

During this period he developed a "terrific craving for the movies. Moving pictures were opium for me." There he could forget himself completely. He entertained pleasurable erotic phantasies, moreover, about the beautiful actresses on the screen.

At sixteen years he began to be troubled with headaches and thereafter became progressively ill with a variety of hypertensive symptoms. The immediate emotional background was a struggle with his family over the question of his going to work, and becoming a breadwinner, instead of remaining a "burden" to his sisters. At eighteen years, a medical examination revealed elevated blood pressure. His physical distress included headache, pains in his legs, knees, mostly on the left, chilly sensations, trembling, and exhaustion. He felt his knees were wobbling and buckling under him. To him this signified he had a "weak left side. I was almost paralyzed with fear. I always had a fear of disaster, but now it seemed right on top of me."

Sometime later a married woman whom he loved romantically at a distance committed suicide. He felt as if he had died with her. "Losing what I had was less painful than losing what I wanted. After she died I became very old. It's like the Unfinished Symphony—more beautiful because it's unfinished."

Skin Disorder and Family

The family experience of a juvenile patient afflicted with a chronic neurodermatitis is illustrative of another psychosomatic illness. This patient exhibited prominent emotional and social disturbances which seemed clearly related to the perpetuation of her skin disorder, if not to its cause.

A fourteen-year-old girl suffered from a recurring and intractable rash. She complained of itching, restlessness, and poor sleep. When she was two, the skin disorder erupted as eczema. From that time on, the eruption alternately subsided and recurred but never disappeared. The patient scratched her body more or less continuously but during periods of emotional tension engaged in an orgy of scratching. The scratching caused her skin to become tough and leathery. When the rash was severe, the patient was markedly constipated.

The patient was a tall girl, overdeveloped for her age. The rash affected most of her body. She was intelligent and alert, but an agitated, destructive tomboy. When angry she was a spitfire, abusive and profane with abandon. She was a bed-wetter. She engaged in daring and dangerous exploits. She flaunted herself before the eyes of surrounding men. The affliction of her skin was a lifelong curse. She was intensely cynical; she was convinced that she would not ever be cured. She felt she would "just as soon die or be killed." She was at times euphoric, at other times morose or depressed.

The patient was the third in a family of four children. She loved her father and brother, hated her older sister but was protective of the younger one. When the patient was two years of age, her mother died during the birth of the fourth child. All the children were placed in an orphan asylum. For the years between two and nine, the patient was irregularly boarded out in foster homes. Between the ages of nine and fourteen, she lived in an orphan home. She had assumed up to the age of nine that her aunt was her mother. For the first time at nine years of age she was informed that her own mother had died in childbirth.

This was a critical turning point in her life. Her entire behavior became transformed. Having believed that her aunt was her mother, she felt bewildered when her younger sister was given over for adoption. Before this, she had had vivid dreams to the effect that her real mother had died. She was unable to divest herself of the suspicion that the dream told the truth. On questioning her aunt, she discovered that her surmise was well-founded. She learned that her aunt had other children of her own. She became secretly convinced that she, herself, had caused her mother's death. She became distant to her aunt, and believed her father would no longer care for her. She said: "Before that, I loved him and he loved me. Afterwards, everything changed—life changed."

With this metamorphosis, her feeling toward herself, her family, assumed an utterly new aspect. Because of her guilt feeelings, she phantasied that she, too, must soon die. Her skin malady became the curse of God for having killed her mother. Having heretofore been a well-behaved girl, "an angel," she abruptly gave way to the devil. She became a trouble-maker, wayward and vicious. She no longer "gave a damn." She imagined herself a criminal and expected severe punishment, even mutilation of her body. Her interpretation of the menstrual function was in harmony with her obsession with punishment. She regarded it as eczema of her genitalia.

Being bad, to her, meant being bad sexually. She launched deliberately on a career of sex. She courted sex in its every morbid guise. She felt drawn to all kinds of perverse sexual activity. She did not masturbate genitally but played with her breasts.

In another way, the patient did penance to her dead mother. She was frightened by visions of nightly visitations by the ghost of her mother. She lay awake imagining her mother had lain in the same bed. She sought signs of blood stains on the sheet.

Her relationship toward her father changed. She now shunned his kisses and felt an annoying impulse to sterilize her face. She thought her skin erupted more viciously following his kisses. She feared that he might be contaminated by her bad skin. Were she to kill herself she did not want her father to be lonely. Therefore, the only satisfactory solution was first to kill him, and then herself.

She toyed continuously with the idea of suicide. On one occasion she cut her wrists and, on another, hung precariously from a window ledge six stories high. At still another time, while submitting to sexual advances, she careened recklessly over the edge of the roof.

Her emotional disturbance and skin disorder are deeply interwoven. The skin of her face, neck, upper thorax and arms showed deformations, caused by habitual scratching. Usually, she was not satisfied to cease scratching until her skin had begun to bleed freely. Her skin seemed to itch most when she felt "nervous," "bitchy," "very mad." She scratched when absorbed with thoughts of her parents' death or when sexually aroused. She described herself as a girl "who wants what she wants when she wants it." If she doesn't get it, she gets very mad, her face gets red, her blood "circulates too fast, too hot." Then she has a "fit of spite." When the fit of scratching is finished, she is exhausted but has a sense of relief; her anger subsides.

She felt that all people shunned her, for fear of contagion. Even children called her "scratchy," "lousy," "rat poison." She fantasied herself horribly crippled but with a clear skin, and being loved. Often she imagined herself a mere torso, without arms and legs, but with a normal skin. Some time later she became an unmarried mother. Such was the "curse of God."

The perpetuation of the skin disorder seemed closely related to her furious scratching. She masturbated her entire body in a boiling rage. She disfigured her skin, made herself ugly and repellant. In this way she created an impassable barrier between herself, her father, and other people. Her mutilated skin became the symbol of her relentless pursuit of guilty self-destruction.

Asthma in Children

In reviewing a series of experiences with the psychotherapy of children with asthma, I was impressed that in most cases the asthmatic reaction disappeared in the course of the psychotherapeutic experience. To be candid about it, in certain phases of the therapy I became so wrapped up in the treatment of the child I forgot about the asthma. Now and then, I got a rude reminder of the asthma, not from the child, however, but rather from the child's mother. I cannot recall a single instance in which the child complained of respiratory distress. It was always the panic-stricken, guilty mother with death fears, who imagined her child choking to death. The harassed mothers expressed their amazement that the child never seemed to worry about distressed breathing. This in itself was interesting in that it offered a possible clue to a form of omnipotent defense in the child against the mother's death anxieties. The child often seemed to deny completely the existence of a death threat.

In any case, most of these children were cured of their asthma although I do not know specifically how it happened. To be sure, I learned something of the interrelationship between the somatic and emotional aspects of this phenomenon, but still cannot say precisely how or why the asthmatic reaction subsided. I do have a general impression that, where successful, I was able not only to modify the anxiety response of the child, but by working directly with the emotional interaction of child and mother, I was able to improve the relationship.

The literature on the psychosomatic aspects of asthma points up certain relevant phenomena. Specific allergies are frequently present though not universally so. Respiratory and dermal allergies frequently coexist, though again not universally. Some writers distinguish between a true immunological allergy and a clinical allergy. The allergic factor may be constitutional; it may exist prior to birth, but there is some evidence to suggest that it may be conditioned by experience in the early months of life. In other words, certain deviant reactions of the autonomic system may be learned. But this conditioning may occur so early in life as to be, in effect, irreversible. It is also hypothesized that strong emotional influences may lower the threshold of allergic sensitiveness. It is believed by some that in asthma a specific parasympathetic hyperfunction is involved, and that this innervation has a regressive pattern. Alexander speaks of a "vegetative retreat." Lthamon and Saul emphasize that the regressive process need not be of the total personality but only of certain component reactions.

Particularly relevant is the concept that a failure of motor discharge in the voluntary neuromuscular system may result in a shunting of energy into the autonomic system, *i.e.*, a failure of effective motor release causes an overflow of autonomic nervous stimulation to certain internal organs. From still another point of view, there is a question of possible hypersensitivity of the end organs in the bronchioles. Another interesting observation is the tendency to mutual exclusiveness of asthma and psychosis. They may alternate, but they usually do not coexist. In those cases where there is both asthma and psychosis, the asthma disappears during the psychosis, and tends to reappear when the psychosis subsides.

In recent times, there is less enthusiasm for seeking specific correlations between psychosomatic disorders and personality type, or between these disorders and the symbolic content of conflict. There is rather more tendency to try to understand specificity in psychophysiological phenomena in terms of disorganization of specific adaptive mechanisms of personality, *i.e.*, in deviant ego operations and in pathological formations of defense against external danger and inner anxiety.

Regarding asthma, French and Alexander[2] say.

> The inhibition of the urge to cry seems to be the nuclear emotional factor in these cases. The function of crying in the infant is to call for maternal help and attention. Later, the same effect is achieved by more complex physiological functions (speech) which, like crying, evoke the expiratory phase of respiration. The inhibition to confess has been

established by these studies as a superimposed factor upon the inhibition to cry. The fear of being separated from mother or the maternal figure brings the urge to regain maternal love through confession of forbidden thoughts and impulses. If the urge is inhibited, the patient who has an allergic sensitivity may respond with a typical disturbance of the respiratory function known as asthma—the psychological factors appear usually in combination with specific somatic factors (allergic sensitivity). The coexistence of both factors explains why in many cases the symptoms may disappear by bringing about changes in either one of these two types of factors, psychological or allergic. In most cases only the combination of both types of factors produce the illness.[1]

It does seem true often that asthmatic children are unable to communicate their emotional needs through the act of crying. But that does not seem to be all. This particular inhibition should perhaps be reassessed in the context of a wider inhibition of expressive behavior. To be sure, there are signs of suppressed oral aggressiveness. There is constraint of the mouth. Such children do not achieve full release of their ambivalent hostility in an oral attack on mother. But more than that, they appear aloof, detached. They wear a kind of poker face or a far away anxious expression; the facial expression is often blank, stripped of affect, frozen or anxiety filled. They endeavor to deny their dependent cravings, and substitute an attitude of detachment and exaggerated compensatory self-sufficiency. Often they show compulsive patterns, but these are not stable, well-integrated defense operations. The compulsive mechanisms operate erratically and are interspersed with episodes of explosive aggression or with signs of withdrawal and suspiciousness.

The capacity of these children to use their body for aggressive control of the environment is impaired; the use of the body is awkward and variably constrained. Asthmatic children tend not to show a sustained spontaneity in motor behavior, but may show periodic, agitated, poorly regulated explosive releases of tension through body activity. At the other pole, when gratified, they are often unable to show a spontaneous happiness or enthusiasm. Thus, it appears, there is variable constraint of emotional release in crying, and also in other forms of motor expression, in speech and in the body musculature. The body talks, to be sure, but through the vegetative nervous system, rather than through systems of voluntary motor expression.

Such behavior is nonadaptive. Adaptive behavior is intended to preserve life, to insure a continuous supply of vital needs. The choked breathing of the asthmatic child accomplishes no such purpose. What is implied here is a significant break in the organism's adaptive connection with the environment. The loss of control of environment is accompanied by a parallel process of homeostatic imbalance within the organism, and a shunting of emotional energy into the autonomic nervous system. This reaction spells a selective disorganization of the basic processes of biosocial adaptation. The question is: How do the normal adaptive aspects of emotional, nervous, and motor reactivity become perverted to a form of nonadaptive behavior which menaces the continuity of life?

The behavior of one such patient is illustrative. Her craving for warmth, closeness and a protective maternal attitude is all too transparent; nevertheless, her attitude is a defensively aloof one. Her emotional behavior reflects the urge to deny these needs, nor can she assert them in words. She does not cry, her face masks her feeling, her body posture is fixed and immobile, she exclaims desperately in a tense, tightly squeezed whisper, "I can't talk, I can't breathe, in fact I'm choking." After the repetition of a number of such episodes, she discovered that she could break the respiratory crisis by kicking out or engaging in a generalized, explosive squirming of her whole body. Ultimately, she reached out her hand to grasp the therapist's hand and draw him toward or into herself, i.e., to incorporate him. When finally able to express this urge as if by magic, there was an instantaneous subsidence of the respiratory choking, and a rapid restoration of normal breathing. Simultaneously she was impelled to confess feelings of guilt and badness, to provoke the therapist into saying he disliked her, or wished to disown or punish her in other ways. It seemed as if in the very act of taking hold of the therapist she was inciting him to turn against her. The impression was striking that this was a reliving of a phase of the child's ambivalent, dependent relationship with mother.

Another asthmatic child, treated in a joint interview with her mother, also wore a frozen face; she sat stark still, eyes glued to her mother's face. Her mother was given to fits of agitated, pressured talking. She literally gave the child no chance to open her mouth. She outtalked the child, interrupted her, took the words right out of her mouth, and at times seemed, figuratively speaking, to jump down the child's throat. This child simply could not spit as well as her mother. At this level of competition the child could never win. The mother devoured successfully; the child's mouth was just not that efficient. Yet in other ways, child and mother were rather alike. There was an underlying closeness which both unconsciously conspired to deny. The child expressed this denial in her detached attitude, in her passive, perverse obstinacy, in her occasional belligerence, and in her effective foiling of the mother's need to aggrandize her personal vanity through the child's achievements. In this case, interestingly enough, during one such ambivalent crisis in the relationship, the mother had an acute attack of asthma; she never had had asthma before, nor has she had asthma since.

In the family of this asthmatic child, the mother filled a role of child-wife. She expected her husband to cater to her needs first. The child craved the love interest of her father, but the demands of the child-wife inserted a barrier between child and father.

In other child-mother pairs the mutual torment and "wolfing" is perhaps not so dramatic, yet, essentially the same interactional pattern seems to prevail. The child's ambivalent hostility to mother is sometimes articulated in speech but more often expressed in non-verbal behavior. Beneath this level of mutual struggle and opposition there is a concealed and unadmitted layer of intimacy. The love tie is a close but a traumatized one. What is this pattern of child-mother union which is disrupted, perverted and tortured into an over-lying pattern of intense mutual opposition?

In attempting to understand these reactions I tried to correlate the emotional patterns of the child at each stage of development with the family experience as a whole, with particular attention to the unfolding of the asthmatic response as related to the interaction of child and mother. Within this context, it was necessary to examine the maternal role as influenced not only by the mother's character structure, but also by the paternal role, the interaction between the parents, and the dynamics of the family group as a unit. This made possible a more careful scrutiny of the conditions which precipitated the attacks of asthma, the role of trauma, the specific effects of mother upon child, and the factor of vulnerability as determined by the vicissitudes of early family conditioning.

Incomplete as they are, I should like to sketch briefly some partial hypotheses regarding the early emotional conditioning in the child-mother relationship. There is some critical disturbance in the phase of symbiotic union of child and mother. This disturbance emerges mainly in the preverbal, preambulatory phase of personality development, and involves some impairment of the omnipotence feeling which rests on a secure child-mother union, also some impairment of the child's emerging body image. This disturbance is influenced by special qualities of maternal behavior. The mother is aggressive, but ambivalently detached and guilty, has the urge to grasp the child, to make it part of herself, but is inhibited in this urge for fear of doing the child injury. The mother allows some closeness with the child, but from time to time unpredictably wheels about, and assaults the child by a sudden withdrawal of herself. The child moves part way toward a positive identification with mother through oral incorporation but the mother's ambivalent hostility arouses a self-protective passive negativism; the child can neither fight effectively nor wholly withdraw, and the identification process becomes distorted. Accordingly the child experiences acute episodes of separation anxiety. In reacting to this anxiety, the child does not succeed in using the motor equipment of the body or speech for mastery of the mother. The child fails in this manner to convey need, or to control the mother in satisfying that need. The release of emotional communication through facial expression or speech, or through the voluntary muscle system is variably inhibited, though there may be intermittent explosive eruptions. What is implied here is some partial selective disorganization of immature ego functions, with distortion of the emerging body image, and some failure of the early control mechanisms of personality.

The child seems to achieve a partial symbiotic union with mother but this is neither secure nor sustained. The continuity of this union is unpredictably and traumatically disrupted by the ambivalent, treacherous withdrawals of the mother. The feeling of security and confidence in the child deriving from magic omnipotent union with mother is therefore damaged. The child is impelled to react with unstable and alternating efforts to restore omnipotent union with mother, or to withdraw. It seems possible, therefore, to conceive the asthmatic reaction as a nonadaptive, ineffectual effort to re-establish the needed symbiosis with mother and, with this, to restore the sense of omnipotent control. The variable failure of these efforts may bear some relation to the tendency to explosive, aggressive release, irritability and to the final recourse to emotional detachment. It may bear a specific relation also to the interchangeability of asthma and psychotic episodes. The somatic reaction itself seems to prevent a complete break of emotional control. In any case the child, unable to enforce a continuous supply of vital needs from the maternal environment through voluntary activity, through speech or through crying, discharges tension in a shunted path through the autonomic nervous system. In this connection, it seems possible that there is an early and special conditioning of the responses of the autonomic system.

The episodes of asthma seem to follow traumatic experiences. The common denominators in these are the following: severe anxiety reactions to separation, the abrupt confrontation of a menacing aggression in the mother figure and the sudden disruption of habitual security patterns.

Inevitably, the question arises: Is there anything specific for asthma in these precipitating experiences, or in the patterns of vulnerability determined by early child-mother conditioning? My frank answer can only be, I don't know. I question whether there is a signficant factor of specificity in the external danger situation. The self-same patterns of response to perceived external danger are associated with other psychosomatic conditions. I am less certain regarding the conditioning of specific psychodynamic patterns that may be established in early child-mother interaction. Here, there may be demonstrated some partial elements of specificity but these are to be sought in the vicissitudes of the mechanisms of emotional control, rather than in specific components of conflicted basic drives.

I have raised the same critical question of organ specificity in my studies on character structure in hypertensive persons. There, too, I could not be sure whether the patterns of vulnerability observed in the character structure of these patients were specifically related to the hypertensive reaction, or whether they simply offered a clue to predisposition to psychosomatic breakdown in general, regardless of the organ system involved. To a large extent, the issue of organ specificity persists as an unsolved mystery.

Part 3

THERAPEUTIC ASPECTS

CHAPTER 16

PSYCHOTHERAPY TODAY

THE PSYCHOTHERAPEUTIC ROLE in the community is an old, established one. It is, in fact, as ancient as history itself. Sometimes honored, sometimes pilloried, it has nonetheless been an indispensable community function. Only in the last half century, however, has there emerged a "scientific psychotherapy," one which purports to rest on a true science of human behavior. But, despite the remarkable advances of recent years in psychopathology and psychotherapy, we cannot claim even now a consensus on the question of what psychotherapy is. Definitions of psychotherapy are notoriously ambiguous. It is an urgent necessity, therefore, to spell out with clarity some of the troubled areas of contemporary psychotherapeutic practice.

A number of schools of thought with conflicting theories and techniques have emerged on the present scene, each competing with the others. Each holds a different theory of personality and trains its disciples accordingly. Each tends to apply its own single method to a variety of disorders. The sheer multiplicity of these different approaches suggests that no one of these systems can be complete in itself.

A variety of researches on the results of psychotherapy have emerged, endeavoring to lend the prestige of science to otherwise doubtful claims concerning the effectiveness of this or that brand of psychotherapy. Considerable time and effort is expended, but by and large such studies are peculiarly disappointing. Regardless of the particular treatment method or the procedure of evaluation that is employed (when one omits technical niceties), the statistical findings are roughly equivalent: one-third of the patients are substantially improved; one-third show some degree of improvement; one-third remain unchanged.

Such figures are conspicuously lacking in eloquence; they prove nothing. The scientific matrix of such studies is suspect. The methodological issues are extremely complex and have not yet been solved. Almost universally the investigations are inadequately controlled for a number of factors: (1) the validity and accuracy of standards of clinical diagnosis; (2) the accuracy of definition of the treatment method; (3) the factor of psychological specificity, *i.e.*, the specific relatedness of a given treatment method to a given pathological condition; (4) the criteria for therapeutic change; the means of measurement and the persons judging such change; (5) the differentiation of changes due to growth and environmental influence from changes specifically induced by psychotherapy; (6) the personal equation, *i.e.*, differences among individual therapists and differences of empathy and interaction among particular pairings of patient and therapist.

Surveying the field at large, the quality of psychotherapy currently practiced could surely be improved. The statistical approach to the assessment of results may be premature. It seems more useful at present to test the quality of therapeutic change through a process of consensual validation between the patient and the therapist, the patient and his family, the patient and his community.

Rather impressive are the private convictions of individual therapists themselves. Typically, the phantasies of psychotherapists cluster about two extreme poles: either the therapist secretly lacks confidence in his therapeutic powers or he harbors the secret delusion that he and he alone can cure, all other therapists being totally inadequate. He may lack faith in what he does or he may bear a magic faith not in the method per se but in his private talent and skill as an individual craftsman. How then shall we weigh the importance of the psychotherapeutic principle itself?

It is certainly true that psychotherapy will always depend on an element of personal skill, on the art of the individual therapist. Therapists do differ one from the next in the quality of talent expressed in their use of themselves in the psychotherapeutic role.

It is true also that for centuries psychotherapeutic practices have had deep roots in religion and art. They have also reflected genuine wisdom about the ways of man. On the contemporary scene, we like to think they are science too. Probably healing of the mind will always depend on an element of faith in miracles. Initially patients tend to expect the therapist to play the role of God, to be omniscient and omnipotent. In this primitive matrix, the therapist is somewhat akin to a "magic helper." As therapy progresses, the demand for magic protection diminishes and increasing trust in the therapist as a human being emerges, but nonetheless the infantile need of magic security and miraculous cure persists as a latent element in the relationship for a long time.

A further problem, much neglected, is the unique quality of empathic union and identification of particular pairs of patients and therapists. Some pairs click instantly and others fail regardless of long effort. The quality of emotional relatedness between a particular patient and a particular therapist creates a factor above and beyond their individual personalities.

All told, there is probably an irreducible minimum of art and religion in all forms of psychotherapy. The religious component is highly individual. The art is a precious possession and, like all fine art, is relatively rare. Spiritual faith and artistic talent cannot be taught; they are given. It is only the scientific foundation of psychotherapy, the part that provides systematic insight into human behavior, that can be taught and can add a new dimension to the age-old practice.

For we would all agree, certainly, that in the healing of mental illness religion and art are not enough. Psychotherapy is handicapped to whatever extent it fails to be buttressed by scientific knowledge. And here we confront the arduous struggle. As scientific method, modern psychotherapy is hardly clear. As scientific process, it seems to be in a peculiar state of neurotic irresolution. It cannot make up its mind and is indecisive about a number of fundamental questions. And for a clearly recognized reason: we do not yet possess an integrated theory of human behavior. At best, we have only partial theories for partial behavioral phenomena, not a systematic, holistic theory. The confusion that currently prevails is immediately transparent in certain polarities of orientation: the biological versus the social determinants of behavior, past versus present, unconscious versus conscious, intrapsychic versus extrapsychic. The tendency is toward an either/or attitude—either the inside of the mind or the outside, either the past or the present.

Generally, in this psychoanalytically oriented age, troubled persons turn inward to solve their problems and discover themselves; they become absorbed in the search for the "real self." At the same time, they turn away from the outer world. It is interesting that one-sided concentration on the inner self followed closely the sharp disillusionment with the efficacy of exclusively social treatment methods. Social therapy unsupported by systematic insight into the dynamics of personality proved insufficient, thus, the sharp swing to individual psychotherapy. But this too, of itself, is insufficient. To know thyself is fine, but it is equally imperative to know thy world. The one kind of insight has not been able to go very far without the other. We see, for example, that the social product of some forms of psychoanalytic therapy reflects certain limitations of individual treatment. Paradoxically, the patient as an individual may markedly improve, and yet in some respects his social relations may remain almost as bad as they ever were. Facetiously speaking, everything in the patient is cured except his human relations. Or, in the words of one analyst, "On completion of analysis, the patient is wiser but sadder and lonelier." More specifically, what are the unfortunate affects of this inner-directed therapy that ignores the world outside?

Let us take, for example, the case of the wife who campaigns to get her husband to enter therapy for sexual impotence, threatening to leave him unless he is cured. The husband yields and is treated, and the symptom of impotence is quickly alleviated. The therapist, pleased with his success, is shocked to discover that directly after the husband restored his potency his wife deserted him. This is a paradoxical response, to be sure, but it can and does occur. Individual psychotherapy may help the individual, but under certain conditions it fails to ameliorate the pathology of a family relationship.

It is by no means rare to see one member of the pair get better in individual treatment as the other gets worse. One partner matures and becomes sexually more adequate, the other regresses. Or one responds to analytic therapy with an increased capacity for closeness and the other reacts with depression. It is apparent that in some circumstances the increased strength or health of personality of one family member becomes a threat to another. This can occur when only one member of the family pair is in therapy or when both are in therapy with separate therapists.

Yet professional opinion varies widely on the solution to this problem. When neurotic family pairs need psychotherapy, the most efficient form of integration of the psychotherapies would seem to be achieved in the mind of a single therapist. Strong objections have been offered to such practice, however. The premise seems to be that two members of a family, interdependent but mutually distrustful and competitively destructive, would vie with each other for the therapist's favor and that this rivalry would jeopardize therapeutic control. Therefore, the argument goes, provisions for separate treatment are preferable. But this argument overlooks the difficulty of integrating the two therapies and the further problems that arise out of the failure to relate the psychotherapy of the neurotic pair to the total dynamics of family life.

Furthermore, we must not deceive ourselves with the thought that the patients' suspiciousness will be disarmed by the mere fact of having separate therapists or that the tensions of the family relationship will take care of themselves.

It is true that when two members of a family are locked in pathological conflict, with a deep layer of mutual suspicion and a strong propensity for destructive motivation, treatment by separate therapists may be indicated. But all too often such treatment is begun without adequate clarification of the interpersonal level of disturbance, without sufficient emotional preparation of each partner, and without laying a foundation for effective collaboration between the two therapists at later stages.

Indeed, as the principle of separate treatment is generally applied at present, it is most difficult to pursue the goal of integrating the two therapies. Both in child and family guidance centers and in private psychiatric practice, effective collaboration is extremely rare. Often mere lip service is paid to the principle. Still more often psychiatrists openly declare that it is intrinsically undesirable. Thus, the two therapeutic experiences tend to get dissociated, and, although the intrapsychic conflicts of each person may be ameliorated, successful readaptation to family relationships nonetheless fails.

It becomes apparent, therefore, that a clinician confronted by a person locked in marital conflict must make some delicate decisions, despite the fact that with present knowledge it is hardly possible to predict with any real confidence the effects of psychotherapy on one partner or on the other or on the marital relationship itself.

The present state of affairs in the area of child therapy presents other kinds of complications. In the contemporary community psychotherapeutic services for children hold a place of special importance. Still, procedures take many forms and the process is not clearly defined. Neither the goals nor the methods are standardized. Treatment is carried out by specialists from a variety of professional groups, each of which reflects a distinct form of training—by psychiatrists, pediatricians, psychologists, social workers, educators, and lay psychoanalysts. The line of demarcation between child treatment and child education is unclear. There is a variety of schools of child psychology, each expounding its own favored theory while arguing the weaknesses of competing theories.

But it is remarkable, and a matter of more than passing interest, that the results of child psychotherapy turn out to be much the same regardless of the particular method employed and the wide differences in professional training of therapists. The general impression is that therapeutic results are often favorable whether one type of treatment is used or another. Is it possible that child psychotherapy, currently represented in a wide range of diverse procedures, is lacking in specificity and that favorable therapeutic results derive as much from the sincerity and devotion of the therapist to the needs of the child as from any other factor? Assuming that this is so, it brings home sharply the primary importance of one aspect of the therapist's role—his assumption of the functions of auxilliary parent in an improved version.

Is it possible, too, that the impression of favorable results is in part due to the fact that more attention is directed to the families of child patients than to the families of adult patients? Because of the very nature of the child his outer world is given consideration as well as his inner self? It is certainly true that in child guidance practice, therapeutic work is still restricted primarily to the mother, with occasional or rare contacts with the father and with no systematic or sustained approach to the family as a whole or to the shared responsibilities of parenthood. It is also true that a sweeping glance at the prevailing practices in the therapy of mothers in a variety of child guidance clinics brings the prompt conclusion that there is little uniformity or consistency in diagnostic appraisal, orientation of therapy, or application of corrective measures. And the results of therapy range from one pole to the other, from dramatic success to flagrant failure, carrying with them no dependable factor of predictability.

Clinicians treating disturbed mothers project short-term goals and long-term goals, use surface therapeutic techniques and depth techniques. Some give direct advice; others do not. Some believe in parent education; others scoff at it. Some hold the conviction that child and mother should always be treated by separate therapists; others experiment with therapy of child and mother by the same therapist. Some focus their corrective efforts sharply on the child-rearing attitudes and conduct of the mothers; others prefer to approach the mother as an individual, pointing their efforts specifically toward the mother's neurotic conflicts and showing only an incidental interest in the child-rearing behavior. Still others embark on group therapy for mothers.

Certainly the extent to which the psychotherapies of child and mother are coordinated varies tremendously, as is the degree to which the therapy of the mother is child-oriented. Some mothers talk in psychotherapeutic sessions of their child and their child only. They seem obsessed with worry over the child and with the need to control and punish the child. Accordingly, they are motivated to exploit the social worker or therapist as the agent of their punitive attitude. They use their preoccupation with control of the child's behavior as a resistance to real understanding of their maternal role and as an escape from facing their personal responsibility for the child's disorder.

At the opposite pole, there is a group of mothers who begin their psychotherapeutic experience with a concern for the child but soon seem to forget him altogether and become exclusively preoccupied with themselves. They exploit their therapeutic interviews for dealing with a variety of personal problems, their marital difficulties, their conflicts with their own parents, but rarely with the issues of their relatedness to the child. His behavior difficulties are dropped wholly on the lap of the child's therapist with an attitude of "Let the therapist worry about him."

In all probability these polar forms of resistance in mothers of disturbed children are influenced in part by the differences in orientation of different psychotherapists. But in either case, in a program of separate treatment effective access to the disturbance moving between child and mother is rendered more difficult if not impossible. The therapeutic orientation seems to move all too quickly to an exclusive preoccupation with the child as an individual and with the mother as an individual. It moves too quickly away from the level of real relationship experience to the level of unreal emotional experience and irrational unconscious conflicts. There is a conspicuous trend toward by-passing interpersonal levels of disturbance and plunging immediately into the intrapsychic conflicts of the individual patient.

Indeed, it is not uncommon to hear protests against this course of treatment from patients themselves. Thus when a child in therapy denies having emotional problems and insists, "It is my parents who are upset, not me," the child may be resisting therapy to be sure; but the implied demand, "Do something about my parents," is certainly not without justification. For example, the only son of a self-centered but highly successful attorney is in therapy because he is emotionally isolated and withdrawn and chronically fails in his academic work even though he has a superior intelligence. He is weak and unassertive but passively resists his father's ambitions for him. He does not feel like a person in his own right but rather like a piece of his father. He accuses his father of pursuing him constantly and expresses the conviction that his father needs the psychiatrist more than he. He is partly right.

A mother of a disturbed child projects blame on the father; the father turns it back on the mother. In effect, the mother says to her psychiatrist, "Why blame everything on me? My husband should be your patient," an attitude which may be promptly chalked down by the psychiatrist as the mother's projection of guilt. So it is, but more often than not such an accusation carries with it an important core of truth as well. For example, a rather masculine woman with a social work professional background is married to a weak man, whom she belittles because he has "hips like a woman and suffers hysterical fits." They have an emotionally disturbed child. The woman denies personal problems placing the main responsibility for the child's difficulty on the father's neurotic fears. She offers to collaborate with the therapist in treating her husband. This woman resists therapy for herself, to be sure, but there is a basis in fact for her insistence that her husband should receive therapy.

When, in cases such as these, father, mother, and child each enter therapy with a different therapist, the areas of reality and the areas of irrational projection all too often tend to remain obscure. The various therapists have abundant opportunity to differ in their evaluations of the situation and in their prescriptions, and the therapy of each patient proceeds without an opportunity for reality testing.* For example, a woman teacher married to a gifted musician brings her

* Bela Mittelman has drawn attention to this problem in an article on the simultaneous psychoanalytic therapy of husband and wife. In the procedure he describes, husband and

disturbed child to the therapist for treatment. She herself is acutely depressed and enters therapy, laying the blame for her depression at her husband's door. She complains bitterly that he failed to earn an adequate living, although earlier he had been highly successful as a musician. She says that he no longer tries hard enough, that he ought to pocket his artistic vanity and go out and get any work he can, no matter what, because he owes it to his wife and child. She sounds vindictive almost to the point of violence, confesses to refusing her husband sexual satisfaction, and has calamitous fears of the imminent break-up of her marriage. When asked whether she had directly expressed these feelings to her husband, she demurs, saying, "No, it would hurt him too deeply, irrevocably."

Meanwhile, her husband expresses to his therapist his deep distress concerning his wife's rejection of sex relations and, at the same time, his unwillingness to force himself upon her. He is trying earnestly to get suitable employment; his temporary failure is no doing of his own but rather the result of a critical turn in the economy of the music industry. Yet he gets no support from her in these trying days. He cannot understand the reasons for her depression and her rejection of him. When asked whether he has attempted to explain the economic situation to her, he replies, "No, she should not be troubled by such matters, especially when she is so depressed and the child is upset, too."

It is conceivable that both therapies could have continued on this level of mutual misunderstanding for many months, but in this particular case a joint interview was arranged after considerable resistance on the part of both patients, each of whom feared that it might precipitate the destruction of the marriage. Actually it did nothing of the kind; on the contrary, it cleared the air of unreal accusations and distorted projections and if anything saved the marriage. The wife was stripped of the alibi for her depression. She was attaching her hostility and guilt to the wrong person and for the wrong reasons, for the real object of her hate was her mother. She could no longer falsely project onto her husband the reason for her bitterness, and she recognized her irrational urge to exploit her husband's unfortunate professional situation for the purpose of humiliating him as a man and making him crawl before her eyes. She was able to admit that her real fear was loss of sexual pleasure with the approaching menopause, a fear that had been profoundly strengthened in her by an earlier traumatic family experience in which her mother played the chief part. Yet had the two therapies gone their

---

wife are treated by the same psychoanalyst, thus violating the traditional psychoanalytic fashion of husband and wife being treated by different analysts. Mittleman points out the advantageous position of a single therapist for both marital partners in being able to discern accurately the irrational projections of each partner onto the other, and thus achieving a clear definition of the reality of the marital relationship. Using in each patient's therapy information derived from the therapy of the other can, of course, be done only with the full knowledge and consent of both. This is a therapeutic plan in which collaboration is truly achieved in the mind of a single therapist.[1]

separate ways, the true cause of the depression and the marital crisis might not have been discovered soon enough to save the marriage and relieve the interpersonal tensions that were disturbing the child.

It seems increasingly apparent that individual therapy cannot be the sole answer to the mental health problems of our time. When each member of a family is given individual treatment and these therapies are not related to one another, the effects on the family are all too often indirect and nonspecific. Such concomitant psychotherapy may bring improvement in family relations, but it may on other occasions worsen the conflicts. Whatever the outcome, it is still therapy for individuals, based on individual diagnosis, and aimed at goals of individual improvement. It is not a therapy of family relationships or of family groups.

CHAPTER 17

TECHNIQUES OF PSYCHOTHERAPY

PSYCHOTHERAPY TODAY has a number of useful techniques at its command—supportive therapy, ventilating therapy, counseling, guidance, social case work, psychoanalysis, and group therapy. Others are being and will be developed. Family treatment by its very nature leads to a new form, the treatment of pairs, threesomes, etc. Still in an experimental stage, this type of multiple treatment, which stands somewhere between the extremes of individual psychoanalysis and group therapy, must be further developed and refined.

At the present time, however, the therapist has two primary methods—individual and group—of which the others are derivatives. A careful comparison of the two as they are now utilized will, I think, indicate their usefulness in various situations and the ways in which they can be mobilized for the special needs of family therapy. At the outset, it should be clear that no therapist ought to discard any method that may alleviate distress; the rigidity that obtains in some therapeutic orientations overlooks the fact that no two patients can be treated in precisely the same way. Certainly great flexibility is called for by the complexities of family diagnosis and treatment.

In a fundamental sense neither of the primary techniques is complete in itself, for each points to different facets of pathological process. Psychoanalysis exerts its main corrective influence on early disturbance of child-family symbiosis, whereas group therapy focuses its corrective influence largely on conflicts in the adaptation of individual personality to social role.

The dynamic bases of the two are the natural processes of growth of personality within the patterns of the surrounding social milieu. These processes are inherent in the child's early experience of relations with mother, and after that with both parents and the family as a whole. Individual psychotherapy highlights the growth-stimulating and growth-inhibiting potentials of parent-child relations. The two-person psychotherapeutic situation provides a unique experience, in which the earlier child-parent relations are relived and their destructive elements removed.

Group psychotherapy, on the other hand, derives its rationale from the fact that the child's character is influenced not only by processes of child-parent interaction but also by his membership in the family as a group. The multiple interactional and transactional experiences of the entire family also contribute to the molding of personality. The group basis for the organization of personality is influenced by the manner in which the child's dependence on mother is affected in further steps by the mother's and child's relations with the father, the relations of siblings with parents, and the relations of both parent and child with extended representations of family, and the surrounding community.

The child's membership in the family group molds his character over and above the emotional content of his tie to any one member. On emerging from the family the child's character is further modified, though more gradually, by membership in an expanding series of groups, nursery, school, neighborhood, social club, etc. As he grows older and moves from one group to the next, each group plays its part in shaping character traits and dominant modes of social adaptation.

It is self-evident that the spontaneously evolving patterns of interpersonal experience that run parallel to the processes of maturation can be exploited for therapeutic purposes. Just as the dynamic processes of child-mother interaction under controlled conditions may serve therapeutic objectives, so too can relationship experience in groups be utilized and directed for therapeutic aims. Individuals often engage spontaneously in self-therapy by investing themselves in selective group experiences. They seek out unconsciously social relationships which they hope will allay anxiety, reduce tension, promote their emotional welfare and further their development as persons. Through these relationship bonds they seek new levels of identification and a firmer confidence and sense of mastery in meeting new experience. In these spontaneous group involvements of particular importance is not only the search for friendship and a stronger confidence but a quest for a solidification of a preferred personal identity and related values. Such self-therapy plays a significant part in the choice of a marital partner and in the development of new relationships with the marital partner's family. Such progressive group involvements may, however, through intrusion of unrational, unconscious motives, exert injurious rather than healing effects.

In group therapy we would naturally wish to carry over from psychoanalysis the penetrating insights into the inner processes of the individual mind and some partial techniques that have demonstrated their power to induce therapeutic change. However, the utilization of selected psychoanalytic principles in group treatment should bring no confusion of the two methods. They are not identical. Although some partial techniques commonly used in one procedure may be employed appropriately in the other, the two methods must nevertheless remain distinct. It is imperative in the first instance to be clearly aware of the significance of some basic differences of structure in the two treatment situations.

Group psychotherapy uses as the instrument of its therapeutic effects a group of people. To restate the obvious: a group is a social entity in its own right; it has features and properties uniquely its own, over and above the characteristics of the individual units that compose it. Group processes should not be evaluated solely as projective expressions of the individuals making it up; nor should the individuals be judged solely as social atoms. The individual and the group, though interacting and interdependent entities, are each characterized by a specific level of biosocial organization, and accordingly each must be appraised by a different set of criteria.

Psychoanalytic technique as a historically patterned model, omitting the neo-Freudian modifications of recent years, does not provide for a social experience in the usual sense of this term. Although involving two persons it represents essentially a therapy of the private psychic life of one of these persons, the patient. The psychoanalyst, preserving anonymity and acting as a mirror for the patient's irrational projections, does not play the part of a real person. Social structuring of the relationship is delayed. The analyst scrupulously avoids the injection of his own personality into the patient's psychic struggles. The patient on the couch, unable to peer into his analyst's face, is literally in the dark about the person with whom he is interacting. The analyst withholds the usual social cues; therefore, the architecture for the ordinary processes of social interaction is lacking.

The analyst acts as a catalytic agent in energizing the patient's efforts to explore his deeper psychic life and the effects of his past experience. Conflict with the analyst is reinterpreted in terms of conflict with older parts of the self, these parts having been shaped by experiences with mother, father, and siblings. The primary focus is on the patient's disturbed inner orientation to himself, though the instrument used to reveal these disturbances is the analytic relationship. Intrinsic to the nature of this process is the temporary subordination of the role of outer reality. The process is so designed that there is greater range for the play of phantasy and for the selective assertion of irrational perceptions and conflicted needs. This is the dynamic matrix for the unfolding of transference and transference neurosis. For a period the unreality of transference achieves not merely a position of prominence but actually one of dominance over the existing realities. Ultimately, and by successive stages, the irrational content of the transference is worked through and matched against the reality of the analytic situation. The real qualities of the analyst's person are not revealed till the later stages; thus, the check with reality is delayed.

This is a dynamic model of classical psychoanalytic treatment. But psychoanalytic technique is today no longer a single entity. In those modified versions influenced by the concepts of Sullivan, Horney, Fromm-Reichmann, Thompson, Fromm, Alexander, and Kardiner, the dynamics of interpersonal relations are differently viewed: the therapist is a more real person, his personality plays a more definitive role, and the realities of current interpersonal and wider social experience assume an expanded importance.

In a therapy group, on the other hand, there is a great variety of possible interactions, all based on face-to-face relations of the participants. In principle, the structure of the therapeutic group is less conducive to the unchecked assertion of irrational and egocentrically oriented behavior in the individual than is psychoanalysis. A quicker impact between real and unreal is apt to be the rule. In fact, this very feature of the group discourages the emotional integration into the group of those individuals whose irrational needs do not find a congenial reception. In such circumstances, the individuals tend to wall themselves off and hover on the periphery of the experience.

The two-person psychoanalytic situation fosters a reliving of the symbiotic features of the child-parent unity; it reactivates the craving for magic omnipotence and the older patterns of the child-parent conflict. The therapy group, by contrast, facilitates re-enactment of conflicts with the entire family group; it brings rivals into the picture, counteracting the infantile urge for exclusive possession of the parent and diluting the degree of reliance on omnipotent fantasy. From the genetic point of view, then, a deeper level of reliving of childhood is possible in the psychoanalytic relationship than in the group therapy setting. This is the reason why psychoanalytic therapy is the preferred treatment for the resolution of deeply entrenched psychoneurotic symptoms.

I am suggesting the theory that psychoanalysis and group psychotherapy, differently designed in structure, exercise their selective effects most potently at different genetic levels of personality organization: psychoanalysis on conflicts emerging from the autistic, magic-minded component of the psyche rooted in the early child-parent symbiosis, and group psychotherapy on later levels of disturbance emerging from the socialization process. In this sense, psychoanalytic technique may be conceived as serving mainly the purpose of removing autistic elements in individual pathology that block the socialization process.

In a therapeutic group, a structured human situation evolves, which epitomizes an individual's relation with society. The group is a micro-society. It is in some respects different from a family. The moment a psychoanalyst assays the task of applying psychoanalytic principles to the objectives of group therapy, he is confronted with the task of designing a unitary frame of reference within which he can encompass the dynamics of the individual mind and the dynamics of group behavior. Simultaneously he must construct within the same conceptual frame, a link between the processes of biological maturation and those of social participation. To do so implicitly is by no means enough; it is essential to make such a formulation explicit. Otherwise, the inevitable result is a trial-and-error form of group therapy, an indiscriminate hodgepodge of group therapeutic techniques, unattached to and undisciplined by an integrated conceptual system of personality and social relations. I do not mean to say that the diverse therapeutic approaches now in use do not exert some therapeutic effects; but therapeutic effects are in no sense the same as cure, and therapeutic effects, in themselves, have never constituted proof of one or another theory of human nature and human relations. From the scientific point of view, such undisciplined forms of therapy eventually move into a dead-end street. To do therapy without a conceptual framework is like playing in the dark; it may be fun at first, but very soon it leads to mounting anxiety and disorganization.

To formulate a theoretical frame within which can be integrated two hitherto separate bodies of knowledge—that which bears on the intrapsychic life of the individual and that which bears on the psychological processes of the group—poses a special difficulty because the traditional aspects of psychoanalytic theory focus on the individual rather than on the group, on the internal economy of personality rather than on social relations. In keeping with Freud's orientation, psychoanalytic technique approaches the determinants of individual behavior from inside outward, beginning with the private and biological core of the individual's experience, and moving out from there to society; social interaction, therefore, tends to be interpreted as a projection of biologically fixed disposition.

Kardiner demonstrates Freud's conceptual error in attempting to evaluate social phenomena with the same criteria as individual personality. He asserts the view that the adaptive processes of individual personality and of society are geared to two different dimensions. On the other hand, in placing priority on the processes of social interaction, the neo-Freudians are in danger of playing down the significance of the relative autonomy of individual personality, its intricate internal mechanisms, and the role of specific biological drives. Franz Alexander endeavors to bridge this gap by giving recognition to the role of both the biological and the social determinants of personality. He takes the view that the child's personality is the product of biological tendencies shaped environmentally by the specific characters of the parents, which are in turn molded by the culture patterns.

There are, moreover, as Sullivan has inferred, certain limits to that abstraction we label individual personality. The original symbiotic union of infant and parent epitomizes the individual's dependence on the social group. Predictable patterns of personality are themselves contingent on a predictable social environment. With unexpected and radical changes of the environment, the operations of individual personality become less predictable. (Witness the behavior of prisoners in a concentration camp and the progressive changes in personality seen in persons subjected to prolonged unemployment.) We are compelled to recognize that the borders of the psyche are semipermeable, that personality is characterized by an autonomy that is only relative, and that the characteristic qualities of personality are characteristic only as the environment remains roughly the same. Therefore, I conceive of personality as an expression of a biopsychosocial continuum, in which behavior is influenced in a parallel way by inner physiological experience and by the processes of social participation. A further extension of these principles requires us to view the phenomena of personality in the context of the behavior of the colony; in other words, the functions of personality need to be defined within the frame of a broader theory of social process.

We must make the working assumption that there are common denominators in all forms of psychotherapy, but that these specific therapeutic devices exert their effects on different integrative levels of personality functioning in accordance with the levels of interpersonal experience that are systematically exploited for the therapeutic alleviation of anxiety. And because anxiety is activated by a failure of psychic assimilation of the discrepancy between real and unreal experience, we must be fundamentally concerned with these questions: What is the reality of the given therapeutic experience? How does the patient perceive it? How much anxiety is generated by the discrepancy between what is and what the patient perceives? We must, of course, be aware that the quality of the patient's perceptions is profoundly affected by his inner needs and the inner state of his psyche. And it is just here that psychoanalysis and group therapy differ in some critical respects. In psychoanalysis, the personifications of reality are purposely kept vague to encourage a maximum of free association and great elasticity in the projections of conflicted need. In a group, certain patterns of social reality are an ever-present force, though their fluidity may vary from group to group and from time to time in the same group. The perceptive responses of the patient are therefore differently conditioned by the two therapeutic situations, and the discrepancies between real and unreal with the corresponding anxiety responses must be differently evaluated.

This brings us immediately to another fundamental qualifying factor. In the two-person psychoanalytic situation, whatever the patient's anxiety, he is offered an implicit immunity against interpersonal retaliation. There is no true group pattern, no social reality in the conventional sense, no representation of punishing social authority. In fact, the analyst constricts himself as a person, minimizes himself as a symbol of threatening external reality, does not judge, approve or disapprove—all on the supposition that social reality exercises a threatening and prohibitive influence on individual expression. This tradition reflects Freud's projected image of paternal authority and his hypothesis of basic opposition between the individual and the surrounding culture.

We recognize now, however, that there need not be a constant state of opposition between the individual and the group. Such relations may be either oppositional or complementary, exactly as is the case in the varying relations of infant and mother. The selective nature of the interactional processes determines this variation. The complementary aspect of the relations of patient and therapist, whether in psychoanalysis or group therapy, becomes finally a potent force for therapeutic change.

In a therapeutic group it is not readily possible to offer the same artificial immunity against retaliative hurt that psychoanalysis provides. An anxious patient integrates his emotional self in the group or fails to do so, reacts or withdraws in accordance with his perception of the reality of the situation. Social reality is tangible; it is there, however fluid in form. The patient feels it quickly and inescapably. It is much more difficult to deny or suppress this than in psychoanalysis. Social reality in the group is represented in the multiple interpersonal patterns and value orientations that vie with each other for relative dominance in the group proceedings. Out of this process of spontaneous interaction the group evolves its form. It unfolds its aims, emotions, values, rules of conduct, paths of satisfaction, and paths of danger. It is this that Redl had in mind, I believe, in stating that a group develops something like an ego, superego, and id. Something like, but not identical with! In psychoanalysis, the patient deals largely with projected images of social authority. In group therapy, the patient deals with both projected and real images of social authority.

It is the patient's perceptive image of the group patterns that determines the quality of his feeling attitude and participation. Is the group as he sees it congenial or inimical to his personal needs? Will it be receptive to the expression of his conflicts, sympathetic and supportive or antagonistic and menacing? Will it oppose or complement his self-assertion? The patient is driven by the struggle between the pressure to find satisfaction of personal needs in the group and the fear of exposure, treacherous hostility, and consequent injury. On this acute struggle hinges the quality of the patient's emotional integration in the group. But the part of self which the patient exposes is selectively determined by the interaction between the pressure of personal need and anxiety associated with his perceptive picture of the group. There is nothing akin here to "free association" facilitated by the sense of immunity which comes with assurance against retaliation, as in psychoanalysis. There is rather a selective living out of specific sets of conflicted urges. In the group, then, access is achieved not immediately to the salient pathogenic components of the inner psychic life but to those specific aspects of self which become selectively involved in the group interaction and the associated conflict patterns. In other words, access to personality is partial and selective. Yet over time, with shifts in level of participation, shifts in the phases of self which become integrated in the group experience, access may be achieved gradually to progressively wider segments of the personality and associated conflict experiences. The quality and relative effectiveness of the process will depend in part on the plasticity of the patient's role adaptation in the group, this being a function of the nature of the group and the make-up of the patient's personality.

It should be clear then that three distinct, though overlapping levels of phenomena are implicated and that the group therapist must have disciplined knowledge of all three levels: (1) the processes of social structuring of the group; (2) the processes of emotional integration of the individual into the group; (3) the inner processes of the individual psyche.

The interplay of these three levels of phenomena conditions those phases of self that become dynamically involved in the group experience and accessible to therapeutic influence. In this connection it must be borne in mind that a two-way process is involved, that the group selects from the individual what its processes require and the individual selects from the group experience what he needs.

At this point it is useful theoretically to view the dynamics of group therapy as a movement from outside inward in contrast to psychoanalysis as a movement primarily from inside outward. It is necessary, furthermore, to set up hypotheses for the dynamic relations of individual personality and social role. Only along this conceptual path is it possible to correlate intrapsychic events with interpersonal ones, to correlate the image of self projected into the group role with the perceived image of the group reality, and, in this context, to evaluate the specific effects of anxiety on behavior.

It is unlikely that therapeutic change in an individual setting, as in psychoanalysis, and therapeutic change in a group, are dependent on unique psychological influences; rather the basic processes of therapeutic change are the same but are differently integrated and balanced in accordance with the differences of social structuring in the two situations. The common denominator of all forms of psychotherapy is composed of a series of interrelated and overlapping processes: an emotional relationship is developed between patient and therapist involving a dynamic "give and take" between them; through this relationship, the patient derives emotional support; in the interchange between patient and therapist opportunity is provided for the release of pent-up emotion and conflicted drives and for reality testing. Through this release and the related phenomena of reality testing, it is possible to diminish guilt and anxiety. Reality testing involves several partial processes: the examination of the immediate clash between a particular image of self and the image of prevailing interpersonal realities; the examination of the appropriateness of this image of self and the appropriateness of the image of the other person or persons involved in the interaction; and, finally, a progressive correction toward reality of the process of assimilating those conflicting images. The emotional working through of the implications of the impact between real and unreal provides the means for a gradual modification of the interpretation of interpersonal experience, particularly that which involves conflict and fear of injury. It is in this dynamic, interpersonal context that the significance of transference, resistance, and defense must be weighed. Through systematic implementation of these partial processes of interpersonal experience, psychotherapy may bring about a more correct understanding of self and more appropriate relations with the personal environment and thus make possible a more realistic and healthier adaptation.

Do the specific structural characteristics of the group qualitatively alter the balance of relations between these partial processes? My answer is affirmative. The contrast in social structuring of the two situations—psychoanalysis and group psychotherapy—predetermines a different balance in the interplay of these partial processes, modifies their form of expression, and alters the quality of the working through of these partial phenomena to the point of resolution. In particular, the processes of transference, resistance, and defense are differently organized in a group. They are structured and molded in a selective manner by the dynamics of role participation in a given group. The spontaneous interaction processes, multiple and overlapping, patterned in specific ways by the experiences of shared emotion, by currents of empathy, identification, and opposition, have the effect of selectively enhancing some components of transference and inhibiting others. The attachments, the antipathies, and the complementary and oppositional relations that spontaneously emerge in the group give the transference reactions their specific coloring. Analogous influences are brought to bear on the structuring of resistance and defense behavior.

The role of the group therapist, personifying the objectives of group, must be different from that of the psychoanalyst in some fundamental respects. He has face-to-face relations with the participants. His social identity is revealed. His emotions and counter-emotions are more exposed. He is therefore a more real person, a less magical figure; less omnipotent, less immune. He cannot be so exclusively the stimulus and object of the patient's irrational projections, nor can he be the exclusive catalyzing agent for the processes of reorientation to the meaning of interpersonal experience. Instead, he capitalizes to the full on the potentialities of the multiple interactions in the group, uses these to activate the processes of revelation of self, neutralizes any excesses of aggression, promotes the aim of mutual support and mutual constructive interpretation of the patients' conflicts. In this context, my earlier theoretical suggestion becomes more understandable, *i.e.*, the psychoanalytic situation reawakens the infantile experience of symbiotic, magic, omnipotent unity with the parent, whereas the group epitomizes in larger measure the realities of social relations. In my opinion this is the main reason that psychoanalysis is better fitted structurally to deal with those aspects of intrapsychic pathology that have a deep egocentric core and involve a distorted psychic relation to the infant-parent image and to the own body, whereas group psychotherapy has its sharpest effects on disturbances in socialization and interpersonal relations. These dynamic principles have specific applicability to the problems of interpersonal disturbances in family relationships.

The Therapy of Mothers

Let us now consider more specifically how these principles may be applied to disturbances of mothering. Mothers conceive of their emotional troubles with their children in different ways. A mother may view her difficulties as arising out of conflict with her child, or her husband, or her mother; or, by contrast, she may be convinced that the deficiency in her maternal behavior lies mainly within herself, her character, her history, or her specific personal conflicts and anxieties relating to womanliness and sexual development. In the latter instance, she may be aware of a need for therapy for herself as a whole person, not merely for her special behavior in the role of mother. In any case, a preliminary period of exploratory contact or a period of educational guidance of the mother is often necessary before a specific psychotherapeutic program can be initiated.

Disturbances of mothering behavior may be appropriately approached at several levels, according to the main determinants:

1. Therapy for deviations in the mother role, deriving mainly from conflict in a particular family pair: (a) conflict with the child; (b) conflict with the child's father; (c) conflict with the mother's mother or equivalent authority figure.

2. Therapy for deviations in the mother role, which are in the main consequences of distortion in the psychosocial structure and mental health of the family as a whole (*e.g.*, a family in which there had been no intention to bear children, or a socially disintegrated family, or a family whose psychological balance is disrupted by crisis—illness, accident, death, financial reverses, etc.).

3. Therapy for deviations in the mother role, related in the main to clashes be-

tween the requirements of the mother role, and other significant familial and extrafamilial roles (*i.e.*, clashes between the roles of mother and wife, mother and occupational or other social role).

4. Therapy for deviations in the mother role, related in the main to long-standing individual pathology of the mother's personality.

When the disturbances in the mother role are chiefly the consequence of interpersonal conflict in a specific family pair (mother-child, mother-grandmother, mother-father), the most appropriate technique is usually the joint treatment of the family pair who are locked in conflict, for the unit to be influenced is the relationship rather than one partner in isolation. The therapeutic influence is pointed directly to the interaction of the family pair, and the therapist energizes spontaneous emotional interchange between the two persons and with himself. Of special relevance are processes of distorted perception of self and other family members, mutual frustration and disappointment, mutual conflict and recrimination, denial, projection of blame, and scapegoating.

Deviations of mothering that are largely symptoms of abnormalities in the psychosocial structure of the family suggest the need for systematic psychosocial evaluation of the family group and the application of appropriate corrective measures at both the social and psychological levels. These measures might at first be most appropriately on the social work level—social welfare, guidance, and casework are sometimes necessary. Once the social factors have been clarified, it is possible to move ahead with a program of family psychotherapy.

When the deviation of mothering reflects an irreconcilable clash between the requirements of the maternal role and other roles, a two-way examination of the failure in role adaptation is needed: (1) an evaluation of the clash of role requirements within the frame of a psychosocial diagnosis of the family group, *i.e.*, how the patterns of family relationship and the adaptation of family to community contribute to the clash of role requirements and what can be done about it; (2) an evaluation of the integration of the mother's personality into the several roles she fulfills in order to discern the motivational content of the clash. What can be done to lessen the inner conflict of the mother? Can she drop one of the conflicting roles, or assign it a subordinate position, or modify the expectations of conflicting roles so as to lessen the intensity of the clash? In the more extreme cases, when the mother is mentally ill, it may be necessary for the therapist to see that one of the roles is dropped, thus relieving pressure and a feeling of excessive responsibility in order to achieve access to other levels of disturbance. In less extreme cases, it is possible to modify the balance of anxiety so that the mother is less threatened and better able to function in all her roles. For example, a woman who has difficulty integrating her roles of mother and sexual partner can be helped by parallel treatment of the mother-child relationship and the husband-wife relationship. Such treatment can be focused in such a way that she becomes aware of her escape into an exclusive mother-child relationship as a way of retreating from sexual contact and is helped to adjust the two roles in accordance with her new perceptions.

Finally, when the deviation of mother is largely an expression of long-standing pathology of the mother's personality, a form of individual psychotherapy specifically suited to her pathology must be the ultimate goal, although a certain amount of supportive therapy or counseling or two-person treatment may be necessary before intensive individual treatment can be begun.

Or we may approach the whole matter of therapy for disturbed mothers in another way—by establishing a rough hierarchy of levels of contact, categories of psychotherapeutic process differentiated in accordance with the depth of influence to be exerted on the personality.

1. Guidance or re-education
   a. by support
   b. by emotional release
   c. by clarification of attitudes
2. Reorganization of the conscious functions of personality integrated into the maternal role
   a. by use of authority, command, advice, persuasion
   b. by the reorientation and re-education of conscious attitudes through intellectual clarification; by giving factual informaiton with respect to problems of mothering and child development
3. Reorganization of the unconscious functions of personality as they impinge on the integration of personality into the maternal role.
   a. by a deliberate utilization of transference and knowledge of the unconscious forces of the personality to promote a redirection of the mother's destructive urges away from the child to another personal object, or a redirection of these urges into other activities, for example, work; by the exploitation of known patterns of defense, reaction formation, and sublimation to relieve the child of an excessive load of the mother's hostility
   b. by the establishment of the goal of basic character change in the mother: a systematic, intensive psychotherapy at the level of psychoanalysis, which involves a deeper, more complete therapeutic experience, systematically employing the technique of dealing with transference, resistance, dreams, and the ordered interpretations of unconscious sources of conflict and anxiety.

It is apparent that these various levels of therapeutic approach can be combined in whatever manner seems suitable for the individual patient. Certain mothers must be approached mainly on a supportive level, where the therapeutic gain rests chiefly on the added security that the patient gets from a sustained and reliable dependence on the therapist. Other mothers respond well to a combination of support and emotional release. The exclusive use of the supportive level of treatment might be suggested by the presence of a dull intelligence, by weak integrative functions in the personality (*i.e.*, a deficient capacity for synthesizing emotional experience), by the presence of rigid emotionality, extreme egocentricity, fixed, inflexible infantile traits, irreversible physical defects or disease, advanced age, a deteriorated family, or other reality factors.

A combination of support and emotional release might be indicated where there is poor or mediocre intelligence, limited capacity for emotional rapport and for insight, rigid emotionality, and other circumstantial factors. A combination of support and repression might be suggested by the presence of a weak or deteriorated ego, by the presence of severe affect disorders and lack of self-control.

A combination of support, release, and some active effort toward reorganizing the conscious functions of personality may be used in persons with a good intelligence and a good coordinative capacity. A measure of emotional flexibility is also required for the use of such therapy. Within limits, this type of treatment may be applied to those persons who depend habitually on intellectual control for competence in dealing with life's problems.

The deepest form of therapy involving support, release, and the use of transference, resistance, and insight mechanisms is indicated for disorders having important sources in unconscious conflicts, particularly those that result in specific symptom formation. Such therapy requires a good intelligence, capacity for ego integration, and a capacity for emotional rapport.

Of course, no one of these methods is feasible unless the mother is suitably motivated to seek out help. But assuming sufficient motivation, the therapist must respect the mother's own attitudes toward her problems of mothering and the quality of her incentive for help. How does she perceive her difficulties and feel about them? How does she try to help herself? What level of help does she seek from the therapist? What a mother wants and what the therapist believes she needs may not agree, but once a clear understanding of goals is reached, the appropriate kind or kinds of therapy can proceed.

The Therapy of Children

Therapy of children, of course, poses somewhat different problems at the outset. As we have seen, the child is brought to the therapist with very little idea of what psychological help from this strange adult may mean to him. Therefore, the techniques of child therapy are, in a sense, qualitatively different. The role of the therapist is threefold: (1) auxiliary parent; (2) educator, promoting growth and increasing mastery of new experience and positive mental health; (3) therapeutic agent, facilitating the expression, relief, and fuller understanding of pathogenic conflict and anxiety in the child.

It is the therapist's duty to be a partner to the child's parent in providing care, protection, and affection to the child. He provides for the child a feeling of acceptance, respect, and security against danger. He offers gratification of the child's need to be understood and loved. He must often provide for the child the emotional satisfactions of which he has been deprived within his own family. To this extent, the therapist, as an auxiliary and improved version of parent is a provider of positive emotional experience with an adult, of the kind in which his family relations have been deficient.

Because the child is immature, in process of growth, and not yet integrated into society, the therapist plays a part with the parents and teacher in socializing the child and training him to meet the responsibility of integrating into the social community. The therapist must exercise discriminatory ethical judgments about permitting or restraining certain impulses and actions. He is permissive of the release of harmless and safe forms of destructive activity in order to achieve access to conflict, guilt, and anxiety in the child, but he does not condone destructiveness. Where destructive urges become a real threat to the child's security, the therapist's person, or valuable property, the therapy intervenes with firm restraint.

The therapist's responsibility is to foster the development of a firm close emotional relationship with the child which facilitates communication, mutual acceptance, and understanding. This takes time. A child's trust of a therapist cannot be anticipated in the beginning. It must evolve gradually as the child tests again and again the therapist's intentions toward him.

Play activity is used often, since it is the natural medium of expression in a child. Play activity is closely tied to the child's tendency to communicate through body expression and motor activity. Play fulfills a significant role for a child in testing reality, and in expanding his mastery. It is also a form of communication. The therapist talks with the child through play. The pattern of play dramatizes the child's emotional experience, his conflicts, his guilts and fears and reflects the gap between what is real and what is phantasy in the child's mind.

As the relationship unfolds and the child, with numerous testings of the therapist's intentions, feels more secure and trusting, the therapist achieves increasing access to the child's inner emotional life. Through the device of interpretation, the therapist translates to the child the unreal foundations of his conflicts and fears and thus relieves the child of this burden.

But this very role of auxiliary parent presents a special problem to the child therapist. Disturbed children are often the victims of emotional deprivation, true enough. They suffer an emotional deficiency, but this condition cannot be equated to a simple deficiency disease. The deficiency in emotional nutrition is a complicated one. Such children are emotionally starved and acutely in need of love and yet are often unable to receive it. They distrust a show of love from an adult person; they tend not to believe it is genuine. They are frequently guarded and suspicious and test an offering of warmth and affection many times over before they risk accepting it. When they finally do, they may feel guilty and undeserving, commit some provocative act to incite punishment, and thereby undo the value of the love offering. If the fear and suspicion are intense, the child may deny his oral dependent need, cease to reach out for love, and substitute an attitude of emotional detachment. If the therapist breaks through this defensive detachment prematurely, the child may strike out aggressively. Occasionally, the provocative lashing out of a disturbed child is a disguised way of expressing the child's underlying emotional hunger.

Such considerations as these confront a child therapist with a special challenge: "to give or not to give love—and how?" The problem of love hunger in a disturbed child must be clearly conceptualized. It is easy for a therapist to fail in his understanding and use of the concept of "giving love." A misuse of the giving of love in child therapy can arise in three ways: from an inadequate knowledge of normal and psychopathological child development; through the intrusion into the relationship of inappropriate attitudes arising from unconscious needs in the therapist, however rationalized they may be; from a sheer deficiency in therapeutic skill.

The giving of love to an emotionally hungry child cannot be a therapeutic "technique." It must be a genuine and sincere warmth. And a therapist can provide this love satisfaction to a child only as he removes, step by step, the suspicion and defensive barricade which the child has built around him. The mistrust and provocative aggression of a disturbed child constitute a roadblock that prevents the child from pursuing the path of friendship and affection. Now and then, the defensive aggression of the child may get out of control. When it does, the therapist must provide control from without in the form of passive physical restraint. Such restraint is indicated if a panicked, angry child lashes out blindly, and there is danger of the child inflicting self-injury, injury to the person of the therapist or causing damage to valued property. If such outbursts are controlled by passive physical restraint, without any vindictive motive on the therapist's part, it lessens the child's guilt and gradually makes him more ready to receive the therapist's warmth as a genuine show of understanding and love. It is well to realize that a child therapist cannot ever compensate or make up for a lack of love that a child may have experienced in infancy. This is past and done. It cannot be magically undone. What the therapist can do is gradually modify the child's anxiety-ridden perceptions and emotional expectations so that here and now he may learn to accept love as love, profit by it, and ultimately return it.

In meeting this problem, a child therapist should be alerted to the risk of intrusion of a variety of inappropriate unconscious motives on his part, which may become expressed consciously as an urge "to give love," but really contain in disguise less salutary motives: a need to control or intimidate the child, to shut off the flow of the child's hostility; a neurotic need to be loved or aggrandized by the child; a fear of the child's rejection; an uncontrolled overidentification with the child, expressing rivalry with the child's love need or his destructive rebellion; a fear of therapeutic failure; the urge to "give love" as a device for bribing or disarming the child or as a device for expressing in disguise a competitive hostility to the child's mother or other child therapists.

In psychotherapy as in life, an offering of warmth, interest, and affection must be a true offering, not a manipulative technique. It should be well timed, when the child's suspicion, fear and hate are neutralized and the matrix of the child's emotional life is properly receptive.

The Therapy of Adolescents

The treatment of the disturbances of adolescents likewise involves the therapist in the role of auxiliary parent; this role demands great flexibility and serves to document further the usefulness of various techniques. Of course, there are some who claim that the special features of adolescent personality, the rapid sexual maturation, the instability of the self-system, the erratic, unpredictable changes in social conduct, the acute anxiety over sexual conflict, tend to hinder the accessibility of adolescents to psychotherapeutic influence. There are others who emphasize the self-absorption and high narcissism of this period as deterrents to therapy; therefore, they counsel patience and argue for a postponement of therapy to the period of adulthood.

I am convinced, on the basis of personal experience, that adolescence is an era strongly favorable for therapy. The fluid, dynamic qualities of adolescent behavior, although injecting an element of risk in the outcome of therapy, may in the end, if correctly exploited, be advantageous for therapy. The adolescent personality, being mobile and suggestible, is highly amenable to interpersonal influence, including the therapeutic one. This is especially so if a concurrent program of therapy of the family is joined to the direct psychotherapy of the adolescent as an individual. Thus, therapeutic interviews with the adolescent and his parents and with the parents alone are indicated as one of the useful techniques.

In the beginning, certain factors may make the task of establishing rapport more difficult: the adolescent's characteristic mistrust of adults, his shift of allegiance to his peers, his egocentricity, evasiveness, and belligerence. I have found often that at the start the transference problems are touchy, delicate, and frequently quite complicated. Access to the adolescent's significant experience is difficult to achieve, and the flow of contact may be erratic. The adolescent's sense of responsibility to the therapeutic situation may be unsteady. Also, if the therapist does not prove himself worthy in the initial tests and unintentionally injures the patient's self-esteem, he may easily lose the patient. These are all serious potential risks for the therapy.

If, however, the therapist skillfully pilots his way through these early dangers, the therapeutic tie becomes intensely strong and reliable and is able to withstand even serious crises. In the later stages of therapy, adolescents show extraordinary powers for the working through of conflicted emotions; they have unusual capacities for perception and for the development of new insights into unconscious processes. Once past the early hazards of the therapeutic relationship, it is my experience that adolescents become excellent patients and benefit enormously.

For selected cases, psychoanalytically oriented psychotherapy works exceedingly well. I make this statement with some qualifications; the analytic technique must be carefully adapted to individual adolescent need. Because the patient's reality testing capacities are often inadequate, the therapist must personify the tangible reality of the surrounding social environment. Wherever the orientation to the external world proves defective, the therapist should be ready and able to translate reality for the patient in a simple, easily assimilated, and unthreatening way. This is vital to the adolescent's effort to build an integrated control over his emotional drives.

Therapy conducted on an easy, flexible, informal basis makes the adolescent as comfortable as possible and allows the broadest possible range of adaptation to rapid changes in situation and behavior. The therapist must assume a strongly supporting role; he is required by the adolescent's need to be a direct parent substitute. Through the feeling of protection which the adolescent derives from this relationship, he is encouraged to face the anxiety that he feels in expanding experiences and relationships. It is important for the therapist continuously to counteract potential threats of injury to the patient's self-esteem and thus carefully guard the adolescent's personal pride.

Of particular importance is the working out of the confusion and anxiety that is associated with the patient's striving for a more secure sexual identity. In this struggle, the adolescent requires sustained help in achieving adequate control over his sexual urges and the associated aggression. Frequently, a patient is excessively preoccupied with sexual need but is completely unready for sexual experience due to specific emotional distortions and generalized immaturity. It is the therapist's function, in such situations, to help the patient to see clearly his unreadiness and thus win the patient's cooperation in waiting until he is ready. Often such patients are deeply relieved by being told directly that they are not yet prepared for such experiences.

The issue of the therapist's identification with the patient is, of course, of central significance. The patient sorely needs the feeling that the therapist is on his side, feels his emotional pain; but empathy must be controlled and regulated to keep faith with therapeutic objectives.

For the majority of emotionally disturbed adolescents, it proves substantially helpful to provide an experience in group psychotherapy as a supplement to individual psychotherapy. The group experience has special value in relation to the need for an exchange of experience with peers. In many instances, the usefulness of working out conflicts through identification with other adolescents in a group therapeutic experience is unique and irreplacable. Indeed, the most striking aspect, by far, in the behavior of adolescents in group therapy is their yearning to complete their incomplete selves. They simply do not feel whole, and from this feeling arises a painful tension. Transparent indeed is their effort to extract selectively from their group experience that which they lack, so that they may be strengthened and enhanced and in their own eyes more closely approximate their ideal image of themselves.

In the proceedings of group therapy two related dynamic trends stand out sharply, the adolescent's reactions to shifting images of self; propelled from within by the physiological processes of maturation, and from without by the demands of the outside world. On the one hand, they must accommodate to the pressures of sexual need, to changes in physique and appearance; on the other hand, they must accommodate to what others expect of them. In this last respect they are influenced in two ways: by their beliefs as to what the opposite sex wants of them, and what members of the same sex expect of them, particularly those whom they admire and wish to emulate. The adolescent personality is squeezed between those several conflicting pressures. This is the pivot around which much of the therapeutic interaction in the group proceeds. On this stage of conflict is reflected the confusions and anxieties relating to sexual identity, the feelings of inferiority associated with awareness of physical difference, the compensating aggressive reactions to anxiety. On this stage, too, emerge responses of guilt and shame; guilt deriving particularly from conflicted sexual temptation and aggressive impulses, and shame deriving from exhibitionistic urges, preoccupation with shortcomings and failure to live up to the idealized image of self. In this connection the dread of ridicule and humiliation is often intense.

Again and again conflict with personal authority intrudes on the scene, literally loaded with the ambivalent emotions of unresolved dependence, the urge to demonstrate self-sufficiency, and the apprehension of one or another form of castration. It is not true, however, that the stage of adolescent conflict represents purely the reactivation of unresolved oedipal conflict. What one observes actually is a reactivation of all significant previous levels of conflict, oedipal and pre-oedipal as well. Clearly dramatized here are the deep formative influences of the "oral" and "anal" levels of personality on the later emerging genital conflicts. Equally transparent are the patterns of defense mobilized aaginst guilt and anxiety deriving from these conflicts.

The therapeutic group provides a social testing ground for the distorted, inappropriate perceptions of self and relations with others, deriving from all the stages of maturation. On this testing ground the adolescent has opportunity gradually to put his confusion to one side and to achieve some dependable, stable clarity in his personal identity. A biweekly group experience is conceived as a supplement to individual therapy, not as an independent therapy.

I have found that in some instances individual therapy is a necessary preparation for the group, especially when the initial psychiatric examination reveals serious illness. In other cases, however, group therapy can be considered as emotional preparation for individual therapy. Generally, this judgment is best reached by mutual discussion between patient and therapist.

Ideally, the group itself consists of eight or ten adolescents. In my own practice the responsibility for treatment is shared by several therapists who treat some of the members on an individual basis. Attendance is voluntary (though absences tend to be rare and, when they occur, unavoidable). The composition of the group varies: old patients leave; new ones are added; a member marries and brings the spouse; visitors are welcome, whether they be friends of members or interested professionals. Diagnostically, all categories of personality are included except frank psychoses. Altogether the group is an extremely mobile and flexible unit.

The various types of reaction displayed by adolescents to the suggestion of group therapy may of themselves be used for therapeutic purposes. At one extreme are the patients who react initially with fright and dread of attack, exposure, and ridicule, who seem dominated by anticipatory phantasies of aggressive dangers lurking in such an exposed experience. Obviously the intensity of this initial reaction derives from the projection of their own aggressive impulses and they react with a strong urge to retreat. At the other pole are those rarer individuals who burst with delight at the anticipation of group experience, who indulge in pleasant phantasies about a grand and glorious landing in the group, of creating a tremendous impression. These are the adolescents with a strong push toward impressing others with their superior attributes, their sexual finesse and triumphs. They are the aggressive, impulsive exhibitionists who hide their anxiety behind their competitive aggressive drive—and the group is a useful instrument for taming these bold ones.

Between these extremes is every intermediate type. Usually the reaction is an ambivalent one: the appetite for direct gratification of personal need in the group is whetted while at the same time the excitement is tempered by the stirring of anxiety connected with anticipatory phantasies of exposure, betrayal, and humiliation. One possible factor in this reaction may derive from certain components of transference: the patient extends from the individual therapist to the group his repressed hope of getting direct gratification of sexual need, as well as his guilt, fear of punishment, and urge to retreat. In certain instances, the mere suggestion of group therapy energizes the working through of specific problems previously undisclosed. In this sense the very anticipation of group therapy holds some potential for enhancing individual sessions.

Specifically, as we have already seen, a group situation provides a spontaneous interaction process quite different from that provided by individual psychoanalytic therapy. This interaction may show itself even before the beginning of a formal therapy session. Who sits next to whom and why? If the sexes sit apart, it may indicate disguised sexual tension or the awareness that someone is "making a play" for someone else. If a particular boy seats himself next to a particular girl, he excites admiration, envy, competitive maneuvering, and barbed jokes. The special role of the therapist causes further interaction. His readiness to begin the session may produce a hushed silence and the tension of suspense. Who will make the first move to expose himself? Will the therapist "pick on someone"? The danger of hurtful consequences from exposure seems ever present. The mutual suspicion of the two sexes is striking. The boys shove the girls into the open; the girls shove the boys; they tease each other. Each wants the other to uncover; each wants to see and be seen but fears being hurt in the process. Sooner or later the tension cracks and someone opens up. Whatever the subject matter, the members listen with rapt attention, envious of the person holding the center of the stage but constrained by a sense of fair play—though, with true ambivalence, if offered the floor they will often demur.

In a typical instance, the adolescent covers himself by couching his problem in social terms, obscuring the specific psychological content, until the influence of the group and the therapist strip away the protective garb and achieve a clear, straightforward definition, articulated and revealed in personal terms. Some members may immediately be tempted to exploit the patient's personal exposure for attack; the greater the personal anxiety, the greater the temptation to seize this way of releasing hostility. Frequently, the patient is pleasantly surprised and rewarded by a show of support and encouragement, often from unexpected quarters. In any case, the problem is batted back and forth, and bit by bit the emotional content becomes more precisely and nudely revealed. The very process of interaction focuses the problem with speed and clarity. The group itself has become a therapeutic agent.

The therapists' contribution has several facets. Words as words are anathema, but it is his effort that reaches behind the words to the genuine emotion being experienced. With calculated intention he ignores the talk that is mere talk. He must be intensely attentive to nonverbal patterns of behavior, facial expressions, body posturings, quick shifts in motor behavior as patients react to the stimuli of group interaction processes. The therapist's spirit in reaching out for genuine emotional communication is contagious and affects the attitudes of group members; the push for more honest self-revelation is accelerated. Occasionally, the therapist interprets an obvious expressional attitude or encourages the group to do so by arousing their curiosity. For example, a girl yawns at the very moment a boy points a personal sexual comment her way; the escape motive in the yawn is interpreted. Or a girl repeatedly brings flame to her cigarette lighter and promptly blows it out; she is intensely castrative toward boys, and the implications of her gesture are discussed.

Of particular importance in the group atmosphere is the shedding of conventional social hypocrisies. Adolescents detest polite dishonesties and are genuinely grateful for a group experience in which they can shrug off the unpleasant burdens of conventionality and the sanctioned patterns of deception in social relations. It is of significant cathartic value, and it adds something to their strength and dignity to be accepted for their real selves rather than for their conformity. The group develops an ethos and morality of its own but of an open, flexible, growing kind.

Altogether the interaction processes of the group lend themselves effectively to the purpose of pointing out the distortions in the patient's interpretation of both self and group reality. It is this phenomenon that has impelled me to attempt a formulation of the dynamic relations of individual personality to group role. Access to personality in the group is partial, not total. The level of access achieved is the dynamic content of the patient's role adaptation in the group, i.e., the self-image projected into the group at a particular time and under particular interpersonal circumstances. As temporal and situational factors change, so does the patient's role adaptation. Over a period of time, therefore, it is possible to achieve therapeutic access to a series of integrative levels of personality functioning.

Although such access is of particular importance during the "unstable" period of adolescence, its value to any sort of therapeutic intervention is obvious. Indeed, the special comments made here about therapy of mothers and adolescents are to a large degree pertinent to the therapy of fathers and marital pairs as well. Adequate motivation, a clear understanding of goals, a flexible use of the primary techniques and their derivatives are all necessary to the success of any psychotherapeutic undertaking.

CHAPTER 18

GOALS OF PSYCHOTHERAPY

THE SINGLE, all-encompassing goal of therapy is cure. But what is cure? The question poses many problems: the multiple meanings of the term "cure"; the relations of cure to changing conceptions of illness and health, to the specific illness and person being treated, to the conditions of treatment and the nature of the curing process itself. There are also the further problems of assessing the quality of the cure, its quantity, partial or relatively complete, and testing the reliability of the cure.

At the present stage, it is safe to assume that standards for cure and the relations of cure to illness and to the curing process are by no means uniform. In these respects there are in our day wide divergences of orientation among the various schools of psychotherapy and among individual therapists themselves. In one sense each therapist evolves a relatively personal set of criteria for the goals of therapy and the signs of cure. From one point of view, this will perhaps always be the case; from another, it reflects a present state of affairs which is by no means ideal.

Insofar as psychotherapy is a healing art that expresses the therapist's unique use of his personal talents in the curative role, there must always be striking variations from one therapist to the next in the practice of this art and in the corresponding judgments of the attainment of cure. Going one step further, the therapist's creativity as an artist will achieve varying expression in accordance with the unique interpersonal stimuli by which he is confronted in his relation with each of his patients. The form of his art and the conviction of cure will vary in each instance. The final portrait must always be molded both by the particular patient who is the model and the gifts of the particular artist. Psychotherapy as art is highly personal and cannot, should not, be reduced to a stereotype. But that component of psychotherapy that is the healing art cannot go very far unless it is solidly buttressed by scientific knowledge of personality, psychopathology, interpersonal relations, and the dynamics of therapeutic process. In principle the psychotherapist labors under a critical handicap unless his talent rests securely on scientific training, experience, and wisdom.

The fate of any psychotherapeutic undertaking is influenced by at least four factors: the character of the patient, the character of the therapist, the unique features of emotional communication between them, and the impingement of environmental forces on both persons and on what goes on between them. Today, of necessity, any discussion of these issues must be incomplete because our understanding of cure and the curing process reflects the same lag that prevails in our understanding of the processes of illness and health. The definitions of goals of therapy must inevitably mirror these changing conceptions. Therefore, present hypotheses must be considered to be tentative and provisional. Yet they must be thoughtfully evaluated.

It is commonly known to clinicians that a considerable gap has grown up between clinical diagnosis and therapy. Traditional categories of clinical diagnosis seem to be of small value in planning therapy. Specificity in the treatment of psychiatric disorders is difficult to achieve. The conceptual gap between diagnosis and therapy is due in one sense to the fact that the knowledge of therapy seemed to spurt forward faster than diagnosis. Systems of psychiatric classification are now outmoded. There is another pertinent issue, however, which has to do with the basic relations between diagnosis and therapy. By its very nature, diagnosis needs to be a total, comprehensive definition of a disturbance, whereas therapy is generally a partial, selective intervention on certain levels of the disturbance. With presently known treatment methods we can only intervene selectively on certain facets of the phenomenon of illness. We do not know how to alter its entirety. Thus diagnosis is total, complete, whereas therapy is partial. This principle has special relevance for the treatment of a disturbed individual and his family.

The term "cure" implies, first of all, the therapeutic removal of symptoms, those specific signs of disordered functioning that characterize a particular illness. For some therapists this removal constitutes the sole meaning of cure; it is conceived as a significant result, sufficient unto itself. Perhaps for certain forms of mental illness, this outcome is good enough. For many therapists, however, and for a great variety of disturbances of mental health, this first meaning is too limiting. A second implication of cure is the dissolution of vulnerability to illness. Treatment is expected to strengthen personality so that the patient will not again fall ill, to provide immunization against a further invasion of illness. Third is the idea that the personality of the patient must have undergone a basic change, signifying not only increased adaptive strength and capacity for resistance to illness but, in a positive sense, the ability to realize potential, to capitalize on personal resources so as to feel free and happy, satisfy personal needs, and be an efficient, productive person. Finally, cure may also mean that the individual, freed of crippling anxieties, can now unfold his capacity for loving others, can share with them both pleasure and responsibility, and can experience the full gamut of satisfaction in making a positive contribution to the welfare of family, friends, and community.

Thus, the goals of therapy and the connotations of cure constitute a hierarchy of meanings, which may be applied with flexibility and discrimination to a wide assortment of illnesses and psychotherapeutic undertakings. In some it may make sense to rest content with a lesser cure; in others it is fitting and right that we aspire to a more complete and superior cure.

But how do we know? What in any given case constitutes the proof of cure? We must build a set of criteria by which to test the adequacy of cure in those several hierarchical meanings. The first criterion is the easiest. The evidence for the disappearance of structured psychopathological symptoms is certainly basic to cure and least equivocal. As soon as we move on to evidence for the strengthening of personality and immunization against recurrent illness, we are on less sure ground; the standards grow hazy, and differences among therapists mount. Some speak vaguely of the signs of "ego-strengthening" or increased maturity and stability. Others erect more stringent and specific criteria, centering around favorable directions of change in anxiety response, ways of coping with conflict, control of emotion and impulse, defense operations, affectivity, self-esteem, interpersonal relations, and reality perception. Finally, if we inspect those criteria that demonstrate increased capacity for self-fulfillment and healthier interpersonal relations, we discover almost as much diversity among therapists as there are therapists themselves. The ultimate test of the validity of the quality of cure is the individual's adaptation to family and community. It is exactly here that we find so great a range of difference in therapists' evaluations.

One way of testing progress toward cure is the patient's increasing understanding of his relationship with his therapist. Step by step, as the twists of transference are worked through and a more appropriate image of self and therapist emerges, we may feel increasing confidence in the cure. Mistrust of psychotherapy cannot be dissociated from mistrust of the therapist and mistrust of the self. Mistrust in the patient expresses itself in avoidance of a close relationship, in the defensive preservation of a certain detachment from the therapist. Emotional alienation from the therapist is usually paralleled by the patient's alienation from his own emotions. This tends to express itself in specific patterns of resistance, self-protective behavior that reflects a fear of exposure to hurt, and apprehension of exploitation or betrayal by the therapist. In this context, the patient reveals a lack of faith in the possibility of therapeutic change. He enters therapy, yet he cherishes his secret belief that therapy is some magic hoax that does not really change anyone. The patient sets out to relieve his suffering and change himself but clings privately and paradoxically to the belief that the powers of psychotherapy are nil. Often at a point nearing termination of therapy these deeper suspicions and resistances become critically intensified and, unless the therapist is vigilant, may nullify the results of therapy. The patient often harbors the secret motivation of mollifying the therapist and escaping from the relationship untouched. He may treasure the phantasy of outwitting the therapist, so that he may stay exactly as he was.

Regardless of critical waves of suspicion and resistance, effective and secure progress toward cure must be mirrored in a tangible forward movement in the patient-therapist relationship, expressed in several ways: diminution of evidences of emotional alienation, increased intimacy, heightening of the quality of emotional communication, increased sincerity and spontaneity, progressive clarification of the image of self and image of the therapist.

Assuming some measure of success in the lessening of anxiety, the resolution of pathogenic conflicts, the removal of symptoms, the melting of regressive defenses, and the repair of damaged self-esteem, the therapist must keep a close watch for tell-tale signs of growing trust and intimacy and an increasing sense of equality. The greater openness, spontaneity, and honesty of the patient take the place of the earlier mistrust and fear of exposure and hurt at the hands of the therapist.

As the patient enters this stage, there is progressively less discrepancy between his verbal utterances and his affective behavior. Words are used not to hide but to reveal. Verbal statements, body movement, action patterns, and affectivity begin to reflect something approaching a harmonious whole. Whenever there is a significant incongruity between the several levels of behavior, it is invariably an index of the disproportionate pressure of anxiety and the prevalence of pathological defense behavior. Under such condidtions, effective emotional communication is interfered with. As trust in the therapist increases and emotional communication improves, the patient draws previously dissociated components of his psyche into one piece; he is, in effect, pulling himself together. In a parallel trend, instead of investing himself in the therapeutic relationship in a partial, segmented, and compromised way, he commits himself more totally to the relationship. Accordingly, verbal utterances, body behavior, and affective expression merge perceptibly into a unity. At the same time, he is better able to assimilate evidences of unconscious tendencies, particularly as revealed in dreams. All these trends converge to a point of optimal trust and acceptance of the therapist as a helping person, a friend rather than an enemy, a supporter rather than a punitive authority. Full trust of the therapist comes late and with a show of great stubbornness. When genuine trust emerges, the therapist's sincerity and benign purposes have already been tested in innumerable ways. The therapy may then be said to be really beginning and also approaching its end.

In the course of this process, the patient's inner face and the face he presents to the outer world tend to merge and at the same time, he reaches a clearer and more accurate perception of surrounding realities. These critical shifts in the interpersonal experience of patient and therapist are increasingly reflected in the patient's performance in real life, in work, in personal relations with family, friends, and community.

Because by its very nature psychotherapy is a shared experience, any decision as to the goal of therapy and the proof of cure must take into account the patient's strivings as well as the therapist's standards. Such judgments, as well as the timing of termination, should not be made arbitrarily or unilaterally by the therapist but should rather reflect a consensus between patient and therapist.

If we accept the premise that a logical relationship exists between ends and means, then the means of cure—the psychotherapeutic relationship and communication process—must correspond to the goal of therapy. If the goal of therapy is cure in its several meanings, then the therapist must himself be properly cured. It is the ethical obligation of a therapist to do everything conceivable to get cured, stay cured, and continue to grow as a person. To paraphrase Erich Fromm, the only tool a psychotherapist has is himself, and as a surgeon cares for his knife so must a therapist keep himself clean and sharp. Only as he fulfills this responsibility can he achieve his goal with his patient.

The therapist, through his own being, must provide the proof to his patient that mental health is no mirage, that it can be achieved. The patient uses his therapist as a model, a test for his faith in psychotherapy. Does mental health really exist? Do people really love? Is it possible, after all, to reconcile one person's strivings for satisfaction with the needs of others, or is it inevitable that in asserting oneself one hurts another? When a patient seeks an answer to these questions, he takes a close look at his therapist. The therapist personifies the ideal of mental health as reflected in his behavior as an individual, as a living representation of healthy patterns of human relations. In this sense, through his attitudes, goals, values, and interpersonal relations, he epitomizes a standard of a healthy social being. Through the emotional interaction of patient and therapist, it becomes possible to correct the patient's distorted image of self and also his view of social reality. The ultimate test of cure is, of course, the patient's performance in life itself, the alleviation of his suffering and dread, his confidence and courage in facing life, his capacity to grow, to live fully, to love and share with others the great adventure of the only life he knows. Thus, the therapist, as he looks at his patient, must also look at the broader outlines of his life. He must consider the patient's sharing of life with significant other persons. He must hold any cure partial and incomplete that does not produce a healthy patient in a healthy family.

As we move away from the traditionally narrow concern with the individual and the internal economy of personality to interpersonal adaptation and the relations of individual to family and society, our scientific knowledge becomes progressively less precise and we enter that no-man's land of the relation of values to mental health. As soon as we think of cure not merely as the elimination of mental disease but also as the promotion of positive health in relations with self and other persons, we are confronted with the search for meaning. The meaning of life can only be discovered in the alignment of one's conception of self with the significant relations with others. Meaning is not to be found in the isolated individual; for one who walls himself off, life becomes more and more empty. Values are derivatives of social relations and serve as guideposts for social action. They reflect basic life attitudes, ideals, and motivations, upon which we base our actions toward desired goals. They structure the individual's orientation to his place and role in his family and wider community. They are functions of the interaction of self-image, image of others, and perception of social reality.

Values and the direction and quality of the corresponding social actions are symptomatic of healthy or unhealthy mental functioning. To quote Burgum, "it is impossible to define mental health apart from considerations of appropriate action toward common good. Common good may be between parent and child, husband and wife, friend and neighbor, workers on a job, members of a community." [1] Assuming such premises are valid, it follows that the goals of psychotherapy and the appraisal of evidences of cure will be directly affected by the interaction of the respective value orientations of patient and therapist.

To make the issue concrete, can a therapist consider a patient cured if his values remain oriented to a goal of self-realization at the expense of others? Can a patient be cured if his self-esteem remains tied to a form of competitiveness and ruthless aggression which threatens injury or destruction to other persons? When therapists encourage patients in self-assertiveness, it behooves them to consider the interpersonal matrix in which the self-assertion is expressed. When "strengthening of self-assertion" is translated into harm of another person, the therapist must take heed. To encourage this is to cripple the patient's self-esteem, for to build oneself up by tearing another down brings shame, mortification, and a crippling of capacity for effective action. The therapist's goal is not to unharness such destructiveness but rather to modify the image of self and others and the related values so that the patient may learn for the first time the satisfaction of self-expression in consonance with the good of others, rather than in opposition.

When a patient asserts a claim on the therapist for unconditional acceptance and love, it usually reflects a need to deny inner guilt concerning destructive motivation. The patient demands an uncritical tolerance of the bad as well as the good in himself. It is the therapist's task to win the allegiance of the healthier and more reasoning parts of the patient's personality in the struggle to modify the sick and destructive parts. The patient needs to discover that the therapist understands and accepts him as a human being although he rejects the sick part, the destructiveness, and the related distortions of value attitude. When a manipulative patient treats people as things, it is not in the interest of cure for the therapist to accept this value.

There is discernible today an increasing need among therapists to consider cure not merely in terms of bringing about the "return of the repressed" or expanding awareness of intrapsychic conflict but also in terms of dissolving distortions of self-identity and corresponding distortions of interpersonal relations. The sharp increase in preoccupation with ego psychology, group dynamics, and the theory of interpersonal communication bears testimony to this. The growing investigations of problems of interpersonal communication all move in the same direction. Within this broader conceptual frame, the role of values becomes less ambiguous. Cure becomes an experience in which the assertion of individual needs, whether for security, self-esteem, power, or sexual fulfillment, complements the needs of other significant persons, rather than the achievement of satisfaction at the cost of another. Acquiring a healthy image of self involves a correct perception of the images of others and of their needs, a respect for the dignity, integrity, and worth of others, a growing capacity for equality in human relations, as opposed to an orientation to power and exploitive relations between human beings. As we learn more about the relation of values to mental health, we may find in psychotherapy a way to diminish the tensions of interpersonal adaptation, particularly in those spheres in which an individual experiences the clash of requirements of different life roles. For example, we may be able to lessen the tensions of the woman who must harmonize the role requirements of wife, mother, and career. Inevitably, a therapist must concern himself with the problems of joining value and action, action and consequence.

The clash of values between patient and therapist provides an effective basis for the working through of residual components of disturbance. This need not mean in any sense that the therapist engages in a mission of moral conversion of the patient to the therapist's value position. It does mean that the patient is challenged to examine critically the implications of value conflicts within himself and between himself and the therapist if he is to get well and realize his human potentials.

It is in this broader context that we must weigh the elusive problem of the relation of psychotherapy to ethics and values. The patient's emotionally barricaded, egocentric orientation gradually gives way to the development of a true social bond, a friendship between patient and therapist. The patient becomes increasingly motivated to cultivate a two-way relationship with the therapist as he achieves relief of his internal distress and his social disablement. The patient's orientation becomes sociocentric rather than egocentric, as the relationship moves toward mutuality of interest and respect.

As this occurs, the issue of value orientation comes more and more into the foreground. The patient begins to ask what kind of person he is, matching his view of himself against the kind of person the therapist is. The link between personal identity and value orientation comes into focus. It is this exploration of the significance of differences in identity and values between patient and therapist that spurs further movement in the emotional interaction of patient and therapist. At this stage, then, patient and therapist wrestle with the meaning of differences in perspective on life and human relations. The patient asks what is the meaning of becoming well in relation to a particular view of life. The goals of psychotherapeutic cure become linked to image of self, image of others, and the related life values.

CHAPTER 19

INTEGRATIVE FAMILY THERAPY

LOGICALLY VIEWED, a systematic therapy of the family must encompass techniques directed at the multiple interpenetrating relationships within the family and the processes of adaptation of family to community, as well as techniques for psychotherapy of individual family members. In this context, the therapeutic approach to the family group per se is primary and the psychotherapy of individual members secondary. In other words, the relation of individual psychotherapy to the therapy of the family is the relation of the part to the whole. Family therapy must therfore rest on a unified diagnostic formulation for the dynamic processes of family life within which is included the adaptation of the individual personality to the respective family roles.

A therapeutic approach to the emotional disturbances of family life must begin, therefore, with a psychosocial evaluation of the family as a whole. Next must come the application of appropriate levels of social support and educational guidance and a therapeutic approach to conflicted family relationships. Only then is it possible to consider individual psychotherapy for selected family members, and this therapy should initially be oriented to the specific dynamic relations of personality and family role and to the balance between intrapsychic conflict and family conflict. Thus, in a very real sense, individual psychotherapy is auxiliary to and dependent upon an integrated therapeutic program for the family as a social unit. Obviously crucial to such a program are the appropriate levels of entry and the timing of such entry to affect in sequential stages specific components of the family disturbance.

On an empirical, exploratory basis, a certain range of procedures has been tentatively developed. In a step-by-step sequence, family diagnosis and therapy move ahead through a series of planned office interviews. Such interviews involve separate sessions with the primary patient interspersed with joint interviews of the patient together with other family members. Because the primary patient is viewed both as an individual in ˙distress and as a symptomatic expression of family pathology, the disturbance of this patient becomes the fulcrum or entering wedge for the appropriate levels of intervention into the disorder of the family relations. The sequence of office interviews is arranged with a view to further elucidation of the interrelations of the primary patient's affliction with the psychopathology of the family and the corresponding interplay between the primary patient's intrapsychic conflict and family conflict. The aim is to define the conflicts in which the patient is locked with other family members, to assay the disturbances in the bond of individual and family identity and the interdependence of stability of individual personality with the balance of role relations in family pairs and the family as a whole. It is possible, then, to mark out the patterns of family interaction that are potentially available for solution of conflict or for restitution.

Insights gained in clinical evaluations during office visits and intimate observations resulting from home visits provide the data necessary for assessing the need for and timing of intervention with any number of techniques—social therapy, educational guidance, psychiatric first aid, psychotherapy for conflicted family pairs, individual psychotherapy for selected family members. In acutely disturbed families where loss of emotional control brings increasingly disorganized behavior, the assignment of a professionally trained person to live temporarily with the family succeeds in restoring emotional balance in family relations and has a preventive as well as a therapeutic value. Occasionally, the use of such a device for first aid achieves a seemingly miraculous effect in calming a chaotic and violent family atmosphere and thus reducing substantially the destructive effects on individual adaptation. This is especially pertinent to the protection of emotionally vulnerable children and for adults with a latent tendency to psychotic breakdown.

It is important to appraise the extent to which family conflict is controlled, compensated, or decompensated and how far family conflict induces progressive damage to salient relationships, impairs complementarity in role relations, and therefore predisposes to breakdown of individual adaptation. In this connection, complementarity in reciprocal family role relations is of special importance insofar as it assures mutual satisfaction of need, avenues for solution of conflict, support for a necessary self-image, and crucial forms of defense against anxiety. Impairment of complementarity undermines the stability of emotional integration into family. It aggravates the internal stress of the primary patient, weakens his control of intrapsychic conflict, and intensifies his psychiatric disablement. Some forms of family conflict are temporary and benign; they may indeed deepen and enrich family ties and spur further maturation of family members. Other forms of family conflict that are prolonged, severe, inadequately neutralized move toward alienation in family relations and progressive damage to individual adaptation. The support of constructive forms of complementarity in family role relations is of central importance therefore in family therapy.

Can family integration be preserved despite conflict, or does conflict tend to destroy the link of individual and family identity and thus magnify the malignancy of individual pathology? Some forms of family conflict are transitory, enhance family unity, and promote the growth of its members. The question must always be raised: Is the conflict pathogenic or healthy? Within the frame of family conflict, what are the vicissitudes of the individual's opportunities to resolve or at least mitigate the destructive effects of intrapsychic conflict? What chance is there to discover a new and improved level of family role complementarity and with this a better level of individual adaptation? In the final analysis, the issue is one of interdependence between the individual's defenses against anxiety and the patterns of control and stabilization operating in family relations.

The appropriate cues to the sequential involvement in therapy of multiple family members are derived from the above described orientation to the delicate dynamic balance between intrapsychic conflict in the individual and interpersonal conflict in family relationships. Of necessity, the proper sequence of diagnostic and therapeutic interviews involving individuals, family pairs or the entire family group varies from family to family. In the case of a child patient the interviews may, for example, take the following order: an interview with the child and mother together, an interview with the child alone, an interview with child and father, and, finally, an interview with the two parents without the child. It might also entail at an appropriate point an interview with the child and both parents, or the child and sibling together with one or both parents.

In the case of an adult patient, the interviews might begin with the primary patient, then this patient and the marital partner, and possibly after that the patient with parent and/or sibling. The need and the sequence depend, of course, on the cues derived from the continuing process of family diagnosis. An unfolding of exploratory therapeutic interviews of this kind has the desirable effect not only of mobilizing receptivity to therapeutic influence in the primary patient; it also promotes in family relationships a more favorable climate for the progress of therapy. It makes clear, too, the patterns of benign and malignant psychiatric distortion in the various individual members of the family and allows the psychiatrist an opportunity to draw discriminating judgments about the timing of involvement of other family members in a therapeutic undertaking.

At certain stages, it may be appropriate to work concentratedly with mother and child together, husband and wife together, or even mother, father, and child together. In this setting one is able to deal directly with certain distortions of perception of family members of one another. Working at this level through a process of reality testing, mediated by the participation of the therapist, one is able to dissolve away various irrational projections of one family member upon another. If at a certain stage, the malignant phase of conflict among family members is ameliorated; it becomes possible to resume systematic individual therapy of one family member with the expectation of an attitude of receptivity to therapeutic influence and with a reduction of resistance. Again one may find at a still later stage that tension and conflict in family relations agitate the primary patient to a state of resistance and again one may choose to deal with this resistance through a therapeutic interview of the relevant family pair, the primary patient with the involved family member.

Thus a pattern of procedure evolves that is a flexible combination of individual psychotherapy and group psychotherapy, involving salient family pairs or threesomes or the entire family group. The planning of sessions with individuals and sessions with two or more family members must be discriminatingly timed in accordance with indications that derive from the active and flexible implementation of the principles of family diagnosis. From one stage of therapy to the next, as the balance of reciprocity in family role relations shifts and the focus of pathogenic disturbance moves from one part of the family to another, the therapist must be ready to institute corresponding shifts of the level of therapeutic intervention into the family disturbance.

Family therapy is obviously complex. It deals with multiple levels of conflict. It may require a division of labor in which various phases of the therapy are carried out by different members of a clinical team. But these therapists do not function in isolation with individual family members. On the contrary, the involved therapists must meet together periodically with the entire family group to deal with certain layers of shared conflict.

The clinical team, furthermore, must work together constantly, for diagnosis and dynamic evaluation, to be effectively utilized for therapeutic purposes, must be on-going processes. Diagnosis and dynamic evaluation of deviant behavior embrace the totality of human experience; they assess derailment of life processes in time and space, in depth and on the surface. Psychotherapy, on the other hand, intervenes only in certain parts of life experience. By its very nature psychotherapy is a partial, selective kind of intervention. Therefore, in order to assure its appropriate and successful use, we can never separate it from diagnosis. Particularly at the complex level of family therapy is this conjunction necessary.

A Family Study

Perhaps the most satisfactory way to make explicit some of these generalized ideas is to look at another specific family that typifies disturbances and problems common to a very large number of contemporary American families. The concepts of family diagnosis and therapy can thus be seen in actual use.

The initial referral for psychiatric therapy in this family was the oldest son Bill Brown, age eight. Bill suffered from fears of body injury. His father, a confirmed hypochondriac, resisted the idea that his son was "abnormal." He came reluctantly to see the psychiatrist about his son but was pressured by the boy's mother. Mrs. Brown was anxious for the boy to have psychiatric help. Mr. Brown, while admitting the boy's terror of physical hurt and bleeding, nevertheless asserted that such fears were "normal" and that the boy would "grow out of it." He said that the boy was exactly like himself; he seemed alarmed both for himself and his son. In alluding to his hypochondriacal anxieties, Mr. Brown said he was not sure whether he had inherited them or got them "by osmosis." At first suave and glib in manner, he soon became acutely anxious. He cast furtive glances about the room, complained of the draft, feared catching cold, and clutched his coat tightly about his body. He was suspicious, guarded and testy. He made plain his fright that psychiatry might harm his son and sought exacting assurances that the psychiatrist was at the top of his profession.

But Bill had other symptoms: acute anxiety on being separated from his parents, bedtime rituals, and nightmares. He had fears of being physically attacked at night and stabbed. If he fell and scratched himself, he became panic stricken. In his first year of life, his parents became alarmed by a medical rumor that the boy had an enlarged heart. They took Bill from one doctor to the next and were finally reassured that he had no heart disease. Their fears for his health continued however. In the early years, Bill was cared for mainly by a nurse. Whenever his parents felt exhausted by the care of home and children, they went off on vacation, leaving the children with a nurse. At four years of age, following the birth of his sister, Bill began to stammer, but this disturbance soon subsided.

Mr. Brown had felt no strong desire for children. But Mrs. Brown moved quickly to have one child after another, not because of a craving for motherhood, but rather to escape her husband's clinging dependence, his fussy demands for attention, and his contagious, panicky fears of illness.

This is a family of means. It consists of the parents and two children, Bill and his younger sister. In its external aspects this family appeared close-knit but family relations were strained, forced, and unnatural. The parents were joined in their excessive anxiety for their children, but family unity was superficial and more pretended than real.

Mr. Brown presented a romantic and unreal picture of his family. He described his relations with wife and children as idyllic. Actually there was an undercurrent of severe sexual conflict and a deep rift between the parents. Mr. Brown had a dependent, guilty tie to his mother; his father had died in an accident. Mrs. Brown also had a dependent but hostile and guilty attachment to her mother. Mrs. Brown resented both her own and her husband's mother and ridiculed Mr. Brown for being a "mama's boy."

Mrs. Brown's attitude toward her children, though conscientious, was detached, cool, and undemonstrative. She was manipulative and held them to a rigid schedule. Mr. Brown hovered over them anxiously and oversolicitously. He was competitive with them in his demands for the mother's exclusive attention. He participated in their activities in an intense, pressured way. He lived their experiences vicariously with them. His attitude with them seemed self-conscious and forced. When Mr. Brown joined the children, Mrs. Brown stood silent at a distance or removed herself from the scene. She retired in sullen anger leaving him to be the sole parent.

The activities of the family were routine and excessively organized. There was little spark or vitality. The life of the family was dampened by the mother's heavy hand. Bill and his sister competed with one another.

About three months after the initiation of Bill's treatment, Mrs. Brown's mother died a sudden, accidental death. Mrs. Brown was interviewed the same day. She was shocked, agitated, and talked in a weird, pressured, elated way. She looked tormented. She wore an inappropriate grin, something more like a leer. She just knew that her mother had to die; she felt deeply troubled, and yet felt freed of an enormous burden. She was "laughing on the outside, crying on the inside."

During this same period increasing tension was building up between Mr. and Mrs. Brown over Mrs. Brown's sexual coldness. Mr. Brown pressed his wife to get psychiatric help. She resisted. She had the conviction that if she once opened up to a psychiatrist she would explode and all hell would break loose in her relations with her husband. She proved true to her word. One night she had a severe outburst against her husband. She screamed that she hated both him and his mother, that sex relations were an ordeal, that she had only pretended to respond. She declared that she never wanted to sleep with him again. This eruption took place despite her conscious resolve to keep the lid on her rage. Mr. Brown reacted with a transitory shock and depression.

Following this episode, she confessed her outburst to the psychiatrist, behaving as if she had been a naughty child. She asserted her deep, magically tinged belief that she had the power to demolish her husband. She admitted being cruel and yet said it was a great relief. She wore an eerie grin, expressing phantasies of destruction of her husband just as she did following the sudden death of her mother. She spoke of her severe irritation with her husband's sexual demands, his fussiness in the home and recurring catastrophic frights of illness.

"I know I married my father," she said. Mr. Brown was the man that her mother had picked for her—a self-made man and an outstanding member of the country club. She wove visions of herself as being a rich, comfortable matron in a swank home, envied by other women. Two weeks before her marriage she came to know her fiancé's hypochondriacal fears, his panicky retreat to bed and temporary invalidism. She identified him with her mother, who behaved similarly. On discovering this frailty in her fiancé she froze emotionally but nevertheless went through with the marriage. She was frigid sexually but play-acted the part of a responsive wife. She busied herself with her children to evade closeness with her husband. She admired his capacity to make money but was otherwise contemptuous of him. At home she made all decisions for him. Her sense of power over him gave her a secret elation.

After the shock of the marital crisis that followed Mrs. Brown's outburst, both partners showed distress. They felt as if the entire house was tumbling down over their heads. They hurried to appease one another. A truce was established. The parents continued to share their home, social life and children; they maintained the outward semblance of an intact family, but sexual relations decreased almost to the vanishing point.

This is a family born out of the reciprocal relation of the sick emotional needs of two people. Here is a woman who marries a promise of economic security and social aggrandizement and a man who marries a pretty picture of a woman who will adorn him publicly and be a doting mother. The central striving is for social success, money and power. The relationship between these persons was emotionally unreal and impersonal.

The superficial unity of this couple rested mainly on a sharing of common social strivings. They complemented one another's dependency and power drives and cooperated in maintaining a façade of social conformity. The sharp emotional and sexual barrier between them impelled each to veer toward the children. They lived out their needs vicariously through the children. Their son, Bill, became the pawn for their conflicts. The balance of parental relations was precarious. It was critically upset by two interlocking events: the sudden death of Mrs. Brown's mother and Mrs. Brown's violent explosion and sexual rejection of her husband. When she admitted to herself the similarity between her husband and her mother, she could no longer tolerate him as a man.

The value orientation of this relationship is essentially a coercive and manipulative one. It contains in it a deep streak of hypocrisy. It is a relationship in which the balance of role relations between husband and wife cannot be steady. There is difficulty in maintaining a stable, joined identity through time. The capacity to control conflict in this relationship is exceedingly poor. The potential ability to adapt to change, to learn from new experience and to achieve further development is minimal.

Bill's fears of body injury were symptomatic of a neurosis deeply intertwined with the marital maladjustment of his parents. Both parents treated the children as extensions of themselves, but they competed for the children. Mrs. Brown rejected the role of wife and marital partner. She reduced her husband to the position of a weak child. She asserted omnipotent control over husband and children. She displaced to her son the hostile rejection she did not openly express to her husband. She suffocated Bill with her rigid routines. She allied herself emotionally with her daughter against her son.

To contrast with this, Mr. Brown was seductive with Bill and overidentified with him. He demanded of Bill the warmth and affection he did not get from Mrs. Brown. But he also competed with and effeminized his son. In this setting it is easy to see Bill's role as a pawn in the unsolved conflicts between the parents.

Bill's psychotherapy posed special problems. It called for therapeutic intervention at two main levels: direct therapy for Bill's inner conflicts and therapy for the foci of disturbance in family relations, especially the core of disorder in the marital relationship. The cues to the multiple foci of conflict in this family group became quickly apparent. These cues indicated the need for therapy for both parents as well as for the boy. In this instance, however, the father was already in treatment with another psychiatrist. Therefore, individual therapy was arranged for Bill and for his mother by the same psychiatrist; beyond that therapeutic sessions were arranged at appropriate times for the parents as a couple, for disturbances in the relations of boy and mother, boy and father, boy and both parents, and, finally, occasional sessions involving the boy, his sister, and his mother. Direct therapy for Bill was undertaken first. Three months later his mother was engaged in therapy.

Significant trends in Mrs. Brown's personality will be summarized first for their relevance to Bill's conflicts. Mrs. Brown did not at first admit to herself the presence of significant neurotic distress. Consciously she thought of herself as a successful and satisfied woman. She dealt with her problems mainly by avoidance and magic denial. She barricaded herself against conscious anxiety. Through her compulsive preoccupation with routine duties she was able to repress awareness of conflict concerning her destructive urges. Concealed in her ritualized daily program was a motive of doing penance for hatred of and death wishes for her mother. Her attitude toward her father and other men was ambivalent. In one sense she was contemptuous of men for their weakness and for their easy victimization by women. In another sense she was envious and competitive toward men; she was power-driven. She allied with her sisters in a kind of militant female army against the weak-kneed men whom they exploited. Beneath the surface defenses, there was a core of chronic depression, a hostile renunciation of parents and family, and guilt and anxiety about mutilation and death. In a sample dream she reduced to shrunken mummies every member of her family group.

She existed as if half-dead; she was detached. She had little zest for life and narrow interests; her daily routine was hollow and devoid of meaning. She placed herself and her family in a straight jacket, an emotional prison, but deluded herself that she was living a snug, comfortable life. She made no real decisions, only empty, cautious, mid-line compromises. She affected an attitude of resignation to the nothingness of her life.

Psychotherapy mobilized her dormant conflict, her fears of death and destruction, and her sacrificial attitude toward life. She consoled herself mainly with her sense of grandiose, magical power over her husband and children. Her role as a hurt, lonely child was concealed beneath this façade of omnipotence. As her therapy progressed, she detached herself more and more from her husband, struggled with her inability to love a man and her cynical, exploitative attitude. She was relieved of the necessity to displace on her son her omnipotent, emasculating attack on her husband. Despite her total rejection of her husband, she nevertheless wanted to have her cake and eat it too. She wanted to preserve the façade of security and unity in her family, retain her home, preserve her place as mother of her children but could not get herself to be sincere with her husband.

As the therapy of Bill and his mother progressed, Bill became less anxious and began to unfold freer and healthier emotional attitudes. At the same time, however, the marital problem became more critical. In effect, the displacement of the family conflict onto the boy was undone, and the focus of disturbance shifted back from Bill to the relations between his parents.

The treatment of Bill had begun with sessions involving both him and his father. In order to achieve access to Bill, Mr. Brown's fears of harm needed first to be neutralized. In the beginning Bill verbalized little. He wore a sad, anguished facial expression. He showed little initiative or spontaneity. He kept a close watch on both his father and the therapist. In these initial sessions the father's behavior was characterized by two main attitudes: the urge to get reassurances that the psychiatrist would not hurt his darling son and the urge to exhibit the boy. He made glowing and grandiose references to Bill's handsome face, his appeal, and his brilliant mind. Gradually, as Mr. Brown's anxieties eased, the boy also relaxed.

After a few such sessions, Mr. Brown became sufficiently reassured and withdrew. Bill then came to his sessions alone.

The therapist's attitude was one of quiet acceptance of Bill. He showed interest but was not intrusive. At first Bill acted with considerable constraint. Bit by bit, as his security increased, he explored the room and became a more active participant. He engaged in a game of catch ball. In this game he quickly dramatized his fear of physical injury. When the ball was thrown toward him, he ducked or showed a startle response. Frequently, when he caught the ball, he held up high the tip of his finger as if it had been painfully wounded. He whined, cried, pouted, and refused to play. The therapist looked at the finger and remarked that he could see nothing. This was followed by an interchange concerning Bill's conviction that the therapist was intent on hurting him. Bill's whining complaints and irritability became increasingly exhibitionistic. He openly accused the therapist of conspiring to injure him. Nevertheless, he committed himself to increasing participation with the therapist.

Bill personified the therapist in a male doll and identified this doll as a spook or a ghost, later as a superman. He proceeded to try to destroy this doll in a fire. He built bigger and bigger fires but never succeeded in completely destroying the doll. The therapist interpreted to Bill that he felt too weak and too fearful to destroy the superman. In effect, Bill was too small to fight his parents or the therapist.

Bill then disclosed his fears of being attacked in the dark by a strange person with a knife. He displayed increasing excitation in building fires in which he tried over and over to annihilate the spook or superman once and for all. But against this enemy the boy felt powerless.

During this activity Bill spontaneously revealed an experience he had at home with his mother. He asked his mother to stir up the fire in the fireplace in order to excite a brighter flame. His mother agreed but instead, while pretending with the poker to stir a bigger flame, actually snuffed out the fire. Discussion of this episode induced Bill to elaborate in great detail his suspicion of his mother, his fear and conviction of her betrayal of him. He then personified the spook as his mother and tried to consume her in hot fire.

In the meantime, the boy revealed his own fear of being burned. He showed an excited interest in the therapist's cigarette smoking and in his talent for blowing rings. He indicated a desire to light a cigarette himself but feared being burned. Again Bill treated the therapist as a persecutor. Discussion of Bill's suspicion of the therapist eased his fears of attack and injury. He became bolder in experimenting both with lighting his own matches and smoking cigarettes. He displayed increasing elation in his newfound manliness as a cigarette smoker. This identification with the therapist's masculinity expanded. Bill talked more about his father, describing his father's fear of his mother's angry outbursts. He also described how much more affectionate his father was than his mother. He enjoyed playing with his father. But this play was intensely competitive. His father urged him into boxing, wrestling, or fencing matches. In the midst of such activity the father often agitated the boy with intense tickling. This aroused in Bill a mixture of pleasure and acute fear. The therapist advised Bill's father to forego this kind of play.

While at first Bill was extremely chary of body contact with the therapist, he gradually relaxed and began to take pleasure in it. He transformed his fears of body injury into a kind of facetious, dramatic play which evoked outbursts of elated cackling. In this joking mood he dramatized phantasies of biting off his fingertip or toe, or elated expressions of pleasure in licking up dry deposits of sweat between his toes. In a similar vein he dramatized his feeling that he was like a chicken with his head cut off. He was not permitted to use his own head. His mother always arranged his appointments for him. He had no memory. At the same time, he became increasingly free in accepting goodies from the therapist: candies, cookies, etc. Gradually he became much more confident and acted much more the part of a man.

Bill became increasingly free of his mother's domination at home. In this setting, therapeutic sessions were conducted with Bill and his mother. At first Bill expressed in a timid, cautious way his fear of the mother's rage. Gradually he became bolder and expressed more openly his hostile criticism of her. Finally he reached a point where he could make believe he was beating her bodily. His mother took these reproaches in a tight, sullen silence, but she did not retaliate. She seemed immobilized. Bill felt that he could be more secure in these sessions with mother because she would not dare attack him in the psychiatrist's office. But he still feared her vengeance at home. As the mother's anxiety and defensiveness diminished, this fear also subsided. Over a period of time, the sessions with Bill and his mother enabled him not only to release his anxiety-ridden hostile feeling for her but also his underlying desire to win back her affection. A new kind of intimacy unfolded between the boy and mother, which gave pleasure to both of them.

Therapeutic sessions were also conducted for Bill and his father during which it became plain that the boy allied himself with father against mother. There was a more open display of affection between son and father. But Bill took his father to task for being so frightened of mother and for his father's failure to protect him from mother's hostile control.

Ultimately there were sessions with Bill and both parents in which the boy once again expressed his disappointment in his father's timidity. He usurped the position of the man in the family and proceeded to chastise his mother as if he were his father. He undertook to fight father's battle with mother. Bill's manly assertiveness gave courage to the father to express more directly his dissatisfaction with his wife.

During this period Bill talked with increasing freedom and security of his curiosity concerning sexual relations between his parents and his phantasy that his mother might harm his father's genitals. This led to discussion of his interest in masturbation and fear of harm to his own genitals, and this anxiety was relieved.

Other levels of therapeutic intervention into the patterns of family conflict involved sessions with Bill, his sister, and his mother, and also home visits which dealt with acute tensions in the entire family group.

The outcome of Bill's treatment was excellent. His fears melted. His positive development as a young man with growing strength and confidence was impressive. The therapy of the residual disorder in the marital relationship proved a thorny challenge. Efforts to deal with the basic marital conflict met with only limited success. The mother secretly harbored the vision of eventual divorce but chose to delay action in the interests of her children. The father, though increasingly open in his expression of dissatisfaction, continued to fear the mother. An uneasy truce persisted, with tacit agreement to avoid discussion of the sexual rift. But this family problem was no longer projected on Bill, whose improvement continued.

Part 4

WIDER
PERSPECTIVES

PROBLEMS OF FAMILY RESEARCH

THE GROWING NUMBER of researches on the mental health of family life is ample testimony to the importance of the subject. As the emphasis shifts from the lone individual to the individual within his family group, we appreciate how inadequate is our present-day understanding of family dynamics. Although the belongingness of individual to family is universal, we have thus far been unable to pin down in any specific, meaningful way the exact relation between the two. The tendency has been either to be severely reductionistic and study minor variables unrelated to the whole, or to be general and vague in the description of family phenomena. Neither fulfills the need for progress in the theory of behavior and its applications to clinical problems.

This book is devoted to conceptualizing the processes of family relationships. The objectives are both clinical and theoretical: to evolve a set of clinical concepts, however tentative, for interrelating individual and family health in diagnosis and therapy; to build a theoretical framework within which new and testable hypotheses can be constructed at a lower level of abstraction, which may then be tested in studies of a more rigorous and systematic nature. Eventually, it may be possible to classify families in relation to their capacity to influence the mental health of family members. This, of course, has wide ramifications for the problems of diagnoses, treatment, prevention of illness and promotion of positive health.

Surely, in facing these problems, more is required than the individual case study. It is true, certainly, that a considerable body of empirical observations concerning family life is now available. But the usefulness of such knowledge is limited. We do not know how far, how accurately, how safely we can generalize. We have no adequate criteria for prediction. Too much is left to chance, and so progress is hindered.

No two families are alike any more than any two individuals. Yet there are dimensions of family dynamics as of individual dynamics which are inherent in the life history of all families. We need to know the universals in the structure and functions of family, and we need to know how family processes vary with the culture. As we move from the larger society to families in the subcultures, we find more commonality in the patterns. Whatever our goals may be in theory and the application of theory to the problems of living, a clearer definition of the dynamic interrelations of individual and family group is essential; but we can achieve this only through effective selection for study of the more significant common variables. This is a complex task because of the tremendous scope and range of family processes, the dearth of dependable knowledge, the difficulties of gathering valid data, and the special problems of hypothesis construction and testing. In confronting the breadth, depth, subtlety, and complexity of family processes, how shall we view the question of erecting scientific standards to study the problem?

Research effort is represented mainly in three phases: conceptualization of the problem, organization and the carrying out of the method of study, and interpretation of the results. All three phases are interdependent and complementary. The problems of method and procedure are secondary to the definition of the problem. The step-by-step structuring of method and procedure, however, often has the effect of stimulating further clarification of the problem. The final stage of interpretation of the results rests on an accurate understanding of the potentials and limitations of the given method and the ability to integrate the findings within the frame of broader knowledge of the problem.

The first priority is accurate conceptualization of the nature of the problem. If this goes awry, all else fails. A single incorrect premise in the initial formulation may lead to a whole series of errors.

Research is concerned with the expansion of knowledge, dependable and valid knowledge. But the primary source of knowledge is not research but experience. Knowledge accumulates through experience; it is handed down from one generation to the next. This is a form of learning which derives from observation of life events, and the testing of the validity of these observations against reality. The accuracy of empirical knowledge is also checked for its predictive value. Such processes are in general the root of common sense.

In everyday living we lean heavily on knowledge which rests on common sense. The dependability of such knowledge is, however, often limited. It can be misleading. Experience tells us that it is possible time and time again for people to share in an illusory sense perceptions of events, incorrect ideas, false judgments of reality—even on occasion to support mass illusion. The fact of agreement between the perceptive interpretations of several observers (consensual validation) does not by itself prove the truth of the interpretation. The real issue concerning knowledge is not so much how it is obtained. This does not count for much. Knowledge may accumulate in many different ways: The real question rather is its ultimate reliability, the final test being the power of prediction.

In general the validity of knowledge is subjected to not one test, but many different tests. Research is one way of testing knowledge. It is a method of checking the validity of old knowledge or what is presumed to be knowledge; it also leads to new knowledge. But it is surely not the sole test; the ultimate test is destiny itself. In the long view, it is the accumulated truth of life itself, the collective wisdom of shared experience in human relations, which provides the ultimate test of knowledge.

In the field of human behavior, concepts of research and scientific method are undergoing significant change. There is the influence of the shift from Aristotelian to Galileon principles and the resulting re-evaluation of the definition of a law of nature. The basic Galileon distinction between regularity or frequency of an event and a true law of nature places statistical studies in a different light. Field theory (Kurt Lewin) and the emphasis on study of the properties of an object within a concrete situation influences present-day approaches to problems of human behavior.

Is there one scientific method or many? Can it be said that a single set of rules applies to all forms of scientific investigation or do these vary depending upon the nature of the problem and the level of participation of the researcher himself? Some students of the subject give strong support to the latter point of view; for example, Northrup[1] suggests that the scientific method may not only vary but that it must vary in accordance with the type of problem under study. He distinguishes three main categories of scientific investigaton: (1) the study of the laws of physical nature; (2) the study of social facts as they exist (factual social theory); (3) the study of social relations as we would wish them to be (normative social theory).

He makes out a strong case for the need to formulate a specifically appropriate set of rules for each of these distinct categories of problem. He declares unequivocally that scientific methods suitable for study of phenomena in the physical world are not appropriate to investigation of problems in human behavior. The study of social and physical processes must be distinct. Beyond this, he establishes a further differentiation between methods of research applicable to social and psychological events as they occur in actuality, and such events as they ought to be, or as we would wish them to be.

A. H. Maslow[2] also points out the pitfalls of applying the principles of physical science to psychology. He provides eloquent support for a holistic-dynamic approach to human behavior rather than an atomistic-mechanical one.

These general principles have relevance for the tasks of research on the role of family in mental health. In the field of family life much of what we now know derives from a vast accretion of human experience, which is the cumulative product of direct observations of the phenomena of family life: family interaction in its endlessly changing forms, and the processes of child development. Both lay persons and professionals have contributed to this aggregate of empirical knowledge. However, only a small fraction of these ideas has really been put to the test. Their accuracy varies all the way from high to low. It is difficult to sift truth from illusion. Much of what is handed down from one generation to the next represents a kind of shared mythology of family life.

In the field of mental health there is a growing body of knowledge based on the accumulation of experience. The greater part of this knowledge comes from a variety of specialists—psychiatrists, psychologists, social workers, social scientists, educators, etc. Here, too, only a small fraction has been tested in research.

Nonetheless, a considerable body of data has been put together on various types of mental illness, the symptoms and social behavior associated with such illness, the course and likely outcome. Through empirical study of a variety of methods of psychotherapy, much has been learned too of the dynamic interpersonal processes by which the course of certain mental illnesses may be modified. The body of knowledge which exists today is, however, in the main limited to the expressions of illness in individual persons; the group expressions of illness are only vaguely defined.

Traditional forms of clinical research have thus far focused almost exclusively on individuals examined and cared for in isolation from their families.* There are both advantages and disadvantages to clinical research on individual patients. It is no doubt true that intensive understanding can be obtained from close study of a single case. Depth studies of the internal processes of personality are extremely useful in getting insights into motivation, in the testing of certain aspects of behavior theory, and in constructing new hypotheses. Often ideas for specific researches are derived directly from such intensive case studies. Clinical understanding of human behavior is in great part true understanding. It is a matter of urgent importance to harness the faculty of clinical intuition, but clinical research has its distinct limitations, too.

To be considered are the factors of personal bias in the clinician, the role of chance in some forms of clinical observation, and the dangers intrinsic to the

---

* A significant exception is the work of H. B. Richardson, *Patients Have Families* (New York: The Commonwealth Fund, 1945).

drawing of broad generalizations from the study of a single case or very few cases. It is also true that the observations of a clinician working alone can almost never be checked or duplicated by another person. Finally, there are the special complications that arise in the study of individual patients removed from their idiosyncratic family environment within which specific forms of behavior have been induced.

Research pointed to the relations of family and mental health involves people and families. The intrinsic nature of the subject matter introduces particular kinds of difficulty. Persons and families change over the span of time. From one point in time to another they are no longer the same; they are continuously evolving entities. The problem then arises as to when to study the family, at what point in time, and over what span of time. To some extent, depending upon the specific focus of study, the procedure must be accommodated to the particular stage of evolution of the family.

Family processes by their very nature are extremely complex. They are almost global in scope. There is the question of assuring correct interpretation of the balanced relations of the parts to the whole. There is the need to describe, define, and classify whole families on a single continuum, rather than describe parts on many continua. The variables are extremely numerous, interdependent, and overlapping. One cannot establish simple one-to-one relationships because they do not exist. If one attempts to simplify the research by narrowing the field and excluding certain pertinent variables, one introduces an element of arbitrary distortion of the results. Therefore, a central challenge in this form of study is that of selecting the more significant variables and respecting the essential interdependence of these variables.

Inevitably in psychiatric research on the family there is the problem of instituting system and exactness into a field where pertinent clinical observations are of first importance and yet by their very nature are subjective, evaluative and inexact. This is a paradox which must be constantly borne in mind. On the one hand, there is the effort to make such study less impressionistic and less dependent on the study of single cases. On the other hand, it often happens that in the search for measurable variables the dynamic essence of the family phenomenon is lost. The striving for exactness rigidifies some research procedures in such a way as to take the very life from the family picture. Though the precision of certain partial study procedures may be enhanced, the accuracy of evaluation of the total family phenomenon is in the end impaired. Scientific method is not an end in itself. It is a tool. The first priority is the study of meaningful problems. We want exactness of formulation, to be sure, but we cannot afford the luxury of keeping busy with measurement of wrong or unimportant things. The testing of trivial hypotheses, which remove a piece of behavior from its contextual family relationships, may often mislead us. As Maslow[3] points out, a disproportionate absorption with means, methods, and techniques contributes to the weakness of psychology and social science.

It is extrememly difficult to categorize or type families. The network of complex emotional processes within the group, between group and community, and within each person belonging to the group creates a uniqueness which we must learn to pin down. Each family must be thoroughly investigated as an entity.

Another problem of family research is the question of the use of descriptive terms which are of doubtful scientific value. In the field of mental health and family, we are burdened with a plethora of descriptive terms, but they remain hazy and poorly defined. There is a special need in this connection both to broaden and specify such terms so as to cover the range or variations from one family to the next. It is necessary to work out concrete, specific, usable definitions so that both the procedures and the results of study are communicable.

In family study there is also the need to define explicitly the bases for judgment in the analysis of the data. It is necessary to indicate in a definitive way how the evaluation of individual and family performance is measured according to the family's own expectations and also according to a dynamic model of ideal performance in a defined culture. The ideal of individual and family performance against which deviations are measured must vary from one culture to the next in accordance with differences in social structure, human relations patterns, and value orientation. Also to be taken into account is the element of bias which may be introduced by the cultural position of the observer and analyst of the data.

Of central significance is the influence of the observer on the very phenomena which he is observing. The observer participates in the events he is recording. He intervenes, catalyzes, and changes these events even as he makes his observations. Where the researcher is also the clinician, his first duty is to the welfare of his patient. He cannot maintain experimental conditions where this conflicts with the needs of his patient. He can, however, uncover much that is significant by a process of exploratory study. The levels of intervention of clinician and researcher are not identical, but they can be complementary.

Research on mental health and family life requires: (1) an economic conceptualization of the problem which highlights the most pertinent variables; (2) the construction of specific hypotheses; (3) the formulation of method and collection of data; (4) the analysis of the data and the use of specific criteria for testing the validity of the hypotheses.

The area of research is huge. For practical purposes it must be divided up in appropriate ways. There is no one correct way of dividing the task of research; nor can one study everything at once. The appropriate division of the tasks of research is influenced in two ways: by the nature of the problem, and by the special interests, preferences, and capacities of the individual researcher.

There are multiple levels to be considered: the biological and social components of family experience; heredity and processes of socialization; predisposition in childhood and traumatic experience in adulthood. There is first a natural division of this problem into the role of family in the mental health of the child and the role of family in the mental health of the adult person. At one pole there is the problem of evaluating the group dynamics of the family as an integrated unit. At the other pole there is the question of assessing individual behavior. Intermediate between the two is the question of evaluating the joined functioning of such salient family pairs as man and wife, parent and child, child and sibling. There is then the question of relating these various levels of behavioral performance within the totality of family life to a set of criteria for the assessment of mental health: the relations of family conflict and family defenses to individual conflict and individual defenses; the relations of failure of family role complementarity to adaptive disorganization and mental illness.

In order to mark out the lines of relation between the emotional functioning of an individual or a family pair and the emotional functioning of the family as a unit, it becomes necessary to make use of systematic concepts. We have earlier suggested a group of such concepts: psychological identity and value orientation, and the stabilization of behavior, evaluated by the continuity of identity in time, the control of conflict, and the capacity to change, learn and achieve complementarity in new role relationships.

In establishing correlations of individual and family behavior four levels need to be kept in mind: intrapsychic processes, interaction among family members, the dynamics of the family group as a whole, and the relations of the family with the larger culture.

As has been indicated, because of the tremendous scope and ramification of the problem, no single study can suffice. It is necessary to organize a series of studies each of which applies a different focus. Such studies can be so formulated as to be sequentially interrelated stage by stage. Each such study would call for a particular set of hypotheses depending upon the focus which is selected. At each level a method of investigation must be accommodated to a set of specific objectives and to the particular hypotheses which are being tested.

The collection and organization of the data must be oriented to definitive goals and hypotheses. The data can be organized in a systematic conceptual framework which allows for a clear definition of terms, explicit commitment to criteria which form the basis of evaluative judgments and includes consideration of the role and influence of the observer. This form of approach recognizes the principle that the kinds of data obtained depend upon the process by which they are obtained, and the quality of participation of the investigator.

The final step is the testing of specific hypotheses. This is a difficult but indispensable task. Where it is possible to test systematically the validity of a group of hypotheses, such testing lends itself to the correction and improvement of behavior theory and the application of theory to clinical work. Such hypotheses, adequately tested, can be applied to the special clinical responsibilities of diagnosis, treatment, prediction of behavior, prevention of illness, and promotion of positive health.

Who is to do such research? That is the question! Part of the difficulty in the mental health field is that research is mostly carried out by persons other than clinicians. A clinician provides the raw data and the initial hunches and interpretations of his data. After that, most often, the researcher goes to work. This is an unsatisfactory arrangement.

The relations between clinicians and researchers are a problem of the first importance. It has sometimes looked as if clinicians and researchers live in separate worlds. The barrier between them has often been a serious impediment. They have mistrusted one another, used different languages and talked across a chasm. Neither psychiatrists nor social scientists can go it alone, however. Psychiatrists possess valuable insights into human behavior. In their everyday work they are close to the live human material but are untrained in the intricacies of research technique. To contrast with this, the researchers are very much at home with the problems of technique but are sometimes removed from persons and the intimate psychological content of everyday human experience. It is an urgent necessity that psychiatrists invest their empirical knowledge in systematic research.

But practicing psychiatrists are often suspicious of the idol worshipers of scientific method. They accuse the researchers of keeping busy with researching the wrong problems or the unimportant ones. They are skeptical of statistical method. They rest their security and conviction on empirical observations of behavior. They hold the belief that human beings cannot be made the subject of scientific experimentation. They point to the inherent difficulty of experimental duplication of human situations. They emphasize the extraordinary complications of setting up rigorous controls.

The pure researchers, in turn, accuse the clinician of undue subjectivity, personal bias, unsystematized thinking, and the exercise of broad license in the method of drawing conclusions. They point particularly to the dangers of drawing large generalizations from observations based upon the study of a single subject. It is self-evident that there is a valid core to both sets of criticisms; something needs to be done about it.

There are two paths open to a possible solution of this problem: bring the clinician and pure researcher together in team study; or bring the two kinds of thinking together inside a single mind. In the latter instance either the pure researcher must acquire clinical background to fortify his technical knowledge of research, or the clinician himself must have specific training in research method.

What we wish to learn from the clinical point of view are the dynamics of the family group which predispose to disorder and mental illness on the one hand, and immunity against illness and positive emotional health on the other. In particular, we want to establish the correlations of components of family life with specific mental illnesses; also, the relation of components of family experience to the course of illness and response to therapy. For such purposes auxiliary studies of the processes of family change associated with a variety of stresses, both usual and unusual patterns of stress, would be most helpful; for example, the advent of a new child, a geographical shift of the family, or the death of a family member.

In examining these phenomena, we may require standards or norms for family mental health against which to judge a wide range of family processes. The concept of a family norm for mental health, seldom made explicit, is nonetheless a part of everyday evaluation. An effort to reach an explicit formulation of such a norm may be made in three ways: (1) A norm of healthy family life in terms of an average or the statistically dominant form of family adaptation in a given community. (2) A norm in terms of the individual family's own standard of healthy and successful fulfillment of family strivings. At different points in time and at different stages of family development, the actual performance of the family in health and fulfillment of family strivings may be measured against the family's own standard of optimal family functioning. In this sense, at different stages of family evolution, the family may be judged to be farther from, or closer to, its own ideal of healthy and happy living. (3) A norm in terms of a dynamic model of ideally healthy family life related to the structure of the surrounding community, the culture pattern, and corresponding values.

A thorough consideration of the issue of a standard in mental health in family life must take into account all three components.

The statistical approach is useful in the elucidation of some parts of the phenomenology of illness and health. However, the search for the subtler aspects of illness and health in family living cannot rest exclusively on a statistical approach. The statistical method has limitations which are familiar to students in the field. From the psychiatric point of view, all too often patterns of family relationship and associated value attitudes that represent common trends in a given community are nonetheless conducive to mental ill-health. For this reason we cannot be satisfied with an exclusively statistical formulation of a norm of health. We must also conceptualize a norm in other ways. It is useful, therefore, to consider the family's own standard for health, and a dynamic model of ideal family health which is influenced by the prevailing conditions of social existence and the values of a particular culture.

The standard of health which a particular family sets for itself derives from its own idiosyncratic background, its history and tradition. It is what is handed down from generation to generation. It is the individualistic aspect of family constellation. It is reflected in specific value judgments as to healthy and preferred forms of family adaptation to community and the desirable forms of relation of man and wife, parent and child. It is best illuminated in long-term clinical studies of individual families.

A dynamic model of ideal family health related to the existing social and cultural patterns and associated values epitomizes the belongingness of the individual and family to society, and defines the kinds of persons and families which are required to carry out the main functions of a given society.

A healthy family group can be hypothesized in terms of the kind and degree of success the family achieves in the fulfillment of its basic functions. But the paths to health in family living in our culture are many and varied. Regardless of this multiplicity and diversity, certain basic conditions are essential. A family achieves health insofar as it fulfills the biological potentials of parent-child relations and husband-wife relations. It must be a workable unit, providing protection from danger and the material satisfactions necessary to survival. It must belong to, and be externally integrated with, the community. It must be internally integrated, cohesive, and self-stabilizing and fulfill the potentials of growth. It must preserve a fluid, resilient capacity to adapt to change. The family as family must have values and goals which are realistic, appropriate, and capable of achievement. It must provide an interpersonal climate, within which the psychological identity and value strivings of its members can be brought into harmony with the psychological identity and value strivings of the family as a group, while it assures an appropriate range of freedom for individuation. Family roles must be sex-appropriate, well-defined, and capable of fulfilling the essential needs of its members in a reciprocal role interaction. Where conflict and frustration of personal needs emerge, the family must have psychological resources for reaching a correct perception of the problem. It must be able to find appropriate means for the solution of conflict, in a way which satisfies need and promotes the health and growth of its members. The potential for empathic identification of individual and family provides support for individual striving and the cultivation of individual autonomy and creativity. Child-rearing must reflect the understanding of the psychological and physical needs of the child and render superfluous any critical competition between the needs of the child and the needs of the parents.

The emphasis in this conception of family health is not so much toward the elimination of conflict, but rather the constructive use of conflict to foster further emotional growth. Creative complementarity of the family role relations of man and woman, and parent and child, rather than the absence of conflict is the cue to a healthy configuration of family relations.

In view of the complexity of the problem, do we throw up our hands in a gesture of surrender? Do we resignedly concede that research on mental health and family is impossible? No, certainly not! We must seek out new approaches.

A detailed exploration of fifty families,* each of which had two or more members in psychotherapy, were used to develop and clarify many of the concepts outlined in this book. No clear techniques have yet been developed to compare families or to place them on a continuum. It did seem possible, however, to mark out relatively healthy and unhealthy areas of family functioning, the balance between them and the specific restitutive or compensatory trends in the family relationships. Thus far we have identified tentatively a small group of forms of family adaptation, which is by no means complete. We state these as theoretically pure types, although in actuality there is considerable overlapping.

1. The externally isolated family group, characterized by excessive isolation from the community, few or no friends, and some or no contact with members of the extended families. The essential pattern is one of failure of emotional integration into the community.

2. The externally integrated family group, characterized by active participation in the community, friends, and contact with extended families. In many instances, this external integration is compensatory for a basic failure of unity in the internal life of the family. The family has an incomplete or fragmented internal life.

3. The internally unintegrated family group, characterized by failure in internal unity with mutual alienation of the two parents or conflict of both. In some instances the effort to compensate takes the form of a mutually protective alignment of the members of one family pair, sometimes parent and child or parent and own sibling, which sets itself against another family pair.

4. The unintended family group, characterized by a primacy of the parents' motivations and needs and the subordination or exclusion of the needs of the child. Sometimes there is a mutually protective alliance of the parents with emphasis on sexual and social satisfaction but no intent to build a family or to have offspring and no goals for the family as a group. The goals of egocentric fulfillment of each parent's individual needs is paramount.

5. The immature family group, characterized by immaturity of the parents, each one parentifying the other. The immature, dependent needs of each parent are fixated to the grandparents and the responsibility for fulfilling family roles

---

* Of the fifty families, thirty-six were urban, lower-middle-class, second generation Jewish-American families of children at the Child Development Center in New York City. Six families, in which the primary patient was a child with learning retardation and associated emotional disorders, were studied at the Hunter College Educational Clinic. The remaining families were studied in the private practice of psychiatry. For another approach to this problem, see James Tichener and Richard Emerson, *Some Methods for the Study of Family Interactions in Personality Development* (University of Cincinnatti).

is not accepted. Therefore, the family unit is not independent and tends to lean on the extended family.

6. The deviant family group, characterized by rebellion against community mores, nonconformity in standards and organization, deviant goals and values for family and child rearing and a revolt against standards of extended families. The deviant family group can be divided into two types: (a) internally integrated but consistently in rebellion against community standards; (b) failure of internal integration, with rebellion occurring both inside and outside the family.

7. The disintegrated or regressed family group, characterized by trends that have the potential of breaking up the group, lack of integration, immaturity, excessive conflict, lack of compatibility, mutual attack, mutual isolation and inappropriate and unclear goals.

The problems of studying the relations of individual and family influenced by psychoanalytic therapy poses some special problems but may be a fruitful line of investigation. This can be illustrated with a study I propose of those families, in which a young adult member is undergoing psychoanalysis. This study would divide itself into two complementary parts: (1) the therapeutic analyst's study of the dynamic relations of personality structure and adaptation to family roles; (2) the concurrent study of the psychosocial processes of the patient's family life, carried out by an interdisciplinary team.

Parallel study of what goes on in the patient's mind in therapy and what goes on outside, in the patient's daily family experience, would provide a special check on the definition of internal processes of the mind against external projection of the mind in family interaction. Each set of observations would provide checks on the other. The analyst's record of his observations of treatment process could be made independently of the team study of the processes of family interaction.

There are undoubtedly some in the profession of psychoanalysis whose orientation to psychoanalytic theory and technique impels them to oppose a study of this kind. They may hold the conviction that the analyst's primary focus on intrapsychic distortion, especially the expressions of unconscious conflict, would be impaired if the analyst interested himself too far in the realistic aspects of the patient's relations with family. I disagree with this. My conviction moves precisely in the opposite direction. I believe that the understanding of the patient's deeper mental distortions would be greatly enriched if the analytic therapist disciplined himself to systematic examination of the relations between the internal processes of the patient's mind and the concurrent processes of the patient's adaptation of his personality to specific family roles, as these are molded by his daily interaction with family members.

In the study I propose, the concurrent process of investigation of family dynamics can be conducted by a research team, which excludes the patient's analytic therapist. The family aspect of the study has the purpose of defining the relations of the patient's personality to his behavior in the required family roles, and the mental health functioning of the family as a whole. Here, however, the relevant processes are illuminated by direct observation of family interaction. Such observations can then be checked back against the therapeutic analyst's observations of related emotional processes going on inside the patient's mind.

The family aspect of the study can be conducted by an interdisciplinary team composed of a psychiatric caseworker, social psychologist, and a psychoanalyst who is not the patient's therapist. It involves: (1) periodic interviews of the individual undergoing analytic therapy by a selected member of the research team; (2) direct observation of patterns of family interaction (a) in visits of the family group to the office of the research team, (b) through the special techniques of home visits.

Such procedure ultimately enables a research group to integrate a picture of change in one person undergoing psychoanalytic therapy with change in the configuration of family relationships. It can shed light on the integrative functions of personality as these are involved in the adaptation of individual personality to the tasks of family role adaptation; the levels at which the day-by-day interrelations of individual and family influence treatment process, the patient's accessibility or resistance, recovery from illness, or the precipitation of a relapse. It would provide a further test of our present powers of prediction of change in behavior of patients undergoing psychotherapy.

Our understanding would also be enhanced because: (1) it would provide data which reveal a family's perception of change in an individual in therapy, the response of family members to this change, and their integration of the patient's therapeutic experience into family living; (2) it would offer a check on the process of change in the patient's perception of family and his response to this, making possible a comparison of the research team's view of change in the patient and change in the family with the psychoanalyst's view of these same processes of change and also a comparison of the research team's view of change in the patient with the patient's own view of change in himself; (3) it could provide a further basis for examining the relations of illness and health in one person with illness and health within a family group. Of particular interest is the light such study might shed on processes of adaptation to new experience and the conditions required for further growth of personality.

There is a continuing need to learn to specify the rationale for clinical statements and judgments, to determine the specific influences in patient-therapist interaction and to introduce more systematic thinking and methods into procedures of diagnosis and therapy. Systematic research would serve these purposes, add to our knowledge of the dynamic relations of social health and mental health, and bring us a step closer to the goal of promotion of positive health in the community at large.

CHAPTER 21

VALUES, FAMILY STRUCTURE, AND MENTAL HEALTH

MENTAL HYGIENE hides its adherence to ethical preconceptions behind a scientific façade. . . . The unconscious assumption of the dominant ethic (the philosophy of private initiative, personal responsibility and the individual achievement) together with the psychologistic interpretation has served to obscure the social determinants of mental disease, and especially the effects of invidious relationships. . . . Mental hygiene seems to be limping along on one foot because if there are social determinants these are not being discovered and utilized in prevention," writes Kingsley Davis.[1] Vigorously propounding the distinction between mental hygiene as a social movement and mental hygiene as an applied science, he sets forth the premise that mental hygiene has used the Protestant ethic as a basis for advice about those forms of conduct which are conducive to mental health and personal happiness. Mental health workers have indulged in preachment of conformity to the prevailing social system and the related values under the guise of "science."

More recently William H. Whyte, in his book *The Organization Man*, argued that the traditional Protestant ethic is steadily yielding to the organizational or bureaucratic ethic, in which the earlier values of individual salvation through hard work, thrift, and competitive struggle become submerged under the pressure toward conformity with the group. He describes the organizational ethic as representing a belief in the group as the source of creativity, a belief in "belongingness" as the ultimate need in the individual, and a belief in the application of science to achieve the belongingness. Except as a unit of society man is isolated and meaningless.

How are mental health workers to view these problems of adaptation to present-day society? Can they define the issues clearly and accurately or do they seek avenues of escape? They may blind themselves to the pathogenic trends in the structure of contemporary social patterns and seek solace in the mental hygiene approach of helping individual persons; or seek comfort in the doctrines of the more restricted and traditional aspects of psychoanalytic theory that stress the past over the present; or contrariwise deny the valid psychoanalytic truths regarding childhood conditioning and blame everything on the "social system." (This last represents a pattern of wishful escapism into radical political philosophy, unchecked by factual acquaintance with the science of psychopathology.) Here are two extremes, each representing a serious danger to correct orientation of mental health workers. Both attitudes represent closed systems of thought, in which effective scientific analysis of the relevant facts is no longer possible. To take flight into either of these blind alleys is no solution. It is a confession of defeat.

More realistic is the approach being made by those professional groups that have recognized the need for a complete re-evaluation of mental hygiene principles. History has challenged us to examine with special care the pathogenic features of the present-day social structure, the phenomena of group tension, the role of conflict and anxiety in interpersonal relations, and the social psychopathology of family life. The anthropological principle of the relativity of behavior has forced us to a critical reassessment of Freudian theory.

One aspect of the problem deserves special emphasis. In an effectively functioning, well-organized social system, the task of adjustment requires that people conform on a selective and flexible basis to the mores of their community. In order to integrate themselves with the group, they must identify with the dominant ethics of family and society. Just as children identify with their parents, so people integrate the dominant ethics of their social system, incorporating it into their growth as persons and making it a functioning part of their self-structure. A healthy conformity to a healthy group need not suppress individual expression and development. It may even enhance it. If, however, the social system is disorganized, unstable, and unpredictable and provides too little security, they cannot conform. If value attitudes are profoundly confused, it is difficult to fit into the group. The tragedy is not, as Davis implies, that people conform to the dominant ethics; it is rather that the prevailing social conflicts and instability make it extremely difficult to conform, or people simply discover that it does not pay to conform.

Dynamically, the problem is analogous to certain elemental aspects of the child-parent relationship. If a parent does not offer enough security to a child, the child neither identifies with nor conforms to the ethics of the parent. The relationship of the adult to his surrounding society is much the same. The striving of adults is basically to conform to the dominant ethics of the prevailing social system. They simply cannot do so if there is too little security in the pattern of group living. Where social ideals and human values themselves are in a state of disorder, it is hazardous for adult persons to identify with such values; it becomes inexpedient to conform. This is surely the case in our time. But we must remember, too, that it is important to distinguish between an emotionally healthy conformity and a superficial, defensive type of conformity which serves the purpose of neutralizing feelings of insecurity but does not represent a true integration of the individual into the group.

Blatantly in evidence are the disorganizing trends in contemporary family life, the conflicts and failures of complementarity in man-wife relations and parent-child relations, the signs of disintegration of the moral and ethical core of family relationships. Whereas fifty years ago people were troubled by an overstrict conscience and crushed by an excessive weight of guilt, today many are amoral, fickle, and destructive in their human relationships. They act out their hostile impulses without any dependable sense of ethical responsibility. It behooves all mental health workers, therefore, to re-examine the entire area of values—in their own lives and their own work, in their patients, in the culture and the society from which they and their patients come. No matter how technologically sound our principles, no matter how well-implemented our techniques, we cannot expect to progress toward a mentally healthy community until values are clarified and value systems defined.[2]

Values are personal and yet they are social too. They do not have a private origin, but they become privately treasured. An individual may defend his values as he defends his own self. He may even sacrifice his life to protect these values. Values are born out of the assimilation of the individual into group living. They provide orientation to the relations of individual, family, and society. They give meaning to a person's position in life. They are the compass which provides a sense of direction in the maze of social relations from birth to death.

Value orientation begins within the family group. It is within the family that the personal identity of the individual is first formed. As the individual grows and differentiates his separate being within the matrix of his childhood family experience, he gradually establishes his personal identity. The psychic center of gravity for the individual is this identity and a corresponding set of standards, strivings, and values. Beginning with family and moving out as the individual matures, to each new group in turn, values undergo further change. They are in no sense static; they are linked to the evolving identity of the person. Each successive level of group identification—the family of childhood, nursery, school, neighborhood, social club, place of work, and ultimately the new family created in marriage—requires some measure of adaptive modification of personal identity and values.

Moving from one group to the next engenders conflict between the older perception of self with its connected values and the newer ones. In this way orientation to self and other persons and the associated values are intimately connected with the roles a person fulfills within each successive group of which he is a part. Conflict in values is therefore related to a shift of groups and roles within these groups. As the individual moves through time, his perspective is influenced by this continuously evolving process of value change, which parallels his membership in a progressive series of changing groups. This process involves conflict between the representations of the old and the new. Conflict is an intrinsic part of living and growing. It is the progressive resolution of conflict that contributes to growth and mental health. But the struggle with conflict may fail, and the result is adaptive breakdown. Thus, the effects of conflict may be healthy or unhealthy, constructive or destructive. They may catalyze the development of the individual or paralyze it.

Psychological identity and value orientation are nuclear representations of the functioning of both individuals and groups. They lend color and character to social behavior. Values are influenced by a wide range of factors: age, sex, personal endowment (physical, emotional, intellectual, etc.), and also social and cultural position.

It is by a recognition of values that we attach meaning to differences among people. It is thus that we define the subjective content of these differences between the light and dark skinned, young and old, male and female, Jew and Gentile, rich and poor. But difference and sameness are two sides of one coin. The confrontation of difference leads ultimately to the recognition of underlying sameness and eventual reconciliation.

Values are influenced by human relations both in time and space. The young and old hold different values. Values are distinct for each era of life: childhood, adolescence, adulthood, and old age. Regardless of chronological age, some people feel young, others feel old. In the passage of time they attach different subjective meanings to change in themselves and their life situations. Some live for the future, some live in the past, some live only for the moment. Some people count as important only their time on earth. Others, in contrast, seek their salvation in the hereafter. Values change with change in the space relations of people. Regardless of actual distance, people may feel close or far away. A sense of abandonment or isolation in human relations alters values, as does the experience of closeness and intimacy.

In accordance with such variations, people love life or are soured on it.

Some hope and dream, others dare not. Some believe life is for living, others for hoarding. Some take a view of life that is expansive; they treasure the intensity of every living moment; they look upon life as an exuberant, exciting adventure; they want the full cup. Others fear life and shrink back from it.

Values, by their very nature, tend to be polarized in sets of opposites. They present a problem in choice which may readily be illustrated in a series of pairs:

Creativity	versus	Destructiveness
Freedom	versus	Compulsion
Strength	versus	Weakness
Independence	versus	Dependence
Courage	versus	Caution and retreat
Adventure	versus	Security
Cooperation	versus	Competition
Social responsibility	versus	Self-indulgence
Orderliness	versus	Disorderliness
Generosity	versus	Parsimony
Inner reality	versus	Appearance
Spiritual enrichment	versus	Material acquisition
Equality and mutual regard	versus	Inequality and a striving for power
Respect for the human being	versus	The human being as a thing, a pawn, a tool

The psychological identity of individuals, families, and communities varies according to an orientation to such a scale of polarized values. The crucial questions are: What roles do psychological identity and value choice play in mental illness and health? How do they affect the forces of social contagion toward the one or the other state of being?

We have said that values emerge through the organic relatedness of individual and group. Human striving requires the organization of a point of view toward the experience of life, a personal philosophy, the setting of a system of priorities in goals and values, which is adapted to the conditions of living. Values are shared; they are neither born nor maintained in a state of isolation. Where there is a conflict of values, a person seeks out allies to defend his values against opposed ones. At every point in life, values are linked to an image of family group or its equivalent. It is within this framework that specific meanings are attached to differences among people—differences of age, sex, physique, social position, etc.

Such meanings are first patterned within the family fold. Values and the meanings of difference are molded in the shared experiences of salient family pairs—man and wife, mother and child, child and child. They are affected, too, by the mutuality of influence of emotional interaction of one family pair upon another, man and wife upon mother and child, and vice versa.

The polarization of values is related to a basic question in human relations: Do the differences of mother and child, or man and wife enhance each partner in the family pair, or are they inimical? Do the needs and actions of the one complement those of the other or do they clash? At some points in life and in connection with specific problems, the needs of mother and child, man and woman, do seem to conflict. The crucial question, however, is not the presence or absence of conflict related to difference; it is rather the choice of direction for the solution to conflict. Is it oriented toward the end-goal of achieving a new level of sharing and union, which furthers the continued development of each partner, or is it oriented toward an irreversible alienation? Fundamentally, are the partners of the family pair friends or enemies?

As far as the evidence goes, they should be friends. The basic needs of mother and child, man and woman, do not clash; they complement one another. Mother and child are in mutual need of one another. Each is incomplete without the other. The baby need not expand at the expense of the mother. The same may be said of the relations of man and woman. What is good for the one is ultimately good for the other. One sex need not fulfill itself at the cost of the other. Healthy individuation rests on the foundation of a healthy union both in the male-female pair and the mother-child pair. When the processes of the relationship move toward irreversible alienation we have somewhere violated human nature.

Yet in our culture certain features prevail which predispose toward alienation. The healthy balance of these joined processes of union and individuation becomes derailed. The organic oneness of family relationships is somewhere lost. Mother is pitted against child, man against woman, family relations move into a state of imbalance. The intermittent episodes of conflict do not move where they ought—to a new and better level of togetherness and mutual complementation. Instead competitive dominance and individual acquisition of power become the supreme goal. When this happens, the persons are treated not as human beings but rather as articles of property or things.

Were we able to examine minutely over the course of time the processes of mother-child interaction and man-wife interaction, we could trace the path of equilibrium of the dual processes of emotional union and individuation for each member of these family pairs; we could then take the further step of attempting to correlate dynamically with this the evolution of value attitudes. The continuous evolution of value attitudes is intimately tied to the delicate equilibrium between the processes, on the one hand, of emotional union and identification, and on the other, of individual differentiation. If we could understand this set of relationships more fully, it would be possible eventually to design an interpersonal theory of the development of values in the interactional and transactional processes of family life.

It is a basic law of nature that difference emerges out of an original sameness. In the differentiation and further development of the individual out of the primary family pairs of mother and child, and man and wife, the basic issue is this: does individual differentiation take place in a setting of love, mutual understanding and support, or in a setting of mutual opposition? In other words, with respect to the evolution of value attitudes, the significant question is whether the changing equilibrium between togetherness and separation, sameness and difference is influenced by a prevailing climate of love or hate and fear.

From the genetic point of view, the infant, to begin with, has no values. Values emerge only as the child differentiates its separate self from the mother's self. The emergence of values and socialization are parallel processes. Without values there can be no socialization; without socialization there can be no values. The development of value attitudes is organically linked therefore to socialization and the establishment of personal identity.

In the original symbiosis of mother and child, the child lives within the sphere of the mother's values. The child grows and achieves increasing confidence through the security of this union. The mother's resources for providing food, protection, love and social training are at the disposal of the child's needs. Healthy individuation of the child rests on the dependability of the feeling of togetherness with mother. Too often, however, the child's trust is traumatized by an unpredictable rupture of this union; the mother abruptly turns on the child, and breaks the line of togetherness. This sets the stage for early conflicts in identity. It influences the quality of emotional separation from mother, the child's perception of mother's relations with father and siblings, and in turn the child's own receptiveness to new relationships with family members other than the mother. The child's movement away from exclusive union with mother into an expanding series of family relationships initiates the establishment of personal identity and ushers in the process of value orientation and value change. This is the fluid, interpersonal matrix for the evolution of values. Thus the child learns what his parents stand for and what they expect of him. As he moves away from mother and invests his emotions in a broader weave of family relationships, his differentiation of personal identity is further affected by the balance of forces that prevails in these other family relationships. The equilibrium is a delicate one. Any distortion of it is promptly echoed in the quality of emergence of his personal identity and value attitudes. In the entire process there is a close link between orientation to identity and values and predisposition to states of emotional health or illness.

As we shift focus from the individual to the family group, we recognize analogous processes. Each family unit has a life and growth of its own: a characteristic psychological and social identity, an inner face and outer face, and corresponding strivings, values, and expectations; a pattern of unity and stability, and a configuration of family role relationships uniquely its own. The character and the development of the family through time derive from its levels of joined experience of family members. The integrative pattern of the family molds the levels of reciprocity in family pairs. It patterns the approaches to solution of family problems. It shapes the likely patterns of family conflict and the corresponding forms of restitution. It likewise determines the specific forms of behavior required of family members in their various relationships in order to carry out the family functions. In this way is molded the psychological identity of male-female pairs, parent-child pairs, and the patterns of child-rearing behavior. It is the evolving family structure that reflects the family's way of adapting to new experience, its capacity to change and to achieve new growth. And it is within this design for family living that the potentials for individual development and creativity unfold.

In these overlapping processes is structured a fundamental point of view toward people and the problems of human relations. The dominant value attitudes of the family group may, in the main, be true or false, positive or negative, creative or destructive. It is the identity and value content of a family group that determines the quality and the quantity of support that the family contributes to the maintenance of mental health in its individual members.

We have already seen that families vary greatly in the extent to which family functions are oriented to one group of values or another. Even the casual observer can readily discern significant differences insofar as the emotional climate and the valued preferences of a particular family offer a sharp contrast with other families. Man-wife relations, parent-child relations, and the functional orientation of the family to its wider community, strongly reflect such differences. Thus the emotional climate and preferential strivings of one family accentuate the values of love, creativity, adventure and freedom, whereas the qualities of another family are dominated by values of static security, competition, and exploitive aspirations in human relations.

It is easy to illustrate this theme in a wide range of component value trends, as expressed in the functioning of contrasting types of families. There are families where the dominant value orientation emphasizes the inner spiritual life of the family, a dedication to the worth, dignity and personal development of each member. There are others which accentuate the outer façade of the family, its external image in the eyes of the surrounding community. Such a family often pays scant interest to the internal relations among family members. Sometimes its outward appearance presents the semblance of a fine, stable, closely-knit group; it may earn for itself in the community the reputation of a well functioning, respectable family group, whereas actually its inner emotional substance may be rotten to the core.

There are some families whose component value trends stress pleasure, the joys of the moment. By contrast, others live off the glories of their past; they cherish the reminiscences of the family attainments of long ago. Still others concentrate on building for the future.

The value orientation of some families reflects a striving for freedom of expression, spontaneity and creativity. Others emphasize discipline, duty and self-control. Occasionally such families reveal a profound defensive antipathy to pleasure. They fear it as a dangerous contamination.

There are those families in which the dominant value orientation is to power, status and money. Family relations are structured according to a hierarchy of prestige representations, mainly molded by the power position of each family member. Competition is intense; it is each man for himself and the devil take the hindmost. The striving is for success, whatever the cost to the emotional health of family relations.

In some families where such strivings are defeated, the family epitomizes social degradation and failure. The members of such families are contagiously invaded by the atmosphere of family failure. They become deeply identified with it. A sense of inferiority pervades the personal identity of the members; in consequence of this they feel profoundly ashamed of their families.

To contrast with this, there are the families in which the value trends accentuate a bond of family closeness, devotion, cooperation, and sharing. Here the identity and value orientation of individual and family are intimately connected. Strong trends toward family unity may reflect a condition of positive emotional health, or a negative, suspicious, defensively toned value pattern which reflects a fear of life.

In its positive aspect, family cohesion is expressed in warm, close, cooperative family relations; this may lead to a strengthening of its members and promote free and creative personal development. In its negative aspect, a compensatory and excessive barricading of the family group may intensify the anxieties of its individual members. It may enormously magnify their perception of the outer world as harsh and dangerous. Under such conditions, individual members of the family may not derive a sense of protection from the family closeness. Instead they may feel choked by it. Their excessive dependency may be linked to intensive resentment toward their families, which ultimately induces a sense of alienation and disrupts the family unity.

Family configuration in these terms affects the destiny of salient family pairs: man-wife, parent-child, and child-sibling. The internal alignments of family members fall into one design or another. Trends toward alienation create emotional splits, which set one family segment against another or one family pair against another or which alienate one parent from the rest of the family.

The design for family living, epitomized in family identity and values, determines the degree to which a given family is an open or closed social system. Some families provide open avenues of transaction with the outer community. Others are closed corporations, shutting their members within and reducing to a minimum significant interchange with the outer world. This design affects the members' image of people in the wider world as being the same or different, friendly or menacing. It molds the pattern of emotional receptivity toward outside persons, strangers; it may foster attitudes of warm, trusting welcome or of suspicion, fear, rejection, and hostility.

This aspect of family functioning raises a crucial problem: the dynamic interrelations of values, family structure, emotional health, and prejudicial behavior.[3] Prejudice may be regarded as a variably sick emotional attempt to repair damage to self-esteem. But this psychological device for self-repair often backfires; in the end, it aggravates the basic affliction which it is intended to counteract, the maimed sense of self, the heightened sense of vulnerability to attack, and the longing for close human relations. The psychological essence of prejudice is the need to build oneself up by tearing the other person down. The deeper the irrationality of the prejudice, the closer does the individual's image of human relations approach a pattern of master and slave. In this view, the one person is perceived as big, powerful, overbearing; the other as small, weak and meek. Master and slave together form a symbiotic bond. They interact parasitically. The power of the one is aggrandized as the other is crushed. The pleasures of the one are enhanced at the expense of the other. The relation of master and slave requires the immolation and sacrifice of one partner to serve the omnipotent grandiosity of the other. To sustain such a pattern requires the belief that there is not enough of anything to satisfy the needs of both persons, not enough food, love, pleasure and power; therefore, one must surrender to the other. Should the slave rebel, the reciprocity of the pattern is broken.

The link of identity and values between individual and family group molds tendencies to prejudice. Where the link of individual and family identity is solid and the foundation of self-esteem is firm, there is less need of prejudice. Where the link of individual and family identity is weak and deformed and the foundation of self-esteem is injured, there is fertile ground for a severe form of prejudice.

Irrational prejudice is a destructive force in human society. It expresses a master-slave image of human relations. It exalts power for its own sake, as the instrument of exploitation. When one person exists only to serve the grandness of another, we have the germ of perversion—perversion of interpersonal relations from a striving for trust, love, and mutuality of interest to purposes of destruction.

The vicissitudes of family living expressed in these differences of psychological identity, interpersonal climate, and value orientation, influence profoundly the family's capacity for maintaining effective emotional equilibrium, fulfilling essential family functions, and promoting the growth and welfare of its members. Such patterns determine the potentials for achieving complementarity in family relationships, for effective solutions to conflict, support of the self-image of individual family members, and support for needed forms of defense against anxiety.

It is the value orientation of the family group that determines what is shared in family relations. Family values mold orienting attitudes toward the goals of security, pleasure, mastery, personal maturation, and self-fulfillment in new experience. Values influence the contagion of family emotion that predisposes to health or illness. It is in this sense that we see the relation of values, family structure, and mental health.

Mental illness and mental health are, in large part, a product of contagion in human relations. In our country today, in matters of physical health, the trend is to move beyond a concern with disease process per se to treat the patient as a whole person within his life situation. In the field of mental health, however, we are still mainly focused on the negative goal: the control of individual cases of mental illness.[4] The rising tide of mental contagion brings a threat of epidemic. But we are not yet finding our way to the sources of contamination in human relations so as to build immunity against illness and promote positive mental health.

An exclusive program of individual therapy for emotionally sick persons is by itself critically inadequate. For each such person treated and cured, there are numerous others who raise their heads clamoring for help. It is like riding forth to do battle with a many-headed hydra. We lop off one head and six others rise to take its place. To destroy the monster completely we must arm the entire community.

The structure of family echoes disordered values in the larger pattern of human relations. Family and society are organically intertwined. Do we have a sick society? We must seek an answer to this question. Perhaps it is possible to shed further light on this question by putting to more rigorous tests the several hypotheses suggested here: (1) mental illness and health are contagious phenomena; the elements of illness and health act like germs; they are passed from person to person in human intercourse; (2) the elements of contagion exist both inside persons and between persons; they pervade the functioning of groups as well as individuals; (3) the principle of relativity applies both to the concept of mental illness and positive mental health. The striving for mental health may take many forms. It is social process which determines the standards of health in a given community.

If these hypotheses are valid, we must determine where in the complicated machinery of human relations and social structure to look for those links in the chain which are relevant to the protection of the mental health of the community. What is contagious and pathogenic in the behavior of particular individuals, families and communities? Where in this intricate weave of human relations do we seek the most virulent carriers of pathology? How do we trace the path from the conditions of living to the balance of forces between illness and health?

Surely one significant link in this chain is the line of identification and value orientation which joins individual, family and society. Some values promote emotional illness, others promote health. Whether they do one or the other can be judged only in a defined life situation. In every society there will always be value differences and value conflicts. This insures personal freedom. But what degree of freedom? No freedom is bad. Too much freedom may cause too great a strain and bring about disorganization. What is the optimum of personal freedom for the promotion of health?

It is our ultimate responsibility as mental health workers to discover and define this optimum and to make it a real and vital force in human relations patterns, within the family, and in the wider social community. As society moves forward into the age of nuclear energy and control of outer space, we must anticipate a revolutionary transformation of social patterns. To prepare for this, we need a better understanding of human nature, of the interrelations of individual, family, and society, and of the role of values in the promotion of health. Albert Einstein has said: "Common sense may be construed to mean a deposit of prejudices laid down in the mind prior to the age of eighteen." In order to pierce the subtleties of the mental health challenge of our time, we must advance beyond the "common sense" of an eighteen year old. We surely need that rare "uncommon sense" with which leaders in science and social philosophy are fortunately endowed. It is this uncommon sense, the capacity for elegant synthesis, which makes for new discoveries and new attitudes toward age-old problems in human relations.

REFERENCES

Introduction:

Mental Health, Social Change, and Family

[1] Arnold Toynbee, New Vistas for the Historian, *Saturday Review*, January 7, 1956.

[2] See, *e.g.*, the brochure on statistical facts regarding mental illness in the United States prepared by the National Committee Against Mental Illness (January 1957) and the chapter Prevalence of Mental Illness, in *Practical Clinical Psychiatry;* by Jack R. Ewalt, Edward A. Strecker, and Franklin G. Ebough (New York: McGraw-Hill, 1957).

[3] Karl A. Menninger, *The Human Mind*, 3d ed. (New York: Knopf, 1947), p. 2.

[4] Erich Fromm, *Escape From Freedom* (New York: Farrar & Rinehart, 1941), p. 138.

[5] See the Constitution of World Health Organization.

[6] Marie Jahoda, Toward a Social Psychology of Mental Health, in *Problems of Infancy and Childhood*, ed. Milton J. E. Senn (New York: Josiah Macy Foundation, 1950).

[7] Andreas Angyal, *The Foundations for a Science of Personality* (New York: Commonwealth Fund, 1941), p. 3.

[8] Jurgen Reusch, in *Toward a Unified Theory of Human Behavior*, ed. Roy R. Grinker (New York: Basic Books, 1956), p. xi.

Chapter 1

The Psychodynamics of the Family

[1] Otto Klineberg, *Social Psychology*, rev. ed. (New York: Holt, 1954).
[2] Arthur Miller, Family in Modern Drama, *Atlantic*, 197: 35-41, April 1956.

Chapter 2

Freud and the Psychoanalytic View of the Family

[1] Ian Suttie, *The Origins of Love and Hate* (New York: Julian Press, 1952).
[2] J. C. Flügel, *The Psycho-analytic Study of the Family* (London: Hogarth, 1926).
[3] Anna Freud, Psychoanalysis and Education, delivered at the New York Academy of Medicine, May 5, 1954.

Chapter 3

Freud and Changing Conceptions of Personality
—A Personal Synthesis

[1] Robert Waelder, Problems of Infantile Neuroses: A Discussion, in *The Psychoanalytic Study of the Child*, Vol. IX (New York: International Universities Press, 1954), p. 56.

[2] For an excellent statement of these concepts, see George L. Engel, Homeostasis, Behavioral Adjustment and the Concept of Health and Disease, in *Mid-Century Psychiatry*, ed. Roy R. Grinker (Springfield, Ill.: Thomas, 1953).

[3] *New York Times Magazine*, May 6, 1956, p. 37.

[4] For a concise summary, see Murphy's Biosocial Theory, in Calvin S. Hall and Gardner Lindzey, *Theories of Personality* (New York: Wiley, 1957).

[5] See A. H. Maslow, *Motivation and Personality* (New York: Harper, 1954), p. 57.

[6] Thomas French, *Integration of Behavior* (Chicago: University of Chicago Press, 1952), p. 116.

[7] Abram Kardiner, Libido Theory—The Cultural Point of View, paper delivered to the American Psychoanalytic Association, St. Louis, Mo., 1954.

[8] Eric Erikson, *Childhood and Society* (New York: Norton, 1950), pp. 90, 91, 60.

[9] Jules Masserman, Psychoanalysis and Biodynamics, *Internat. J. Psychoanal.*, 30:1953.

[10] Ian Suttie, *The Origins of Love and Hate* (New York: Julian Press, 1952).

[11] Ruth Munroe, *Schools of Psychoanalytic Thought* (New York: Dryden Press, 1955), p. 121.

[12] Max Planck, *Treatise on Thermodynamics* (New York: Dover Publications, 1945), pp. 104-105.

[13] Ralph Girard, Brain Physiology: A Basic Science, in *Changing Conceptions of Psychoanalytic Medicine*, ed. Sandor Rado and George E. Daniels (New York: Grune & Stratton, 1956), pp. 31-43.

[14] Herbert Birch, Sources of Order in the Maternal Behavior of Animals, *Am. J. Orthopsychiat.*, 26:279-284, 1956.

[15] Ralph Girard, *op. cit.*

[16] Robert G. Heath, Electroencephalograms and Subcortigrams Recorded since 1952, Addendum E, in *Studies of Schizophrenia* (Cambridge, Mass.: Harvard University Press, 1954), pp. 579-583.

Chapter 5

The Homeostasis of Behavior

[1] Walter B. Cannon, *Wisdom of the Body*, rev. ed. (New York: Norton, 1938), p. 305.

[2] *Ibid.*, p. 286.

[8] Andreas Angyal, *Foundations for a Science of Personality* (New York: Commonwealth Fund, 1941), p. 32.

[4] Margaret Ribble, *The Rights of Infants* (New York: Columbia University Press, 1943).

[5] Therese Benedek, Personality Development, in *Dynamic Psychiatry*, ed. Franz Alexander and Helen Ross (Chicago: University of Chicago Press, 1952), pp. 63-113.

Chapter 6

Family Identity, Stability, and Breakdown

[1] See, *e.g.*, Don D. Jackson, The Question of Family Homeostasis, *The Psychiatric Quarterly Supplement*, Vol. XXXI, Part I, pp. 79-90; Gregory Bateson *et al.*, Toward a Theory of Schizophrenia, *Behav. Sci.*, 1:251-264, 1956.

[2] Murray Bowen *et al.*, Study and Treatment of Five Hospitalized Family Groups Each with a Psychotic Member, paper delivered to the American Psychiatric Association, 1957.

[3] See, *e.g.*, Erich Lindemann, Symptomatology and Management of Acute Grief, *Am. J. Psychiat.*, 101: 141-148, 1944.

[4] Gerald Caplan, Some Comments on Family Functioning in Its Relationship to Mental Health, paper delivered to the American Orthopsychiatric Association, 1956.

[5] See, *e.g.*, Florence Rockwood Kluckhohn, Family Diagnosis: Variations in the Basic Values of Family Systems, *Social Casework*, 39:63-72, 1958; John P. Spiegel, New Perspectives in the Study of the Family, *Marriage and Family Living*, 16:4-12, 1954.

[6] Seymour Fisher and David Mendell, The Communication of Neurotic Patterns over Two and Three Generations, *Psychiatry*, 19:41-46, 1956.

[7] Gerald Handel and Robert D. Hess, Family Themes and Patterns of Alignment, paper delivered to the American Orthopsychiatric Association, 1956.

[8] See, *e.g.*, Nathan W. Ackerman, Interpersonal Disturbances in the Family: A Frame of Reference for Psychotherapy, *Psychiatry*, 17:No. 4, 1954; Nathan W. Ackerman and Marjorie L. Behrens, A Study of Family Diagnosis, *Am. J. Orthopsychiat.*, 26:No. 1, 1956; Nathan W. Ackerman, An Orientation to Psychiatric Research on the Family, *Marriage and Family Living*, 19: 68-74, 1957; M. Robert Gomberg, Family Diagnosis: Trends in Theory and Practice, *Social Casework*, 39: 73-85, 1958; as well as other studies listed in the Bibliography.

[9] See William Goldfarb and Marilyn M. Dorsen, *Annotated Bibliography of Childhood Schizophrenia* (New York: Basic Books, 1956).

[10] Adelaide M. Johnson and S. A. Szurek, The Genesis of Antisocial Acting Out in Children and Adults, *Psychoanal. Quart.*, 21: 323-343, 1952.

Chapter 8

Behavioral Disturbances of the Contemporary Family

[1] Iago Galdston, personal communication. See also his Social Implications of Dynamic Psychiatry, in *Social Medicine* (New York: Commonwealth Fund, 1949)

and The American Family in Crisis, paper delivered to Pennsylvania Mental Health, Inc., May 1957.

[2] E. R. Mowrer, The Study of Family Disorganization, *The Family*, 8: 85-87, 1927.

[3] Talcott Parsons and Robert F. Bales, *Family, Socialization and Interaction Process* (Glencoe, Ill.: Free Press, 1955), p. 4.

[4] E. W. Burgess, The Dilemma of Family Relations in a Changing Society, paper delivered to the American Orthopsychiatric Association, 1957.

[5] Margaret Mead, American Man in a Woman's World, *New York Times Magazine*, Feb. 10, 1957.

[6] Emil Durkheim, *Suicide* (Glencoe, Ill.: Free Press, 1951).

[7] Erich Fromm, *The Sane Society* (New York: Rinehart, 1955).

[8] David Riesman, *The Lonely Crowd* (New Haven, Conn.: Yale University Press, 1950).

[9] E. W. Burgess, The Family in a Changing Society, *Am. J. Sociol.*, 53: 417-422, 1948.

[10] Eric Erikson, The Problem of Ego Identity, *J. Am. Psychoanal. Assn.*, 4: 56-121, 1956.

Chapter 10

Disturbances of Marital Pairs

[1] The work of Bela Mittelman on this problem is helpful. See, *e.g.*, Complementary Neurotic Reactions in Intimate Relationships, *Psychoanal. Quart.*, 13:No. 4, 1944; and Concurrent Analysis of Married Couples, *Psychoanal. Quart.*, 17: 182-197, 1948.

Chapter 11

Disturbances of Parental Pairs

[1] Gerhart Piers and Milton S. Singer, *Shame and Guilt* (Springfield, Ill.: Thomas, 1953).

Chapter 15

Psychosomatic Illness and Family Disturbance

[1] Although available material is limited, the following may prove useful: C. A. Binger *et al.*, *Personality and Arterial Hypertension* (New York: American Society for Research in Psychosomatic Problems, 1945); Nathan W. Ackerman, Character Structure in Hypertensive Persons, *Life Stress and Bodily Disease*, 29: 1950; Nathan W. Ackerman, Personality Factors in Neurodermite, *Psychosomatic Medicine*, 1: No. 3, 1939; Lawrence E. Hinkle, Jr., and Harold G. Wolff, Health and the Social Environment, in *Explorations in Social Psychiatry*, ed. Alexander H. Leighton *et al.* (New York: Basic Books, 1957).

[2] Thomas Morton French and Franz Gabriel Alexander, Psychogenic Factors in Bronchial Asthma, in *Psychosomatic Medicine Monographs,* 1941.

Chapter 16

Psychotherapy Today

[1] Bela Mittelman, The Concurrent Analysis of Married Couples, *Psychoanal Quart.,* 17: 182-197, 1948.

Chapter 17

Goals of Psychotherapy

[1] M. Burgum, Values and Some Technical Problems of Psychotherapy, paper delivered to the American Orthopsychiatric Association, 1955.

Chapter 20

Problems of Family Research

[1] F. S. C. Northrup, *The Logic of the Sciences and the Humanities* (New York: Macmillan, 1947), pp. 255-264.
[2] A. H. Maslow, *Motivation and Personality* (New York: Harper, 1954).
[8] *Ibid.*

Chapter 21

Values, Family Structure, and Mental Health

[1] Kingsley Davis, Mental Hygiene and the Class Structure, *Psychiatry,* 1: 55-65, 1938.
[2] In this connection, see John Spiegel, New Perspectives in the Study of Family, *Marriage and Family Living,* 16: 4-20, 1954; Florence Kluckhohn, Family Diagnosis: Variations in the Basic Values of Family Systems, *Social Casework,* 39: 63-72, 1958; and John Spiegel and Florence Kluckhohn, Integration and Conflict in Family Behavior, Report No. 27 (Topeka, Kan.: Group for the Advancement of Psychiatry, 1954).
[8] See, *e.g.,* Nathan W. Ackerman and Marie Jahoda, *Antisemitism and Emotional Disorder* (New York: Harper, 1950); Nathan W. Ackerman, The Psychology of Prejudice, paper delivered at meeting of The Society of Medical Analysts, New York Academy of Medicine, March 1955.
[4] See, *e.g.,* Marvin Opler, Cultural Anthropology and Social Psychiatry, *Am. J. Psychiat.,* 113: 302-311, 1956; The Social Responsibility of Psychiatry, Report No. 13 (Topeka, Kan.: Group for Advancement of Psychiatry, 1950).

BIBLIOGRAPHY

In addition to the sources cited in the notes, the following books and articles provide useful background material for professional work with family problems.

Abrahams, Joseph, and Varon, Edith. *Maternal Dependency and Schizophrenia.* New York: International Universities Press, 1953.

Abrahams, Ray H. The Concept of Family Stability. *Annals Am. Acad. Pol. and Soc. Sci.,* 272: Nov. 1950.

Ackerman, Nathan W. The Diagnosis of Neurotic Marital Interaction. *Soc. Casework,* 35: No. 4, 1954.

———. Interpersonal Disturbances in the Family: Some Unsolved Problems in Psychotherapy. *Psychiatry,* 17: 359-368, 1954.

———. An Orientation to Psychiatric Research on the Family. *Marriage and Family Living,* 19:68-74, 1957.

———. Psychoanalytic Principles in a Mental Health Clinic for the Pre-School Child and His Family. *Psychiatry,* 19: 63-76, 1956.

———. Psychotherapy and "Giving Love." *Psychiatry,* 7: 129-137, 1944.

———. Group Dynamics: 1. "Social Role" and Total Personality. *Am. J. Orthopsychiat.,* 21: 1-17, 1951.

———. The Unity of the Family. *Archives of Pediatrics,* 55: 51-62, 1938.

———, and Behrens, M. L. Child and Family Psychopathy: Problems of Correlation. *Psychopathology of Childhood,* ed. Paul H. Hoch and Joseph Zubin. New York: Grune & Stratton, 1955.

———, and Behrens, M. L. A Study of Family Diagnosis. *Am. J. Orthopsychiat.* 26: 66-78, 1956.

———, and Neubauer, P. B. Failures in the Psychotherapy of Children. In *Failures in Psychiatric Treatment,* ed. Paul H. Hoch. New York: Grune & Stratton, 1958.

———, and Sobel, Raymond. Family Diagnosis: An Approach to the Study of the Pre-school Child. *Am. J. Orthopsychiat.,* 20: 744-753, 1950.

Adams, E. M. The Philosophical Approach to Marriage and Family Research. *Soc. Forces,* 29: 62-64, 1950.

Adler, Lita M. The Relationship of Marital Status to Incidence of and Recovery from Mental Illness. *Soc. Forces,* 32: 185-194, 1953.

Allen, Frederick H. Dynamics of Roles as Determined in the Structure of the Family. *Am. J. Orthopsychiat.,* 12: No. 1, 1942.

Altman, Charlotte H. Relationships Between Maternal Attitudes and Child Personality Structure. *Am. J. Psychiat.,* 28: 160-169, 1958.

Anderson, Harold H., and Anderson, Gladys L. Social Development. In *Manual of Child Psychology,* ed. Leonard Carmichael. 2d ed. New York: Wiley, 1954.

Anshen, Ruth. *The Family, Its Function and Destiny.* New York: Harper, 1949.

Appel, Kenneth. Anxiety Problems Within Cultural Settings. *Am. J. Psychiat.*, 113: 526-529, 1956.

Austin, Lucille N. Failures in Social Casework. In *Failures in Psychiatric Treatment*, ed. Paul H. Hoch. New York: Grune & Stratton, 1948.

Bain, Read. Making Normal People. *Marriage and Family Living*, 16: No. 1, 1954.

———. Needed Research in Parent-Child Fixation. *Am. Sociol. Rev.*, 10: 208-216, 1945.

Baldwin, Alfred L. Changes in Parent Behavior During Pregnancy: An Experiment in Logitudinal Analysis. *Child Develop.*, 18: 29-39, 1947.

———. Differences in Parent Behavior Toward Three- and Nine-Year-Old Children. *J. Personality*, 15: 143-165, 1946.

———. Socialization and the Parent-Child Relationship. *Child Develop.*, 19: No. 3, 1948.

———, Kalhorn, J., and Breese, F. H. Patterns of Parent Behavior. *Psychol. Monogr.*, 58: No. 3, 1945.

———. The Appraisal of Parent Behavior. *Psychol. Monogr.*, 63: 4 (No. 299), 1949.

Bales, Robert F. *Interaction Process Analysis.* Cambridge, Mass.: Addison-Wesley, 1951.

Beaglehole, Ernest. A Critique of "The Measurement of Family Interaction." *Am. J. Sociol.*, 51: 145-147, 1945.

Behrens, Marjorie L. Child Rearing and the Character Structure of the Mother. *Child Develop.* 25: No. 3.

Benedek, Therese. Psychobiological Aspects of Mothering. *Am. J. Orthopsychiat.*, 26: 272-278, 1956.

———. The Psychosomatic Implications of the Primary Unit: Mother-Child. *Am. J. Orthopsychiat.*, 19: 642-654, 1949.

Bennett, Edward M., and Johannesen, Dorothea E. Some Psychodynamic Aspects of Felt Parental Alliance in Young Children. *J. Ab. and Soc. Psychol.*, 49: 463-466, 1954.

Berdie, Ralph F. The Parent as a Rival Sibling. *J. Clin. Psychol.*, 8: 95-96, 1952.

Bergler, Edmund. *Divorce Won't Help.* New York: Harper, 1948.

———. Six Types of Neurotic Reaction to a Husband's Request for a Divorce. *Marriage and Family Living*, 8: No. 4, 1946.

———. *Unhappy Marriage and Divorce.* New York: International Universities Press, 1946.

Berkowitz, Sidney. An Approach to the Treatment of Marital Discord. *J. Soc. Casework*, 29: No. 9.

Bettelheim, Bruno. Individual and Mass Behavior in Extreme Situations. *J. Ab. and Soc. Psychol.* 38: 417-452, 1943.

Bion, W. R. Experiences in Groups. *Human Relations*, 1: Nos. 3, 4, 1948; 2: Nos. 1, 4, 1949; 3: Nos. 1, 4, 1950; 4: No. 3, 1951.

Bird, H. Waldo, and Martin, Peter A. Countertransference in the Psychotherapy of Marriage Partners. *Psychiatry*, 19: 353-360, 1956.

Bishop, Barbara Merrill. Mother-Child Interaction and the Social Behavior of Children. *Psychol. Monogr.* 64: No. 11, 1951.

Bobbitt, Joseph M., and Clausen, John A. Psychotherapy and Its Public Health Implications. In *Psychotherapy: Theory and Research*, ed. O. H. Mowrer *et al.* New York: Ronald, 1953.

Boggs, Marjorie. Family Social Work in Relation to Family Life. *The Family*, 15: No. 5, 1934.

Bossard, James H. S. The Law of Family Interaction. *Am. J. Sociol.*, 50: 292-294, 1945.

———. *Parent and Child: Studies in Family Behavior*. Philadelphia: University of Pennsylvania Press, 1953.

——— (ed). Toward Family Stability. *Annals Am. Acad. Pol. and Soc. Sci.*, 272: Nov. 1950.

Bott, Elizabeth. Urban Families: The Norms of Conjugal Roles. *Human Relations*, 9: No. 3, 1956.

Bowen, M., Dysinger, R. H., Brodey, W. M., and Basamania, B. Study and Treatment of Five Hospitalized Family Groups with a Psychotic Member. Paper delivered at Am. Orthopsychiat. Assn. meetings, Chicago, March 8, 1957.

Bowlby, John. *Maternal Care and Mental Health*. World Health Organization Monograph Series No. 2. Geneva: WHO, 1952.

———. The Study and Reduction of Group Tensions in the Family. *Human Relations*, 2: No. 2, 1949.

Bowman, C. Research in Family Dynamics: A Criticism and a Proposal. *Soc. Forces*, 34: 201-207, 1956.

Briffault, Robert. *The Mothers*. New York: Macmillan, 1927.

Brim, Orville G. Jr., Brieland, Donald, and Harris, Dale B. Research on Parent Education. *Marriage and Family Living*, 19: No. 1, 1957.

Brodey, W. M., and Hayden, M. Intrateam Reactions: Their Relation to the Conflicts of the Family in Treatment. *Am. J. Orthopsychiat.*, 27: 349-355, 1957.

Brody, Sylvia. *Patterns of Mothering*. New York: International Universities Press, 1956.

Brown, Andrew W., Morrison, Joan, and Couch, Gertrude B. Influence of Affectional Family Relationships on Character Development. *J. Ab. and Soc. Psychol.*, 42: No. 4, 1947.

Burgess, Ernest W. The Family as a Unity of Interacting Personalities. *The Family*, 7: 3-9, 1926.

———. The Family in a Changing Society. *Am. J. Sociol.*, 53: 417-422, 1948.

———, and Cottrell, L. B. *Predicting Success or Failure in Marriage*. New York: Prentice-Hall, 1939.

———, and Locke, Harvey. *The Family from Institution to Companionship*. New York: American Book, 1945.

Burgum, Mildred. The Father Gets Worse: A Child Guidance Problem. *Am. J. Orthopsychiat.*, 22: 474-485, 1942.

Burrow, Trigant. The Basis of Group-Analysis, or the Analysis of the Reactions of Normal and Neurotic Individuals. *Brit. J. Med. Psychol.*, 7: Part 3, 1928.

———. *The Biology of Human Conflict: An Anatomy of Behavior, Individual and Social*. New York and London: Macmillan, 1937.

———. Emotion and the Social Crisis: A Problem in Phylobiology. In *Feelings and Emotions*, ed. Martin L. Reymert. New York: McGraw-Hill, 1950.

———. Our Mass Neurosis. *Psychol. Bull.*, 23: 1926.

——. *The Neurosis of Man: An Introduction to a Science of Human Behavior.* New York: Harcourt, Brace, 1949.

——. Our Social Evasion. *Med. J. and Record,* 123: 1926.

——. *A Search for Man's Sanity.* New York: Oxford University Press, 1958.

Buxbaum, Edith. *Your Child Makes Sense: A Guidebook for Parents.* New York: International Universities Press, 1949.

Calhoun, A. W. *Social History of the American Family from Colonial Times to the Present.* New York: Barnes & Noble, 1945.

Cameron, N. *The Psychology of Behavior Disorders; A Biosocial Interpretation.* Boston: Houghton, Mifflin, 1947.

Cass, Loretta Kekeisen. An Investigation of Parent-Child Relationships in Terms of Awareness, Identification, Projection, and Control. *Am. J. Orthopsychiat.,* 22: 305-313, 1952.

——. Parent-Child Relationships and Delinquency. *J. Ab. and Soc. Psychol.,* 47: 101-104, 1952.

Cava, Esther Laden, and Rausch, Harold L. Identification and the Adolescent Boy's Perception of His Father. *J. Ab. and Soc. Psychol.,* 47: 855-856, 1952.

Chance, Erika. Measuring Changes in the Family of a Four-Year-Old During Treatment. In *Emotional Problems of Early Childhood,* ed. Gerald Caplan. New York: Basic Books, 1955.

——. Measuring the Potential Interplay of Forces Within the Family During Treatment. *Child Develop.,* 26: 241-265, 1955.

Chisholm, George Brock. Social Responsibility. *J. Soc. Issues,* Suppl. Ser., No. 1, Dec. 1948.

Classification of Disorganized Families for Use in Family Oriented Diagnosis and Treatment, St. Paul, Minn.: Community Research Assn., Inc., 1954.

Clausen, John A. *Sociology and the Field of Mental Health.* New York: Russell Sage Foundation, 1956.

——, and Yarrow, M. R. (eds.) The Impact of Mental Illness on the Family. *J. Soc. Issues,* 11: 3-64, 1955.

Cleveland, E. J., and Longaker, W. D. Neurotic Patterns in the Family. In *Explorations in Social Psychiatry,* ed. Alexander H. Leighton *et al.* New York: Basic Books, 1957.

Cohen, Mabel Blake, Baker, Grace, Cohen, Robert A., Fromm-Reichmann, Frieda, and Weigert, Edith V. An Intensive Study of Twelve Cases of Manic-Depressive Psychosis. *Psychiatry,* 17: No. 2, 1954.

Cole, Nyla J., Shaw, Orla M., Steneck, Jack, and Taborof, Leonard H. A Survey Assessment of Current Parental Attitudes and Child-Rearing Practices. *J. Am. Orthopsychiat.,* 27: 815-822, 1957.

Community Service Society. *The Family in a Democratic Society.* New York: Columbia University Press, 1949.

Cottrell, Leonard S. New Directions for Research on the American Family. *Soc. Casework,* 34: 54-60, 1953.

——, and Dymond, Rosalind F. The Emphatic Responses: A Neglected Field for Research. *Psychiatry,* 12: No. 4, 1949.

Crawley, Ernest. *The Mystic Rose.* Rev. Basterman. 2 vols. New York: Boni and Liveright, 1927.

Davidson, H. B. The Psychosomatic Aspects of Educated Childbirth. *New York State J. Med.*, 53: 2499, 1953.

Davis, Kingsley. The Sociology of Parent-Youth Conflict. *Am. Sociol. Rev.*, 5: No. 4, 1940.

Despert, Louise J. *Children of Divorce*. Garden City, N.Y.: Doubleday, 1953.

Deutsch, Albert. *The Mentally Ill in America*. Garden City, N.Y.: Doubleday, Doran: 1937.

Deutsch, Helene. On the Genesis of the Family Romance. *Psychoanal. Rev.*, 23: 104, 1956.

———. *The Psychology of Women*. 2 vols. New York: Grune & Stratton, 1945.

Dunn, Halbert L. Points of Attack for Raising the Levels of Wellness. *J. Nat. Med. Assn.*, 49: No. 4, 1957.

———, and Gilbert, Mort. Public Health Begins in the Family. *Public Health Reports*, 71: No. 10, 1956.

Dymond, Rosalind. The Relation of Accuracy of Perception of the Spouse and Marital Happiness. *Am. Psychologist*, 8: 344, 1953.

Eisenberg, L. The Fathers of Autistic Children. *Am. J. Orthopsychiat.*, 27: 715-724, 1957.

Eliot, T. D. Interactions of Psychiatric and Social Theory Prior to 1940. In *Mental Health and Mental Disorder*, ed. Arnold Rose. New York: Norton, 1955.

Engels, Friedrich. *The Origins of the Family*. Kerr, 1910.

English, Spurgeon O. The Psychological Role of the Father in the Family. *Soc. Casework*, 35: 323-329, 1954.

Fairbairn, W. Ronald D. *An Object-Relations Theory of the Personality*. New York: Basic Books, 1954.

Faris, R. E. L. Cultural Isolation and Schizophrenia. *Am. J. Sociol.*, 40: 155-164, 1934.

———. Interaction of Generations and Family Stability. *Am. Sociol. Rev.*, 12: 159-164, 1947.

Farnham, Marynia F. *The Adolescent*. New York: Harper, 1951.

Felix, Robert H. Evolution of Community Mental Health Concepts. *Am. J. Psychiat.*, 113: 673-679, 1957.

Field, Minna. Maternal Attitudes Found in Twenty-five Cases of Children with Primary Behavior Disorders. *Am. J. Orthopsychiat.*, 10: 293-311, 1940.

Fischer, A. E. Sibling Relationships, with Special Reference to the Problem of the Second Child. *J. Pediatrics*, 40: 254-259, 1952.

Fischer, Sarah Carolyn. *Relationships in Attitudes, Opinions, and Values Among Family Members*. University of California Publications in Culture and Society, Vol. II, No. 2, pp. 29-100. Berkeley and Los Angeles: University of California Press, 1948.

Fisher, Seymour, and Mendell, David. The Communication of Neurotic Patterns over Two and Three Generations. *Psychiatry*, 19: 41-46, 1956.

Flesch, Regina. The Problem of Diagnosis in Marital Discord. *Soc. Casework*, 30: No. 9, 1949.

Fonesca, O. W. Emergent Social Structure Among Short-Term Psychiatric Patients. *Internat. J. Social Psychiat.*, 11: 132-140, 1956.

Foote, Nelson N. Love. *Psychiatry*, 16: 245-251, 1953.

——, and Cottrell, L. S. *Identity and Interpersonal Competence: New Directions in Family Research.* Chicago: University of Chicago Press, 1955.

Frank, Lawrence K. Adolescence and Public Health. *Am. J. Public Health,* 31: No. 11, 1941.

——. The Things We Live By. *Family-Community Digest,* 1: No. 2, 1945.

Freeman, Howard E., and Showel, Morris. The Role of the Family in the Socialization Process. *J. Social Psychol.,* 37: 97-101, 1953.

Frenkel-Brunswik, E. Patterns of Social and Cognitive Outlooks in Children and Parents. *Am. J. Orthopsychiat.,* 21: 543-558, 1951.

Freud, Anna. *The Ego and the Mechanisms of Defense.* New York: International Universities Press, 1946.

——. *The Psycho-analytical Treatment of Children.* London: Imago, 1946.

Freud, Sigmund. Contributions to the Psychology of Love. In *Collected Papers,* Vol. IV. London: Hogarth, 1934.

——. *The Question of Lay Analysis.* New York: Norton, 1950.

——. The Passing of the Oedipus Complex. In *Collected Papers,* Vol. II. London: Hogarth, 1924.

Friedlander, K. Neurosis and Home Background. In *The Psychoanalytic Study of the Child,* Vol. 4, New York: International Universities Press, 1949.

Friend, Maurice R. Family Diagnosis and Treatment: Points of Reference for the Analysis of Family Process. *Casework Papers, 1957, from the National Conference of Social Welfare.* New York: Family Service Assn. of America, 1957.

Fries, Margaret. Interrelated Factors in Development. *Am. J. Orthopsychiat.,* 8: 726, 1938.

Fromm, Erich. *The Art of Loving.* New York: Harper, 1956.

Fromm-Reichmann, Frieda. Notes on the Mother Role in the Family Group. *Bull. Menninger Clinic,* 4: No. 5, 1940.

Frumkin, Robert M. The Indirect Assessment of Marital Adjustment. *Marriage and Family Living,* 14: 215-218, 1952.

Galdston, Iago. Dynamics of the Cure in Psychiatry. *A.M.A. Archives of Neurology and Psychiatry,* 70: Sept. 1953.

——. The Place of Psychoanalysis in Modern Medicine. *Canadian Psychiat. J.,* 1: No. 2, 1956.

——. *Social Implications of Dynamic Psychiatry.* New York: The Commonwealth Fund, 1959.

—— (ed.). *Beyond the Germ Theory: The Role of Deprivation and Stress in Health and Disease.* New York: Health Education Council, 1954.

Galt, William. Our Mother Tongue: Etymological Implications of the Social Neurosis. *Psychoanal. Rev.,* 30: No. 3, 1943.

——. The Principle of Cooperation in Behavior. *Quart. Rev. Biology,* 15: No. 4, 1940.

Gardner, George E. Present-Day Society and the Adolescent. *Am. J. Orthopsychiat.,* 27: 445-461, 1957.

Glauber, I. Peter. The Mother in the Etiology of Stuttering. *Psychoanal. Quart.,* 20: 160-161, 1951.

Glick, Paul C. The Family Cycle. *Marriage and Family Living,* 9: 58, 1947.

Goldfarb, W. Effects of Psychological Deprivation in Infancy and Subsequent Stimulation. *Am. J. Psychiat.*, 102: 18, 1945.

Gomberg, M. Robert, and Levinson, Frances T. (eds.). *Diagnosis and Process in Family Counseling: Evolving Concepts Through Practice.* New York: Family Service Assn., 1951.

Greenacre, Phyllis. Child Wife as Ideal: Sociological Consideration. *Am. J. Orthopsychiat.*, 17: 167-171, 1947.

Greig, Agnes B. The Problem of the Parent in Child Analysis. *Psychiatry*, 3: 539-543, 1940.

Gross, Llewellyn. A Hypothesis of Feminine Types in Relation to Family Adjustment. *Am. J. Orthopsychiat.*, 20: No. 2, 1950.

Grotjahn, Martin. *Beyond Laughter.* New York: McGraw-Hill, 1957.

Groves, Ernest R., and Groves, Gladys H. *Sex Fulfillment in Marriage.* New York: Emerson, 1942.

Hallowitz, D., Clement, R. G., and Cutter, A. V. The Treatment Process with Both Parents Together. *Am. J. Orthopsychiat.*, 27: 587-607, 1957.

Hamilton, Gordon. *Theory and Practice of Social Case Work.* New York: Columbia University Press, 1951.

Handel, Gerald, and Hess, Robert D. The Family as an Emotional Organization. *Marriage and Family Living*, 17: No. 2, 1956.

Harris, D. B. Social Change in the Beliefs of Adults Concerning Parent-Child Relationships. *Amer. Psychologist*, 3: 264, 1948.

Harvey, William A. Changing Syndrome and Culture: Recent Studies in Comparative Psychiatry. *Internat. J. Soc. Psychiat.*, 2: No. 3, 1956.

Henry, Jules. Family Structure and the Transmission of Neurotic Behavior. *Am. J. Orthopsychiat.*, 21: 800-818, 1951.

———, and Warson, Samuel. Family Structure and Psychic Development. *Am. J. Orthopsychiat.*, 21: 59-71, 1951.

Herbst, P. G. Analysis and Measurement of a Situation: The Child in the Family. *Human Relations*, 6: No. 2, 1953.

———. The Measurement of Family Relationships. *Human Relations*, 5: No. 1, 1952.

Hess, Robert D., and Handel, Gerald. Patterns of Aggression in Parents and Their Children. *J. Genetic Psychol.* In press.

Hill, Reuben. The American Family: Problem or Solution? *Am. J. Sociol.*, 53: 125-130, 1947.

———. *Families Under Stress.* New York: Harper, 1949.

———. Social Stresses on the Family: Generic Features of Families Under Stress. *Soc. Casework*, 39: Feb.-Mar. 1958.

———. Marriage and Family Research: A Critical Evaluation. *Eugenics Quart.*, 1: March 1954.

———. Review of Current Research on Marriage and the Family. *Am. Sociol. Rev.*, 16: No. 4, 1951.

———, et al., *Eddyville's Families.* Chapel Hill, N.C.: Institute for Research in Social Science, 1953.

Hollis, Florence. *Women in Marital Conflict: A Casework Study.* New York: Family Service Assn., 1949.

Horney, Karen. The Flight from Womanhood. *Internat. J. Psycho-anal.*, 1926.

Huxley, Julian. *Man in the Modern World.* New York: New American Library, 1952.

Ingersoll, Hazel L. Transmission of Authority Patterns in the Family. *Genetic Psychol. Monogr.*, 38: 225-302, 1948.

Jackson, Don D. Family and Sexuality. In *Psychotherapy of Chronic Schizophrenic Patients.* Boston: Little, Brown, 1958.

———. A Note on the Importance of Trauma in the Genesis of Schizophrenia. *Psychiatry*, 20: No. 2, 1957.

Jackson, James, with Grotjahn, Martin. The Current Psychotherapy of a Latent Schizophrenic Husband and His Wife. *Psychiatry.* In press.

———. The Efficacy of Group Therapy in a Case of Marriage Neurosis. Presented at the Annual Meeting of the American Group Psychotherapy Association, New York, Jan. 1958.

Jahoda, Marie. *Current Concepts of Positive Mental Health.* New York: Basic Books, 1958.

Jansen, Luther T. Measuring Family Solidarity. *Am. Sociol. Rev.*, 17: No. 6, 1952.

Johnson, Adelaide M., with Szurek, S. A. The Genesis of Antisocial Acting Out in Children and Adults. *Psychoanal. Quart.*, 21: 323-333, 1952.

———, Falstein, Eugene I., Szurek, S. A., and Svendsen, Margaret. School Phobia. *Am. J. Orthopsychiat.*, 11: 702-708, 1941.

Jones, Maxwell. The Treatment of Personality Disorders in a Therapeutic Community. *Psychiatry*, 20: No. 3, 1957.

———. *The Therapeutic Community.* New York: Basic Books, 1953.

Josselyn, Irene. Cultural Forces, Motherliness and Fatherliness. *Am. J. Orthopsychiat.*, 26: 264-274, 1956.

———. The Family as a Psychological Unit. *Soc. Casework,* 34: Oct. 1953.

Kanner, Leo. *In Defense of Mothers.* Springfield, Ill.: Thomas, 1941.

Kardiner, Abram. *Sex and Morality.* Indianapolis: Bobbs-Merrill, 1954.

———, et al. *The Psychological Frontiers of Society.* New York: Columbia University Press, 1945.

Kasanin, J., Knight, E., and Sage, P. The Parent-Child Relationship in Schizophrenia. *J. Nervous and Mental Disease,* 79: 249-263, 1934.

Kaufman, Irving, Peck, Alice L., and Tagiuri, Consuelo K. The Family Constellation and Overt Incestuous Relations Between Father and Daughter. *Am. J. Orthopsychiat.*, 20: 266-279, 1950.

———, Rosenblum, Eleanor, Heims, Lora, and Willer, Lee. Childhood Schizophrenia: Treatment of Children and Parents. *Am. J. Orthopsychiat.*, 27: 683-690, 1957.

Kephart, William M., Ehrmann, Winston, and Kirkpatrick, Clifford. Research on Marriage and Sex. *Marriage and Family Living,* 19: No. 1, 1957.

Keyserling, H. *The Bankruptcy of Marriage.* New York: Harcourt, Brace, 1946.

Klein, Melanie. *The Psycho-Analysis of Children.* 3d ed. London: Hogarth, 1949.

Kohn, M. L., and Clausen, J. A. Social Isolation and Schizophrenia. *Am. Sociol. Rev.*, 20: 265-273, 1955.

Komarovsky, Mirra. Cultural Contradictions and Sex Roles. *Am. J. Sociol.*, 52: No. 3, 1946.

————. *Women in the Modern World: Their Education and Their Dilemma*. Boston: Little, Brown, 1953.

Koos, Earl L. Class Differences in Family Reactions to Crisis. *Marriage and Family Living*, 12: No. 3, 1950.

————. *Families in Trouble*. New York: King's Crown Press, 1946.

————. *The Middle Class Family and Its Problems*. New York: Columbia University Press, 1948.

Kronhausen, Eberhard W., and Kronhausen, Phyllis E. Family Milieu Therapy. *Psychoanalysis*, 5: No. 3, 1957.

Kuhn, Anne Louise. *The Mother's Role in Childhood Education*. New Haven: Yale University Press, 1947.

LaBarre, Weston. Appraising Today's Pressures on Family Living. *Soc. Casework*, 32: No. 2, 1951.

————. *The Human Animal*. Chicago: University of Chicago Press, 1954.

Lang, Olga. *Chinese Family and Society*. New Haven: Yale University, 1946.

Lasko, Joahn Kalhorn. Parent-Child Relationships: Report from the Fels Research Institute. *Am. J. Orthopsychiat.*, 22: 300-304, 1952.

Leary, Timothy F., and Coffey, Hubert S. Interpersonal Diagnosis: Some Problems of Methodology and Validation. *J. Ab. and Soc. Psychol.*, 50: No. 1, 1955.

Leichter, Elsa. Participation in Treatment by Both Parents. In *Diagnosis and Process in Family Counseling*. New York: Family Service Assn. of America, 1951.

LeMasters, E. E. Social Class Mobility and Family Integration. *Marriage and Family Living*, 16: No. 3, 1954.

Levinson, Daniel J., and Huffman, Phyllis E. Traditional Family Ideology and Its Relation to Personality. *J. Personality*, 23: No. 3, 1955.

Levy, David M. *Maternal Overprotection*. New York: Columbia University Press, 1943.

————. Psychosomatic Studies of Some Aspects of Maternal Behavior. *Psychosom. Med.*, 4: 223, 1942.

————, and Hess, Audrey. Problems in Determining Maternal Attitudes Toward Newborn Infants. *Psychiatry*, 15: 273-280, 1952.

Levy, John, and Monroe, Ruth. *The Happy Family*. New York: Knopf, 1938.

Lewin, Kurt. *A Dynamic Theory of Personality*. Trans. Donald K. Adams and Karl E. Zener. New York: McGraw-Hill, 1935.

Lewis, Nolan D. C. Historical Roots of Psychotherapy. *Am. J. Psychiat.*, 114: No. 9, 1958.

Lewis, Oscar. An Anthropological Approach to Family Studies. *Am. J. Sociol.*, 55: 468-475, 1950.

Lidz, T., *et al*. The Intrafamilial Environment of the Schizophrenic Patient: 1. The Father. *Psychiatry*, 20: 329-342, 1957.

Lindemann, E. The Wellesley Project for the Study of Certain Problems in Community Mental Health. In *Interrelations Between the Social Environment and Psychiatric Disorders*. New York: Milbank Memorial Fund, 1953, p. 165-185.

Linton, Ralph. *The Cultural Background of Personality*. New York: Appleton-Century, 1945.

————. *The Study of Man*. New York: Appleton-Century, 1937.

Lu, Yi-Chuang. Home Discipline and Reaction to Authority in Relation to Marital Roles. *Marriage and Family Living*, 15: 223-225, 1953.

———. Parent-Child Relationship and Marital Roles. *Am. Sociol. Rev.*, 17: 357-361, 1952.

———. Parental Role and Parent-Child Relationship. *Marriage and Family Living*, 14: 294-297, 1952.

Lumpkin, Katherine. *The Family: A Study of Member Roles*. Chapel Hill: University of North Carolina, 1933.

Lundberg, F., and Farnham, M. F. *Modern Woman: The Lost Sex*. New York: Harper, 1947.

McCord, W. and J. *Psychopathy and Delinquency*. New York: Grune & Stratton, 1956.

McGavran, Edward G. Scientific Diagnosis and Treatment of the Community as a Patient. *J. Am. Med. Assn.*, Oct. 1956.

McGuire, Carson. Conforming, Mobile and Divergent Families. *Marriage and Family Living*, 14: No. 2, 1952.

MacIver, Robert M. *Social Causation*. New York: Ginn, 1942.

———, and Page, Charles H. *Society: An Introductory Analysis*. New York: Rinehart, 1949.

Madow, Leo, and Harvey, Sherman E. Incidence and Analysis of the Broken Family in the Background of Neurosis. *Am. J. Orthopsychiat.*, 17: 521-528, 1947.

Mahler, M. S. On Child Psychosis and Schizophrenia: Autistic and Symbiotic Infantile Psychoses. In *The Psychoanalytic Study of the Child*, Vol. 7. New York: International Universities Press, 1952.

Malinowski, Bronislaw. *The Sexual Life of Savages*. New York: Halcyon House, 1929.

Marmor, Judd. Psychological Trends in American Family Relationships. *Marriage and Family Living*, 13: 145-147, 1951.

Martin, Peter A., with Bird, H. Waldo. An Approach to the Psychotherapy of Marriage Partners: The Stereoscopic Technique. *Psychiatry*, 16: 123-127, 1953.

Maze, J. B. On Some Corruptions of the Doctrine of Homeostasis. *Psychol. Rev.*, 60: 1953.

Mead, Margaret. The Contemporary American Family as an Anthropologist Sees It. *Am. J. Sociol.*, 53: 453-459, 1948.

———. *Male and Female*. New York: Morrow, 1949.

———. Some Theoretical Considerations on the Problem of Mother-Child Separation. *Am. J. Orthopsychiat.*, 24: No. 3, 1954.

Meadows, Paul. Balance-Imbalance in Human Social Adjustment. *Soc. Forces*, 22: No. 4, 1944.

Mendell, David, and Fisher, Seymour. A Multi-Generation Approach to Treatment of Psychopathology. *J. Nervous and Mental Disease*, May 1958.

———. An Approach to Neurotic Behavior in Terms of a Three Generation Family Model. *J. Nervous and Mental Disease*, 123: No. 2, 1956.

———. Multigeneration Family Patterns. *Med. Sci.*, 3: No. 2, Jan. 1958.

———. The Spread of Psychotherapeutic Effects from the Individual Patient to His Family Group: An Exploratory Attempt to Validate Family Model of Disturbed Behavior. *Psychiatry*, 1958.

Menninger, Karl A. Psychological Aspects of the Organism Under Stress. Part I: The Homeostatic Regulatory Function of the Ego. *J. Am. Psychoanal. Assn.*, 2: No. 1, 1954.

————. Psychological Aspects of the Organism Under Stress. Part II: Regulatory Devices of the Ego Under Major Stress. *J. Am. Psychoanal. Assn.*, 2: No. 2, 1954.

Merrill, Barbara. A Measurement of Mother-Child Interaction. *J. Ab. and Soc. Psychol.*, 41: 37-49, 1946.

Midelfort, Christian F. *The Family in Psychotherapy*. New York: McGraw-Hill, 1957.

Miller, Nathan. *The Child in Primitive Society*. New York: Brentano, 1928.

Mittelman, B. Analysis of Reciprocal Neurotic Patterns in Family Relationships. In *Neurotic Interaction in Marriage*, ed. Victor W. Eisenstein. New York: Basic Books, 1956.

Mooney, Ross L. Creation, Parents, and Children. *Progressive Education*, 31: No. 1, 1953.

Moore, Eleanor A. Casework Study in Marriage Counseling. *Soc. Casework*, 24: No. 6, 1953.

Moreno, J. L. *Who Shall Survive: A New Approach to the Problem of Human Interrelations*. Washington, D. C.: Nervous and Mental Disease Publishing Co., 1934.

Motivation in Health Education: The 1947 Health Education Conference of the New York Academy of Medicine. New York: Columbia University Press, 1948.

Motz, Annabelle Bender. Conceptions of Marital Roles by Status Groups. Marriage and Family Living, 12: 1950.

Mowrer, E. R. Recent Trends in Family Research. *Am. Sociol. Rev.*, 6: No. 4, 1941.

————. The Study of Family Disorganization. *The Family*, 8: No. 3, 1927.

————, and Mowrer, Harriet. The Social Psychology of Marriage. *Am. Sociol. Rev.*, 16: 27-36, 1951.

Mowrer, Orval Hobart, *et al. Psychotherapy: Theory and Research*. New York: Ronald, 1953.

Mumford, Lewis. *The Transformation of Man*. New York: Harper, 1956.

Murdock, George. *Social Structure*. New York: Macmillan, 1949.

Murphy, Gardner. Human Potentialities. *J. Soc. Issues*, Supp. No. 7, 1953.

————. Personality: *A Biosocial Approach to Origins and Structure*. New York: Harper, 1947.

Neiman, L. J. and Hughes, J. W. The Problem of the Concept of Role: A Re-Survey of the Literature. *Soc. Forces*, 30: No. 2, 1951.

Oberndorf, C. P. Unsatisfactory Results of Psychoanalytic Therapy. *Psychoanal. Quart.*, 19: 393, 1950.

Oltman, J. E., McGarry, J. J., and Friedman, S. Parental Deprivation and the "Broken Home" in Dementia Praecox and Other Mental Disorders. *Am. J. Psychiat.*, 108: 685-694, 1952.

Opler, Marvin K. Cultural Anthropology and Social Psychiatry. *Am. J. Psychiat.*, 113: No. 4, 1956.

Parsons, Talcott. Psychoanalysis and the Social Structure. *Psychoanal. Quart.*, 19: 371-384, 1950.

———, and Bales, R. F. *Family: Socialization and Interaction Process.* Glencoe, Ill.: Free Press, 1955.

———, and Shils, Edward A. (eds.). *Toward a General Theory of Social Action.* Cambridge: Harvard University Press, 1952.

Pearse, Innes, and Lucy H. Crocker. *The Peckham Experiment: A Study in the Living Structure of Society.* London: Allen and Unwin, 1944.

Pechey, B. M. The Direct Analysis of the Mother-Child Relationship in the Treatment of Maladjusted Children. *Brit. J. Med. Psychol.,* 28: 101-112, 1955.

Penrose, L. S. Mental Illness in Husband and Wife: A Contribution to the Study of Associative Mating. *Psychiat. Quart.,* Supp. 18: 161-166, 1944.

Plank, Emma N. Reactions of Mothers of Twins in a Child Study Group. *Am. J Orthopsychiat.,* 28: 196-204, 1958.

Poincaire, Henri. *The Foundations of Science. Science and Hypothesis; the Value of Science; Science and Method.* Trans. George Bruce Halstead. Lancaster, Pa.: Science Press, 1946.

Pollack, Otto. *Integrating Sociological and Psychoanalytic Concepts.* New York: Russell Sage Foundation, 1956.

———, et al. *Social Science and Psychotherapy for Children.* New York: Russell Sage Foundation, 1952.

Prout, C. T., and White, M. A. A Controlled Study of Personality Relationships in Mothers of Schizophrenic Male Patients. *Am. J. Psychiat.,* 107: 251-256, 1951.

Regensburg, Jeanette. Application of Psychoanalytic Concepts to Casework Treatment of Marital Problems. *Soc. Casework,* 35: No. 10, 1954.

Reichard, Suzanne, and Tillman, Carl. Patterns of Parent-Child Relationships in Schizophrenia. *Psychiatry,* 13: 247-257, 1950.

Rexford, Eveolean, and Van Ameronger, Susan. The Influence of Unresolved Maternal Oral Conflicts upon Impulsive Acting Out in Children. *Am. J. Orthopsychiat.,* 27: 75-86, 1957.

Richardson, H. B. *Patients Have Families.* New York: Commonwealth Fund, 1945.

Richmond, M. E. *Social Diagnosis.* New York: Russell Sage Foundation, 1917.

Roberts, B. H., and Myers, J. S. Schizophrenia in the Youngest Male Child of the Lower Middle Class. *Am. J. Psychiat.,* 112: 129-134, 1955.

Rogers, Carl R., and Roethlisberger, F. J. A Therapist's View of the Good Life. *The Humanist,* 18: No. 5, 1957.

Rose, Arnold. The Adequacy of Women's Expectations for Adult Roles. *Soc. Forces,* 30: No. 1, 1951.

Rosen, Victor H. Changes in Family Equilibrium Through Psychoanalytic Treatment. In *Neurotic Interaction in Marriage,* ed. Victor W. Eisenstein. New York: Basic Books, 1956.

Rubenstein, B. O., and Levitt, M. Some Observations Regarding the Role of Fathers in Child Psychotherapy. *Bull. Menninger Clinic,* 21: 16-27, 1957.

Ruesch, Jurgen. Social Factors in Therapy: A Brief Review. *Psychiatric Treatment,* Vol. XXXI, Proceedings of the Association for Research in Nervous and Mental Disease. Baltimore: Williams and Wilkins, 1953.

———, and Bateson, Gregory. *Communication: The Social Matrix of Psychiatry.* New York: Norton, 1951.

Sacks, Patricia. Establishing the Diagnosis in Marital Problems. *Soc. Casework*, 30: No. 5, 1949.

Sands, Rosalind M. Family Treatment in Relation to a Disturbed Pre-School Child: A Case Presentation. *J. Psychiat. Soc. Work*, 23: No. 4, 1954.

Schemerhorn, R. A. Social Psychiatry. In *Mental Health and Mental Disorder*, ed. Arnold Rose. New York: Norton, 1955.

Scherz, Frances H. What is Family Centered Casework? *Soc. Casework*, 34: No. 8, 1953.

Sears, Robert R. Relation of Fantasy Aggression to Interpersonal Aggression. *Child Develop.*, 21: Mar. 1950.

Selye, Hans. *The Stress of Life*. New York: McGraw-Hill, 1956.

———. Stress and Psychiatry. *Am. J. Psychiat.*, 113: 423-427, 1956.

Seward, Georgene. *Psychotherapy and Culture Conflict*. With case studies by Judd Marmor. New York: Ronald Press, 1956.

———. *Sex and the Social Order*. New York: McGraw-Hill, 1946.

Sherman, I. C., and Kraine, S. S. H. Environmental and Personality Factors in Psychoses. *J. Nervous and Mental Disease*, 97: 676-691, 1943.

Sinnott, Edmund W. *The Biology of the Spirit*. New York: Viking Press, 1955.

Siporin, Max. Family-Centered Casework in a Psychiatric Setting. *Soc. Casework*, 37: April 1956.

Spiegel, J. P. The Resolution of Role Conflict Within the Family. *Psychiatry*, 20: 1-16, 1957.

Spitz, René A. Hospitalism: An Inquiry into the Genesis of Psychiatric Conditions in Early Childhood. In *The Psychoanalytic Study of the Child*, Vol. I. New York: International Universities Press, 1945.

———. Possible Infantile Precursors of Psychopathy. *Am. J. Orthopsychiat.*, 20: 240-248, 1950.

Starr, Philip H. The "Triangular" Treatment Approach in Child Therapy: Complementary Psychotherapy of Mother and Child. *Am. J. Psychother.*, 10: 40-53, 1956.

Stearns, Warren A. Murder by Adolescents with Obscure Motivation. *Am. J. Psychiat.*, 114: 303-305, 1957.

Stein, Herman. Social Science in Social Work Practice and Education. *Soc. Casework*, 36: No. 4, 1955.

Stone, Carol Larson, and Landis, Paul H. An Approach to Authority Patterns in Parent-Teen-Age Relationships. *Rural Sociol.*, 18: 233-242, 1953.

Sullivan, H. S. *The Interpersonal Theory of Psychiatry*. New York: Norton, 1953.

Sumner, William Graham. *Folkways*. Boston: Ginn, 1906.

Syz, Hans. The Concept of the Organism-as-a-Whole and Its Application to Clinical Situations. *Human Biology*, 8: No. 4, 1936.

———. An Experiment in Inclusive Psychotherapy. In *Experimental Psychopathology*, ed. Paul H. Hoch and Joseph Zubin. New York: Grune & Stratton, 1957.

———. New Perspectives in Behavior Study: A Phylobiological Reorientation. *J. Psychol.*, 1951.

Szurek, Stanislaus. Some Lessons from Efforts in Psychotherapy with Parents. *Am. J. Psychiat.*, 296-302, 1952.

Tasch, Ruth Jacobson. The Role of the Father in the Family. *J. Exper. Education*, 20: 319-361, 1951.

Thomas, Alexander. Simultaneous Psychotherapy with Marital Partners. *Am. J. Psychother.*, 10: 716-727, 1956.

Thomas, W. I., and Znaniecki, Florian. *The Polish Peasants*. New York: Knopf, 1927.

Thompson, Clara. Concepts of the Self in Interpersonal Theory. *Am. J. Psychother.*, 12: 5-17, 1958.

Titchner, James and Emerson, Richard. Some Methods for the Study of Family: Interaction in Personality Development. *Am. Psychiatric Assn. Research Reports*. To be published.

Toby, J. The Differential Impact of Family Disorganization. *Am. Sociol. Rev.*, 22: 505-512, 1957.

Toch, Hans H., and Hastorf, Albert H. Homeostasis in Psychology: A Review and Critique. *Psychiatry*, 18: Feb. 1955.

Towle, Charlotte. *Common Human Needs*. Assistance Report #8. Washington: Federal Security Agency.

U. S. Government. National Conference on Family Life. *The American Family: A Factual Background*. Washington: GPO, 1948.

———. Public Health Service. *Psychology of Aging*. Summarizations of eight papers from the Bethesda (Maryland) *Public Health Reports*, 70: No. 9, 1955.

———. Senate of the United States. *Juvenile Delinquency*. Report of the Senate Subcommittee on Juvenile Delinquency, 85th Congress of the United States, 1st Session, 1957. Washington: GPO, 1957.

Van Amerongen, Suzanne Taets. Initial Psychiatric Family Studies. *Am. J. Orthopsychiat.*, 24: 73-83, 1954.

Walker, Gerald. Why Children Kill. *Cosmopolitan*, Nov. 1958.

Walker, Kenneth. *Living Your Later Years*. New York: Oxford University Press, 1954.

Waller, Willard. *The Family: A Dynamic Interpretation*. Rev. Reuben Hill. New York: Dryden Press, 1951.

Wallin, Paul. Marital Happiness of Parents and Their Children's Attitudes to Them. *Am. Sociol. Rev.*, 18: No. 4, 1953.

———. Sex Differences in Attitudes to "In-Laws": A Test of a Theory. *Am. J. Sociol.*, 59: No. 5, 1954.

Westermarck, E. A. *History of Human Marriage*. New York: Macmillan, 1921.

Whyte, William H. *The Organization Man*. Garden City, New York: Doubleday, 1957.

Wiener, Norbert. *The Human Use of Human Beings: Cybernetics and Society*. Garden City, New York: Doubleday, 1954.

Witmer, Helen L. (ed.). *Psychiatric Interviews with Children*. New York: Commonwealth, 1946.

———, and Kotinsky, Ruth (eds.). *Personality in the Making: The Fact Finding Report of the Midcentury White House Conference on Children and Youth*. New York: Harper, 1952.

Wolff, Harold G. What Hope Does for Man: A Scientific Report. *Saturday Review*, Jan. 5, 1957.

World Health Organization. *Measurement of Levels of Health*. Report of a Study Group. Geneva: WHO, 1957.

Young, Florence M. Psychological Effects of War on Young Children. *Am. J. Orthopsychiat.*, 17: 500-510, 1947.

Young, Kimball. What Strong Family Life Means to Our Society. *Soc. Casework*, 34: No. 8, 1953.

Zimmerman, Carle C. *Family and Civilization.* New York: Harper, 1947.

———. *The Family of Tomorrow: The Cultural Crisis and the Way Out.* New York: Harper, 1949.

———, and Broderick, Carlfred B. Nature and Role of Informal Family Groups. *Marriage and Family Living*, 16: No. 2, 1954.

———, and Frampton, M. E. *Family and Society.* New York: Van Nostrand, 1935.

INDEX